Elements of Prospecting for
Non-fuel Mineral Deposits

Elements of Prospecting for Non-fuel Mineral Deposits

Elements of Prospecting for Non-fuel Mineral Deposits

P.K. Banerjee
S. Ghosh

ALLIED PUBLISHERS LTD.

New Delhi • Mumbai • Calcutta • Lucknow • Chennai
Nagpur • Bangalore • Hyderabad • Ahmedabad

ALLIED PUBLISHERS LIMITED
Regd. Off.: 15. J.N. Heredia Marg, Ballard Estate, Mumbai—400038
Prarthna Flat (2nd Floor), Navrangpura, Ahmedabad—380009
3-5-1114/1 Kachiguda Cross Raod, Hyderabad—500027
16A Ashok Marg, Patiala House, Lucknow—226001
5th Main Road, Gandhinagar, Bangalore—560009
17 Chittaranjan Avenue, Calcutta—700072
81 Hill Road, Ramnagar, Nagpur—440010
13/14, Asaf Ali Road, New Delhi—110002
751 Anna Salai, Chennai—600002

ISBN 81-7023-726-2

ASSOCIATE EDITOR	:	JYOTI MEHROTRA
PRODUCTION	:	B.K. DAS
DTP	:	S.J.I. SERVICES
COVER	:	KAM STUDIO

Published by Sunil Sachdev and printed by Ravi Sachdev at Allied Publishers Limited (Printing Division), A-104 Mayapuri, Phase II, New Delhi - 110 064.

Preface

This introductory text is meant for students in the undergraduate and postgraduate geology classes of non-specialist universities, and for prospectors with little access to authoritative volumes. It grew out of the course of lectures on mining geology and geochemical exploration (given by the first author) to the final year postgraduate students of geological sciences at the Jadavpur University, Calcutta. Such a short presentation of all the topics concerning an interdisciplinary, applied subject is not readily available in a single textbook suitable for beginners. It has been our endeavour to keep the presentation as simple as possible and to use illustrative sketches.

Now that the Government of India has thrown open all the 13 scheduled minerals (iron ore, manganese ore, chromite, sulphur, gold, diamonds, ores of copper, lead and zinc, molybdenum ore, tungsten and nickel ores and ores of the platinum group of minerals) so far exclusively reserved for state undertakings to the private sector, it is likely that Indian entrepreneurs will again embark on mining activities in a big way. Prospectors will be in great demand as a result. With changes in the MMRD Act also, the next century may witness a shift to environment-friendly mining activities in our country. It is hoped that this small book will be useful for newcomers to such endeavours.

The list of 'Further Reading' at the end of each chapter is kept as short as possible; access to specialised journals is not easy in many of our libraries. The reader is advised to peruse the publications listed for a proper grasp of the subject. What we have presented are thumbnail sketches of the craft.

We must own up our debts: to the Geological Survey of India, where we received professional training and exposure to different terrains and different mineral deposits over three and a half decades; to our contemporaries—geologists, geophysicists and chemists in the heyday of prospecting by the survey during the fifties and the sixties—who enriched us by their interaction; to Prof. A.D. Mukherjee of the Jadavpur University for providing the enthusiasm to the first author to write a book for beginners; to the Indian National Science Academy for supporting the first author in this endeavour; and to the Director General, GSI for allowing us to reproduce some illustrations from the publications of the GSI. Paraphrasing Montaigne, we have merely made up a bunch of 'other men's flowers.'

Finally, the help and guidance of Suresh Gopal, Publishing Consultant, Allied Publishers is gratefully acknowledged.

P.K. Banerjee
S. Ghosh

Contents

1

Classification of Mineral Deposits for Prospecting

Accumulations of mineral substances within a rock mass in the earth's crust, which are suitable both in quality and in quantity for commercial exploitation, *now or at some later time,* are called Mineral Deposits. These may occur in solid, liquid or gaseous state at different depths in the crust of the earth (down to a few kilometers below the surface). Solid deposits may occur as dispersion of native elements (e.g. Au), compounds (e.g. iron oxides), crystals (e.g. diamond) or rock bodies (e.g. marble). Liquid deposits include oil pools and groundwater. Gaseous deposits include reservoirs of hydrocarbon and of inert gases.

According to their industrial use, mineral deposits are classified into metallic (ore), non-metallic, fossil fuel and mineral water categories. In this book, methods of prospecting for only solid, non-fuel deposits are discussed. Other types of deposits are excluded from its purview, not because those are less important, but because their exploration techniques are substantially different.

ANCIENT USES

Stones (chert, quartzite, etc.) were used by paleolithic man as tools more than 20,000 years ago. From the advent of the Holocene sea level highstand (*c.* 7000 years B.P.) the demand for mineral resources appears to have grown hand in hand with growth of settlements in the Eastern and Western Hemispheres.

An idea about the scale of the mining activities and the variety of applications can be formed from the following facts:

(1) Native copper was first used around 7000 years ago. After the development of techniques for smelting carbonate and oxide ores and the introduction of tin bronze, Cu production became substantial. It has been estimated that cumulative production of Cu from *c.* 4000 to 2700 years ago was approximately 500,000 tonnes (C.C. Patterson. *Econ. Hist. Rev.* 25, 2nd Ser., 1972, 205).

The 4600-year-old pyramid of King Khufu of Egypt is spread over 13 acres of desert and soars up to 150 m from the ground level. It was built manually by mining and ferrying rocks from distant sources. The limestone blocks of the Pyramid of Gizeh average 2.5 tonnes each—and there were 2.3 million of them! In the remains of old pyramids at Dhashur, built by King Khufu's father, King Snofru, whose reign began around 2613 BC and who had built the Bent Pyramid, beads of amethyst and bracelets and anklets of carnelian, lapis lazuli and turquoise have been found in the tomb of his queen.

Emerald was mined in Egypt 5000 years ago (J.R. Sauer, *Emeralds Around the World*, 9, 1992, 33–44, Amsterdam). About 3920 years ago, Egyptians had dug hundreds of shafts along the Red Sea coast in search of emeralds. Some shafts were as deep as 250 m and large enough to permit entry by 400 miners. Egypt had a flourishing mineral industry, extracting turquoise and copper ore from the Sinai, gold from Nubia and the cataracts of the Nile and base metals from Cyprus.

Equally ancient is lead ore mining. The earliest known specimen of lead, dating from 3000 BC (i.e. co-eval with the Egyptian civilisation) is a figure found in the area of the Dardanelles on the site of an ancient city called Abydos. Old pipes of lead have been found in Egyptian monuments. The hanging gardens of Babylon were floored with soldered sheets of lead. The Egyptians also used lead to glaze pottery and to make solder and ornamental objects. Manganese oxide was also used to control the colour of glass.

(2) About 3500 years ago, bronze was used in China and Japan during the period of the Shang dynasty. During the succeeding Chou dynasty, jade was extensively mined for use as *objets d'art*. There are Chinese compilations of minerals dating from the seventh century BC. The earliest tin objects date from 1400 BC and from 700 BC tin foils were used to wrap mummies. The root of the Greek term *cassiteros* is the Sanskrit word *Kastira* which implies that tin was known in India in Vedic times (*c.* 1100 BC).

The Hittites and their contemporaries in Anatolia, Babylon etc. were using the new knowledge of iron smelting from near surface material. Armies of the Egyptian king Amenhotep III sacked the countries east of Egypt and returned with almost 50 tonnes of copper, half a tonne of gold (and captives for use in the gold mines of Nubia!).

(3) Almost 2500 years ago, the Phoenicians of N. Africa, who built a number of trading posts all along the coast of the Mediterranean, used to visit the Scilly islands, southwest of Cornwall (U.K.) to buy tin. Tin mining in Cornwall is still active.

The lead mines of Cyprus, Sardinia and Spain were worked by the Phoenicians; the lead-silver mines of Laurium, Greece were equally famous.

The copper mines at Timna in the deserts of the Negev had reached peak productivity in the latter part of the second millenium BC. State control is deduced from the cartouche of pharaohs, such as Rameses II, carved on rocks at the mine. These mines were made up of a large number of small shafts, rarely more than a few meters apart, linked by galleries at depths between 5 and 20 m underground.

During the first millenium BC there was a great increase in mining activities all over the world—from the Han Chinese, the Greeks and Romans to the Mauryans of Northern and Eastern India. The mines at Agucha, Dariba and Zawar in Rajasthan were worked for silver whereas the copper mines of Singhbhum, Khetri etc. gained prominence both for civilian and defence needs. Radiocarbon dating of the elaborate timber shoring, which was discovered while draining the open cast ancient mine at Dariba, shows that this 300 m long mine reached its peak productivity in the second and third centuries BC, as the demand for punch-marked silver coins in ancient India rose during the Mauryan empire. At Agucha polymetallic deposit, Rajasthan, one of the pits dates to the third century BC. At Zawar, zinc smelting was practised on a large scale from ancient times. A well-preserved system of hollowed tree trunks used for dewatering the lower levels of the mine and the vast heaps of spent retorts used for distillation of zinc at a temperature of 1110–1200°C for four to five hours testify to the use of 'advanced' mining and metallurgical technology nearly two millenia before Europe started smelting zinc in the 18th century (Paul Craddock: Mining and Smelting in Antiquity, 57–73. In: Sheridan Bowman (Ed.) *Science and the Past*, British Museum Press, 1991).

(4) After the early reference in the Vedas (c. 1100 BC) Kautilya (3rd to 4th century BC) wrote a full chapter (Chapter 12, Book 2) giving procedures for prospecting and development of mines and factories. He described the properties and uses of ores of Fe, Zn, Pb, Cu and Au as also of beryl (emerald and aquamarine), diamond, ruby and sapphire mined in and around India. He also included in Chapter 13 the

procedures for testing and beneficiation (A. Haldar & S. Sen Sarma, *Vishveshvaranand Indological Journal*, 27, 1989, 165–88).

Contemporaneous records from Greece include Aristotle's (384–322 BC) *Meteorologica* and Theophrastus's (370–287 BC) *History of Stones.* Greek documentation reached its zenith in Pliny the Elder AD 23–79 who produced five volumes dealing with minerals, gemstones and their treatment.

(5) Around 500–300 BC copper was mined in the Singhbhum copper field from oxidised ore. Megasthenes (300 BC) mentioned gold and diamond mining in India.

In fact, before 1728, when the first diamond mines were opened up in Brazil, the whole diamond supply of the world came from India.

During the time of the Roman Empire, large quantities of heavy metals, especially Pb (80,000–100,000 tonnes per year), Cu (15,000 tonnes per year), Zn (10,000 tonnes per year) and Hg (more than 2 tonnes per year) were required to sustain their civilian and military needs, especially coinage. The main sources were Cyprus, Spain and Central Europe.

(6) In the Western Hemisphere, recent excavations in Ayabaca province, about 110 km north of Lima (Peru) of a pre-Inca period show that Cu, Au, Ag and precious stones were prized during the third century.

Mining activities flourished again during medieval times in Germany from the beginning of the ninth century and in Sweden from the thirteenth century. But none of these reached the level of China, especially during the Northern Sung period (10th–12th century), when Cu production peaked at 13,000 tonnes per year.

Besides these ancient records, references to mines and metals in the writings of Jabir ibn Hayyan (Persia, 8th century), Avicenna ibn Sina (Persia, AD 980–1037), the travelogues of Marco Polo (e.g. the golden towers of Zipangu, Japan) and of Tavernier and in Ain-i-Akbari (AD 1595) of Abul Fazl testify to a long tradition of mining activities globally before pirates from Portugal, Spain, Germany, France and England subjugated and cannibalised the ancient cultures and industries of Asia, the Americas and Africa. It is amusing to recall that in the fifteenth century, Pope Alexander VI had issued a decree, dividing the world into two equal areas of control between Spain and Portugal by a line of demarcation which followed longitude 50° W, known to the European historians as the Division of Tordesillas, 1494. The arrogance of ephemeral power!

Five hundred years later, many such areas of influence have come tumbling down and the old civilisations are recovering their latent creative potential.

At the beginning of the sixteenth century there were extensive mining activities in Germany. It was here that George Bauer published his comprehensive book documenting all aspects of minerals and mining: *De Re Metallica*, under the latinised pseudonym Georgius Agricola.

PRESENT USES

Mineral deposits are used in Ferrous (Fe, Ti, Cr, Mn), Non-ferrous (Cu, Zn, Pb, Sb, Ni, Co), Light (Al, Li, Be, Mg), Scarce (W, Mo, Sn, Hg, Bi, Zr, Nb, Ta), Rare Earth (La, Ce, Pr, Nd, Pm, Sm, Eu, Gd, Tb, Dy, Ho, Er, Tm, Yb, Lu), Noble (Au, Ag, Pt, Pd, Os, Ir), Radioactive (U, Ra, Th) and Byproduct (Sc, Ga, Ge, Rb, Cd, In, Hf, Re, Te, Po, Ac) metal industries.

Non-metallic mineral deposits are used as fluxes for metallurgical requirements (fluorspar, cryolite, calcite and dolomite, felspar and quartz, nepheline); as material for refractories and insulators (graphite, magnesite, chrysotile asbestos, talc, bauxite [diaspore], sillimanite, kyanite, dumortierite, quartzite, chromite, vermiculite); for fertilisers (apatite, phosphorite, potash salts, Saltpetre [nitre], bórates, datolite, glauconite etc); for abrasives (bortz, corundum, topaz, garnet, quartz); for manufacture of chemicals (salts, sulphur, iron pyrite, arsenopyrite, realgar, orpiment, strontianite, calcite, aragonite, celestite, alunite, witherite, barite, fluorite); for dielectrical and piezoelectrical uses (muscovite, phlogopite, quartz, tourmaline); for glass and ceramic industries (white silica sand, pegmatite, kaolin, loam); for pigments and paints (chalk, ochre, barite and other compounds); and as precious and semi-precious stones (diamond, emerald, aquamarine, alexandrite, ruby, spinel, topaz, amethyst, agate, opal, obsidian, chalcedony, jasper, nephrite, jadeite, lazurite, malachite, rhodonite, selenite etc). Besides, a variety of rocks are used as facing stone (marble, granite, charnockite, felsite, rhyolite), binding material (marl, limestone, clay, gypsum), filler and road making (gravel, sand, basalt).

The need for mineral raw materials has been steadily increasing over the centuries. No sudden reversal in demand is anticipated during the next century. According to Vernadsky, man needed only 18 elements in ancient times, which increased slowly to 25 by the dawn of the eighteenth century, 47 by the nineteenth and 80 (not counting the transuranic elements) by the middle of the present century. Who knows how many will be listed a century later!

MINERAL PROVINCES AND DISTRICTS

Minerals and rocks used in modern industries are not found everywhere. Their occurrences are non-random. From the regional, down to the local scale, their occurrences are clustered in discrete areas as follows:

(1) mineral province, e.g. the Sausar Series Manganese ore province of M.P. and Maharastra;
(2) region, e.g. the Singhbhum copper field, Jamda-Koira manganese ore basin of Bihar and Orissa;
(3) district, e.g. Koraput (Mundaguda)-Bastar tin ore district;
(4) field, e.g. Sukinda chromite field;
(5) orebody, e.g. Saruabil chromite orebody in Sukinda.

A SCHEME OF CLASSIFICATION FOR PROSPECTING

The classification of a mineral deposit for the design of appropriate exploration techniques is multi-parametric. The factors include:

(1) origin of the deposit: magmatic, sedimentary, residual, metamorphic;
(2) depth of occurrence:
    (a) top of deposit exposed on ground;
    (b) top of deposit at less than 100 m depth;
    (c) top of deposit at greater than 100 m depth.
    Deposits of types 2(b) and 2(c) are called blind deposits.
(3) morphology of the deposit:
    (a) stratiform/bedded;
    (b) vein and stockwork;
    (c) lenticular;
    (d) pipe or chimney.
(4) Mineralogical composition of the deposit and its immediate wall rocks:
    (a) zoned but identical with the host;
    (b) zoned and different from the host;
    (c) unzoned with gradational margin;
    (d) unzoned (massive) with sharp margin.
(5) Chemical composition of the deposit:

(a) grossly similar to the host but differing in the percentage of major elements, e.g. a cement grade limestone within a carbonate stratigraphy or an iron ore deposit in Banded Haematite Quartzite;
(b) strongly different from the host with sharp chemical contrasts, e.g. a massive sulphide deposit within basic volcanics;
(c) moderately different from the host, e.g. bauxite in a ferruginous laterite cover.

(6) Physical properties of the deposit, e.g. porosity and permeability, magnetism, electrical conductivity, density etc:
(a) sharply different from the host;
(b) gradational with the host;
(c) identical with the host.

(7) Structural history of the deposit:
(a) undeformed;
(b) folded;
(c) faulted;
(d) controlled by pre-existing structures, including unconformities and other barriers/precipitation fences.

A complete understanding of all the parameters listed above is neither a practical scientific pre-condition for exploration nor can it be funded without guaranteed social/economic return. The 'hunch' of an experienced field geologist is a powerful tool, since it distills the total experience intuitively. Whatever be the level of experience, it is essential to document the available information systematically and clearly so that promising indications are not ignored. For example, suppose you are looking for a cement grade limestone deposit in a forested, partly covered area by combined geomorphological-lithological survey. You would not normally use geochemical methods. But if there is a linear stretch of 'gossan' within the area which merits geochemical prospecting to find out whether it is a true or a false gossan, you should note its occurrence in your field sheet. This may escape your memory later, unless your field notes are comprehensive. A well-structured data format is used in many companies and national geological surveys.

It is useful to remember that there are infinite possible combinations in nature. The job of a successful prospector is to progressively eliminate less promising sectors so that maximum effort, both in terms of time and funds, is concentrated towards a comprehensive 3-D delineation of the mineral deposit, its grade variations and its physical-chemical attributes. Before complex geochemical and geophysical probes were available, prospecting usually started with small scale geological mapping, examination of surface expressions of mineral deposits and heavy mineral panning in the drainage system. Large areas measuring thousands of square kilometers were covered by such 'foot soldiers' in search of mineral deposits. The scale of the survey was usually 1: 50,000 or smaller.

Next in sequence came larger scale mapping of the surface expressions, coupled with sampling and pitting or trenching, wherever necessary. This was followed by drilling and exploratory mining in promising fields. The targets for such larger-scale operation were necessarily small, a few tens of square kilometers or less, the scale was larger, from 1: 30,000 to 1: 5,000 and the duration of the program extending longer, for two or more field seasons. In parts of M.P., combined geomorphological and geobotanical observations by geologists of the Geological Survey of India (GSI) in the late forties led to the delineation of concealed limestone deposits, long before such techniques were formalised. In fact, a general rule of prospecting in tropical landscapes is that you must walk over the ground and examine even the most weathered outcrops in detail. 'Hunches' come after long experience in field work, after you have absorbed many types of geological set-ups visually and intellectually; a chair-borne geologist is usually a poor prospector.

Systematic surface examination can be done at less cost than other methods of search. The methods vary from one type of ore to another and in different landscapes. For example, in a region covered by glacial drift, systematic prospecting for gold quartz veins, e.g. in Nova Scotia, followed a different technique from the method used in the deeply weathered tropical field of Serra Pelada in the Amazon rain forest. Tracing floats of mineralised rocks or panning or trenching are effective tools of discovery in poorly explored terrain. While tracing floats, all pieces of float, should be labelled, portions from each piece analysed chemically and locations plotted on the map. Similarly, while panning for economic minerals, it is important to take equal volumes of sediment (usually a level panful) from each sampling point, so that the recovery is semiquantitative and the change from one spot to another provides the prospector with a direction for future search. In trenching, the initial program should be to sink a few trenches or pits as far apart as geologically permissible, concentrating on very detailed study and analysis of the individual layers intersected at very close vertical intervals. If you find that all the rich values are in the upper level of the trench, the source is probably far away; if all the high values are confined to the lower layers, the source may be close by. Such simple tests are often quite revealing.

Deep-seated, concealed deposits or mineral deposits of unusual appearance can be missed by the most careful field geologist. The ultimate test of success is positive intersection of a deposit. This demands correct interpretation of the ground geological set up and systematic laboratory identification and assay. In tropical countries, exposures being few, nuances and subtleties of the rock record are easily overlooked. If your field and laboratory observations are wrong or if you have not undertaken proper mineralogical and structural study of the exposed rocks, expectation for discovery of a new deposit is likely to be low.

It is useful to recall that the first discoveries of ore in Cobalt, Ontario, were made by examination of rock outcrops. Co minerals oxidise to pink erythrite, commonly known as cobalt 'bloom'. The pink colour disappears on weathering but shows up on freshly broken surfaces. Careful examination showed that this is associated with a soft black mineral, CoO, and with nuggets of native Ag!

Virgin deposits with surface shows are now comparatively rare, and rate of discovery is falling off globally. The future prospector will have to devote more time in search of blind deposits and in reaching remote areas on land and below the sea. Metallogenic potential, particularly of granitoids and mafic-ultramafic associations, will have to be refined by fingerprinting such geological and chemical parameters which are indicators of high mineral potential. This means that surface geological studies will have to be integrated with the tools of the geochemist, geophysicist, statistician and microbiologist in genuinely co-operative and interdisciplinary—not multidisciplinary and combative—endeavours. A better mix of generalists and specialists and a better organisation of the data base will be needed.

This point can be illustrated by a few case histories of discovery of blind deposits.

The first example was the discovery by GSI of concealed chromite deposits in the north limb of the Sukinda syncline in Orissa, India. The ore bodies are blanketed by laterite and colluvium. Ground mapping in 1961 led to a structural re-interpretation of the ultramafic field as a westerly plunging synform (Fig. 1.1). The north limb was believed to lie concealed. This led to the focussing of gravimetric survey over the colluvium and duricrust covered area of the north limb. A large number of residual Bouguer anomaly closures were defined, some caused by a tabular orthopyroxenite mass, others by chromite lenses. These two types were then discriminated by pedogeochemical survey, leading to the discovery of blind chromite deposits. The total ore reserve was estimated at around 0.1 million tonnes in 1960 before the GSI program; now it stands at more than 100 million tonnes.

The second example is the Neves Corvo massive sulphide deposit (30.3 million tonnes of ore with 7.81% Cu and 1.33% Zn, 2.76 million tonnes of ore with 13.42% Cu and 1.35% Zn and 32.6 million tonnes of ore with 0.46% Cu, 1.13%Pb and 5.72%Zn) in the Portuguese sector of the Iberian Pyrite Belt. There were two stages

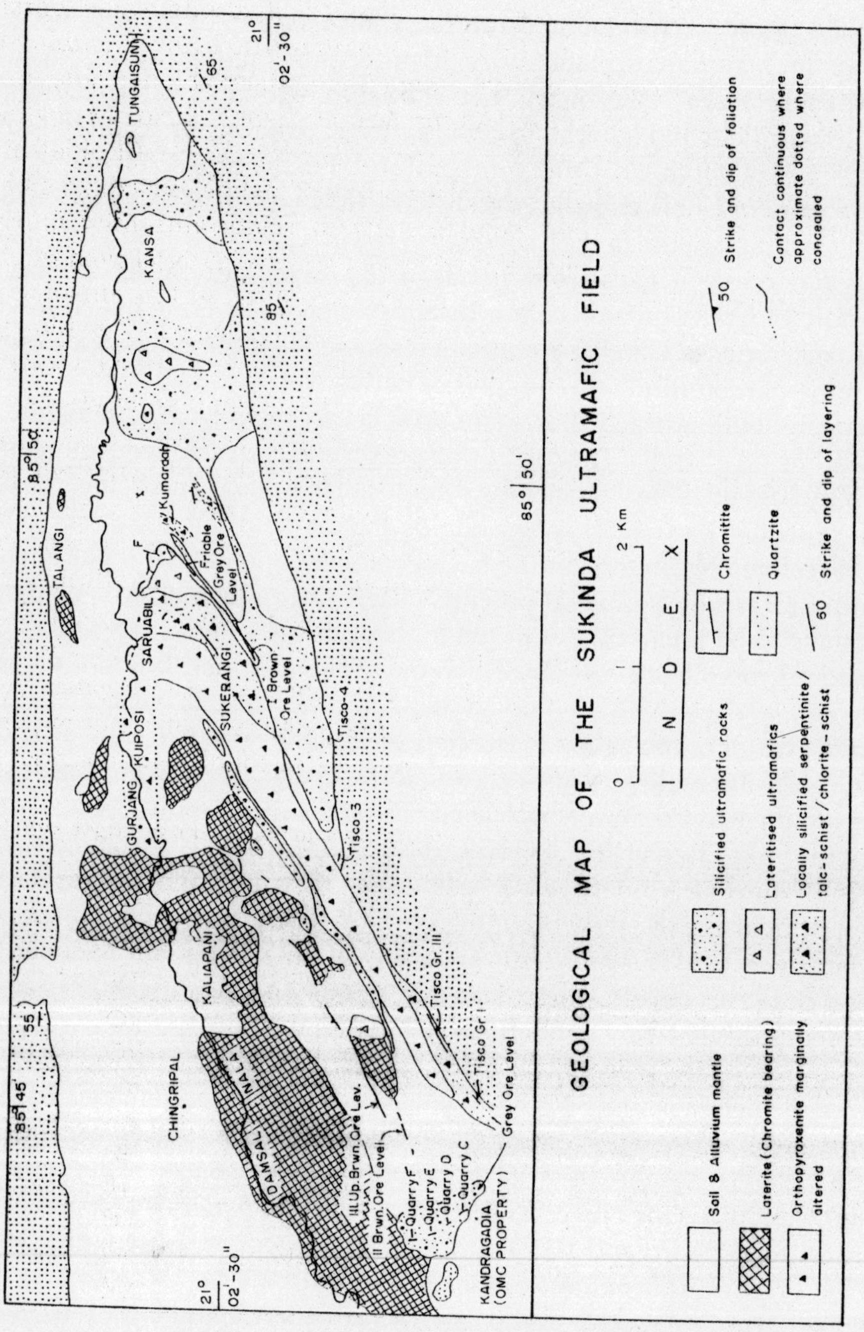

Fig. 1.1: Geological map of the Sukinda ultramafic field.

of prospecting from 1969 to 1977: the first stage, based on gravimetry (1969–73) ended with a barren drill-hole. The second stage (1973–77) involved the collection and synthesis of lithostratigraphic, tectonic, paleogeographic, geophysical and geochemical studies, ending with the first successful drill-hole in 1977: mineralisation was first intersected at a depth of 350 m at Neves and at 570 m at Corvo. Claimants to the credit for the discovery were many. Some in the Rio Tinto Zinc (RTZ) stated that the discovery came about because a certain geophysicist realised that a borehole had not accounted for the gravity anomaly it was supposed to test and therefore insisted on having it deepened (causative body's estimated depth: 80–180 m at Neves and 150 m at Corvo). Others credited a local geologist with careful core logging in the light of modern lithogeochemical knowledge of the attributes of supra-ore barren holes, which suggested that the sulphide body lay deeper than the hole designed to test the gravity anomaly. Deeper drilling was thereafter undertaken.

A recent exposition by G.A. Reynolds (*Exploration Geophysics*, 26, 1995, 547–8) sets the record straight. Gravity survey was of little help. The orebody is low dipping and 'ribbon-like'; the computed gravity anomaly is 0.3 mGal, which is slightly more than the noise envelope (0.2 mGal). Similarly, the geological control was tenuous. The dip of schistosity at surface level is steep, contrary to the low dip of the concealed orebody. During aerogeophysical survey, a strong INPUT anomaly had been picked up. This was followed up on ground by large loop EM 37 profiling on 200 m line spacing along the geological strike. The EM 37 data were modelled using the GEONICS PLATE program in H.P. BASIC developed by the Ontario Geological Survey. A gradient I.P./Resistivity survey defined a single smooth symmetrical chargeability anomaly. Dipole-dipole profiling ($a = 200$ m) confirmed that the source is deep. The first hole was positioned to intersect the source. This passed within 25 m of the orebody, but down hole TEM was also of very little use. The EM 37 survey had shown that the anomaly trends shifted their position by 200 m depending on which side the transmitter loop was placed. Speculating that current gathering could displace the anomaly, the second hole was stepped back. This intersected the Aguas Tenidas East massive sulphide deposit for the first time.

Whether or not this was a fortuitous bonanza is a debatable question; but a bonanza, which was struck by a series of false premises and conceptual models, is the Olympic Dam copper-uranium-gold-silver deposit with a measured and indicated resource of 450 million tonnes, approx 520 km NNW of Adelaide in S. Australia. The story is worth narrating in some detail to illustrate the inherent uncertainties in geological, geochemical and geophysical modelling as well as the advantage of teamwork and good communication among geoscientists in the exploration group.

1969–72: In the course of a research project for the degree of doctor of philosophy at the Australian National University a conceptual model embracing source, transport and mineral precipitation aspects of sedimentary copper deposits was developed.

June, 1972: R. Woodall, chief geologist of the Exploration Division, Western Mining Corporation, initiated a geological literature study of the Proterozoic and Lower Paleozoic rocks of S. Australia and sent a team to Zambia to get details of the geological-geophysical frame of the bedded Co-Cu deposit there.

May–June, 1974: Stage (1): Altered basalts exposed along the southern margin of the Stuart Shelf were considered to be a possible source of Cu. These were interpreted to continue down depth. Stage (2): An area of 43,500 sq.km was targetted for conceptual modelling. Stage (3): Regional gravity high at Olympic Dam, which lies at the northwestern tip of the area together with a magnetic high, 1.6 km to its north, were interpreted as a potential locus for sedimentary copper deposits, because these anomalies were thought to be caused by piles of altered basalts. Similar anomalies were identified in some other sectors of the Andamooka area.

July–September, 1974: A lineament analysis (as a target-defining tool) was undertaken. The analysis confirmed the potential of all the geophysical anomalies and defined some more targets to boot.

May, 1975: Ground magnetic, gravity and seismic traverses over two of the strongest geophysical anomalies, including that at Olympic Dam, were completed.

June–July, 1975: Diamond drill-hole RD 1 intersected 38 m of ore containing 1.05 per cent Cu. After a run of as many as 8 barren holes, RD 10 again intersected 170 m of ore with 2.12% Cu.

Now comes the twist to the tale.

(a) The orebody is a large hydrothermal breccia system, hosted by a granite with U-Pb zircon age of around 1590 Ma. It is not a sedimentary Cu deposit associated with basalts.

(b) The domical Bouguer residual anomaly (ranging from –18 mGal at the base to –8 mGal at the crest) spreads over more than double the area of the ore zone. In fact, the southern half of the Bouguer anomaly ellipse, where the first hole was drilled, is relatively lean. Neither the magnetic nor the Bouguer closure coincides with the disposition of the orebody.

(c) The observed features, notably: (1) paragenetic sequence of pyrite-chalcopyrite-bornite-chalcocite-(native copper)-gold-silica, (2) association of pitchblende with copper sulphides (± fluorite, barite) in colloform and crustiform infillings, replacing or intergrown with other breccia components of the haematite-rich hosts, (3) occurrence of gold near the silicified margins of the haematite-quartz breccias, associated with sericite and chlorite, (4) presence of silver in solid solution with copper sulphides, and (5) REE minerals (bastnaesite, florencite, monazite and xenotime) intergrown with haematite, sericite and fluorite—all testify to:

- widespread fluid-wall rock interaction;
- mixing of hot reduced Fe-rich waters with cooler meteoric waters;
- localised boiling of fluids in near-surface eruptive environment.

(d) The core of the breccia complex is a nearly barren haematite quartz breccia devoid of mafic and felsic dykes and diatremes, which are abundant within the orebody. A complete spectrum of breccia types—from granite rich to haematite rich—are present within the orebody. The network of dykes and volcaniclastic tuff testify to extended eruption, followed by a shallow marine environment, since the cover sedimentaries over this Mesoproterozoic ore deposit are (local) pebble conglomerates, capping parts of the orebody followed by shale with local dolomite.

(e) Fluid inclusion and stable isotope studies suggest that ore deposition took place in the range of 150–350°C, whereas Nd isotopic signature of the ore suggests that the mineralising fluids were derived not from the host granite but from a mantle derived magma. A mystery wrapped in enigma, the history of discovery of the Olympic Dam deposit lying 350 m below flat lying Cambrian and Neoproterozoic limestone, sandstone, shale and quartzite shows the inadequacy of present technology in locating orebodies lying at moderate depth. Numerical modelling by D.W. Haynes et al. (*Econ. Geol.*, 90, 1995, 281–307) shows that fluid mixing was probably the dominant ore forming process here, ground water being responsible for transport of Cu, U, Au and most of S, whereas hotter water introduced most of Fe, Ba, F and CO_2 from below. One has to proceed with imagination and care, reconstruct palaeogeographic scenarios from a few leads, and depend on the prospector's luck for similar possibilities in the basement below the fringes of the Cuddapah, Vindhyan and Chattisgarh basins of India.

Another illustration of modern exploration techniques is the discovery of nearly a hundred kimberlite pipes in the North West Territories of Canada in recent years. The remoteness and harsh subpolar climate of the terrain make exploration extremely difficult. An airborne magnetometer was successfully utilised to pick up the magnetic contrast between kimberlite and the surrounding bedrocks. Ground investigations included sampling of the till and boulder clay for indicator minerals garnet, ilmenite and chromite normally associated with kimberlite (vide Chapter 4). The indicator trains were traced back through streams and glacial drifts to the source rock, frequently with the help of mechanised drills that can operate at temperatures down to minus 40°C for taking samples at the bottom of frozen lakes (E. Stephenson, *The Geographical Magazine*, 1996, 23–5).

PROSPECTOR'S PHILOSOPHY

The guiding rules of Davis (B. Rex Davis: *Episodes*, 11(2), 1988, 105–10) are worth quoting:

- Sound and unbiased field and laboratory observations and measurements are the foundation stones on which to build.
- Data should be critically appraised before accepting current interpretations and authoritarian theories.
- Data for which no coherent genetic mechanism is apparent should not be discarded but continually reviewed.
- When exploration progress is slow, seek and test alternative genetic models for guidance.
- Persistence often brings rewards if all data continue to make good geological sense.
- Be receptive to unexpected experimental results.
- When a revised and better genetic concept emerges, apply it to extend exploration programs.

For a prospector, optimism is half the battle. But the better half of the battle is when he not only knows what to look for and where, but also how. A broad idea about the industrial specifications of the different mineral deposits, an awareness of market prices and global patterns of trade, and a capacity to combine data from different sources into a compatible model are desirable. The conjunction of factors that gives rise to different types of mineral deposits include geochemical, hydrological, magmatic, tectonic, metamorphic and weathering processes besides the vagaries of erosional and depositional patterns and sequences, operating over varying scales of time (from less than 10^4 years to 10^8 years) and space (from a mineral deposit to a continental scale). Many of the endogenic deposits are products of a heat source, a convective circulation system, mixing of fluids of different chemistry and temperature, open system behaviour for some parameters and non-linearity in reaction kinetics. Prediction of the actual path of evolution of such a multi-parametric system by mathematical modelling has so far been unsuccessful, not because of any basic fault in computational procedure but on account of a lack of clear definition of the initial condition which describes the distribution of values for each parameter (temperature, pressure, element concentrations, etc.) at all points of the system at the beginning and the types of boundary conditions which describe the interaction of the system with its surroundings for the entire period.

Such mathematical modelling is carried out in three stages. In the first stage, physical processes are represented in terms of mathematical equations. Both analytical and numerical methods are used to develop mathematical models. Analytical models are more versatile, because the same model can be used for different values of input parameters. But in natural systems of mineral concentration, many simplifying assumptions are needed to make the problem amenable to analytical modelling. Hence it is a common practice to adopt a numerical approach for geochemical modelling. For example, chemical mass transfer modelling is frequently used to analyse the development of multi-component fluid-rock reactions in natural hydrothermal systems. Even here, there are problems of uneven quality of basic thermodynamic data and variable reactivity of the fluid passing through rocks of different composition, creating complex balance between fluid flow and fluid-rock interaction. These require multi-box models. The difficulty is illustrated by the discrepancies between thermodynamic predictions on the one hand and observed brine compositions and mineral assemblages in the Salton Sea geothermal system on the other.

Another obstacle to model-driven prospecting for mineral deposits is the variety of competing genetic models for most of the well-studied epigenetic deposits. Some hypotheses depend mostly on field and structural criteria of association in time and space; some on trace element fingerprints; others on chemical-isotopic signatures. Not all of these are internally consistent in many cases. This results in a plethora of alternative hypotheses which act as veritable mine fields against rigorous modelling. There is a growing awareness that model-driven prospecting provides the key to defining ore expectations on regional to district scale. The power of prediction diminishes steeply as one narrows the search to an individual deposit.

Quantitative prediction and evaluation of mineral resources on the basis of field and laboratory data require the development of expert systems involving many fields of computer science. Chinese geologists have reportedly developed one such system based on comprehensive prediction theory and achieved success in predicting gold deposits in Shanxi and Hebei provinces (Shicheng Wang et al., *Episodes*, 18, Nos. 1 & 2, 1995, 87–90). Even with such expert systems to support the prospecting campaign, one has to choose the right tools in their proper sequence for locating hidden deposits. Sometimes it is found that prevailing paradigms are inadequate. The prospector has to proceed empirically, as in eastern New South Wales, where more than 2 million diamonds have been recovered from alluvial deposits as well as from diatremes of nephelinitic, basanitic and basaltic compositions. Kimberlite and lamproite are not known here and the continental lithosphere is only upto 85 km thick (L.M. Barron et al., *Australian Journal of Earth Science*, 43, 1996, 257–67).

A successful prospector in the next century will not work alone; he will combine the academic aptitude of a post-doctoral research scientist and the innovative knack of a first rate technologist with the physical and mental toughness for prolonged wear and tear in harsh, inhospitable climate and a temperamental preference for discipline and danger. The images of hard drinking, hard living prospectors of the American Wild West are slowly fading out even from the silver screen.

FURTHER READING

A.M. Evans, *Ore Geology and Industrial Minerals, An Introduction.* 3/e, Blackwell Scientific Publications, Oxford, 1993, 390 pp.

V.I. Smirnov, *Geology of Mineral Deposits*, Mir Publishers, Moscow, 1976, 520 pp.

2

Host Rocks of Mineral Deposits

The geologist has an anxious part to play with reference to practical questions. He is instituted more as a concession to what seems but a raising fashion, than from any faith in his knowledge or any understanding of his functions; and thus it happens that he is not consulted when his opinion might be of great service, or, on the other hand, he is called upon to perform what is quite out of his line of business, or twitted for not having done what it would be unwise to attempt unless under special circumstances, and impossible to undertake without special appliances that were not at his disposal. As no one is more aware than himself that the best, if not the only warrant for his existence in his usefulness, such circumstances are very distressing.

—H.B. Medlicott, Suptd. GSI
(in Preface to V. Ball's *Economic Geology*, 1881)

Mineral deposits are integral components of the rock bodies within which they occur. It is, therefore, essential for a prospector to understand the history of evolution of a rock mass in broad detail to design a proper programme of exploration. Conversely, if one is looking for a particular mineral or element, the search has to focus on favourable host rock associations. Mineral deposits develop on or below the earth's surface by complex and abnormal combinations of physicochemical processes, whether it is an early magmatic chromite seam in dunite, a late magmatic pod of vanadiferous magnetite in norite, a high temperature (600–300°C) porphyry copper deposit, a low temperature (less than 300° C) Mississippi Valley Type (MVT)

Pb-Zn-Cu pocket, a tabular mass of flux grade limestone or bauxite in a laterite mesa. In general, such abnormalities leave tell-tale signals in the associated lithologies.

By careful mineralogical, geochemical and structural studies of the rock sequences, an experienced prospector can recognise such signals from a distance and limit his expectations from the framework. A confined shallow basin with abundant indications of anoxia and limited detrital input, a laterite catena over an alumina-rich, relatively permeable basement, a granitic mass intruding into relatively volatile rich rocks, a region of fumarolic activity near a plug-shaped igneous mass, a differentiated mafic ultramafic fragment of the oceanic crust and mantle; such formational environments are prime targets for economic mineral concentration. A classic example is the porphyry copper deposit having a core of biotite ± K felspar surrounded by a zone of quartz + chlorite and overprinted by epidote + albite + chlorite. Even if only the outer zone is exposed on the surface and the boundary between the K-silicate and sericite zones, which carries high temperature copper sulphide accompanied by magnetite is far underground, a careful study of the mineralogy, O and H isotopes of the outer kernel and structure of the rock mass should prompt the prospector to drill a few deep holes to collect fresh samples from deeper zones for fluid inclusion fingerprinting. Inclusions related to porphyry mineralisation form at 700–800°C, are hypersaline (with 40–60 wt% NaCl equivalent) with 250–5000 p.p.m. of Cu, and three-phase (brine + crystals of halite/sylvite + a vapour bubble). In contrast, if the fluid inclusions are of low salinity (1–2 wt% NaCl) but rich (upto 4 wt%) in CO_2 with H_2S, there is a possibility of epithermal Au concentration. If the fluids are slightly more saline (10–15 wt% NaCl eq), the possibility of Pb-Zn-Ag mineralisation has to be looked for. We now know that Au is normally transported as a bisulphide complex; Pb, Zn and Ag prefer transport by Cl complexes and Cu is transported by hypersaline metal-bearing magmatic fluid in a porphyry; the fluids move away from the intrusion and react with cooler country rocks. Such a generalised model affords a clear physicochemical perspective in our search for favourable environments.

Prospecting is not just looking for a mineral body, walking for miles and examining fragments from rock outcrops. The essence of good prospecting is to define the boundary conditions of formation of a mineral deposit which could develop within the given set up. For example, if you are looking for chromite, your target is a group of differentiated ultramafic rocks. If you are looking for tin-tungsten deposit, on the other hand, pegmatites and quartz veins associated with epizonal to mesozonal granitic intrusives afford a prime target. A classic illustration is afforded by the Cornubian batholith in Southwest England. The batholith is a Hercynian emplacement in course of the continental collision of what is now Northern and Southern Europe. It has a strike length of 250 km and a maximum width of about 50 km, extending from Dartmoor in the northeast to Scilly in the southwest. There are five major plutons of coarse grained S-type granite with cross-cutting rhyolite porphyry. Various types of ore (Sn, W, Mo, Cu, Pb, Zn, Ag, Sb, U) minerals occur in steep dipping fractures and lodes across the granite and the country rocks with evidences of multiple episodes of mineralising fluids and concomittant changes in fluid chemistry covering a range of 35 million years (294–259 Ma), a temperature (measured in fluid inclusion) interval of 400°C (500–100°C) and a habitat ranging from skarn and pegmatite deposits to polymetallic fissure veins. (J.T. Chesley, et al., *Geochim. Cosmochim. Acta*, 57, 1993, 1817–35).

The range and diversity of ore deposits associated with the batholith emphasize the following points:

- Complexity of the process of ore formation.
- Long duration of the process.
- Need for a broad comprehension of the complex history of evolution of the ore minerals and the host rocks without the simplifying assumptions of continuity in space and time.
- A model driven approach, firmly anchored on ground data, recognising that 'verification' in the orthodox sense is not possible for models of long-term non-linear geological processes.

Quantitative studies on duration and chemistry of ore-forming processes suggest that many epigenetic deposits form by protracted episodes of mineral formation including locally retrograde dissolution. In most cases, paragenetic conclusions based on ore textures record only the concluding episode and should not be used singly to interpret the total history of the deposit.

For example, the southeast Asian tin belt, extending over 2800 km in Malaysia, Myanmar, Indonesia, and Thailand have four types of mineralisation: hydrothermal infilling or replacement type; pegmatite hosted; skarn; and skarn-breccia-vein type in granite. The temperature of homogenisation of early stage fluid inclusions ranges from 200–400°C. Salt-enriched fluids produced by unmixing from the granitic melts interacted with the cooling rock in four steps:

1. Partitioning of Sn during crystal-melt fractionation of granite magma.
2. Extraction of tin by an aqueous phase.

3. Transport of the metal and its associated elements (Ta, Nb, W, Fe) in hydrothermal fluids.
4. Deposition as cassiterite or less frequently as tin sulphide.

From the Jurassic to the Miocene over more than 200 million years, this complex process acted intermittently with varying intensity in different parts of the tin belt, the host granites yielding dates between 22 and 260 million years (M.O. Schwartz et al. *Earth Science Reviews*, 38, 1995, 95–293). The super-large wolframite-quartz vein deposits of Dajishan-Xihuashan of China are also a four-stage product of accumulation and concentration over 40 Ma (R. Pei and D. Hong, *Episodes* 18 (1 & 2), 1996, 77–82).

At the other end of the spectrum, it has recently been established that episodic hydrothermal activity has been continuing for the past 20,000 years on the massive sulphide mound at TAG (Trans-Atlantic Geotraverse) site, east of the Mid-Atlantic Ridge at 26°08'N, with cycles of precipitation and partial dissolution (S.E. Humphris et al., *Nature*, 377, 1995, 713–16; C. Laiou et al., *Jour. Geoph. Res.*, 96, 1993, 9705–13).

Spatial association is no longer accepted as a sufficient ground for ore genetic conclusions. For example, recent researches on the Mt. Isa ore deposits of Australia (C.A. Heinrich et al., *Econ. Geol.* 90(4), 1995, 705–30), Witwatersrand Au-U deposits of S. Africa (L.J. Robb & F.M. Meyer, *Ore Geology Review*, 10, 1995, 67–94) and Mississippi Valley Type (MVT) ore deposits in mid-continent of N. America and Western Australia (M.S. Appold et al., *Econ. Geol.* 90(4), 1995, 902–19; J.C. Brannon et al., *Science*, 271, 1996, 491–3) underscore the complexity of the source and long duration of the process of concentration.

At Mt. Isa, Proterozoic (1870–1650 Ma) supracrustal rocks host two different ore associations in close proximity: giant, stratiform Pb-Zn-Ag deposits as well as Cu mineralised breccias free from Pb and Zn. The deposits 'evolved by metasomatic exchange between two chemically contrasting rock reservoirs: a large volume of copper-rich metabasalts of the Eastern Creek volcanics that underwent progressive oxidation through several episodes of infiltration of sulphate bearing fluids and a smaller volume of anomalously dolomitic, carbonaceous, pyritic and already Pb-Zn mineralised metasediments of the Urquhart shale, which acted as a local reductant and partial sulphide source for high grade copper ore deposition. Mass transfer was driven by advection of fluids from one additional reservoir, which provided water, unusually high Br/Cl salt providing metal transporting ligands, ^{34}S-enriched sulphate as an oxidant. Downdraw of surface derived fluids by seismicity of the Mt.

Isa fault zone or by deep thermal convection appear more feasible than upward focussing of deep metamorphic or magmatic fluids.' (Heinrich et al., *op.cit.*).

Such crustal recycling is also manifest in the Paleozoic MVT deposits of the Central Appalachians. These formed by mixing of 'a more saline, calcium rich fluid with final melting temperatures between –42°C and –29°C and a less saline or calcium poor fluid with final melting temperature of –24°C to –12°C' (Appold et al., *op.cit.*). Around Missouri, Kansas, Oklahoma and Kentucky, ore deposition took place between 251 and 272 Ma, indicating a considerable time span. MVT deposits in the Upper Devonian reefs of Western Australia indicate events of ore formation at 357 Ma and again at 325 Ma. Besides, it has now been recognised that MVT deposits can form not only by gravity-driven fluid flow by compressional tectonism but also in rift environments, where fluid flow is forced by rapid sedimentation during subsidence.

We are now facing a paradigm shift. It appears that the mineral-bearing potential of a region or district is directly *and not inversely* proportional to the duration and complexity of the operative processes and variety of the accessible sources of anions and cations. A classic demonstration of this is the Witwatersrand Basin of South Africa. Sediments from mixed granite-greenstone detritus of ancient Archaean province accumulated here intermittently for about 360 My. Later it was intruded by Au- and U-rich granitoids. Detritus from the granitoids favoured the formation of paleoplacer deposits. At 2500 Ma, authigenic pyrite formed. Hydrocarbon-bearing fluids, derived by maturation of organic material, permeated the paleoplacers 200 My later. This led to radiolytic fixation of bitumen around detrital uraninite. After about 300 My, there was a high-intensity metamorphic flushing. This resulted in widespread re-distribution of Au and the development of a number of secondary sulphides (Robb & Meyer, *op.cit.*).

Quantitative geochemistry and radioisotope dating techniques may reveal similar complexity in the genetic history of the Karnataka sulphide deposits, of the epigenetic deposits within the remobilised fringe of Proterozoic assemblages wrapping around the granulites of the East Coast of India (P.K. Banerjee, *Mem. Geol. Soc. Ind.* 8, 1988, 199–216) and of the base metal deposits in Cuddapah-Kurnool Proterozoic sedimentary basin of A.P. Such studies may provide a road map of future discovery of concealed mineral deposits as well. In the case of giant gold deposits like Kalgoorli (Australia) and Timmins (Canada), however, the favourable combination was host rock chemistry, thickness and mechanical properties, regional scale faults (which allowed highly focussed fluid flow) and PT conditions in a greenstone architecture. Factors such as high heat flow, large fluid reservoir, efficient fluid focussing had to couple with large and compositionally favourable lithology. Since the probability of conjunction of all favourable parameters is very low, a high system efficiency to form such giant deposits is achieved only rarely (G.N. Phillips et al., *Ore Geology Reviews*, 10(3–6), 1996, 295–317).

As narrated in Chapter 1, there are many instances of discovery of deposits on the basis of wrong correlation and many more of hopeful models without resultant discoveries. But prospecting cannot do without conceptual models.

A large number of mineral deposits are found in diverse rock associations. Copper provides an extreme example: Cu deposits occur in association with all types of igneous, sedimentary and metamorphic rocks. It is more difficult to prove that an area is barren of all types of mineral deposits than to prove a mineral deposit, if you get a lead. The history of mineral exploration is replete with instances of success after repeated initial failures, e.g. at Kambalda (Australia), Malanjkhand (India) etc.

It is important to bear in mind that surprises are the bread and butter of prospecting. Sometimes intelligent guesswork is rewarded. Thus the first discovery of gold in bauxite-laterite of Australia owed much to the perception of the mining geologist who first asked for analysis of Au in a bauxite sample on the suspicion that a product of residual weathering could as well be enriched in elements of low solubility and higher 'clarke' in the parent material (greenstone), like Au besides Al. A new type of resource for Au was thus thrown open all over the tropical belt. A prospector has to retain an open and logical mind to understand the turns and twists of behaviour of a mineral deposit. It may pinch off; it may have been cut out by a fault; folded back on itself; or the elements of interest substituted by other compatible elements over a stretch. In each case, the design of further search will be different. Failure to diagnose correctly is a sure way to miss the extension of a mineral deposit. The need for using the time-honoured concept of Multiple Working Hypothesis cannot be ignored.

Table 2.1 provides a framework of the usual rock associations of different mineral deposits. The listing is not exhaustive, although it covers a majority of the known ore types.

Table 2.1: Industrially Useful Minerals and Their Host Rock Associations

Element	*Constituent minerals in minable material*[1] *and their composition*	*Host rocks*	*Associated elements*	*Indian example*
a	*b*	*c*	*d*	*e*
Li	Spodumene: $LiAl(SiO_3)$; Lepidolite: Li-mica; Zinnwaldite: Li-Fe mica; Amblygonite: $LiAl(F\,OH)PO_4$	Pegmatite (Peg); Granite (Gr); Greisen (G); Wad.	Rb, Cs, Be, Nb, Ta, Bi, B, P, F, Sn, W, Mo, REE, U, Th	Bastar pegmatites, M.P.
	Petalite: $LiAl(Si_2O_3)_2$			Koira valley manganese oxide deposits, Orissa.
	Eucryptite: $LiAlSiO_4$			
	Lithiophilite: Li(Mn, Fe)PO			
Rb	Lepidolite: Li-mica Carnallite: KCl, $MgCl_2 . 6H_2O$	Peg, Gr, G, Evaporite.	Cs, Li, Ta, Nb, Be, Sn, P, F, K, Li, W, Na, Ca, Mg	Bastar Peg.
Cs	Pollucite $(Cs, Na)AlSi_2O_6 .nH_2O$	Peg; Granite.	Li, Rb, Be, Sc, Y, REE, Nb, Ta, Zr, W, Ga, Tl, Sn, B, P & F.	
Sn	Cassiterite: SnO_2 Stannite: Cu_2S, FeS, SnS_2 Teallite: Pb SnS_2 Cylindrite: $Pb_3 Sn_4 FeSb_2 S_{14}$	Pegmatite; Granite; Skarn; Quartz veins; Lodes in greisen; Disseminations in acid igneous flows and ignimbrites; Placers.	W, Ta, Nb, Bi, As, Be, REE, B, F, Li, Rb, Cs, Mo, Pb, Zn, Fe, Cu, Cd, Bi, Ag, Au, Sb, In, Tl	Mundaguda, Orissa; Bastar, M.P.; Tosham, Haryana.

[1]Grade of minable material depends on: (1) international market value; (2) cost of mining and processing; (3) form and presence of associated economic/deleterious material; (4) distance from market; (5) accessibility and political stability; (6) current technological status of mining, beneficiation and metallurgy; (7) scale of mining, etc. Hence, specifications of grade including the nature and concentration of acceptable impurities change with time and place; vide Chapter 11.

(Contd)

Table 2.1: ***(Contd)***

a	*b*	*c*	*d*	*e*
W	Scheelite: $CaWO_4$ Wolframite: $(Fe, Mn)WO_4$	Pegmatite; Aplite; Skarn; Quartz veins; Placers.	Mo, Sn, Cu, Nb, Ta, Bi, Li, Be, REE, F, Rb, Cs, B, Sc, Mn, Zn, Pb, Ag, Au, Fe, U, Cd	Chendapathar, W.B.; Degana, Rajasthan.
C	Graphite	Schists		Khondalite belts of Eastern Ghats.
	Diamond[2] Bort	Kimberlite; Lamproite; Placers.	Cr, Nb, Ba, Ti	Panna, M.P. ; Vajrakarur, A.P.
Si	Quartz	Quartzite; Sandstone; Quartz veins and void fillings.		Semi precious varieties include: (i) Agate, e.g. Rajpipla mines obtained from the amygdaloidal flows of the Deccan Trap. (ii) Rock crystal, e.g. Thanjavur, T.N. (iii) Amethyst, rose quartz, onyx in Deccan Trap geodes

[2]Diamond is not necessarily a high pressure polymorph. Chemical vapour deposited (CVD) diamond forms at ambient pressure (L. Chow et al.: *Appl. Phys. Lett*. 66, 1995, 430). Diamond has been grown under hydrothermal conditions (800°C and 1.4 kbar) from mixtures of 95 wt % glassy carbon, 2 wt % diamond seeds and 3 wt % powdered nickel (Xing-Zhong Zhao et al.: *Nature*, 385, 1997, 513–5). Recently, diamond bearing ophiolitic peridotites have been described from Tibet (R.G. Coleman & X. Wang, ed., Ultrahigh Pressure Metamorphism, *Cambridge Topics in Petrology*, 1995, 528pp, Cambridge University Press, New York). Diamond is also reported to form when carbonaceous material is irradiated by the spontaneous fusion products of uranium. Carbonado, a polycrystalline porous aggregate of fine-grained diamond, found in placer deposits, is also believed by some to form by this method of irradiation. On the other hand, graphite in rocks like khondalite could form in lower crust by reaction between water and abundant CO_2 or from Archaean methanotrophs.

(Contd)

Table 2.1: (*Contd*)

a	*b*	*c*	*d*	*e*
Be	Beryl: $Be_3Al_2(SiO_3)_6$ [3] Chrysoberyl: $BeAl_2O_4$ Bromellite: BeO Phenacite: Be_2SiO_4 Euclase: $HBeAlSiO_3$ Bertrandite: $H_2Be_4Si_2O$ Gadolinite: $Be_2FeY_2Si_2O_{10}$	Pegmatite; Granite; Greisen; Skarn.	Li, Rb, Cs, Sc, Nb, Ta, Mo, W, B, Sn, Bi, F, U, Th, REE	Pegmatites of Hazaribagh, Bihar; Bolangir, Orissa; Nellore, A.P.; Tonk, Ajmer-Merwara and Mewar, Rajasthan.
Mo	Molybdenite: MoS_2 Powellite: $Ca(Mo, W)O_4$ Wulfenite: $PbMoO_4$	Pegmatite; Aplite; Greisen; Quartz vein; Skarn; Acid porphyry.	W, Re, Cu, Sn, Be, B, F, Zn, Bi, Fe, Li, P, Au, Ag, Zn, Cd, As, Pb	Karadikuttam, Tamil Nadu.
Nb–Ta	Columbite-Tantalite $(Fe, Mn)(Nb, Ta)_2O_6$ Pyrochlore $(Na, Ca)_2(Nb, Ti)_2(O, F)_7$ Niobian Perovskite ? $Ca(Ti, Nb)O_3$	Granitic and syenitic pegmatite; albite-riebeckite granite; Carbonatite; Placers.	Sn, W, Sb, Bi, Li, Be, Ti, Rb, Cs, U, Th, REE, P, F, Zr, Hf, Sr	Hazaribagh pegmatites, Bihar. Dharmapuri carbonatite, Tamil Nadu. Sung Valley & Samchampi alkaline complexes, Assam-Meghalaya.
Zr-Hf	Zircon: $ZrSiO_4$ Baddeleyite: ZrO_2	Placers; Carbonatite.	Ti, Th, REE Sn, W, U	Chattarpur, Orissa & Chavara, Kerala placer deposits[4]

[3]Gem varieties are emerald and aquamarine; some emeralds are costlier than diamond. Bolangir, Orissa has reportedly yielded pegmatites with good quality emerald. Emerald is the Cr/V-rich variety of beryl; Colombian emeralds have a value a thousand times more than gold and are especially prized for the intensity of their colour. These are found in sedimentary rocks formed at 290–360°C under 1.1 Kbar pressure from basinal sulphate-bearing hydrothermal brines interacting with black shales and limestones. Be, V and Cr are derived from the shales. (T.L. Ottaway et al., *Nature,* 369, 1994, 552–4; A. Cheilletz et al., *Econ. Geol.* 89, 1994, 361–80). Large crystals of beryl with clear parts which might be cut as aquamarines are known to occur in Bihar and Nellore mica belts, at Pattalai near Kangayam, Coimbatore dt., Tamil Nadu, associated with clevelandite, in Toda hills (Rajasthan) and in Skardu tehsil of Kashmir.

[4]Marketable grade of zircon concentrate contains 66% ZrO_2. Semiprecious, sherry-coloured zircon occurs in the Mogok Stone Tract, Myanmar.

(Contd)

Table 2.1: ***(Contd)***

a	*b*	*c*	*d*	*e*
REE (La to Lu) & Th	Bastnaesite, a fluocarbonate of REE, mostly Ce; Monazite: (Ce, La, Dy) PO_4 with ThO_2	Veins in Carbonatite; Phosphorite; Placers.	Th, Ba, Sr, Zr, P, Cu, F, Ti, U, Sc	Manavalakuruchi placer sand, Kerala; Ambadongar, Baroda dt., Gujarat.
Sc & Y	Thortveitite: $(Sc, Y)_2 Si_2 O_7$ Fergusonite: Metaniobate and tantalate of Y with Er, Ce, U; xenotime: YPO_4	Complex pegmatites; Pyritic quartz pebble conglomerate; Placers.	U, Th, REE, Au, Ag	Hazaribagh pegmatites, Bihar. Fluvial placers over granitic tract of Bihar, M.P. etc.
U	Uraninite (Pitchblende): Uranyl etc. uranate; Brannerite $(UO, TiO, UO_2) TiO_3$ Carnotite $K_2O. 2U_2O V_2O_5. 3H_2O$	Calcite-fluorite-apatite veins; Disseminations in black shales and schists; Sandstones in rolls and pinchouts; Quartz pebble conglomerate.	P, F, Nb, Ta, Ti, Zr, Hf, Cu, Mo, Sc, V, Th, Y, REE, Au, Ag	Jaduguda, Singhbhum, Bihar.
F	Fluorite: CaF_2 Cryolite: Na_3AlF_6 Topaz[5]: $(AlF)_2 SiO_4$	Greisen; Veins, lodes, pockets in acid igneous rocks; Carbonatite and alkaline igneous rocks; stratiform deposits in limestones & sandstones.	P, U, Th, Zr, Ti, Mo, REE, Ba, Sr, Pb, Zn, Sn, W, Be, Ba	Ambadongar, Gujarat
P	Apatite (including collophane, a microcrystalline variety) $(CaCl) Ca_4 (PO_4)_3$ $(CaF) Ca_4 (PO_4)_3$ Vivianite: $Fe_3P_2O_3 . 8H_2O$ Wavellite: $4AlPO_4$ $2Al (OH)_3. 9H_2O$	Veins and segregations; Marine phosphorite; Bog phosphate; Guano; Phosphatic nodules.	REE, Ti, Zr, Fe, Nb-Ta, Th, U, F, V, Mo, Zn, Ag	Bayanbil (Singhbhum) apatite magnetite veins; Mussoorie phosphorite; Kavaratti island (Laccadives); Perambalur taluk of Trichinopoly dt., Tamil Nadu. Semi-precious variety includes green apatite, e.g. in Vishakhapatnam dt., A.P.

[5]Gem variety topaz has perfect crystal faces, transparency and is wine yellow in colour.

Table 2.1: *(Contd)*

a	*b*	*c*	*d*	*e*
Ba	Barite: $BaSO_4$ Witherite: $BaCO_3$	Veins and replacements; Bedded deposits; Residual enrichments in karst and sinkholes.	Ca, Sr, Mg, Fe, Mn, Pb, F, Nb, REE	Mangampeta and other localities in Anantapur and and Cuddapah dts., Andhra Pradesh; Katni, Jabalpur dt., M.P.
Sr	Celestite: $SrSO_4$ Strontianite: $SrCO_3$	Veins and lenses in volcano-sedimentary basins/evaporite.	Pb, Zn, Fe, S, F, Ba	Uttattur beds of Tiruchirapalli Cretaceous.
Al	Bauxite: $Al_2O_3 . nH_2O$ Corundum[6]: $Al_2 O_3$ Emery[7] (Corundum) Kyanite[8] (Al_2SiO_5) Cordierite ($Mg_2Al_4 Si_5O_{18}$) Alunite: $K_2Al_6 (OH)_{12} (SO_4)_4$	Tropically weathered residual cappings. Pegmatite; Nepheline Syenite; Limestone; Skarns. Acid igneous rocks altered by H_2SO_4 fluids.	Fe, Mn, Au, Ti, V F, Pb, Zn, As	East Coast Bauxite, Orissa. Hazaribagh Pegmatites; Padar Sapphire Mine, Kistwar, J&K State; Gem variety kyanite occurs at Narnaul, Patiala. Gem variety cordierite occurs in Vishakhapatnam Hill Tracts and near Udaiyapatti and Kiranur, Tiruchirapalli dt., Tamil Nadu.
Ti	Rutile, Anatase, Brookite: TiO_2 Ilmenite; $FeTiO_3$ Titanite: $CaTiSiO_5$	Gabbroic anorthosites; Alkali syenite; Placers. Residual tropically weathered laterite.	Fe, V, P, REE	Chattarpur & Chavara placers; West Coast Laterites

[6]Gem variety of corundum includes ruby and sapphire.

[7]Used as abrasive.

[8]Kyanite and its polymorphs—sillimanite and andalusite—are used as refractories. Large deposits of kyanite occur at Lapsa Buru, Singhbhum dt., Bihar. Sillimanite is now abundantly recovered as a placer mineral from Chattarpur (Orissa) & Chavara Coast (Kerala). Massive sillimanite occurs at Nongstoin, K & J Hills and Pipri (Rewa). Andalusite deposits occur in Rajasthan.

(Contd)

Table 2.1: ***(Contd)***

a	*b*	*c*	*d*	*e*
V	Patronite: VS_4 Roscoelite: Vanadium mica Carnotite: $K_2O . 2U_2O. V_2O_5. 3H_2O$	Vanadium bearing uranium deposits in sandstone; Oxidised parts of polymetallic sulphide deposits.	U, Mo, Fe, Ti, Cu, Pb, Zn	
	Vanadiferous magnetite	Titaniferous magnetite bodies within gabbro and anorthosites.		Dublabera-Betjharan, Bihar-Orissa.
Hg	Cinnabar Metacinnabarite HgS Livingstonite: $HgS, 2Sb_2S_3$ Native Hg	Fissure veins; Stockworks; Disseminations in sedimentary and volcanic rocks along zones of dislocation.	As, Sb, Cu, Pb, Ag, Au, Zn, Se, Te, Mo, W, F	Arnala Hg show, Maharashtra; Simlipal, Orissa.
Sb	Stibnite: Sb_2S_3 Tetrahedrite: $3Cu_2S.Sb_2S_3$ Boulangerite: $PbS.2Sb_2S_3$ Jamesonite: $2PbS.Sb_2 S_3$ Bournonite: $2PbS. Cu_2S.Sb_2S_3$ Pyrargyrite: $2Ag_2S. Sb_2S_3$ Polybasite: $9Ag_2S.Sb_2S_3$	Massive Cu-Zn-Pb sulphide deposits and veins/lodes in volcanic, plutonic & sedimentary rocks; Pb-Zn-Ag deposits in phyllites, limestones, black schists; stibnite deposits in quartz veins; porphyry copper-molybdenum deposits; Residual enrichment in karst; gold-quartz veins & stockworks.	Cu, Pb, Zn, As, Au, Ag, Mo, Fe, Cd, Bi, Hg, S	Bara Shigri stibnite, Himachal Pradesh; Dariba-Rajpura polymetallic sulphide deposit, Bhilwara dt., Rajasthan.

(Contd)

Table 2.1: *(Contd)*

a	*b*	*c*	*d*	*e*
As	Realgar AsS; Orpiment: As_2S_3; Arsenopyrite: FeAsS; Niccolite: NiAs; Rammelsbergite: $NiAs_2$; Loellingite: $FeAs_2$; Enargite: $3Cu_2S. As_2 S_5$ Proustite: $5Ag_2S.As_2S_3$ Sperrylite: $PtAs_2$	Quartz veins: Volcanogenic Au deposits; Porphyry Cu & massive sulphide deposits; Au deposits in slate and graphitic schists; Pyrite bearing quartz pebble conglomerate; Skarn type Au deposits; Differentiated basic igneous plutons.	Cu, Pb, Zn, Sb, Cd, Ag, Au, Mo, Ni, Co, Sn, W, Te, Se, Bi, PGE	Kolar Au field, Karnataka; Lashteal quartz arsenopyrite vein, Baramulla dt., Kashmir.
Bi	Bismuthinite: Bi_2S_3 Tetradymite: $Bi_2 (Te, S)_3$ Cosalite: 2 PbS, Bi_2S_3	Pegmatites; Aplites; Quartz veins; Highly altered acid flows and ignimbrites; Skarn deposits; Polymetallic sulphide deposits.	Li, Rb, Cs, Be, Cu, Sn, W, Au, Ag, Mo.	
Cd	Greenockite: CdS	With Pb-Zn deposits; Phosphorite.	Fe, Cu, Ag, Mn, Ni, Co, Ba.	Dariba-Rajpura, Rajasthan.

(Contd)

Table 2.1: *(Contd)*

a	*b*	*c*	*d*	*e*
Cu	Bornite: Cu_5FeS_4 Chalcopyrite: $CuFeS_2$ Covellite: CuS Chalcocite: Cu_2S Cuprite: Cu_2O and a large number of other oxides, carbonates etc.	Stratiform disseminations in shales, sandstones and conglomerates; Porphyry copper deposits. Volcanogenic massive sulphides with Zn. Disseminations with Ni & Co in gabbros, norites & anorthosites; Carbonatite; Felspathised mafic granulites.	Ag, Zn, Pb, Mo, Au, Ni, Co, As, Sb, PGE, Se	Singhbhum Copper belt, Bihar; Malanjkhand Copper deposit, M.P.; Khetri-Dariba Copper deposits, Rajasthan. Sargipalli, Sundargarh dt. Adas, Sambalpur dt., Orissa.
Ag	Argentite: Ag_2S Dyscrasite: Ag_2 Sb Many other complex sulphides	Native Ag deposits associated with Au & Pb-Zn deposits; In Cu-U-V deposits; With Ni-Cu arsenide deposits.	Pb, Zn, Cd, Hg, Cu, Au, Te, As, Sb, Ni, Co, Bi	Zawar Pb-Zn sulphide deposits (Rajasthan); Kolar gold field, Karnataka.
Au	Petzite: $(Ag, Au)_2$ Te Sylvanite: (Au, Ag) Te_2	Skarn; Pegmatites & granites; Stockworks with SiO_2; Veins, lodes in K-rich/desilicated/carbonate rich/albitised zones within deformed volcanics; In BIF and quartz pebble conglomerate; Placers; Laterite and other residual enrichments.	Ag, As, Te, Bi, Se, Ba, B, W, Mo	Kolar Au field, Karnataka; Kerala laterite near Wynaad Valley.

(Contd)

Table 2.1: *(Contd)*

a	*b*	*c*	*d*	*e*
Pb	Galena (PbS) and a large number of complex sulphides	Mississippi valley type replacement in carbonates; Disseminations in sandstone and shale; Skarn type deposits; Veins and lodes in recrystallised carbonate sequences with barite and sphalerite.	Ag, Zn, Cd, Ba, As, Sb, Bi, Hg	Dariba-Rajpura & Zawar, Rajasthan & Sargipalli, Orissa.
Zn	Sphalerite: ZnS; Willemite: $Zn_2 SiO_4$ and a large number of carbonates, oxides	Same as for Pb; also massive sulphide deposits with Cu and Ag.	Cd, Pb, Fe, Cu, Ag, Au, Ba, Mn, Ni, Co	Zawar, Dariba-Rajpura, Rajasthan; Gainta, Riasi Jammu.
Cr	Chromite (Fe, Mg)O, $(Cr,Al)_2 O_3$	Dunite; Peridotite; Pyroxenite; Placer.	Ni, Co, As, PGE	Sukinda-Nausahi, Orissa; Jojuhatu, Bihar; Byrapur, Karnataka.
Ni	Pentlandite: (Fe, Ni)S; Millerite: NiS; Niccolite: NiAs; Chloanthite: $NiAs_2$; Gersdorffite: NiAsS, Garnierite: H_2 (Ni, Mg) $SiO_4 . nH_2O$ Nepouiter 3 (Ni, Mg)O. $2SiO_2$	Massive sulphide deposits; Veins & lenses in basic and ultrabasic rocks; Supergene enrichments in (a) serpentine, (b) laterite.	Co, Fe, Cu, Au, Ag, PGE, Cr Co, Mn, Cr	Mosabani copper mine, Singhbhum field (Bihar). Sukinda (Kansa) oxidic nickel deposit (Orissa).
Co	Cobaltite: CoAsS; Smaltite: $CoAs_2$; Linnaeite: $Co_2 S_4$; Carrollite: $CuCo_2 S_4$; Skutterudite: $CoAs_3$; Safflorite: $CoAs_2$; Glaucodot: (Co, Fe) AsS	As in Nickel; also in bedded deposits with Cu in shales (Zambia) and with Pb-Zn ore veins.	Ni, PGE, Fe, Cu, Ag, Au, Se, Mn, Cr, Pb, Zn, Cd	Madan-Kudan deposit, Khetri, Rajasthan.

(Contd)

Table 2.1: *(Contd)*

a	*b*	*c*	*d*	*e*
Fe	Haematite: Fe_2O_3 Magnetite: Fe_3O_4 Goethite: $Fe_2O_3 . H_2O$ Siderite: $FeCO_3$	Residual enrichments from BHQ and Shales; Skarn deposits; Small bodies in mafic igneous rocks and carbonatites.	Mn, Al, P, S, Si, Cu, Nb	Bonai, Orissa; Bailadila, MP; Sandur, Karnataka.
Mn	Pyrolusite, Polianite] MnO_2 Psilomelane: Hydrous Mn manganate Bixbyite: $(Fe, Mn)_2O_3$ Manganite: $Mn_2O_3 . H_2O$ Hausmannite: Mn_3O_4 Braunite: $3Mn_2O_3 . MnSiO_3$ Franklinite: $(Fe, Zn, Mn) O . (Fe, Mn)_2O_3$ Wad: Hydrous Mn Oxide	Residual enrichments; Bedded deposits; Veins and lenses in different rocks; Deep sea nodules.	Fe, Ba, Li, Cu, Co, Ni, Mo, W, Ag, P, S	Balaghat and Bhandara dts., Maharashtra; Koira-Jamda valley, Orissa; Garivedi, A.P.; Central Indian ocean lease area.
Platinum Group Elements including the highly refractory IPGE (Os, Ir & Ru) and more volatile PPGE (Pt & Pd)	Sperrylite: $PtAs_2$ Cooperite: $Pt (As, S)_2$ Braggite: $(Pt, Pd, Ni)S$ Laurite: RuS_2 Stibiopalladinite: $Pd_3 Sb$	Minor concentrations with Cu, Ni sulphides in differentiated mafic-ultramafic plutons and their sheared, remobilised derivatives.	Cu, Ni, Co, Au, Cr, Te, Se, Sb, Ag, As	Singhbhum copper deposits, Bihar (in trace amounts).

(Contd)

Table 2.. (*Contd*)

a	*b*	*c*	*d*	*e*
Ruthenium, rhodium, palladium, osmium, iridium & Pt (contd)		Trace concerntrations with volcanogenic copper / silver / gold lodes and veins.[9] Sediment hosted Cu deposit[10] & metalliferous black shales. Fractures & breccia fillings of U-Au-PGE below, above or across unconformity. Porphyry copper ores. Quartz pebble conglomerates and placers. Gossans and residual deposits.		

[9]Unlike Os, Ru. & Ir (IPGE) which are highly refractory metals, Pt and Pd (as well as Au) have enhanced mobility with increasing temperature and concentration of Cl, OH and S in the fluid phase. Hence their chalcophile nature. All platinum group elements as well as gold and rhenium are generally grouped under *Siderophile* elements. Iridium and platinum are heavy platinoids, whereas ruthenium, rhodium and palladium are light platinoids. The earth's upper mantle is over-abundant in these elements relative to what would be expected from equilibrium with the metallic core. This has led many geochemists (vide K. Kamura et al., *Geochim. Cosmochim. Acta*, 38, 1974, 683–701) to conclude that these elements were partly introduced by meteorite bombardment during the Hadean era of the earth's history, but after separation of core.

[10]PGE, U & Au are byproducts of recovery from some Kupferschiefer & Zambian deposits (*USGS Bull.* 2049A, 1994).

FURTHER READING

M.L. Jensen and A.M. Bateman, *Economic Mineral Deposits,* 3/e, John Wiley & Sons, New York, 1981, 593 pp.

R. Edwards and K. Atkinson, *Ore Deposit Geology,* Chapman and Hall, London, 1986, 466 pp.

R.W. Boyle, Elemental Associations in Mineral Deposits and Indicator Elements of Interest in Geochemical Prospecting. (Revised). *Geological Survey of Canada Paper,* 74–45, Ottawa, 1974, 40 pp.

3

Geological and Geomorphological Prospecting

Geological and geomorphological prospecting is divisible into a number of categories:

1. Regional scale prospecting covering thousands of square kilometers of virgin or poorly explored territory;
2. District scale, covering the whole or a large part of a known ore district;
3. Local scale, covering one or a few small leaseholds, the total area being less than fifty square kilometers.

REGIONAL SCALE PROSPECTING

Such efforts should start in the office with examination of satellite imageries of the area, and if available, aerial photographs before proceeding to the field. It is useful to focus search on favourable tracts, although remote sensing is not a substitute for field work. Satellite imageries and aerial photographs show ancient planation surfaces, fold closures, fault linears (comparatively resistant formations standing out and indicating lateral displacement under favourable circumstance), zones of contrasting lithology, fracture patterns, vegetation, possible access routes in poorly known tracts, etc. Even where toposheets are available, satellite imageries and aerial photographs provide useful supplementary data for maximum definition in map making. For example, in the Bihar mica belt, there are several granitic plutons of various sizes and shapes, some being porphyritic having sharp contact with the surrounding metamorphic rocks, others non-porphyritic with gradational contacts.

The majority of the mica pegmatites are sited around the non-porphyritic granites, whose photo characters on Landsat imagery are distinctive (P.K. Guha and S. Chakravarti, *ITC Journal*, 1983, 13–16). In the Sukinda reserve forest, chromite bands could be clearly picked up on aerial photographs of scale 1:25,000 in 1961 through the then-thick (now partly destroyed) canopy of the Sal *(Shorea robusta)* forest by a combination of characters—a subtle contrast in shade, absence of undergrowth over the chromite seams and a sharp micro-relief. All these features could be identified as diagnostic for chromite bodies only during actual field work; this resulted in accurate delineation of all the exposed chromite masses over an area of 20 sq.km in a very dense, wild-animal-infested jungle within a period of 3 months.

In the Amazon rainforest of Brazil, the first indications of large ore districts were provided by photogeological interpretation. The region is thickly forested except for the mesa type clearings standing about 350 m above m.s.l. During the Araguaia Project (1966) the clearings were initially identified; and in August 1967 geologists of Companhia Meridional de Mineracao first discovered iron ore in the course of a regional prospecting program for manganese ore in one of the clearings in Serra dos Carajas district. There were no roads in this area nor navigable rivers; access was only by air. After the first find, many more mesas were delineated through additional photogeological interpretation. Between 1970 and 1972, intensive exploration was undertaken. This included aeromagnetic survey (34,000 sq.km on reconnaissance scale and 18,000 sq.km on detailed scale), topographic surveying of the iron ore district, drilling of 277 holes with an average depth of 134 m using 15 drill machines and ensuring a minimum core recovery of 80%, excavation of 13 exploration galleries totalling 3,392 m and 87,400 chemical analyses. Because of the dense forest surrounding the mesa tops, ground geological and geophysical mapping was undertaken concurrently on traverse lines, which had to be cleared by machete. The work included 1,022 km of detailed geological mapping (on drill-hole and exploration gallery sections), 567 km of regional geological mapping, 400 km of geophysical survey, besides study of thin and polished sections, routine XRD identification and screening tests of the ore samples (bulk) etc.

This prospecting programme proved the existence of high quality reserves of haematite. Next came the stage of pre-investment viability study for defining the technical problems associated with large-scale iron ore mining and cost-benefit studies. One of the deposits, N4, was identified for this exercise. Detailed work continued from 1972 to 1979. The main items of work included:

- Drilling of 10,176 m in 123 holes;

- Excavation of 4 exploration galleries with a total length of 602 m;
- A 108 m long raise connecting a gallery with the surface along a previous borehole course;
- A pilot plant assembly for undertaking different screening and crushing tests on representative ore samples.

The prospecting work led to the estimation of about 35 billion tonnes of iron ore, out of which N4 deposit itself carries 2.6 billion tonnes of 66.6% Fe and 0.55 billion tonnes of 61.1% Fe. The discovery of such a large ore district would have been long delayed without the photogeological leads.

The Brazilian programme during the sixties and the seventies illustrates the following aspects of regional geological prospecting:

(1) Intelligent application of geomorphological features, it being common knowledge all over the Gondwanaland fragments that deposits of iron and manganese oxides over Banded Iron Formation occur within uplifted and dissected peneplains, now exposed as mesas.

(2) The advantage of saturation prospecting using a large team, having almost 800 workmen in the months of greatest activity, operating from different camps. This was possible by allotting a large budget to the effort within a well-defined time frame and combining the resources of Companhia Vale de Rio Doce with Companhia Meridional de Mineracao.

(3) Total utilization of modern technology all down the line from transhipment of the exploration personnel by air, utilization of aerogeophysical techniques with different grid intervals and levels of flight, use of aerial photographs for designing the prospecting programme, comprehensive use of laboratory facilities at Belem, 550 km from Carajas Iron Ore district, regular and real time feedback from the laboratory to the field parties by telecommunication facilities etc. A byproduct of this operation resulted in the discovery of an earthy, ferruginous, friable bauxite with an average thickness of 4.5 m in the N5 plateau area, while searching for clay suitable for brick making! It was a standard practice to send all samples to the Belem laboratory for routine physical tests by X-ray diffraction before chemical analysis of each sample. XRD revealed the presence of strong gibbsite peaks, and the field geologist was alerted immediately to define the bauxite area by close sampling.

(4) Efficient management of time and resources in exploring a thickly forested and remote terrain. The whole regional prospecting programme covering about 10,000 sq.km conceived in 1966 was completed by 1972—an enviable record by any standard.

The Carajas experience is however not the standard model in Regional Exploration. Where the work is undertaken by Government Survey Agencies in developing countries, operations are limited by availability of funds, equipment and personnel; and saturation prospecting is hardly possible. What is worse is that the linkage between field and laboratory operations is not usually comprehensive and close, resulting in many wasteful endeavours. Aerial photographs and satellite imageries as well as aerogeophysical maps reveal many subtle traits of ground, which are not otherwise discernible. The British Geological Survey uses a system for turning air photos into digital data, using a powerful work station, to create 3-D images at all factors of magnification, and very high resolution digital elevation models. Rock outcrops and micromorphologic contrasts are defined even before field work begins; this helps not only in faster ground survey but also in identifying changes in underlying rocks, fault zones, etc. in relatively open areas. Even in areas with thick vegetation cover, sharp changes in vegetation pattern and subtle changes in shade are used for broad correlation of ground features in course of actual field work.

A regional survey is essentially based on wide-spaced traverses; no systematic geological map can be produced. During the early days of the Geological Survey of India in the nineteenth century, the traverses of Medlicott, Ball, Blanford and others across the length and breadth of India illustrate the amount of detail recoverable by such work in an alien land, when no aerial photograph or good topographic sheet was available. During the last few decades there has been a substantial improvement. Topographic maps on scale 1:50,000 became available for the whole country; so also aerial photographs on scale 1:50,000 to 1:25,000; changes in geomorphology during the past decades can be studied by the Landsat satellites, (the first of which was launched in 1972) besides the current series of Indian satellites. The sensors in this group of satellites detect electromagnetic radiation from the visible to the near infrared; and individual scenes have a resolution of approximately 30 m (i.e. objects of this size can be detected). One problem with the older Landsat images is that these are stored on magnetic tapes that can deteriorate or in formats that cannot be read by existing equipment; but the day is not far off when the Global Topography Mission (TOPSAT) of NASA will yield a high resolution, high accuracy (± 10 cm) topographic map of the entire land surface of the globe with the help of synthetic aperture radar (SAR) interferometry in a few months time (*EOS*, June 14, 1994). Other freely available sources of satellite imagery include the SPOT, NOAA and ERS-1 data products as well as the Indian Remote Sensing satellite imageries. The products are offered on different media, such as photographic prints, transparencies, CCTs, floppies, cartridges etc. The photographic prints are available with different enlargements from the NRSA data centre, National Remote Sensing Agency, Balanagar, Hyderabad-500037, India. Many (not all) mineral species have diagnostic features of emission and absorption in electromagnetic wavelength ranges. These are measurable by remote sensing through the atmospheric blanket, particularly the 2000–2400 nm wavelength region which covers a large number of absorption features corresponding to hydroxyl and carbonate minerals. Under favourable conditions, zones of hydrothermal alteration around ore deposits can be picked up by remote sensing, as demonstrated by Hook and others in the Cuprite area on the western edge of Esmeralda County, Nevada, U.S.A. Here they achieved partial success in discriminating among silicified rock, opalised rock and argillised rock zones around epithermal auriferous deposits (S.J. Cook, et al. *Geophysics* 56(9), 1991, 1432–40). In the densely forested, flat to gently undulating tract of the Norseman area, Yilgarn Block, Western Australia, Landsat MSS data were first corrected for geometrical distortion, atmospheric effects, etc. (image restoration) and then subjected to contrast, edge, colour and multi-image enhancement techniques for creating False Colour products by Principal Component Analysis through trial and error to best reveal features of geological significance. The distribution of greenstones and granitoids was clearly revealed as also fault lineaments. Since the greenstones are associated with Archean, vein-type gold deposits, the importance of such studies is apparent. (J.O. Spray & L.A. Burgess, *Geol. Mag.* 122(6), 1985, 587–94).

In another instance, Ford and others used Landsat Thematic Mapper and other images along with aerial photographs to delineate a major fault system in the Mojave Desert, California. Landsat TM images processed by a four-component technique revealed contrasting compositional characteristics of the rocks mostly at IR (infra-red) wavelengths over a 2000 sq.km area, where no detailed mapping had been done earlier. In contrast to low resolution, single band and other types of false colour imageries, which are just different ways of depicting landforms with very little extra information, it was observed that infra-red and visible wavelength band ratios (5/7, 5/4 and 3/1) of the Thematic Mapper emphasize compositional difference of the rocks. High values for band ratio 5/7 general denote OH^+ rich minerals; high values for band ratio 5/4 generally denote rocks rich in Fe^{2+} and high values for band ratio 3/1 generally denote rocks rich in Fe^{3+} (J.P. Ford et al., *Science* 248, 25 May, 1990, 1000–3). In the Tomkinson Range, Western Musgrave Block, Central Australia, Landsat TM multi-spectral imagery furnished a workable method of correlating the weathered surface covers, specially from the reflectance in the infra-red range.

It is however important to bear in mind that the best resolutions from remote sensing are available over arid areas of the world exposing Cenozoic mineral provinces, e.g. Arizona and other parts of the Great Western desert of N. America. In large volcanic or mixed volcanoplutonic fields, space borne imaging radar and X and synthetic aperture radar images are capable of mapping lava flows and other structures like rift zones. The radars illuminate earth with microwaves, allowing detailed observations at any time, regardless of weather or sunlight conditions. Normally, three micro-wavelengths are used: L band (24 cm), C band (6 cm) and X band (3 cm). The multi-frequency data are also useful for measuring large-scale changes, both natural and anthropogenic and are of use in environmental studies as well. Recent flights of the Space-borne Imaging Radar (SIR)-C/X band Synthetic Aperture Radar mission aboard the Space Shuttle Endeavour brought out the usefulness of such images in hyper-arid areas. Paleodrainage systems in old inactive stream valleys covered by thick deposits of windblown sand are revealed in such images. It was found that productive wells were located at the confluence of such old river valleys in the Kufra oasis in southeast Libya. Wherever the country rocks are covered by deep tropical weathering, identification of rock compositions by remote sensing is difficult. But even in such areas, significant geomorphological interpretations are possible, as illustrated by the Carajas experience of Brazil.

There are no standard formulae for successful use of remote sensing data. Major initiatives are necessary for obtaining high spectral resolution and high signal-to-noise in the short wave infra-red band. These imageries are very useful for systematic mapping.

DISTRICT SCALE PROSPECTING

The use of aerial photographs for culling the greatest amount of information before and during field work is also very helpful at this level of operation. In many ore districts, the expressions of mineral deposits are associated with subtle morphologic changes. Mesas in BIF terrains associated with Fe and Mn deposits have already been mentioned; even in base metal areas, like the Broken Hill lode of Australia, a prominent ridge, made up of iron-rich gossan with wall rocks of resistant metamorphites defines the ore zone. The quartz vein of the auriferous Mother Lode of

California stands out in relief. The mesas of the East Coast bauxite deposit in Orissa and Andhra Pradesh appear as clear incised table lands among the undulating ranges of the Eastern Ghats of India. The copper mineralised ground in Singhbhum between Surda and Keruadungri is enclosed within resistant quartzites, which stand out as low, linear ridges facing the Subarnarekha plains to their north.

Not all ore districts are marked by clear ridges. Some mineral deposits are associated with minor depressions, particularly in arid terrains and those associated with limestones or calcite gangue. The blue ground of a kimberlite pipe is normally a depression. Oxidation-shrinkage over porphyry copper deposits in arid tracts results in depression of the land.

In zones of deep tropical weathering, such morphologic contrasts associated with mineral deposits (other than Fe, Mn and Al enrichments) are generally hidden beneath a carapace of laterite. The regolith landscape is divided into residual, erosional and accumulation regimes and the landform units are mapped on the basis of exposed laterite profiles and their erosional/depositional variants. Shallow pits are useful for proper classification into zones of massive duricrust, disintegrated and colluvial duricrust, hardened saprolite etc. Over large parts of the Indian Peninsula, ancient laterite catena are dislocated; and structured/unstructured saprolite is juxtaposed against cavernous laterite due to neotectonic movements, e.g. in the Adash copper sulphide field in Sambalpur district, Orissa. Elsewhere as in the Sukinda ultramafic field, the nickeliferous saprolite is intermittently polished and mullioned along zones of neotectonic movement, and is silicified in linear tracts. Such zones of contrasting weathering are easily identifiable in aerial photos.

The width of surface expressions of a mineral deposit may not coincide with its actual thickness. Downhill creep is very common.

Depressions within uplifted peneplains in deeply weathered tracts are also informative. In Niquelandia, Goiaz province, Brazil, W.T. Pecora of USGS had concluded that the weathering of peridotite to clay on an old erosion surface (the Goiaz upland surface) which shows up as isolated mesas was followed by supergene enrichment of the exposed saprolite layers, and deposition of garnicrite (nickel silicate) in joints and fractures in the underlying peridotite to 20 meters below the present surface, particularly in sites which formed shallow valleys in the Goiaz upland surface. The nickel deposits occur only at lower heights. Subsequent Brazilian work revealed that there are two types of nickel ore in Niquelandia; the garnieritic and the oxide ores, the former originating by decomposition of pyroxenites and the latter from peridotites and dunites. The deposits of garnierite are in the hanging valleys, which escaped erosion. In air photos, such hanging valleys are recognisable in between the succession of N–S asymmetrical ridges of pyroxenites and peridotites of Serra da Mantiqueira.

The task of mineral survey in the course of systematic mapping is to prepare large-scale maps of such sectors with all topographic and geologic details, examine the mineralised ground for its paragenetic history and zonation, and enunciate the framework of the controls and characteristics of the mineral shows.

Modern geological maps are no longer coloured topo-sheets with a few strike and dip symbols marked here and there. The maps represent an integrated interpretation of the geology of the region based on field observations and measurements, laboratory studies and analysis; and is underpinned by airborne geophysical, magnetic and spectrometric data sets, gravity and seismic reflection profiles, data sets from regolith characters, geochemical, geochronological, metallogenic and well log studies. In the Eastern Goldfields of Australia, airborne geophysical survey of 47,000 km along flight lines 400 meters apart and just 100 meters above the ground was completed as a part of geological mapping. Over a large area of the Tanami desert in the Kimberlay-Arunta area, airborne survey acquired magnetic and gamma ray spectrometric data sets 500 meters apart and just 90 m above the ground. Such low flight picks up many high frequency anomalies, related to local features, which would provide clues to ore deposits. A flight deck of 500 m to 1000 m is not meant for hunting for indications of local specialisation of the basement, normally associated with ore deposits (vide Chapter 5). Replacement of the old-style geological maps by modern geological-geophysical-geochemical sheets represents a major investment by the Government, but this is adequately repaid by its use in discovery of new mineral and water resources as well as in land use planning, environmental assessment and natural hazard mitigation.

It is now recognised that a major control of continental metallogeny during the Proterozoic and later periods is the remobilised zone of the upper crust. This provides the framework for all tectonic and magmatic activity; and large funds have been spent in Europe and N. America on the Geotraverse programme during the eighties to outline Proterozoic subduction zones. In the Baltic and Bothnian seismic reflection profiles, zones of megashear, bivergent crustal reflectors and supposed remnants of Proterozoic oceanic crust trapped in the subduction zone, choked by collision of arc have been outlined, similar to many Phanerozoic orogens, like the Alps, Pyrennes, Appalachians and Caledonides (BABEL working group, *Nature*, 348, 1990, 34–8).

In the course of such efforts, it has also been clear that interdisciplinary—instead of multidisciplinary—projects yield greater benefits, because a combined geological-geochemical-geophysical survey is so designed that the fundamental uncertainties in the geological interpretation are reduced to the minimum. Devoid of such an overview, data do not lead to a complete understanding and the maps and overlays, however pretty and impressive, cannot demand custom. In recognition of such emerging perception, a regional 250 km long crustal transect of the Mount Isa inlier by the Land Seismic Group of AGSO is proceeding with complementary studies of the structural history of the region by graduate students of Monash University. Topographic pseudo-3D reflection recordings of several major fault systems, gravity measurements every 240 m and magnetic intensity measurements every 40 m along the seismic lines are concurrently undertaken.

Fundamental to the generation of such interdisciplinary maps is the new mapping technology using multiple digital data sets in Geographic Information Systems (GIS). Such comprehensive databases are not generated in many developing countries even now; but their introduction cannot be far delayed without a risk to the national enterprise.

Equally important is a critical understanding of the history of evolution of the landforms. Recent researches all over the world show that there were many cycles of sea level change during the Neogene-Quaternary period with attendant changes in atmospheric circulation, precipitation and weathering of the rocks. Countries in the cooler climatic belts suffered repeated advance and retreat of glaciers and related isostatic uplift when the weight of the glaciers was removed (e.g. Fennoscandia). The tropical countries were also subjected to isostatic perturbations due to changes in the volume of water on the continental shelf and alternations of arid and humid cycles. These are recorded in the geomorphological, pedological and other records.

For example, parts of the Gondwanaland continents have many landscapes which are at least 300 million years old. The fundamental questions which are relevant to mineral prospecting in such tracts (e.g. parts of the coastal granulite terranes of S. Orissa, N. Andhra Pradesh, and South Tamil Nadu) are: (1) the history of development of the individual landscapes and their weathered cover; (2) mechanisms of physical and chemical dispersion of major and trace elements in such slowly evolving landscapes; and (3) development of three-dimensional models and appropriate prospecting sequence for picking up surface and subsurface expressions of mineral deposits associated with these old landscapes.

In the Himalaya also, such climatic perturbations led to fluctuations in the intensity of precipitation, resulting in cyclic growth and retreat of valley glaciers during the Quaternary period and consequent changes in the rate of uplift and erosion of the Inner Himalaya. In such sectors, there is a continuous competition, as it were, between bedrock uplift and erosion. Small lenticular MVT orebodies get intermittently exposed by landslides and then eroded away rapidly, e.g. at Sersandu (Riasi tehsil) Pb occurrences. In such areas, the heavy mineral assemblage in sediments of uplifted terraces and boulders in the river bed locally carry indications of ore potential. In parts of the Indus river, it has been found that uplift and incision rates are maintained near equilibrium. ^{10}Be and ^{26}Al dating of strath terraces (portions of river channel bottom preserved unweathered on side slopes) yield incision rates from 2 to 12 mm/year (D.W. Burbank et al., *Nature*, 379, 1996, 505–10). Even in rapidly eroding regions like the Indus gorge near Skardu, cutting across the Nanga Parbat-Haramosh Mountains, steep slope gradients hover close to the maximum angle of stability of partially weathered bedrock (around 32°). In the lower Himalaya, on the other hand, heavy rainfall during the monsoon months leads to fast stream erosion. Wherever the threshold of stability is crossed, erosion takes the form of landslides to carry away excess mass efficiently and quickly. In general, wherever incision rate of a river system crosses the threshold of nearly 0.5 mm/year, development of the soil profile (including regoliths carrying oxidic enrichments of Fe, Mn, Al etc.) is arrested and hill slopes adjust by landsliding in place of soil creep and slope wash. A critical analysis of the ground slopes and drainage patterns provides an important preliminary framework for mineral deposit prospecting.

Geomorphological classification on the basis of aerial photographs and topographic sheets can be initiated in the office before actual field work; but walking over the ground carefully cannot be avoided for proper geological correlation. In moderately accessible tracts, this does not pose any problem for sturdy geologists; but in extremely rugged or terrorist-infested or thickly-forested terrains, one faces problems of reaching every outcrop. In the developed countries, modern technology has come to the aid of the geologist. In extremely rugged terrains, accessibility is aided by helicopters with two-man teams using hammer + rope + piton + axe for steep slopes; in thickly-forested terrains, location is now easy with Global Positioning System (GPS) receivers, which provide a good accuracy (± 10 m and less) for detailed mapping. These facilities are generally not available in developing countries. Controlled pacing from well-located points has been the time-honoured practice in thick forests. For steep slopes, it is always advisable to use mountaineering techniques with a two-man team as the unit of workforce, even where modern facilities are otherwise absent.

The useful life of a geological map depends on many factors. Generally, it is about 30 years before it needs revision as a result of new needs or changing ideas. For example, the emerging concern with environment, including pollution, global warming, carbon and nitrogen cycles, ecological sustainability etc. calls for various types of thematic maps, where pedological and geomorphological features assume importance even where you are prospecting for mineral deposits. In many old style maps, geomorphological attributes are relegated to depiction of contours and drainage features. Their significance is not highlighted. For example, tectonic landforms, e.g. fault scarps and annular depressions or karst landforms with sinkholes, caverns, runnels with trenches and pits or zones of creep and landslide can be identified by hummocky or chaotic landforms at the base of the scarps by debris flow. Regolith-landform-geomorphic maps in the form of overlays, one coloured according to dominant regolith type, the other coloured according to dominant landform type complemented by geomorphic features reveal many latent contrasts. These are important features, when a search for mineral deposits on district to local scale is being executed. The design of the mine, ancillary developments, environmental impact assessment—all these are dependent on a proper geomorphic analysis.

Leaving aside such indirect objectives, geomorphologic interpretation is frequently a direct aid to discovery of new ore deposits. Ore bodies are at places marked by clear surface features—like a ridge, e.g. over the Broken Hill lead-zinc deposit in Australia; or ribbed humps on ground, e.g. the quartz vein system of Malanjkhand; or depressions, e.g. at Bisbee, Arizona, which simulates slumping due to mining but is actually due to oxidation shrinkage; or karst-like disposition with interconnecting sinkholes, e.g. some Mississippi Valley Type epithermal base metal deposits of the U.S.A.; or uplifted planation surfaces, which are invariably associated with secondary enrichments of iron, manganese and aluminium oxide deposits in Gondwanaland fragments, e.g. Bonai-Bailadila Iron Ore ranges, the East Coast Bauxite Plateau of Orissa and M.P., Carajas province Iron Ore plateaus of Brazil etc; or channel filling on extensive palaeo erosion surfaces, e.g. uranium deposits of the Colorado Plateau, U.S.A., Witwatersrand gold-uranium deposits of S. Africa, etc. The planar surfaces of Bihar-Orissa Fe ore region at the top of the hill ranges were recognised as remnants of an old peneplain by J.A. Dunn and H.C. Jones of the GSI in the late twenties and early thirties of the century. K.L.V. Ramana Rao & R. Vaidyanadhan (*Ind. Jour. Earth Sci.* 1(1), 1974, 84–95) had demarcated three surfaces—the Kiriburu surface at 830–900 m.a.s.l, Noamundi surface at 590–670 m.a.s.l. and Jamda surface at 424–530 m.a.s.l. and had hinted at Miocene to Pliocene age of these surfaces. An earlier relict surface at more than 1000 m.a.s.l. elevation was suspected to be Middle or Late Eocene in age. Such uplifted planar surfaces have since been identified over almost the whole of Peninsular India. In other fragments of Gondwanaland, broad undulating surfaces with low relief standing out as mesas with a gentle regional dip, as at Carajas in the Amazon rain forest of Brazil, have also been mapped, e.g. in various parts of Australia and Africa. These surfaces truncate a variety of lithologies and structures, and are locally associated with lateritic ore deposits. It is generally believed that some of these surfaces formed since the Cretaceous period. Similar lateritised surfaces at lower elevations could either represent successive cycles of pediplanation and epeirogenic uplift or differentially displaced co-eval surfaces. This debate has not yet been resolved.

The best example of the use of paleogeomorphic interpretation is associated with Waldemar Lindgren. In the Tertiary valleys of Sierra Nevada, he outlined three sequences in 1911—the Eocene valleys with buried gold placers, the intermontane valleys of the Miocene and of the Pliocene which contain little Au. The tropical climate of the area during the Eocene favoured deep chemical weathering of the gold-bearing rocks of the Jurassic batholith and attendant release of gold, which was washed down into the valleys existing at that time (Eocene surface). Burial of these valleys with later volcanic debris ensured their preservation. Exposure is confined to the places where these sequences are intersected by younger valleys. Before this geomorphic analysis, much money was wasted by early gold hunters, tunnelling into many barren valleys.

Careful geomorphologic study of the lateritised terrain at Belhouro in northern Burkina Faso by ORSTOM revealed that gold distribution (particles being upto 0.5 mm in size in surficial sand and gravel) is noticeable within the iron crusts of the middle and low fans. The upland is mostly a thick kaolinic regolith capped by an iron crust. It is barren except close to primary gold quartz veins within Birrimian tuffaceous schists near granites.

Gold panning from the Tertiary quartz pebbles and gravels near the Sonapet anticline over a 50 km stretch of the Subarnarekha river in Bihar is more than a century old; a cottage level operation of the local people. Although the quartzites associated with the Dalma volcanics appear to be the most likely parent, the ultimate source of this gold is still not clear.

Systematic geologic mapping involving continuous examination along the strike of each mappable rock unit is required during this stage of operation. But this is not possible everywhere. In such cases traverse mapping along key sections on a properly controlled space frame (river courses; orthogonal grids; foot tracks and mule paths oriented across the trend of the rock formations) is undertaken in order to understand the stratigraphic sequence. Large-scale geologic mapping covers only the mineral bearing ground to define its lateral continuity and variation in width. Important features of the mineral bearing zones to be observed include:

(a) Nature of rock alteration associated with the mineral deposit;
(b) Stratigraphic level where the mineral deposit occurs;
(c) Specific lithologic associations of the mineral deposit;
(d) Preferred orientation of the planar surfaces, fracture systems and lineaments, if any, associated with the mineral deposit; and
(e) relationship of lithologic contacts and folds of different generations and styles with the mineral deposit.

(a) Rock alteration: Alteration of wall rocks around mineral deposits is very common in many epigenetic and some syngenetic deposits. Even where post-diagenetic changes are absent, variations in the mineralogy of the wall rocks are near-universal, be it a deposit of limestone, chromite, tin-tungsten, gold or lead-copper-zinc. The thickness of the zone may be meters or centimeters, the variation may be gross and striking or subtle and invisible to the naked eye. Careful thin-section study supplemented by X-ray diffraction (XRD) scans and multi-element analysis help to define the variations in detail.

Such mineralogical changes in the wall rocks are brought about by either depletion of some elements from the wall rocks, e.g. in the Saladipura pyrite-pyrrhotite deposit of Rajasthan, where iron from the wall rocks was extracted for the development of pyrite ore bodies; or by incorporation of extraneous elements into the wall rocks, e.g. boron in the hanging wall of the copper lodes of Rakha Mines, Bihar; or by a chemical shift in the depositional basin, with the change expressed in such subtle characters as the texture or the colour of the material, e.g. in the cement and steel melting grade limestone deposits of Gangpur, Orissa.

A large variety of minerals define the outer mineralogical mile posts of an ore deposit. These include: tourmaline, magnetite, garnet, amphibole, pyroxene, biotite, quartz, sericite, chlorite, carbonate, epidote, adularia, alunite, clay minerals and chalcedony. For example, the Salobo 3A copper deposit, north of the Carajas synclinorium in Brazil (estimated reserve of 400 million tonnes of ore of 1.3% Cu with concentrates of 35–40% Cu grade carrying 10 gm/tonne of Au and 0.2% Mo) is flanked by schistose host rocks carrying grunerite—cummingtonite, actinolite, hastingsite and hornblende in addition to almandine, biotite, fayalite, chlorite and schorlite. The hanging wall of the Rakha Mines copper deposit in Singhbhum, Bihar is a very striking tourmaline-magnetite-quartz rock. In the copper sulphide deposit at Adash, Sambalpur district, Orissa, the garnet-diopside granulite host rock was infiltrated by biotite, quartz, carbonate, muscovite and chlorite. At Malanjkhand, the copper ore deposit (chalcopyrite-pyrite-magnetite-molybdenite) localised in a 2.6 km long and 60 m (average) wide quartz vein within granodiorite is flanked by zones of wall rock alteration marked by intense development of K-feldspar, biotite, chlorite and sericite.

Such mineralogical guides are most useful when these are neither very widespread nor rare. For example, there are extensive tourmaline rich tracts in the southern arm of the Gangpur fold (Orissa), stretching over tens of kilometers, but no mineral deposit has yet been found in association; similar instances are the sparsely pyritised clay and chlorite-rich zones in the Andaman ophiolites (with some Cu and Au indications) and the abundant but barren propylitised epidote + chlorite + carbonate zones in some parts of western U.S. These illustrate the inherent uncertainty of this technique at an early phase of prospecting. One has to be cautious and discriminate between the barren and the ore-associated phases of rock alteration. One has also to ensure that the orebody is not a product of different phases of mineralisation; where that happens, as in the Singhbhum copper field, ore shoots of different generation are surrounded by different types and degrees of rock alteration. Blind use of empirical criteria without a clear analysis of the ore genetic history and chemistry of the fluids leads to errors.

A very common surface indicator of an orebody is its oxidation product, manifest in outcrops and old workings as oxides, carbonates and silicates of the main or of associated ore elements in the form of coatings or cellular, leached masses with or without varying amounts of the parent minerals. This is known as *gossan*. In tropical tracts, there are instances where a laterite saprolite was mistaken for a gossan, e.g. at Riamal, Sambalpur dt., Orissa. On the other hand, in glaciated terrains, rapid erosion can remove the earlier-formed oxidised zone and expose primary ore at the surface.

Gossans of iron oxides (composed of geothite and lepidocrocite ($Fe_2O_3 . H_2O$) and haematite (Fe_2O_3) derived from different minerals can be discriminated by careful study. Some of the important varieties are indicated here:

From pyrite

- Nodular or thin crusts, dark in colour, locally iridescent with or without columnar iron oxides formed by evaporation of dripping iron rich acid solutions;
- Cellular cubic or rounded boxwork or sponge of heterogenous pattern (very rare);
- Hard pseudomorphs, mostly cubic, after pyrite;

Fig. 3.1: Polygonal boxwork diagnostic of galena and other associated minerals in the gossan outcrop at Dariba-Rajpura.

- Botryoidal boxwork, simulating laterite crust.

From chalcopyrite

- Coarse to fine, cellular boxwork, brown to brownish black, the iron oxide arranged in quadrilateral webs forming angles of 70° and 110° approximately; soft and friable iron oxide inside the boxworks; as a result, the insides of the cells are commonly empty;
- Cellular sponge, locally chocolate coloured;
- Craggy and cavernous iron oxides with tiny sponges jutting out;
- Very dark brown to black iron oxide films with pitch like lustre.

From pyrrhotite

- Oval cellular boxwork with an underlying hexagonal pattern.

From arsenopyrite

- Arborescent, granular or cellular boxwork; diagnostic mineral in these iron oxide boxworks is scorodite ($FeAsO_4.2H_2O$); also acicular shapes of voids.

From bornite

- Orange to orange yellow, triangular to trapezoidal cellular boxwork or sponge of diverse sized round voids; also orange red kaolinic mass with polygonal shrinkage cracks; or partially coalesced iron oxide granules with a rough surface.

From tetrahedrite

- Cells in boxwork elongate, the length being 2–10 times the width. Diagnostic association is encrustation of colourless to white or yellow spots of antimony oxides.

From sphalerite

- Acute angular (30–55°), coarse to fine, cellular boxwork, the cell walls being firmly joined and coated with small grains of smithsonite ($ZnCO_3$) or calamine (H_2ZnSiO_5);
- Cellular sponge resembling a bath sponge; strongly siliceous.

From galena

- Cleavage boxwork corresponding to the cleavage pattern of galena; walls strikingly parallel;
- Crusts of globular cerussite ($PbCO_3$) with sinter-like crusts of iron oxide granules;
- Boxwork of diamond mesh pattern, usually made up of very thin, intersecting webs, visible under a hand lens;
- Pyramid patterned, slender boxwork;
- Cellular, honeycomb boxwork, orange to dark chocolate coloured where pyrite is dominant.

In areas free from laterite cover, boxwork is a very common surface expression of basemetal sulphide deposits, e.g. Khetri, Dariba-Rajpura (Fig. 3.1) and other fields of Rajasthan. In the central part of the Singhbhum copper field, particularly along the Rakha Mines—Tamapahar sector, boxwork is seen. However, not all sulphides yield boxwork gossan in proportional amounts. Chalcopyrite and sphalerite yield

Fig. 3.2: Gossan veined by silcrete, Ponk, Khetri Cu field.

abundantly; galena less commonly; while pyrite and arsenopyrite hardly yield any cellular boxwork. A critical morphological study of the gossans, supported by mineralogical determinations and trace element analysis is useful in the course of a district survey. Silver, gold and metals of the platinum group, Pt, Pd, Rh, Ru, Ir and Os, are locally enriched in gossans over nickel sulphide deposits; gold is enriched in gossans over massive pyrite/pyrrhotite body. Gold from tellurides and epithermal veins are in very fine particles, frequently not amenable to concentration by panning. This may be totally missed unless the associated gossan is chemically analysed.

Residual enrichment of resistant elements is a common feature of the oxidised zone over mineral deposits near the earth's surface, and is not uniquely diagnostic of gossan. Enrichment in resistant elements is common in lateritic cover also, e.g. over Mundaguda cassiterite deposit in Koraput dt. where the weathered zone carries a higher concentration of SnO_2 than the protore below. A discrimination between gossan and pseudo-gossan has to be based on the concentration of mobile elements like Cu, Zn, Ni etc. (Fig. 3.2). Cellular to honeycomb structure and diagnostic minerals of a gossan (e.g. scorodite over arsenopyrite ore bodies) are also critical (vide Chapter 4 for geochemical fingerprints of hypogene alteration zones).

The development of boxwork gossan is not only related to the pyrite : chalcopyrite (or other copper bearing minerals) ratio of the protore but also to the nature of gangue minerals. If the gangue is reactive like carbonate instead of being inert like quartz, development of boxwork is retarded. Where potash is present, e.g. in a granitic host rock, haematite and jarosite $[K_2Fe_6(OH)_{12}(SO_4)_4]$ are common in the boxwork. Detailed field and microscopic studies of the boxwork can yield a broad idea about the nature of protore, although a quantitative estimate of the grade of primary ore from boxwork composition and texture requires careful initial calibration from surface and sub-surface data. Such an attempt was made in the Rakha Mines sector of the Singhbhum copper belt by the GSI during the late sixties.

This is by no means an uncommon practice. Gossans are generally associated with large ore deposits of massive, disseminated or porphyry type. Where the iron of sulphide is fixed at the original site, it is possible to reconstruct the form and size of the underlying sulphide body. Such iron oxide is called *indigenous* limonite. Cappings over predominantly pyrite deposits are however made up of *transported* limonite, the reason being that free acid from oxidation of pyrite tends to keep Fe in soluble bivalent state, so that it can move out and flood the rock mass as a halo, paint or crust in cracks over barren rocks.

(b) Stratigraphic control: Where a mineral deposit occurs at a given stratigraphic level, search for similar occurrences elsewhere in the ore district becomes easier. For example, at Amjore, Sahabad district, Bihar, pyrite and galena occur as stratiform masses within the Bijaigarh Shale of the Vindhyans, just below the Scarp Sandstone. The pyrite bed is around one meter thick and extends over 150 sq. km, approximately 6–10 m below the base of the Scarp Sandstone. During the late sixties, some galena impregnations were accidentally discovered in the roof of the pyrite workings. Subsequent exploration was considerably simplified by the observation that these disseminations of galena, sphalerite and pyrite occur in a 20–280 cm thick rhythmite at the base of the Scarp Sandstone. Extension of this mineralised zone over an area of 5.21 sq.km within the Amjhore leasehold of the PPCL (Pyrites, Phosphates and Chemicals Ltd.) could be established within a year after the initial find on the basis of 9 underground drill-holes and re-examination of the old drill cores.

In such a stratigraphically controlled ore field, one proceeds with confidence. Detailed measurement of the stratigraphic sequence and of the structures defines the level at which ore is to be found. Actual estimation of resource is then based on well-spaced, measured intersections, since the ore seam cannot be presumed to have uniform thickness and grade all over its extent. In using the stratigraphic frame for predicting orebody behaviour, it is essential to distinguish between syngenetic (including diagenetic) and epigenetic ore formation. Syngenetic deposits of both sedimentary and igneous (e.g. chromite, vanadiferous magnetite) origin which are free from later deformation have regular, stratiform arrangement; an isopach (equal thickness) map of such ore bodies is easily prepared on the basis of regular intersections. In contrast, epigenetic deposits, which have been introduced into the rocks at a later date, are complex. Even where such a deposit is confined to a specific stratigraphic level, its distribution may be irregular and shape and size diverse. For example, the stromatolite-bearing Proterozoic dolomites of Riasi and Almora in the Jammu and U.P. Himalaya are comparable stratigraphically. Both carry Mississippi Valley Type Pb-Zn-Cu sulphides. It is however impossible to predict the ore locations or their dimensions. Nonetheless, stratigraphic knowledge of such epigenetic mineral deposition in an ore district helps to eliminate search over barren sequences and reduce the exploration effort.

(c) Lithologic associations: These are generally of two types: universal and local. An example of universal association is chromite in dunite-peridotite fractions of an ophiolite. Such formulations constitute an essential part of geological studies of an ore district. Local associations are more significant in a search for ore bodies. Favourable formations may be sedimentary, igneous or metamorphic rocks of specific composition like the association of shales with Mount Isa (Queensland, Australia) lead-zinc deposits, the associated limestones being barren; felspathic biotite-chlorite schist with copper sulphide ore deposit at Rakha Mines, Bihar; phosphorite enrichment in some limestone bands of Mussoorie; silver deposits with andesite flows in western Mexico; vanadiferous magnetite deposits in gabbro-anorthosite of Betjharan and Dublabera along the border of Bihar and Orissa; gold in dark grey quartz veins of Kundarkocha (Bihar), etc.

Once it is observed during geological mapping that a particular lithology is favourable for a type of deposit, this information can be used as a good guide in exploration of extension areas. The specific and special conditions of the host rocks accompanying formation of the deposit should be analysed to enlarge the target area and discover unexpected twists.

(d) Fracture systems: Fracture systems are generally classified into two types: shear and tension fractures. Brittle material normally fails along a combination of shear and tension cracks. Usually, shear cracks are parallel to the plane of maximum shearing stress and make angles of less than 45° with the planes of maximum normal stress, while tension cracks develop parallel to the axis of compression. In mineralised zones, it is not always possible to distinguish between shear and tension

Fig. 3.3: Slickensides in quartzite.

fractures of different generations. Replacement and sequential movement blur the picture. But features like slickensided surfaces (Fig. 3.3) or streaks of crushed material are useful guides to identification of shear fractures. Slickensided surfaces are abundantly exposed in the outcrops of kyanite bearing quartzite on the hanging wall of the Rakha Mines copper deposit, Bihar.

In contrast, tension fractures form where the walls are opened up by separation either normal or oblique to the plane of the crack. Mineralised tension fractures are easily identified where blocks of polygonal inclusions within a vein appear to fit back into the walls, if the replacing material is taken out (Fig. 3.4). This is known as domino-breccia; excellent examples of this structure are common in MVT deposits e.g. in the sphalerite body within the Riasi Limestone Inlier at Darabi, Anji Khad, Jammu.

During complex multi-stage fracture fillings and partial dissolution, some breccia zones develop by collapse. These should not be mistaken for tectonic brecciation. For example, in the sulphide mound of the mid-Atlantic TAG site, most of the sulphide cores recovered during Ocean Drilling Program Leg 158 are made up of breccia with clasts of silicified and chloritised basalts. These were initially infiltrated by anhydrite at high temperature, which got dissolved by 'retrograde solubility' at low temperature leading to collapse of the framework and replacement by sulphides.

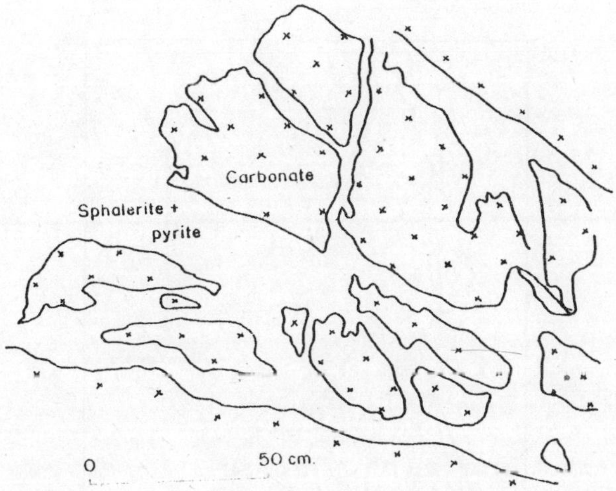

Fig. 3.4: Domino-breccia of sphalerite and pyrite in late carbonate vein, Darabi, Anji Khad, Riasi, Jammu.

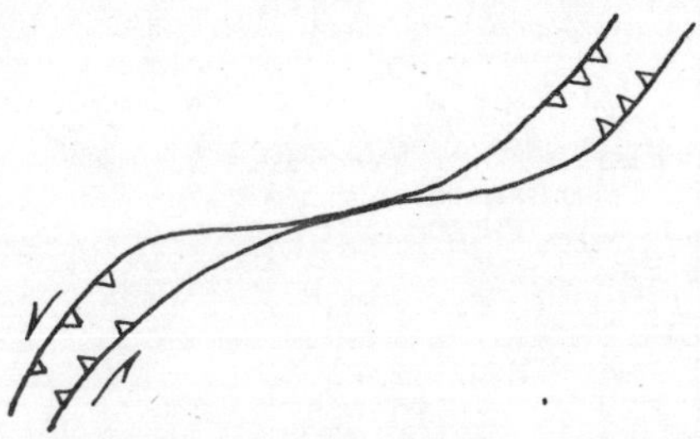

Fig. 3.5: Openings created by shear movements on an uneven surface and subsequent vug filling.

Tension cracks are often lenticular and occur in bundles. Within a shear zone, the presence of lenticular tension cracks arranged in herringbone pattern or *en echelon* tension cracks demonstrate the complex interplay of shear and tensional forces. In fact the same vein may turn from a tension crack filling to a shear crack replacement; and it is important to remember that vugs can form both in tension and shear cracks. Shear movement on an uneven surface would result in openings, which may be partly filled up and partly empty. Thus vugs form (Fig. 3.5).

One has to study the shear and fracture zones very carefully both for indications of abrupt termination of a deposit and for mineralisation channelway (Fig. 3.6).

It is imperative to identify and map the faults correctly: a classic example is the Jharia coal field map of C.S. Fox, where faults were mapped on the basis of surface studies alone and later confirmed by underground mining! In Cornwall, there are

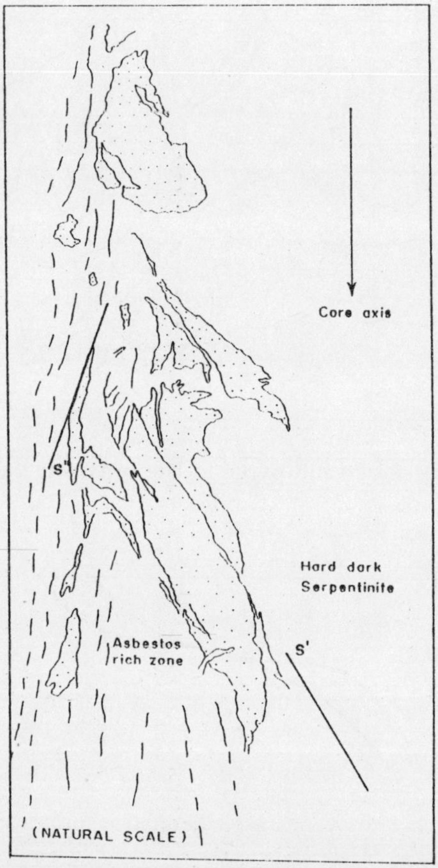

Fig. 3.6: Growth of asbestos along interesecting shear surface and fold closures in hard serpentinite, at 150 m depth of borehole BTB-146, Bhimtangar block, Sukinda ultramafic field, Cuttack district, Orissa.

some standard examples. Two parallel veins dipping towards each other were cut up by a dipping normal fault. On the upthrown side, these were brought much closer to each other. In another example two contrasted pegmatites, broken by a dipping fault, were so faulted as to bring the dislocated part of one vein abutting directly against the other thus concealing the existence of the fault to a casual observer!

Shear zones act as loci of mineralisation at places. The Singhbhum shear zone is a classic example of a host for epigenetic ore bodies of different types: apatite-magnetite, copper sulphides with traces of nickel, platinum, etc., uraniferous-molybdenite ore, local sphalerite disseminations and quartz-kyanite veins. Even after nearly a century of exploration in different parts of this ore district new discoveries are still made.

Such macroscopic-scale features are included within the term lineament, which covers various types of linear patterns, visible in satellite imageries and air photos. Lineaments are observed by the following features:

(1) fractures/faults (Fig 3.7);
(2) contrasts in the density of vegetation;
(3) preferred alignment of drainage courses;
(4) abrupt linear morphologic change, either in topographic or in gravity or magnetic contours;
(5) long and tabular intrusive bodies.

Alignment of tin-bearing igneous intrusives along lineaments in Nigeria and of porphyry copper deposits in the Andes Mountains are well known examples of lineament controlled ore districts.

A combination of linear fractures forming a master set over thousands of kilometers is commonly called a *mega-lineament*, e.g. the Son-Narmada lineament

Fig. 3.7: A faulted contact between magnesite-bearing ultramafite and unaltered pyroxenite near Salem, Tamil Nadu.

extending from the Gaya district in Bihar past Jabalpur and Hoshangabad to the Gulf of Cambay near Broach, marking the boundary between two blocks: the Precambrians of the Dharwarian-BIF sequence with Gondwana grabens on the southern side and Bundelkhand granite-Vindhyan basin to its north. It is actually made up of a series of lineaments, trending ENE–WSW. These fractures are nearly coincident with similar trends in aeromagnetic contour maps and appear to be caused by recurrent movements from the Precambrian.

Another classic example of a lineament is along the 38th parallel of U.S.A.; there are many Mississippi Valley Type sulphide deposits along this lineament.

In the imageries of the Bihar Mica Belt, NE–SW lineaments are correlative with narrow linear zones of high magnetic intensity possibly correlative with mafic and ultramafic bodies.

Although lineaments are not necessarily mineralised everywhere, a regional or district scale survey for mineral deposits has to critically examine such features for tell-tale indications of mineralisation.

Careful mapping of fractures in and around a mineral deposit is also useful for future mining. It has been found that subsidence of ground above an underground mine is essentially controlled along a mean or resultant of the various fracture systems dipping towards the mine opening, their relative roles weighted in order of their abundance and dip angle.

Lineaments on satellite imageries are not necessarily geological in character. For example, there are strong lineaments on the Contai delta plain paralleling the coastline which are essentially induced by different types of cropping pattern causing contrasts in soil moisture from month to month. Vegetation and agriculture are as important in causing lineaments in air photos and imageries as rock characters. Frequently, these are related and could be used interchangeably, e.g. the white patches in the air photos of the Singhbhum shear zone between Tamapahar and Surda are almost always indicative of quartzite which supports very scanty vegetation. But such correlations are made after and not *before* ground survey. This must be remembered. One must guard against the temptation of over-interpreting from imageries and photographs.

(e) Formational contacts and folds: Contacts of meso- and epi-zonal igneous plutons are frequently hosts of mineral deposits, because these are zones of relative weakness, of mixing of fluids of different composition and of steeper thermal gradient. They provide receptacles for deposition of ore metals. For example, the wolframite-bearing quartz veins of Chendapathar (West Bengal) are close to the roof of the

Chendapathar granite, which crops out at a few points in the area. Similarly, in many parts of the world the contact areas around granite porphyry are loci of disseminated Cu-Mo/Cu-Au porphyry deposits.

Even in the case of magmatic ore deposits like chromite, contacts provide favourable zones where the host ultramafic body re-intrudes in semi-solid state, e.g. in the Sukinda ophiolite hosted chromite body adjacent to Mahagiri quartzite (Fig. 1.1). Due to differential flow of silicates (hydrothermally softened), harder chromite masses lag behind and come in contact with the wall rocks in the constricted parts of the channel of re-intrusion; in extreme cases, the originally layered material gets squeezed into diversely oriented, lenticular to 'plums-in-a-pudding' type masses. Such chrome ore bodies are found in the southwestern fringes of the Sukinda ultramafic mass and in the adjoining Katpal enclave.

Even in the case of sedimentary rocks, contacts provide contrasting permeability and are favourable zones of ore deposition. For example, low temperature sulphide deposits of Cu, Pb and Zn of the Mississippi Valley Type frequently occur along zones of different competence in the Riasi inlier of Jammu.

Folds play a variety of roles. Where folding precedes ore deposition and involves rocks of different competence, the host rocks may provide loci for mineralisation, e.g. in the case of flowage folds, involving alternate bands of quartzite and mica schist. Thinning of limbs and thickening of crests may influence ore deposition by: (1) non-uniform distribution of fractures, generated during post-folding relaxation; and (2) creating permeability contrasts and thereby guiding the pathway of fluids.

Where mineral deposits pre-date folding, the fold geometry is relevant for exploration. For example, the north limb of the synform involving the Sukinda chromiferous ultramafic body lies concealed below colluvium: without a targetted search, the deposits of the north limb would have been left untapped; a few of these masses have since been quarried extensively.

Such megascopic folds are important for all types of deposits whereas mesoscopic to microscopic folds are more important for epigenetic ore deposits. Auriferous quartz veins of Kolar provide a classic example of such controls.

In many metamorphic tracts, folds of two, three or even four generations are common. The cycles of deformation overlap cycles of metamorphism and metasomatism. Where ore mineralisation is associated with such metasomatic pulses, it is essential to correlate the cycle of deformation with ore formation both in space and time. Such studies involve careful petrographic and structural analysis of the rock units including the accessible parts of the mineral bodies on all scales. Folds are normally accompanied by fractures. Where such fractures form in course of folding, these are generally tensional in the crests and troughs specially in relatively competent layers. But in polymetamorphic tracts with complex history of deformation, shearing and brecciation could show complex patterns. It is not always possible to resolve the age relationship among different pulses of deformation and ore formation. The Singhbhum copper field in Bihar provides a classic example of the complex relationship on different scales. Here shearing affected different types of rocks which dip towards north and east at moderate angles, paralleling the axial plane of isoclinal folds. Copper mineralisation followed the shear zone on regional scale. But there are different generations of faults and shears in this belt. Besides the ductile shear zone, which parallels the general lie of the rock units, and left its imprint on a package of metasomatised rocks—tourmaline-chlorite-quartz rock, albite-biotite-quartz schist, tourmaline-magnetite rock and quartz-chlorite schist, there are both transverse and strike faults, post-dating ductile shear and copper mineralisation. These faults range in length from meters to kilometers with variable displacement. For example, near the Jaduguda uranium mine, the whole shear zone assemblage is displaced over a few km by a right lateral transverse fault; on the other hand, in the underground workings, e.g. at Surda, individual sulphide veins are cut up by a network of close spaced transverse faults with displacements of a few cm to meters.

Unlike the Singhbhum shear zone, there are areas where strong folding has not obliterated the bedding planes. In such cases, shear fractures follow bedding planes through part of the course, as in the famous saddle reefs of the Bendigo gold field, Australia. The arcuate saddle reefs are thick on the crests of broad, upright, open folds, their thinner prolongations at one end following the bedding plane down one limb of an anticline. At the other end a reverse fault cuts across the upper levels of the other limb (Fig. 3.8a). In the neighbouring district of Ballarat, the folds are overturned, one limb being vertical and the other dipping at 60–70°. The reef geometry is totally different from Bendigo and comprises flat-lying tension gashes (Fig. 3.8b) within the steep dipping limbs. The shear planes passing through the vertical limbs could not provide openings for mineralisation.

Where mineralisation replaces tightly folded beds, the ore shoots normally follow the plunge of the folds, as in Dariba-Rajpura and Pur Banera Pb-Zn-Cu deposits of Rajasthan. Even in such cases the relative roles of primary replacement versus remobilisation during amphibolite facies metamorphism remain controversial.

In gently folded but rugged terrains with local scarps, as in Vindhyan, Cuddapah, Chattishgarh and other basins of Peninsular India, Krol-Tal sequence of the

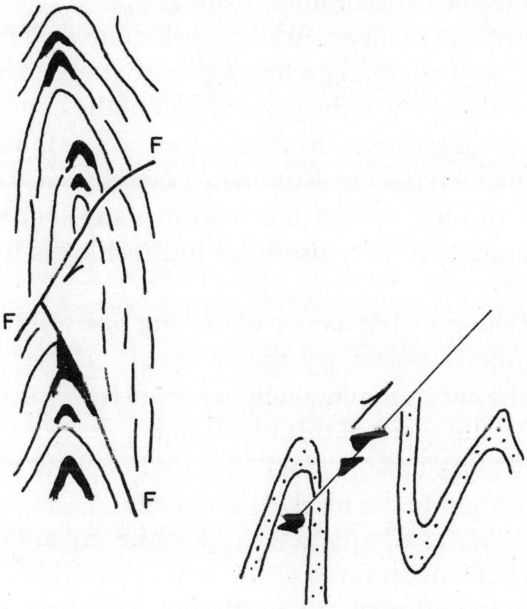

Fig. 3.8: (a) Generalised form of saddle reefs, Bendigo gold field, Australia. (b) Illustrative sketch of tension gashes hosting gold mineralisation, Ballarat gold field, Australia.

Himalaya, etc., rock outcrops are monotonously similar in appearance and structural complexities are infrequent. This may so dull the prospector that he misses a thin but workable strata-bound mineral deposit or impersistent indications of ore unless he is careful to observe the unusual variants: conglomerates, undulations caused by folding, minor differences in colour, grain size, composition, sedimentary structures etc. associated with the mineral forming environment. A district-scale search has to follow Goethe's motto: ohne hast, ohne rast (without haste, without rest).

LOCAL SCALE PROSPECTING

The objectives are as follows:

(a) To find out the mineral potential of a leasehold;

(b) to find extension of the deposit within a leasehold; and

(c) to have an approximate idea of the resource *in situ*.

The following activities are commonly taken up:

(i) A critical examination of all records of work done earlier in the area, including the data (wherever available) on tonnage and grade of material raised.

(ii) Careful geological survey of the ground and of the openings, if any, to form an idea about the geological set up and nature of the mineral deposit, chemical assay of different ore types, measurement of their physical properties, examination of the mine dumps. Where quarries are water-logged, their surface extent and orientation are generally useful as indirect leads to the behaviour of the deposit.

(iii) Formulation of the possible nature of mining operation and the probable cost of such operation.

(iv) Assessment of the environmental impact of past mining operation, and the cost of reclamation in the event of future mining.

(v) Estimation of the amount of capital required for new working and per tonne cost of transportation to the market or smelter.

(vi) Tests for availability of adequate water for human and operational needs and raw material for constructions.

(vii) Feasibility of upgradation of raw material.

In case there are operating mines it always pays to visit such places and have discussions with the mine manager and the supervisor/mate to get a feel of the ground conditions.

Where you are involved in a takeover bid of other leaseholds, you should be doubly cautious about the claims of the present owner. A model questionnaire is given in Appendix I to emphasize the cross-checks necessary before a purchase.

Geological consultancy is now providing an alternative source of employment for many fresh graduates. A good preliminary examination requires caution and experience.

SURFACE AND UNDERGROUND MAPPING

In humid tropical areas with intermittent flat to undulating topography, where soil/laterite cover masks the basement, pits or trenches are sunk at an early stage of prospecting to: (a) expose extension zones of a mineral deposit; (2) to pick up indications of subjacent ore bodies; or (3) to compute depth-wise or soil horizonwise abundance of the economic mineral(s). Where labour is cheap, this is undertaken even before or during large-scale survey of the prospect. Resistant minerals like cassiterite, wolframite and diamond are volumetrically more abundant in the weathered zone than in the primary host rock at places, e.g. cassiterite at Mundaguda, Bastar district, M.P., diamond around Gooty, Jonnagiri, Guntakal and Wajra Karur, which constitute a part of the famous Golconda diamond mines of the historical period. Photographs (annotated) and sketches of the walls of the pits and trenches are essential for future interpretation besides routine analysis of mineralogical and textural attributes of each layer intersected.

Where the survey aims at finding out down depth or lateral extension of the mineral deposit, large scale/detailed mapping of the surface and underground openings and sampling of the mineral deposit are required, although the nature of information/data may vary from one deposit to another. In one field, you may have to take up very detailed lithological-structural mapping on 1:1,000 scale with topographic contouring. In another, it may be enough to lay out orthogonal traverse lines for gridded data collection. Elsewhere, a delineation of the mineralised zone on a well-made plan may be enough. There is no fixed rule; large-scale topographic-cum-geological mapping on 1:1,000 scale is not always essential before a potential target is identified and exploratory drilling is planned. Topographic and geologic mapping is required along the drill profiles for borehole correlation.

To relate the surface geology to the underground workings, you need a large-scale topographic-cum-geological map. Where you have to probe for down depth continuity of the deposit, drilling can be undertaken either from the surface or from underground. If there are underground workings, it is advisable to map the accessible levels as carefully as possible before planning any drilling. Underground geological mapping is more difficult than surface mapping. The first requirement is to prepare a plan of the underground workings, including the drifts, cross cuts, raises and winzes. The second requirement is to adjust your sight to prolonged operation in semi-dark, narrow chambers. The following equipment are needed:

- transit or theodolite for mine surveying
- cloth tape (50 m / 100 m)
- miner's hat with a headlamp/hard hat and 3-cell torch
- aluminium sheet holder (30 cm × 20 cm) with a hinged cover and a blotter and pencil holder with 3H to 6H pencils
- a pocket tape
- chalk or other prominent markers for the wall

- steel pegs and hammer
- crowbar and shovel (for old abandoned mines)
- brunton compass/clinometer
- circular protractor
- hurricane lantern (to check for $C0/C0_2$ pools).

You must reconnoitre the workings first before starting to map. You must also check that the sidewalls arc plotted as accurately as possible in the survey plan with all their angularities. Ideally, this job should be done by a qualified mine surveyor. Otherwise, it may be ensured that the bearing of each drift and cross cut is measured very carefully. Errors are frequent and lead to gross mis-interpretation of the behaviour of the lodes. Fix the stations in such a way that the line of sight, both fore and aft, is as long as possible. The elevation of the track has to be determined at short intervals.

After you have prepared the base map of the workings with the help of either transit and tape or prismatic compass and tape and have determined the elevation of the workings by abney or dumpy level, you should cross-check the total error in distance, bearing and elevation by closing the traverse. If the errors are less than 1%, you can distribute the error according to standard practice.

Errors in bearing are more serious in underground mines than small errors in distance and could create unreal faults (Fig. 3.9).

It is advisable to use loose-leaf notebooks with aluminium covers. The most convenient size is 20 cm × 15 cm. Facts to be noted include the nature of the orebody including rock alteration, pinch out, visible mineralogical change, presence of fault or dyke, caved or covered stretch, splits in vein, strike and dip, drag etc. It is better to avoid making copious notes of descriptive nature only.

The base map should be traced on transparent graph sheet, preferably water proof; the plan of the working should be copied in black India ink on the reverse side of the transparent sheet, so that you can plot the geological features in pencil and use your eraser as needed without disturbing the drawing on the reverse side of the sheet; station locations should be on the top side. When you are mapping a level, either a drift or a cross cut, spend the maximum part of your time in chipping both the walls at close intervals and exposing the fresh material, so that you do not miss the outlines of the vein. Normally, the scale of the underground map is between 1:100 and 1:500, depending on whether you are mapping thin and interlacing vein systems (e.g. an auriferous quartz vein) or thick lodes of sulphide.

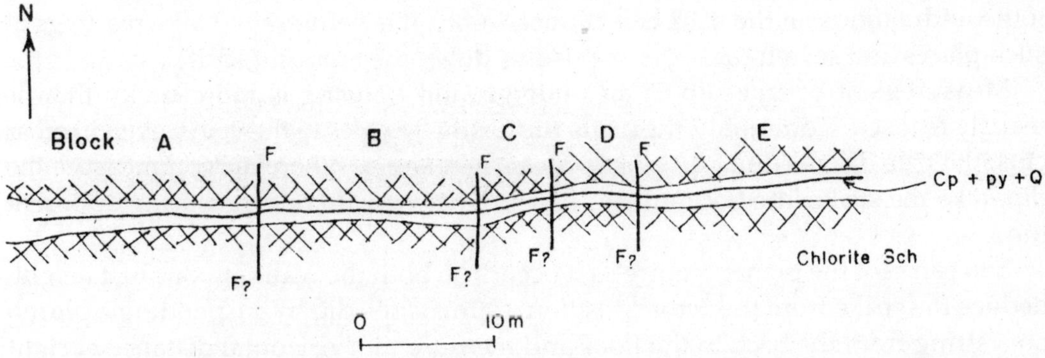

Fig. 3.9: A continuous lode mistakenly mapped as faulted in five discrete blocks (A to E) (F ?) due to errors in bearing by only a few degrees.

Use blue pencil for marking faults; red for veins; and ordinary 3H lead pencil for structural data, like S-planes and lineations.

The plane of projection is normally your belt height, i.e. you have to project all planar features to an uniform horizontal plane. After washing and cleaning the walls, you should stretch the tape on the floor from the nearest survey station and measure the distance of each observation point at the place where the feature intersects your belt height. If the floor is muddy, hang the zero end of the tape on a side wall opposite the survey station and ask a helper to carry the reel end. Use chalk for marking out the contacts and other features as well as zones to be channel sampled before you plot the observations on the sheet. This will prevent errors in plotting.

Such belt-level projection is easy for steep dipping features. Low dipping features could create serious errors. Measurement of both strike and dip in such a situation has to be done with great care. Otherwise estimation of true width of the feature might be wrong.

In all cases, you should try to measure the strike by observing the plane on both the walls at your belt height and read the bearing between these two points carefully. If the feature is exposed on the back (roof) of the drift or if the sidewall is so broken that the surface of the feature is exposed over a considerable area so that you can place your brunton or clinometer on the surface and take a reading, measurement of strike is admissible. Here again, a low dipping surface creates errors on the uneven back and on the exposed slab on the sidewall. If your measurement of strike on the exposed slab is faulty, i.e. due to not holding the compass perfectly level or if the undulations on the back create uncertainty, it is better not to take readings at such places and search for better exposures down the cross cut/drift.

Measurement of true dip in an underground opening is more tricky than is usually realised. Commonly, the drifts run at small angles to the veins; even in cross cuts, the true dip need not be exactly at its right angle. Wherever you measure the dip, take the strike into account and be sure that you are not measuring apparent dip.

You can plot the planar feature as it occurs on both the walls at your belt height, deduce the strike from the actual position, estimate the dip by suspending a plumb on a string from the back to the floor and measure the horizontal distance at right angles to the strike direction between the plumb line and the trace of the feature on the floor. The length of the plumb line divided by the horizontal length on the floor will be the tangent of the dip angle.

Once you have mastered the art of correct reading underground, this procedure is not necessary. You must actually plot the features underground, and record the values of strike and dip at the edge of your worksheet for accurate transfer to a fair sheet at a later date.

Dips are important particularly where the lode is low dipping and regular, e.g in the Mosaboni copper mine (Bihar); any systematic error creates problems in ore zone projection to the lower levels.

For mapping raises, stretch a tape between the top and bottom of the raise, measure the inclination with your brunton compass, count the rungs for calibrating elevation difference and plot the features on your base map. The disposition of the veins on the raise would provide you with additional confirmation about the cross-sectional view of the orebody.

Mapping stopes (Fig. 3.10) is more difficult, since these are invariably irregular; survey plans are not usually available in advance; and you have to locate the points in all three dimensions—two horizontal and one vertical. Use the plane table-alidade method with a cloth tape for both survey and sampling of the stope. Measurements on the stope are read off the stretched tape along the wall and the profile is plotted separately. Intermediate points on the profile are transferred to the plan with suitable corrections for vertical and horizontal distance. You must bear in mind that the features plotted on a stope, say a fault or a particular vein, do not fall in line with the counterpart features you might have mapped on the adjacent levels, since the projection of features gets displaced from one level to the next unless these are vertical.

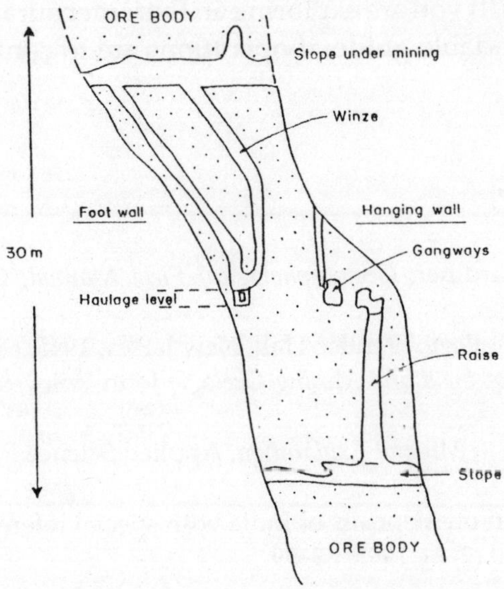

Fig. 3.10: Simplified sketch of developmental openings.

A word of caution is necessary. Whenever you enter an abandoned mine for geological mapping or sampling, you should carry not only torches and ropes but also a hurricane lantern to be aware of pools of C0 and $C0_2$ which might accumulate in depressions (even in deep pits) and could prove fatal. You should also carry some shovels and pick axes to dig your way out, in case exit is blocked by roof collapse.

Underground sampling should be in the form of carefully dug channels across the mineral deposit at regular intervals. The channels should be cut only after cleaning and smoothening the surface. Each channel should be at least 15 cm wide and 5 cm deep on the side wall and back. You should avoid channel sampling from the floor. The channels should be subdivided into sectors of equal curvature and their respective lengths and computed true width should be noted against the corresponding sub-sample. The procedure for sample collection and processing is discussed in Chapter 6.

In a working underground mine, sampling programme is a daily job and has to be as detailed and close-spaced as possible, not only for deciding the mix of advancing mine faces for maintaining as constant a R.O.M (run of mine) grade as possible but also for outlining the extension zones. But for assessment of a prospect, try to obtain past data and collect check samples to see whether the previous data are dependable and whether the grade of the deposit is regular. You should plan only for criticality tests. If you are exploring an Extramensurate deposit, past records of raisings are a dependable guide, if operations are to continue over comparable geological set up.

FURTHER READING

R. Daekombe and V. Gardiner, *Geomorphological Field Manual*, George Allen & Unwin, London, 1983, 254pp.

H.E. Mckinstry, *Mining Geology*, Prentice Hall, New Jersey, 1948, 680pp.

J.D. Forrester, *Principles of Field and Mining Geology*, John Wiley & Sons, New York, 1946, 482pp.

J.H. Reedman, *Techniques in Mineral Exploration*, Applied Science Publishers, London, 1979, 533 pp.

R.N. Mishra, Lateritic iron ore deposits of India with special reference to their exploration. *Rec. Geol. Surv. Ind.* 120 (2–8), 1995, 83–99.

4

Geochemical Prospecting

Geochemical prospecting methods grew out of the recognition that primary and secondary dispersion haloes are associated with ore deposits. Early attempts were made by geophysicists, and included stannometric survey for Sn and Au lodes and for Cu deposits with the newly discovered instrument, the Emission Spectrograph (ES). Almost concurrently, secondary dispersion of ore metals from a deposit into soil, vegetation and water of the neighbourhood was demonstrated in Norway and Finland by Rankama and Vogt.

The spread of geochemical prospecting after World War II, first in the U.S.A., U.K., France, Canada and Australia and later in the newly-independent states of Asia and Africa as well as in Latin America, was basically due to the invention of colorimetry in the U.S.A., atomic absorption spectrometry in Australia and of polyethylene for collection and transport of field samples without contamination and breakage. The reconstruction of war-ravaged Europe, the growing need for metals in the newly-independent developing nations and pessimistic forecasts of global metal shortages by the early years of the next century powered the growth and adoption of improved sampling procedures and statistical methods for anomaly identification, so that concealed deposits would show up clearly in their dispersion patterns. Automated X-ray Fluorescence Analysis (XRF), Instrumental Neutron Activation Analysis (INAA) and Inductively Coupled Plasma Atomic Emission Spectrometer (ICPAES) were invented in the seventies and eighties to provide the prospector with larger options of more precise and extensive multi-element survey. Simultaneously, a parallel revolution in computer software and hardware was going on. Advanced interactive computer graphical methods could be used for integrating geochemical data with remote sensing data from satellites, aircraft, etc. Development of knowledge-based systems for regional geochemical data sets was also pioneered by U.S.A., France and U.K. during the last decade, so that one could conduct both intensive and extensive search for concealed mineral deposits.

With such a diverse array of high cost, sophisticated technology, geochemical prospecting has undergone a sea change over the last fifty years. Initially it was a low cost, low sensitivity but fast technique, thanks to the rapid and moderately sensitive dithizone test for heavy metals. With a few scientists and a larger number of relatively undertrained technicians, large areas were searched, as in many UNDP campaigns. By the end of the eighties, geochemical prospecting, particularly for radioactive elements, noble metals and deep-seated mineral deposits, started utilising high cost, temperature sensitive instruments. These require clean laboratories. With a rapidly changing market for products and a constant demand from city centres for materials, the simple early tools of prospecting have been supplanted (partly through an aggressive sales pitch). However, there have not been many noteworthy successes from these modern instruments in locating large concealed mineral deposits. Also, the special scientific and operational problems of geochemical exploration in tropical countries have defied generalised solutions. The high rate of discovery of base metal deposits by geochemical prospecting in the fifties and sixties came down during the later decades as a consequence of diminishing returns, sharp increase in energy costs, growing environmental concern in the developed countries, increase in the free market price for gold and an intermittent oversupply of base metals in the world markets.

Geochemical prospecting can be broadly classified into the following types:

(1) Stream sediment survey and heavy mineral reconnaissance: for deposits of mobile and resistate elements/minerals, particularly in semi-humid to humid tropics.
(2) Pedogeochemical prospecting: analysis of weathered cover for secondary dispersion.
(3) Till geochemical prospecting: analysis of moraines.
(4) Lithogeochemical prospecting including analysis of host rocks for primary haloes.
(5) Fluid inclusions: Analysis of the composition and homogenisation temperature of fluid inclusions in rock-forming minerals.
(6) Hydrogeochemical prospecting: analysis of water for mobile elements like Zn and U.
(7) Biogeochemical prospecting: chemical analysis of plant ash.

(8) Geobotanical prospecting: visual examination of plants.
(9) Photogeochemical method: By identifying toxic effects of metals on plant population by reflectance ratios.
(10) Geozoological and microbial prospecting: use of animals and micro-organisms, either directly or indirectly, in searching for minerals.
(11) Atmogeochemical prospecting: analysis of vapour phases in the atmosphere.
(12) PEXMEL method: collection of free metallic ions in pots by passing stable d.c. over 8 hrs at 100–700 volts.

None of these methods is universally applicable; some, like stream sediment survey, are useful in the early stages of reconnaissance in the humid tropics, but are of very limited utility in Himalayan tracts, where river currents are fast, the gradient steep and downstream anomaly trains are very short. Others like photogeochemical prospecting or PEXMEL method are only in the developmental stage, and cannot yet be used as a standard tool. Biogeochemical, geobotanical and geozoological methods are not useful in rapid reconnaissance of a large area where the object is elimination of unfavourable ground from further examination by more intensive and often more costly methods.

Thus the options available depend on the stage of prospecting, the nature of terrain, the nature of chemical signals associated with the mineralisation, the nature of analytical tools and methods adopted, and the time and cost permissible for the program. Improved geochemical understanding of a system provides better constraint on the geological model. The poorer the model, the less valuable the data (D.J. De Paolo, *Nature*, 381, 1996, 36).

The first stage in any geochemical prospecting program is an orientation survey. This aims at determining the type and size of the anomalies in the vicinity of a known mineral deposit (taking care to avoid possible sources of contamination) in different media-wall rocks, residual soil, stream sediment, water, plant, etc. In the course of the survey, the best sampling medium is identified; suitable methods of sample treatment and analysis, including determination of the best grain size fraction for anomaly amplification and the choice of metal and extraction techniques are also decided.

A careful and critical orientation survey followed by detailed planning and organisation of the relevant sampling campaign is crucial to the success of geochemical prospecting. Many anomalies, related to sub-economic mineral deposits or bands of high average but uneconomic grade material or past smelting activities (specially near old workings) can clutter up the search, unless orientation survey has correctly defined the target medium and sampling depth. For example, an orientation survey of the residual soil defines:

(a) the strength of the anomaly related to a known orebody;
(b) the width, homogenity and depth-wise dispersion of the metal in different soil zones; and
(c) the dispersion pattern of associated mobile or resistant elements in different size fractions.

Background metal content (for definition see Chapter 6) must also be determined by sampling barren areas in the neighbourhood.

The spread and intensity of geochemical anomaly are influenced by the following factors:

(1) mobility of the elements in the physical and chemical (including biologically cycled) milieu;
(2) depth of the upper, altered tier of the deposit;
(3) shape of the deposit and its size;
(4) strike and dip of the deposit;
(5) permeability, porosity and mineralogical composition of the host rock;
(6) local topography;
(7) hydrologic regime;
(8) nature of the weathered profile;
(9) tectonic movements;
(10) sampling medium;
(11) sampling density;
(12) precision and accuracy of the analytical procedure.

PATHFINDER (ALIAS INDICATOR) ELEMENTS/MINERALS

Pathfinder elements are elements associated with the target element(s) but which for one reason or another can be determined more easily in geologic material than the target element. For example, in Sardine mine, Australia, copper and tin occur together as stannite. Tin determination is more difficult than copper; hence copper was used as pathfinder for tin ore. Similarly, in sulphide nickel deposits associated with ultramafic rocks, copper is a pathfinder, since nickel occupies both silicate and sulphide mineral sites and the fixation pattern remains uncertain unless sequential extraction is undertaken. The absence of sulphide minerals in the Sukinda nickel (oxide) deposits was indirectly confirmed in the early stages of exploration by the low copper values.

Pathfinder minerals are those which can be more readily identified than the target element(s). In the Kolar gold field, scheelite was a pathfinder mineral for the gold-bearing Champion reef.

In the following pages, a brief account of the various prospecting techniques are given as a general introduction. You should consult advanced textbooks for detailed operational guidance.

STREAM SEDIMENT SURVEY

Stream sediments comprise composite samples of weathered and primary rocks in a state of mechanical transportation as unconsolidated material by a river or as chemical precipitates in coatings, cation exchanges in clay fractions, etc. Vast tracts ranging from tropical rain forests to cold mountains have been covered by such reconnaissance surveys on sample density varying from 1 in 200 sq. km (Uganda: 1965–75) to greater than 1 per sq. km (Solomon Islands: 1976–82). In the high and cold terrains of southern Quinghai, China, it is reported that a sample density of 1 per 30 sq. km was sufficient for finding very large ore deposits or outlining the most promising ground in a stream sediment survey program combined with heavy mineral reconnaissance.

Large copper deposits have been discovered by stream sediment survey, e.g. Bougainvile porphyry copper deposit in an acutely dissected terrain of Papua New Guinea; the 70 km long belt of copper occurrences including the 1.13 billion ton orebody at Salobo 3A in the Carajas district of Amazonia, Brazil which lay hidden within an impenetrable rain forest remote from access routes upto the early seventies was also discovered by following up a strong stream sediment signal. The discovery of Salobo 3A deposit illustrates an intelligent application of stream sediment survey to check aligned aeromagnetic anomalies parallel to the Igarape Salobo valley.

Regional geochemical mapping programs are usually based on multi-element analysis of stream sediments. The optimum size fraction of the sediment varies in different environments from coarse in arid tracts to –80 mesh in the warm, humid areas of India and –200 mesh in Warburton Range, Australia.

There are a few general rules:

(1) Over rugged terrains in temperate/cold climates, it is always advisable to collect sediment samples from first (i.e. the smallest channel at the head of the stream) or second order drainages.

(2) In areas of extensive glacial cover, sediment samples should be collected from active medial or lateral moraines.

(3) In many humid, tropical belts, thick forests and deep weathering restrict sampling to second or third order streams. In such terrains clay minerals are likely to be better as sampling media than coarse detrital fractions because of their high cation exchange capacity and deep weathering of the bedrocks. Recent human intervention and population pressure have converted parts of the second or third order valleys in many parts of the Indian countryside into cultivated lands. Some stream courses have been submerged by irrigation projects. Others are seasonally contaminated by pesticides and fungicides sprayed on the crops and plants growing on the banks.

As a precaution against such contaminants and to check the reproducibility of the data, it is advisable to collect stream sediment samples from the upstream and downstream ends of small point bars, as far away from the banks as possible at a depth of approximately 50 cm below the surface.

(4) Another common method is to collect stream sediments, particularly in the dry season, from natural sediment traps along stream courses below confluences or in a three point set around the confluence spaced 10–20 m from one another (Fig. 4.1).

(5) In cool, temperate areas, organic accumulations are likely to provide important leads to ore deposits. For example, in poorly drained areas covered by permafrost, muskeg swamp develops in many places. These are good scavengers of trace elements, comparable to the Fe and Mn oxide films in tropical terrains. Enrichment of Fe oxide in trace metals takes place under varying environments. Fe oxides in fracture coatings resembling gossan carry high levels of Au, As, Sb and Hg, e.g. at Pinson, Nevada. This is different from trace or minor element enrichments in fragmented ferricrete particles in drainage channels. For example, a low level but extensive Pb anomaly (a fan-shaped train extending at least 5 km) was picked up near the Elura Zn-Pb-Ag deposit, Cobar, New South Wales, Australia. The dispersion pattern is believed to be related to the Miocene lateritic weathering cycle here.

It is important to check for the appropriate size fraction of stream sediments for sampling each domain. It is also advisable to collect a duplicate sample from each

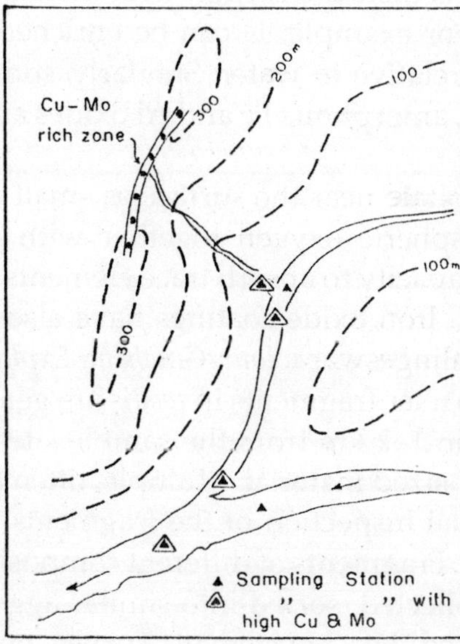

Fig. 4.1: Three-point sampling around the confluence of a river.

spot/station to check reproducibility. Usually the duplicate should be collected 5–10 m away from the original site.

The optimum size fraction for stream sediment sampling varies in diffferent environments. At high latitudes and altitudes, coarse fragments are normally useful for tracing anomalies. Similarly in arid and semi-arid tracts, a coarse fraction plus an ultrafine fraction is appropriate. In lateritised areas, size fractions depend on the nature of mobility of the target element and its affinity for iron oxide nodules, kaolin etc. The preferred range is from +35 mesh to –200 mesh, changing with the type of landscape, its history of evolution, alteration path of the target element etc.

Sample density is normally one per 2–5 sq. km in the reconnaissance stage. Two types of samples are collected at each site: a panned heavy mineral concentrate and a wet-sieved –200 mesh (–75 micron) fraction of stream sediment. The wet seived material is allowed to settle for 10 minutes, decanted and then transferred to a plastic bag, decanted again and air dried.

Re-distribution of elements in a stream involves interaction between bedrock and the weathered cover with water. Chemical elements are variously carried: in the form of detrital particles of rocks and minerals, solutions and organic and inorganic colloids. Colloids in stream sediments play an important role because of their surface charge, which affects their interaction with dissolved ions and their large surface-to-volume ratios. For example, U can be enriched by a factor exceeding 10,000 on organic colloids relative to water. Similarly, some cations are adsorbed preferentially in Mn oxides, amorphous Fe and Al oxides and humic substances, as indicated in Table 4.1.

Mn and Fe oxides precipitate near the surface as small nodules and in streams in equilibrium with atmospheric oxygen together with organic material. Such micro-nodules have large capacity to absorb trace elements, especially the first row transition elements and Ba. Iron oxide coatings have also been reported to carry particulate gold (K. Bheemalingeswara, *Jour. Geochem. Exploration* 52, 1995, 373–80).

In arid, rocky deserts, coarser fragments in *wadis* are generally representative of basement rocks lying within 1–2 km from the sample site. The fragments vary in length from 150 cm to sand-sized material. Multiple, often braided, flood channels characterise the *wadis*. Visual inspection of the fragments is an important step in such prospecting programs. Fragments of different composition, including samples of wall rock and ore are collected, sorted into similar aggregates, and chemically and mineralogically analysed. For a systematic survey, one sample per sq. km is generally adequate in the first stage.

A variant of stream sediment survey of an earlier vintage, but of great practical use is heavy mineral reconnaissance as a guide to ore deposits. Sample spacing varies from 2 per sq. km to 1 per 100 sq. km. The optimum spacing for reconnaissance is 1 sample representing a drainage basin area not exceeding 5 sq. km upstream from

Table 4.1: Relative degree of adsorption of some cations (after Rose, Hawkes and Webb, 1979)

	Mn oxide	*Amorphous Fe oxides*	*Goethite*	*Amorphous Al oxide*	*Humic substances*
	(1)	(2)	(3)	(4)	(5)
Greatest	Cu	Pb	Cu	Cu	Ni-Cu-Co-Pb
	Co	Cu	Pb	Pb	
	Mn	Zn	Zn	Zn	Zn-Mn-Ca
	Zn	Ni	Co	Ni	
	Ni	Cd	Cd	Co	Mg
	Ba	Co		Cd	
	Sr	Sr		Mg	
	Ca	Mg		Sr	
Least	Mg				

the sample locality. This method has been successful in locating deposits of gold, platinum, diamond, zircon, tin, tungsten, chromium, tantalum and rare earths. Heavy mineral surveys are suitable in areas with low relief with a net of contiguous drainage basins. The technique is applicable also to humid areas. Samples for heavy mineral studies, commonly stream sediment or weathered rock, are collected and washed in a prospector's wooden pan or using other forms of manual gravity separation. Panning is the best method so far devised for concentrating heavy minerals in the field. The most suitable and representative size of material is gravel and sand from first and second order streams. The initial samples should be composed of similar-sized particles and of constant weight at different stations. Concentrates may be prepared from approximately 15–20 kg in weight to permit comparative evaluation. Each concentrate is separated into strongly magnetic, feebly magnetic and non-magnetic fractions before seiving. Separate splits from each size fraction are prepared carefully both for multi-element analysis (spectrochemically) and mineralogical grain counts.

The time spent in processing a concentrate in the laboratory is much more than the time spent in collection of the heavy concentrate; but it is the best available method for reconnaissance in tropical humid terrains.

In semi-arid terrains, surveys of well sediments, particularly for the less mobile metals like Pb, Ba etc., are useful as leads to concealed deposits.

In semi-arid areas, well sediment, if available, offers an attractive alternative medium for picking up U, Pb, Zn and other mineral deposits of the neighbourhood (S.P. Vriend et al., *Jour. Geochem. Exploration*, 41, 1991, 151–67).

In India, one of the success stories in heavy mineral reconnaissance and detailed follow up was the discovery by the National Geophysical Research Institute (D. Gupta Sarma et al., Case History of a Kimberlite Discovery, Wajrakarur Area, A.P., South India, in G.D. Garland (Ed.): *Proceedings of Exploration* 87, Ontario Geological Survey Special Vol. 3, 1989, 888–97) of a 400 m long kimberlite diatreme lying under cover of red soil and calcrete and weathered down to a depth of 6–15 m near Venkatampalli, approximately 10 km south of Wajra Karur, Andhra Pradesh. The samples were processed through a Wilfley table and a high intensity magnetic separator, followed by gravity separation using tetrabromomethane. The heavy fraction was then sieved into different size fractions and examined under a microscope. The nature of dispersion indicated a steady increase in pyrope and Cr-diopside as given in Table 4.2.

A commonly ignored but important step in both heavy mineral reconnaissance and stream sediment survey is to ensure representative sampling at all stages of

Table 4.2: Differences in spread of indicator minerals from source kimberlite

Distance from source (in meters)	*Indicator Minerals (Per cent)*		
	Pyrope	*Picroilmenite*	*Cr-diopside*
50	75	19	7
100	65	33	1
1100	46	48	6
2200	24	75	1
5400	100	0	0

sample collection and volume reduction. Wet seiving in the field from a constant weight of sample is recommended. Slurry screening with a minimum of water helps in recovery of fine and colloidal fractions as well. Large initial volumes are essential for Au etc.

Search for deposits of gold, tin, tungsten etc., whose dispersion is spotty from point to point, is generally successful only in the reconaissance stage stream sediment survey. During the follow-up systematic search, there are difficulties in obtaining representative samples. The reasons are: (a) a naturally stochastic distribution of such rare minerals and metals in a sediment sample, where deposition, interstitial entrapment, winnowing and dilution are controlled by the size distribution of the economic minerals within the clay-to-boulder sized substrate of the channel; and (b) differences in particle size between the target mineral/metal and the host sediment, which creates sampling and analytical error. It is well known that grain size, density and shape are the principal factors controlling deposition or entrainment of the different particles moving by saltation or suspension along the channel. In most of the channels, the energy regime fluctuates in different seasons from high to low at different sites. If the geochemist involved in stream sediment survey ignores the variable nature of channel bed sediments, one may end up following false trails during detailed sampling.

To cite an example, it is commonly observed that anomalous concentration of heavy metals is found in coarser-grained sediments like boulder/gravel beds. This is difficult to explain in terms of simple hydraulic equivalence for settling particles, unless it is recognised that the enrichment process is a complex superposition of events over an extended period under varying energy regime of the transporting media.

In all such cases, the optimum sampling size for the economic minerals is sand to clay. One has also to adjust local variability against the substrate characteristic at each sampling site—not just grab a sample and move on!

PEDOGEOCHEMICAL PROSPECTING

Soil is an unconsolidated weathering product, which lies on or close to its source of formation. The temperature dependence of soil weathering reactions acts as a stabiliser for global temperature over geological time. Silicates weather faster at higher temperatures, consuming large quantities of CO_2 and thus causing CO_2 levels and global temperature to drop (J.C.G. Walker et al., *J. Geoph. Res.*, 86, 1981, 9776–82). Where unconsolidated material has been transported over large distances, it is called alluvium. The distinction between résidual and transported soil is important in soil geochemical prospecting; one can only be sure of the residual nature by checking the vertical sections (pits, cuttings, etc.) from the parent rock to the top soil. Where soil creep has taken place, a stoneline, composed of fragments of rocks, is common between B and C zones.

In a soil profile, the soil horizons (Fig. 4.2) can be classified as follows:

A_0 Humus charged top zone.
A_1 Mineral and humus charged zone.
A_2 Leached zone, dry in summer.
B Zone of accumulation of clays and sesquioxides; diagnostic field test: even in dry months samples from freshly dug holes are moist to feel.
C_1 Weathered structureless or layered zone, with or without fragments of bedrock.
C_2 Weathered zone with relict structures from the bedrock.
C_3 Zone of bleached parent rock

Such distinctions within the C zone are clearly seen in soil profiles of humid, tropical areas.

The following minerals are generally present in a soil profile in different combinations, depending on the nature of the bedrock, climate, topography, vegetation, seismicity, etc.

Oxides and hydroxides: boehmite, quartz, goethite, haematite, gibbsite,
1:1 Sheet silicates: kaolinite[1], halloysite

[1] X-ray diffraction shows maxima at 7 Å and 3.5 Å.

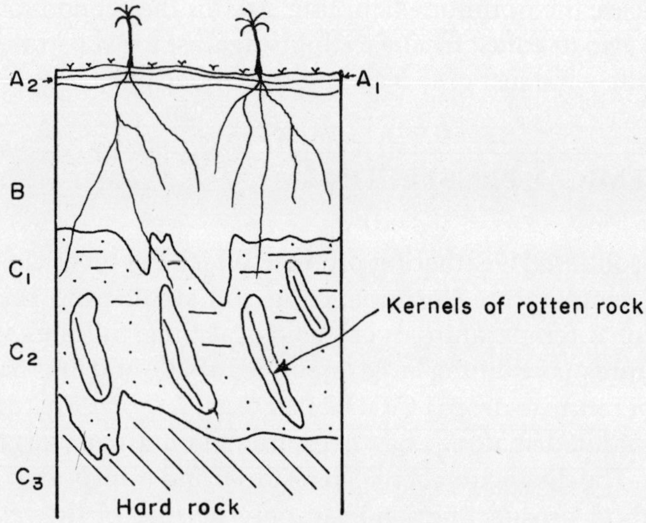

Fig. 4.2: Soil zones.

2:1 Sheet silicates: illite[2], smectite[3], vermiculite
2:1:1 Sheet silicates: chlorite[4].

Specific identification of the clay minerals and a semi-quantitative estimate of their weight per cent require X-ray diffraction studies (XRD) and measurement of the peak areas of glycolated samples. You may consult P.E. Biscaye: *Bull. Geol. Soc. Amer.* 76, 1965, 803–32, for details.

The breakdown of rock forming silicates proceeds in steps: first hydrogen ions exchange with the alkali metal cations of the primary silicates; next the cations are leached from the solid; this leaves behind a layer of amorphous silica, which subsequently reacts with cations from the surrounding solutions to create new minerals. The dissolved heavy metal cations from ore deposits get into the reconstituted residual silicate material by inorganic, organic and biochemical routes (Fig. 4.3).

[2] X-ray diffraction shows maxima at 10 Å and 3.3 Å; not affected by glycolation.
[3] X-ray diffraction shows maxima upon glycolation at 17 Å (001 peak).
[4] X-ray diffraction shows maxima at 14 Å non-expanding and at 4.7 Å.

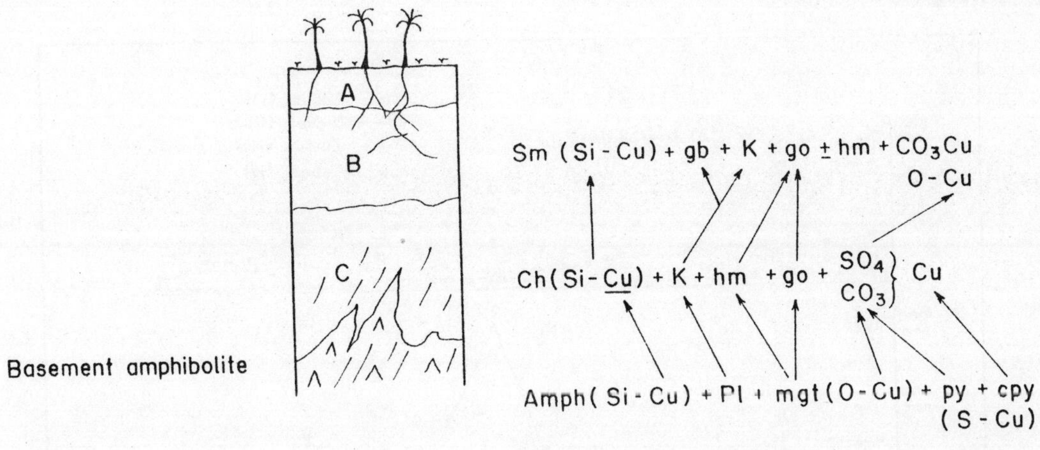

Fig. 4.3: Illustrative routes of transfer of trace metals from bedrock to topsoil (amph = amphibole; pl = plagioclase; ch = chlorite; mgt = magnetite; py = pyrite; cpy = chalcopyrite; k = kaolinite; gb = gibbsite; go = goethite; hm = haematite; sm = smectite).

Amorphous silica has large sorptive capacity, and can sequester quantities of crop nutrient chemicals. It is therefore not advisable to undertake pedogeochemical prospecting near areas of cultivation with artificial fertilisers.

After the target areas are broadly defined, soil samples are generally drawn from the B horizon. This is the beginning of detailed geochemical exploration and is accompanied or succeeded by lithogeochemical prospecting, where required, because anomaly signals in soil and other weathered cover are more diffuse and spread wider than in rocks. A comparison of anomalies in bedrock and overburden in Turamdih, Singhbhum copper field illustrates this point (Fig. 4.4). The upper part of B horizon is generally enriched in trace elements as compared to A horizon, particularly in humid tropical forests. But in poorly drained areas soil samples from A horizon are more informative, since chelates of heavy metals accumulate there. During early summer, deciduous forests in the tropics are subjected to intermittent fire; this burns up dry biomass accumulated on the forest floor. The ash is transported down-slope by summer rains. This explains why the top humus-charged zone of the soil in parts of the tropics is not as enriched in trace elements as the A horizon of cool temperate regions, where high rainfall and high organic activity lead to large-scale development of peat bogs and acid soil and intermittent concentration of trace elements in the A horizon.

Soil sampling has been extensively used in India in various base metal fields, e.g. Agnigundala (A.P.), Malanjkhand (M.P.), Rajpura-Dariba, Zawar Mala, Sawar, Khetri,

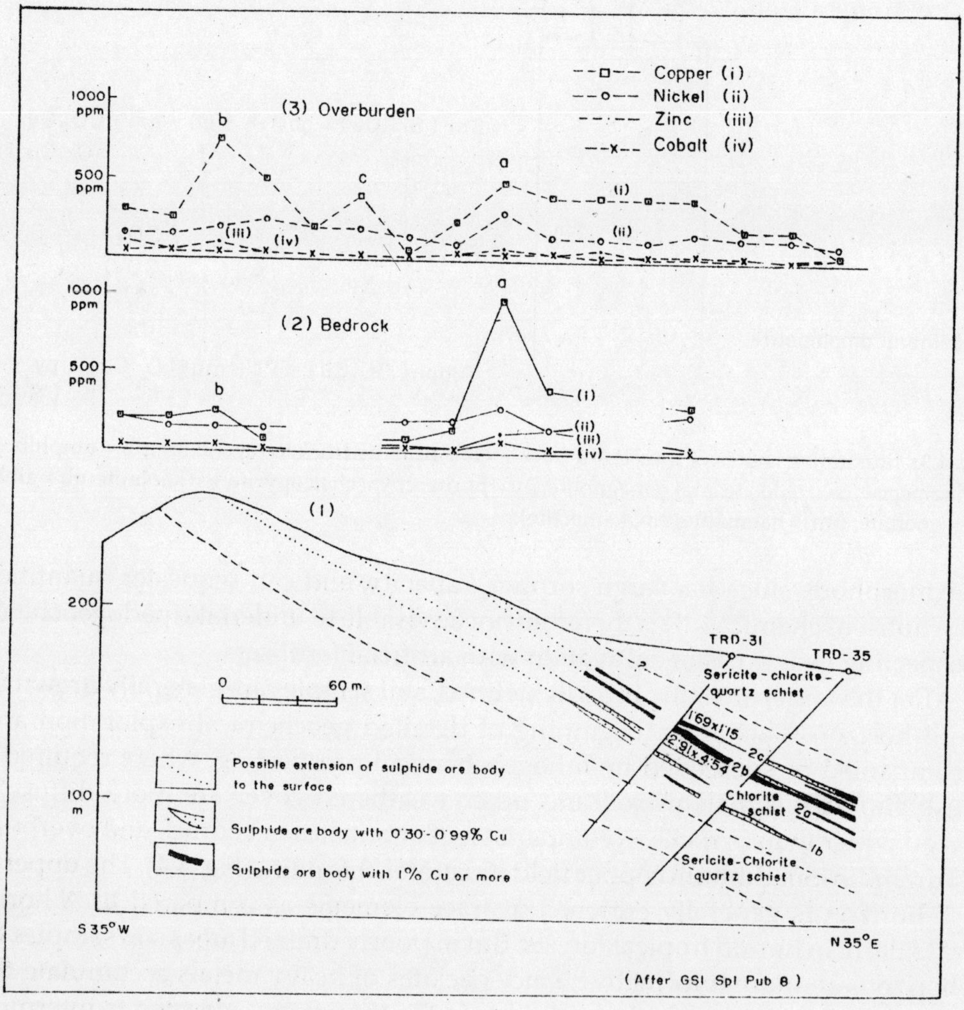

Fig. 4.4: Profile of metal anomalies in bedrock and overburden above sulphide ore bodies in Turamdih, Singhbhum copper field, Bihar.

Pur-Banera, and other deposits of Rajasthan, Singhbhum Copper field, Bihar, Sargipalli Pb-Cu deposit, Orissa, Pular-Parsori Cu occurrence, Maharashtra etc.

High As values (upto 1000 p.p.m.) are present in soil above sulphide-rich Au lodes of Kolar, Karnataka. In the Bodal uranium prospect, Rajnandgaon dt., M.P., feeble U anomalies in soil, 2–3 times the background, were found to be sited over weakly-mineralized (0.01–0.03% eU_3O_8) sheared effusives (P. Krishnamurty et al., *Exploration and Research for Atomic Minerals*, 1, 1988, 139–52).

Soil geochemical prospecting methods for U usually involve the analysis of 2 nuclides in the ^{238}U decay series- ^{238}U and the inert gas ^{222}Rn. The decay products of ^{222}Rn include some relatively longer lived isotopes like ^{210}Pb (half life = 22.3 yrs) and ^{210}Po (half life = 138.4 days). Since ^{210}Po is an alpha particle emitter, it can be detected in the soil sample up to a considerable time after sampling.

In soil sampling, various sampling patterns are used. Square or rectangular grid systems are common. Traverses are laid across the general strike of the mineralised patches. Where extension of mineralised ground is being searched by soil sampling, the width of its anomaly on the known part of the mineral bearing zone is first determined in course of an orientation survey; and the spacing of sample stations on each traverse across the extension zone is kept at half this width or less. For example, if the pedogeochemical anomaly extends over 20 meters across strike in the known mineralised ground, the sample interval on each traverse across the extension zone should not exceed 10 m.

In virgin tracts, where no surface expression of the mineral deposit is seen, the orientation survey should be so designed that sampling is done on variable spacing between 5 m and 50 m. It must however be kept in mind that topography, depth of weathering, degree of soil creep, surface runoff, etc., do not remain constant from one sample station to another. One must adopt appropriate modifications from one field to the other, taking care that sample station interval does not exceed the limit of secondary dispersion of target element(s). In comparatively flat terrains, coincident pedogeochemical and geophysical anomalies afford prime targets for drilling (Fig. 4.5); at places, like the Sukinda Chromite Field, discrimination of gravimetric anomalies (Bouguer) over concealed chromite and pyroxenite masses was possible by pedogeochemical screening of the anomalies. In rugged terrains, ridges and spurs are suitable for soil sampling, since the slopes are largely made up of transported soil and colluvium.

GEOCHEMICAL PROSPECTING OF CONSOLIDATED WEATHERED COVER

The process of weathering creates chemical fractionation at atmospheric P, T and enriches the residuum in resistate, hydrolysate and oxidate components, leaching the carbonate and evaporate ones. When the climate of a region changes from humid to

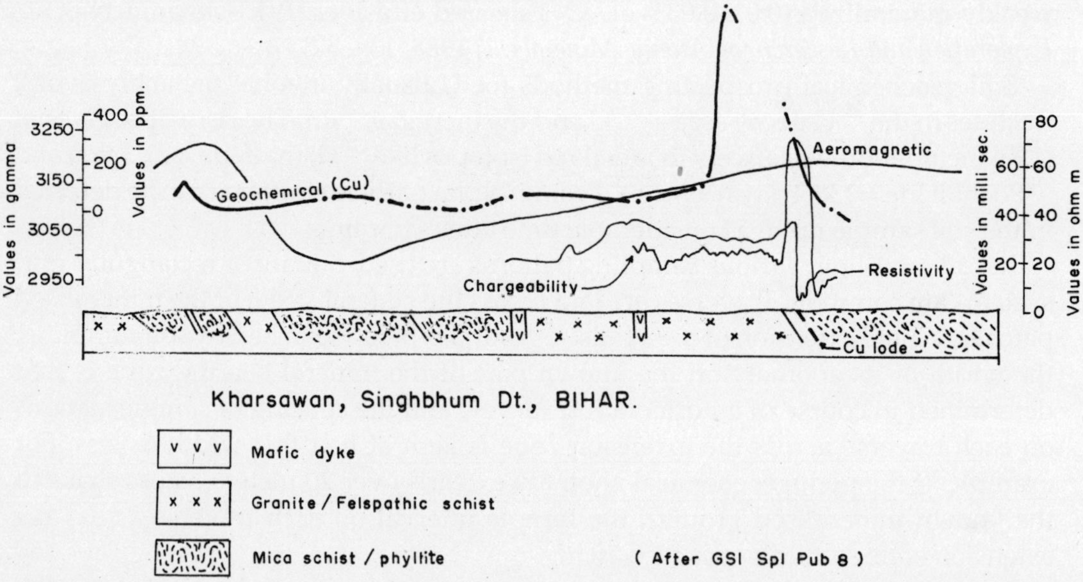

Fig. 4.5: Coincident geochemical and geophysical anomalies in Kharsawan, Singhbhum copper field, Bihar.

arid, the chemistry of weathering and the vehicles of erosion change. If the change is maintained over thousands of years, a new pattern is superposed on the earlier pattern.

Recent paleoclimatic researches have indicated that the earth has been passing through alternate cold and warm periods (glacial and interglacial in temperate belts) at intervals of approximately 10^5 years over the last 5×10^6 years. In the tropical belt, the cold climatic intervals are accompanied by fall in sea level by approximately 100 meters, isostatic uplift of the coastal tracts, severe changes in seasonal rainfall and resultant changes in vegetation and erosion of the rocks including the weathered cover. During the glacial periods, polar climate extended to temperate belts, with advance of glaciers far south into European, Asian and N. American mainlands. Due to stronger thermal gradients in the atmosphere between the equator and the poles, the glacial periods witnessed stronger and more frequent gales and accompanying eolian transport. The interglacial periods witnessed stronger discharge from the rivers, partial isostatic rebound due to withdrawal of ice cover from the high latitudes (a classic case is the Fennoscandian uplift) and resurgence of chemical weathering. Mobilisation of heavy metals fluctuated with changes in: (i) eH and pH, (ii) availability of colloidal organic matter, (iii) manganese and iron oxides, and (iv) relative rates of mechanical versus chemical alteration.

For older soils and consolidated weathered residuum, landscape dating is still not well established. Various techniques like thermoluminescence, palaeomagnetic reversal, radioactive isotopes, varnish cation ratio (R.I. Dorn, *Quart. Res.* 20, 1983, 49–73) have been used, but debate and uncertainty persists: are weathering events episodic with fast and slow modes or essentially continuous? Does the preserved record reflect the total history? Even the credibility of well-established land surface is questioned. Imprints of past climate changes are partially preserved, although intermittent vertical movements have destroyed and displaced these cappings to a large extent. Where old residual crusts have been partly displaced or exhumed, allochthonous geochemical anomalies, i.e. rootless signals, occur locally. Unless care is taken to classify the weathered cover in relation to the evolutionary history of the landscape, search for mineral deposits by geochemical methods may be fruitless. Classification of the landscape and separation of the Late Quaternary weathered cover areally and sequentially are useful in interpreting the heavy metal dispersion data in a proper frame. In favourable circumstances it is possible to reconstruct the paleotopography during the development of the weathered cover. This method of classifying a landscape into homogeneous domains of basement, weathered cover, neotectonic boundary, drainage and vegetational cover is generally described as *landscape geochemistry*. This term is not to be confused with *geochemical landscape*, which means the chemical attributes of bed-rock, stream sediments, soil, groundwater, lake sediments etc. of an area. The discovery of a small copper sulphide deposit beneath the laterite cover of Adash, Sambalpur district, Orissa (India) was possible due to correct understanding of landscape geochemical set up, in spite of rootless base-metal anomalies cropping up far away from the deposit in a displaced laterite catena (P.K. Banerjee et al. *Jour. Geol. Soc. India*, 31(4), 1988, 404–16).

Chemical dispersion of elements is generally weaker in cold climatic belts than in the tropics. Many heavy metals become mobile partly through inorganic and partly through organometallic transfers; oxidation of pyrite, for example, can bring the pH of the circulating fluid down to 4 or less and so mobilise the heavy metals, leaving the weathered residuum totally depleted.

Consolidated weathered cover reflecting different types of palaeoclimatic set up is divisible into the following varieties.

(1) Calcrete: This is a surface crust of residual weathering, where sand and silt are cemented by $CaCO_3$, precipitated directly from groundwater. This is an indicator of arid environment, except over mafic and ultramafic basements, where carbonate nodules are common in soil along river banks.

Some calcretes are silicified; lenses of vesicular opaline silica define zones of sharp pH changes near a past water table.

Under extreme aridity, calcrete grades into playa. Where the surface crust of residual weathering is essentially composed of hydrous iron oxides, *replacing the bedrock,* and precipitated from groundwater, it is known as *Ferricrete.*

In some parts of Australia, calcretes are associated with uranium enrichments. Ferricretes are common along the coastal tract of Orissa. Anomalous concentration of Cu, Ni and Co in calcrete samples above the Jacomynspan copper-nickel prospect, South Africa provides an example of its potential for use as a proximal signal of an orebody in a semi-arid environment.

(2) Silcrete: This is a surface crust of weathering, where sand and silt are cemented by silica. Low relief with a stable groundwater regimen, progressive aridity leading to alkaline condition of the water through excess evaporation and internal drainage are some of the causes for its formation. Silcretes over carbonatites locally carry up to 10% Ti, 0.5% Zr, 200 p.p.m. of Nb, 30 p.p.m. of U etc. In parts of the Khetri copper field, Rajasthan, thin films of silcrete are associated with gossan.

(3) Laterite: A pedogenic product of humid tropical weathering, consisting of goethite, haematite, kaolin, quartz with or without gibbsite and other clay and resistate minerals; in consolidated masses, the material shows cavernous, vesicular, botryoidal and other structures, a progressive change from a nodular, iron oxide rich zone at the top to structureless, clay rich zone at the bottom, nearly devoid of bases. A loose, brown to chocolate latosol occurs at the top. The cappings of laterite carry economic grade enrichments of Fe, Al, Mn, Cr, Ti, V, Zr etc., exceed 100 m in thickness locally and simulate gossan at places.

A pedogenetic laterite catena (Fig. 4.6) starts from clay rich saprolite at the base to the hard iron crust at the top. Ferricrete does not have underclay (Fig. 4.7).

(4) Gossan: It is an iron stone above a sulphide deposit, commonly with a cellular boxwork structure. A complete profile from the parent protore upward includes the zone of supergene enrichment, intermediate carbonate/sulphate/phosphate/arsenate zone and a top iron oxide rich zone with some quartz. Gossans over Pb sulphide with little pyrite-pyrrhotite are poor in iron oxides, e.g. at Sargipalli, Orissa.

Surface features of gossan have already been discussed in Chapter 3. Gossans are generally enriched in base and precious metals, as compared to ferricrete.

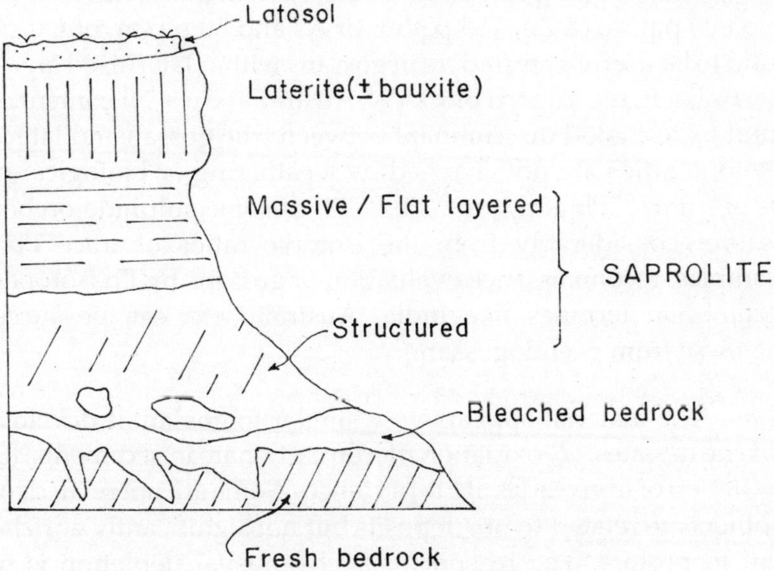

Fig. 4.6: Generalised pedogenetic laterite profile.

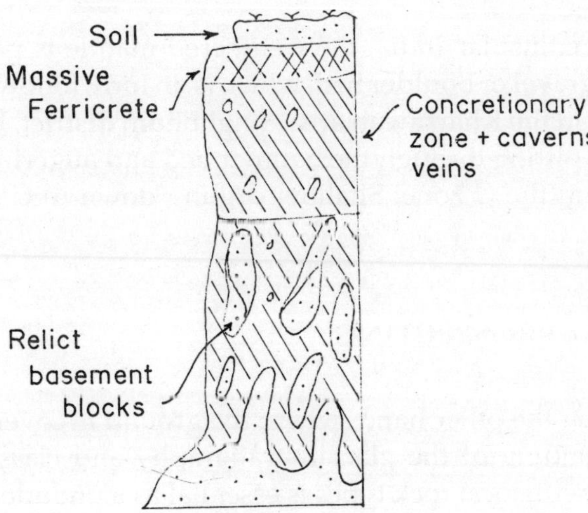

Fig. 4.7: Ferricrete profile near Bhubaneswar over Athgarh sandstone. Note absence of saprolite zone.

The gossan at Bethumni (Rajpura-Dariba field, Rajasthan) carries over 150 p.p.m. of Pb and upto 800 p.p.m. of Zn, 150 p.p.m. of As and 50 p.p.m. of Cu. Se and Pt have been found to be useful pathfinders in gossans within lateritised areas of some parts of W. Australia. In the Yilgarn block (W. Australia) Cu + Ni content of an iron stone was found to be a good discriminant between true gossan and laterite.

Since Pb isotope ratios are not changed by weathering or biological processes and the ratios of $^{206}Pb/^{204}Pb$ and/ or $^{207}Pb/^{204}Pb$ of some sulphide orebodies and their haloes differ considerably from the isotopic ratios of trace Pb in non-mineralised samples, reconnaissance evaluation of gossans by Pb isotopes in non-glaciated Precambrian terranes like India, Australia etc. can be successful in discriminating these from pseudogossan.

(5) Pseudogossan: The material appears very similar to gossan. It develops by: (1) oxidation of pyrite in slates; (2) oxidation of iron carbonate in sediments; (3) migration and precipitation of iron oxides at Eh-pH fences. Some are not related to metallic ore deposits; others are related to ore deposits but not significantly enriched in the metals, present in protore. The reason for such unusual depletion is not clear. Pseudogossans are exposed near Tama Dungri, West Bengal, and in Zawar Mala, Rajasthan (an oxidised product of ferruginous dolomite).

The usual method of sampling weathered crust is to undertake chip or channel sampling on exposures.

In many parts of Peninsular India, the weathered mantle is polyphase: a soil cover, underlain by a gravel or boulder bed, which is, in turn, followed downwards by a laterite layer, e.g. in the Kharsawan area, Singhbhum district, Bihar. Sampling in such cases requires pitting through the boulder bed and augering farther down to recover sample from the C zone. Shallow drilling down to C zone is a faster alternative.

TILL GEOCHEMICAL PROSPECTING

In glaciated terrains, on the other hand, where the ground is covered with glacial drift, a clear understanding of the glacial stratigraphy and classification of the various till sequences with local rock types is essential as a prelude to prospecting. The boulders in the till of different sequences would reveal the extent of local vs long distance transport; and mineralised boulders in any of these till sequences can be traced back to the high topographic elevations, from where these were carried.

Normally, the source is within a few kilometers in the higher reaches of the valley glacier. But if ore particles are present as heavy minerals in sand-to-clay fraction sediment of the till, the source may be as far as 40–50 km away.

In glaciated terrains of the Central Himalaya as well as in many other parts of ice-bound tracts like Siberia, Finland etc., ore bodies lie concealed below glacial moraine. Locally, the drift sequences can be extremely thick—up to 350 m in parts of Siberia. The first step is to decipher the startigraphic ordering of the till. At places there are as many as five separate till sequences. Each sequence has to be analysed separately. A sample of till taken at a given site may be an aggregate of material from many sources, coming from a few meters to a few hundreds of kilometers. Sample spacing has to be reduced with increase in complexity of the dispersal train. There are two different ways to look for signals.

(1) Use of glacial dispersal of clastic components. Where the source is near, comminution by glacial transport is less and the grain size of the material is coarse; as the source gets farther and farther away, one has to look for the indicator minerals/ore minerals in finer fractions. Thus size analysis of the till and a careful mineralogical classification from boulders to clay-sized fractions is essential.

(2) Use of material with high exchange capacity, such as cation exchange resins or 'sorbence' cloth, i.e. cloth woven of material with high exchange capacity, laid out in a grid, which adsorb proportionately more metals over orebodies than in barren areas.

Till geochemical survey has been very successful in Finland, where thousands of pits have been excavated to clarify glacial stratigraphy. Fabric studies, heavy mineral analysis and the distribution of different types of rocks in each stratigraphic unit are carefully taken up to prepare 'probability sections' or zones up the direction of ice movement where more mineralised boulders are likely to be found. Further pitting is confined within these sectors and new probability sections are prepared therefrom up the palaeoslope from the original apex of the boulder train till the source deposit is located. There are many instances of successful discovery of concealed orebodies in Finland from till geochemical prospecting.

The uranium deposit of Pahtvouma, N. Finland was discovered this way. For further details of this approach, you may consult 'Drift Prospecting', *Geol. Surv. Canada Paper* 89–20, 1991.

LITHOGEOCHEMICAL PROSPECTING

Around epigenetic and some syngenetic mineral deposits, the unweathered wall rocks carry abnormal concentration of the target elements. This is known as primary dispersion. Lithogeochemistry aims at detection of these primary dispersion patterns around or associated with mineral deposits. Although lithogeochemical prospecting is normally successful in epigenetic deposits, instances of primary dispersion haloes around syngenetic to diagenetic deposits are also known, particularly around Pb-Zn sulphide bodies.

Another application of rock geochemistry is to evaluate the mineralisation potential of a specific rock body by comparing the concentration of a particular ore element in that rock mass with the corresponding regional average. This helps in defining potentially productive zones. For example, Hesp and Rigby (1974) demonstrated that in the areas of Tasman geosyncline, rocks associated with Sn deposits have 3–10 times the Sn values of barren rocks. (W.R. Hesp and D. Rigby, *Mineral. Deposita* 9, 1974, 49–60). In the Gudzhir Intrusive complex in West Transbaykalia, biotite from granitoids associated with W-Mo deposit was reported to have 2–3 times Rb content (144–631 p.p.m.) over the normal range (73–123 p.p.m.) and 12–360 p.p.m. Sn ($\bar{x}$: 59–176 p.p.m.) as against 5–35 p.p.m.Sn ($\bar{x}$: 15–21 p.p.m.) in barren granites. Similarly, Zn content in biotite ranges from 400–5000 p.p.m. ($\bar{x}$: 1400–3100 p.p.m.) in productive granitoids as against 340–1600 p.p.m. ($\bar{x}$: 540–1350 p.p.m.) in barren granites (Ye. M. Sheremet et al. *Geochem. International* 10(5), 1973, 1125–35). Sometimes indicator (pathfinder) minerals point to ore deposits, e.g. scheelite in the Ramagiri and Kolar gold fields of India (K. Surya Prakash Rao et al., *Jour. Geochem. Expl.* 31, 1989, 307–317).

Instances of syngenetic to diagenetic orebodies having well-defined haloes are also known, e.g. Howard's Pass Pb-Zn deposit, Selwyn basin, Yukon. The footwall carbonaceous mudstones are enriched in Si, Cu, Co, Mo, As, Sb, Zn, Cd, Hg and Pb relative to similar rocks far away from the orebody. Carbonaceous, arsenical shales are associated with the vein and shear zone Au deposits of the Meguma Group of Nova Scotia and in Victoria, Australia.

For a proper design of sampling, a careful mineralogical and textural study of the rock body is a pre-requisite.

GEOCHEMICAL SPECIALISATION

Magmatogenic ore deposits leave their signatures in the host igneous rocks in two ways: either the host body is enriched in ore elements because of a high initial content of these elements in the melt; or it is depleted in those elements by their diversion to form ore bodies. This is known as geochemical specialisation and is a characteristic of all types of ore-bearing igneous suites which distinguish these from similar looking but barren suites.

For a uniformly fine-grained and mineralogically homogenous body, sampling is easy. An average of 40–60 sampling stations per sq. km would afford a general idea about the concentration level of a target element: but if you have a range of grain sizes and variable mineralogy, say a porphyritic granite with dykes of aplite and pegmatite and veins of sheared and vuggy quartz, sampling has to be so designed as to be representative of the different facies, keeping in mind that primary dispersion is influenced by the imprint of the fluid phase in relation to pre-ore and post-ore processes.

As a general rule, the larger the grain size of the rock, the larger is the volume and weight of the sample required. Normally, for a fine to medium grained granite, 1 kg of sample is sufficient. The number of samples per sq. km also increases correspondingly. For a volcanogenic Cu-Zn deposit in Viti Levu, Fiji, it has been reported that a density of 70 samples per sq. km could pick up anomalies in the footwall as far as 800 m below the orebody.

Lithogeochemical prospecting is locally a very powerful tool for locating blind sphalerite deposits at shallow depth. A halo of trace element enrichment is generally present around such deposits although sampling in the Mochia mine of the Zawar Pb-Zn belt did not pick up any noteworthy Pb or Zn anomaly. It is instructive that such deposits are not detectable by most geophysical techniques because of the low conductivity of sphalerite. Where such deposits are associated with pyrite or galena, EM and IP methods (see Chapter 5) could be tried.

Lithogeochemical prospecting has been used extensively in Russia. S.V. Grigorayan (*Int. Geol. Rev.* 16(1), 1974, 12–25) suggested the following procedure for identifying primary geological haloes:

(a) Maximal concentration field. Areas having values of target elements exceeding 10 times the background.

(b) Additive halo: This is constructed by adding the anomalous contents of a group of indicator elements after standardising the digits in terms of background. The standardisation neutralises randon errors in chemical analysis. Some recommend direct summation above background.

(c) Multiplicative halo: This is computed by determining the ratio of the products of the concentration of elements of economic interest (numerator) divided by the products of impurity elements (denominator). In disseminated zones, the multiplicative index is not as clear in defining mineral distribution as in well-defined lode deposits. Computation of multiplicative halo involves the following steps:

1. Obtain the logarithms of the concentrations of target elements.
2. Compute the average of the log transform and the standard deviation.
3. Calculate the background by direct summation of the log values.
4. Use the deviations from the log transformed background for the economic and gangue elements analysed.

In the Wainalaka Cu-Zn volcanogenic deposit, Fiji, multiplicative anomalies of $Mg \times Mn/Cu \times Zn$ and standardised additive ratios of $(Na + Ca + Sr + Mn)/(K + Rb + Mg) \times 100$ were found to coincide with footwall alteration zones (C.S. Rugless, *Jour. Geochem. Exploration*, 19, 1983, 563–86).

(d) Vertical zonality: This is a very important attribute of some sulphide deposits. For example, in the Yakutian sulphide-cassiterite deposits, Pb, Zn and Ag haloes are more prominent in the upper levels whereas Cu, Sn, Co, Mo and W haloes are strong in the lower levels and below the orebody. In the Cu-Ni deposits of the Kola Peninsula, Ba, Ag, and Pb haloes form stronger components in the upper level, getting gradually replaced by Co, Ni and Cu haloes below. On the basis of extensive observations, Grigorayan formulated a vertical zonality series from the top downwards as follows:

Ba-(Sb,As1,Hg)-Cu1-Cd-Ag-Pb-Zn-Sn1-Au-Cu2-Bi-Ni-Co-Mo-U-Sn2-As2-Be-W

For better definition of zonality, Grigorayan recommended use of overall haloes (both additive and multiplicative) in preference to single element haloes.

Around base metal deposits, vertical zonality on the basis of chemical changes in single mineral fractions, e.g. chlorite (which is a hydrothermal product) from different levels and at different distances from the lode margin may prove worthwhile, although in the Mosaboni copper deposit, Grigorayan's concept was tested in a preliminary way on whole rocks without any success.

In China, these concepts have been successfully applied in some deep-seated orebodies, e.g. in the Karatungk Ni-Cu deposits associated with norite and gabbro. Li Yinggui et al. *(Jour. Geochem. Exploration,* 55, 1995, 309–20) reported that the ratio $(As \times Ba \times B) / (Cu \times Ni \times Co)$ can be used in this field in three ways. First, the ratio is useful in evaluating the relative denudation level of Ni-Cu ore deposits, associated with carboniferous mafic intrusives. Secondly, it is useful for recognising significant geochemical anomalies quickly. Thirdly, it can be used to predict the location of blind orebodies. The ratio falls by an order of magnitude for every 100 m depth of the orebody. It is greater than 10 above the orebody; 0.1–10 in the upper part of the orebody, 0.01–0.1 in the upper middle part and 0.001–0.01 in the lower middle part of the orebody.

(e) Zonation Index: Some Russian geochemists advocate use of the following formula on log transformed analytical data for computation of the zonation index:

$$x = \bar{x} \cdot e^{2.651} s^{.2}$$

where x = mathematical expectation of the value of the element;

$\bar{x}$ = the averge of log transformed value

s = standard deviation

The concepts of additive and multiplicative haloes, vertical zonality and zonation index are anchored on the experimental and thermodynamic findings that residual volatiles tend to increase during crystallisation of a magma, and when these move through the adjacent rocks, heavy metals are leached out and deposited. In fact, such solutions need not be magmatic in origin. D.S. Korzhinskii *(Geochim. et Cosmochim. Acta* 17, 1959, 17–20) and H.C. Helgeson (*Econ. Geol. Mon.* 4, 1967, 333–42) demonstrated that during a reaction of acid, chloride rich waters with rocks of granitic composition, destruction of primary silicate minerals releases sufficient ore-forming elements for generating mineral deposits. Subsequent researches have confirmed the validity of such processes even for ocean floor hydrothermal deposits.

Other related terms are as follows:

(f) Coefficient of contrast: This is the ratio of an element at the surface to the element at depth. This is a descriptive parameter without much genetic or interpretative significance; but many Russian geochemists were fond of such frills!

(g) Linear productivity: This is the product of the width of an anomaly in meters and the average content of an element in per cent.

(h) Anomaly ratio: Ratio of an anomalous value to background value.

The trouble with such empirical guidelines is that one is liable to reach misleading conclusions unless the rock geochemical study is carried out hand-in-hand with mapping of the mineralogical zones. Thus, in a tin field of southern New South Wales, it was observed that mineralised granites are depleted in Li and Rb and enriched in Ba in course of hydrothermal destruction of felspars. Similarly, biotite in unaltered granite may carry more F than muscovite in topaz-bearing mineralised granites (K.M. Scott & M. Rampe, *Jour. Geochem. Exploration,* 20, 1984, 337–54)!

FLUID INCLUSION PROSPECTING

This is a comparatively new exploration tool. Fluid inclusions are samples of hydrothermal solution that were trapped in the minerals either during or after crystallisation. There are mixtures of juvenile and meteoric fluids—the meteoric fluids circulating down to 5–7 km below the surface (R.E. Criss et al., *Jour. Geoph. Res.* 96, 1991, 13335–56), whereas the juvenile fluids (H_2O and CO_2) are estimated to disappear below 300 km (S. Kraft et al., *Jour. Geoph. Res.* 96, 1991, 17997; A.B. Thompson, *Nature* 358, 1992, 295). The geothermal fluids have varying intensity of heat flux, ranging up to 4200 ± 500 MW in the Taupo Volcanic Zone of New Zealand and 5300 MW in Yellowstone National Park of the U.S.A. One can derive information about the chemical composition of the hydrothermal fluids, their temporal and spatial variations and the position of the sample with respect to the whole circulation chamber. For example, in epithermal gold deposits, CO_2 is an ubiquitous component of the inclusions. The amount varies, for example, from 20 mole% at Homestake to less than 2% in a typical epithermal deposit. The presence of a water-rich fluid plus CO_2 indicates boiling. Suppose you are drilling for Au-Ag lodes and the fluid inclusions in the drill cores so far recovered show two phases but ore has not yet been intersected. In such a case, you should continue drilling till you cross the lower limit of this two-phase zone, where boiling actually started and where most probably the ore zone lies. The supra-ore and sub-ore situations are also revealed in favourable circumstances from fluid inclusions. For example, adularia often occurs above the boiling zone and carries two-phase inclusions, whereas silicified wall rocks below the ore zone could be associated with one-phase inclusions. Infra red microscopy is suitable for ore minerals like wolframite, stibnite, bournonite etc. where the fluid composition is different from that in the gangue due to boiling of the fluid in course of precipitation of the ore minerals (V. Luders, *Econ, Geol.*, 91, 1996, 1462–1468.

Fluid inclusions in a mineral deposit may provide a powerful prospecting tool. Where such fluid inclusions display a wide range of homogenisation temperature, indications of boiling and fairly high pressure, one may normally expect a major ore field in the vicinity. In the Da Hinggan Mountains of China, where more than 300 metallic ore (Pb-Zn, Ag, Cu, Sn and REE) occurrences have been discovered, Chinese geochemists [Sheng Jifu et al., *Acta Geol. Sinica*, 8(3), 1995, 289–303] noted that the fluid inclusions evolved 'from multi-phase to single phase liquid inclusions and from being gas rich to gas poor and water-poor to water-rich ones' with a fall in temperature, pressure and salinity. In their scheme of classification, they identified the following types of inclusions:

L-type:	Liquid inclusions with less than 50% gas;
V-type:	Gaseous inclusions with less than 50% liquid;
LCO_2 type:	Polyphase inclusions with liquid CO_2, gas and aqueous solution;
S-type:	Polyphase inclusions having gas, liquid and solid, mostly halite;
G-type:	Inclusions of primary melts in the form of glass plus gas and liquid.

The homogenisation temperatures of fluid inclusions in most of the large deposits cover a wide range—from 600°C to 190°C, corresponding to different stages of their growth and recycling—although there are some deposits like the Meng' en Tolgoi Pb-Zn deposit (with Ag) whose T_h ranges between 380°C and 140°C.

In view of the frequent co-existence of primary and secondary fluid inclusions, geochemists use an indirect method for determination of salinity. For liquid rich inclusions, the salinities are determined by the freezing method. Liquid nitrogen is used so that the fluids within the inclusion are frozen. The melting temperature of the frozen material is determined in the course of its natural recovery to the original fluid state by using the thermometric table of the freezing stage. From the phase diagram of the $NaCl–H_2O$ system, the corresponding salinity value of the inclusion fluid is derived. In the case of inclusions with daughter crystals, a heating stage is used. The temperature of melting of crystals at the point of their complete disappearance is measured on the thermometric table and the corresponding salinity values are read on the halite crystal melting curve of the NaCl–H_2O system. Estimation of pressure of the ore-forming environment is normally attempted following Roedder's P-T-D diagram of the system NaCl–H_2O (E. Roedder, *Reviews in Mineralogy*, 12, 1984, 250–90).

Isotopic composition, gas composition, salinity etc. of the hydrothermal fluids are decipherable from the fluid inclusions with the help of ion microprobe. Otherwise, only the composition of the primary fluids (H_2O, CO_2, CH_4, H_2S) is determined with heating and cooling stage. Even such studies are illuminating. For example, A.M. Yerokhin and T.M. Sushcherskaya (*Geochem. International*, 29(12), 1992, 50–61) found in the Iul'tin tin deposit that two different fluids were involved in its formation—the first related to a crystallising granite having an aqueous chloride composition and the second the pore fluid of the heated country rock saturated with volatiles (CO_2 and CH_4). These fluids mixed in the zone where quartz + cassiterite + muscovite + arsenopyrite + wolframite + scheelite + beryl + fluorite formed. The pore fluid got exhausted when the later assemblage of lollingite + arsenopyrite + pyrite + pyrrhotite + chalcopyrite deposited essentially from chloride-rich water. Russian and Indian geochemists found in both Champion and Oriental reefs of the Kolar gold field that there is a gradual increase in temperature of homogenisation (T_h) of fluid inclusions in quartz from 130°–305°C at depth, along with an increase in the salinity of the fluids. In place of the two-phase inclusions (Gas : Liquid = 1 : 7) of the upper levels, multi-phase (with sylvite and halite daughter minerals) and H_2O + CO_2 fluid inclusions with low methane and higher density of the carbonic fluid (1.03 gm/cm^3) are noted in the lower levels. (Y.G. Safonov et al., *Jour. Geol. Soc. Ind.* 25, 1984, 145–154).

Metal concentration in fluid inclusions as small as a few micrometers can also now be determined at parts per million level by Proton Induced X-ray Emission (PIXE) and the X-ray microprobe (vide C.A. Heinrich et al., *Econ. Geol*, 87, 1993, 1566–83; J.B. Lowenstern et al., *Science*, 252, 1991, 1405–9).

It is worth noting that fluid inclusions need not signify only the hydrothermal to pneumatolytic phase chemistry of a system. Magmatic fluids capable of carrying ore metals and volatiles and escaping on depressurisation are well known. In effusive lavas, these inclusions are generally very small in the range of a few microns to a few hundred microns. A combination of scanning electron microscope (for enlarged view), infra red spectroscope (for analysis of bubble composition) and electron probe wave length dispersive spectrometry (for mapping concentration of different elements within the inclusion) was used by K. Yang and S.D. Scott (*Nature*, 383 1996, 420–423) to identify CO_2 rich gaseous phase 2.3 wt% Zn, 7.2 wt% Cu, 1.1 wt% Ni etc. from 5–20 micron size bubbles within melt inclusions, which occur in pyroxene phenocrysts of a vesicular andesite. Compared with dilute hydrothermal fluids (carrying around 6 p.p.m. Zn, 2 p.p.m. Cu etc.) venting on sea floor, the magmatic volatile phase has a much higher concentration of ore metals around massive sulphide deposits and provide a subtle but firm indication of the ore potential of a volcanic fields.

Each mineralising hydrothermal system has its own diagnostic trend no doubt. But a pattern can be established from an orientation study of known deposits; search in extension areas of epigenetic deposits can be more thorough and rewarding.

One of the best explored geothermal systems is at Broadlands, New Zealand, where Au, Cu, Zn, Pb are found in small quantities; and like the 'Black Smokers' in the mid-ocean transform-ridge environments, active ore-forming processes can be observed here. The deep thermal water has indications of mixing of 20% low salinity magmatic vapour with local meteoric water. At the Ohaki pool, precious metals are deposited primarily near the surface and base metals deeper. There is an active graben. Temperature in the deep reservoir ranges from 250°C to 270°C, the maximum being close to 307°C. At the highest temperature, Au is mainly in chloride complexes; at lower temperature (below about 250°C) Au is in bisulphide complexes and the water is highly undersaturated in gold down to 100°C. But this does not stop its precipitation. The main control is oxidation; Eh change plays a more critical role than boiling, pH and T°C.

Hg complexes are stable to slightly higher fO_2; hence mercury deposits are likely to be underlain by Au deposits. There are intermittent shows of Hg along the west coast of India. These coincide with a zone of high heat flow. There could be intermittent polymetallic and Au concentration underground. In fact this could be analogous to late stage waters (70°– >150°C) which still flow through the two largest and youngest epithermal Au deposits (Hishikari, Japan and Lodolane, Papua-New Guinea).

Recently, such studies of fluid inclusions have been extended to mantle xenoliths. Remnants of magmatic melts, migrating through the mantle, wedge beneath island arcs lying along the western rim of the Phillipine plate, as glass inclusions in olivine prophyroclasts of spinel bearing harzburgite xenoliths are found to contain primary H_2O-fluid inclusions and spherical sulphide droplets. On the basis of heating stage experiments as well as electron probe and ion probe analysis of the inclusion material P. Schiano et al. (*Nature*, 377, 1995, 595–600) have concluded that these melt inclusions carry trace element signature of the subducting slab and that the basaltic crust of the subducting slab yielded by a small degree of partial melting giving rise to hydrous siliceous melts which percolated through the overlying depleted mantle wedge and 'refertilised' the depleted peridotites.

Another interesting recent development is the discovery of large reservoirs of CH_4 in layer 3 of the oceanic crust. Between 1979 and 1983 abiogenic methane, forming several per cent of the total gas with an isotopic composition distinctly heavier than that normally produced in the breakdown of organic matter was recovered from high temperature vent fluids of the East Pacific Rise (EPR). In 1987, a 500 m-long core of oceanic crustal layer 3 recovered during drilling at the South West Indian Ridge (SWIR) as a part of the Ocean Drilling Project (ODP), was found to be made up of gabbroic rocks with fluid inclusions enriched in CH_4 as a volatile phase. There are various theories about its origin—some proposing that sea water carbonates yielded CH_4 during transformation of ultramafites to serpentine by infiltration of sea water; others proposing that magmatic volatiles, trapped within inclusions, built up CH_4 from CO_2 and H_2O by inward diffusion of H_2O. Such debates can only be resolved by a thorough isotopic characterisation of the inclusions. Reactions that produce CH_4 from CO_2 concentrate ^{12}C. Therefore the remaining C in CO_2 should get heavier. Of course the possibility of formation of graphite in course of such reactions is a complicating factor.

Lithogeochemical prospecting including fluid inclusion study cannot succeed in locating new deposits on a mechanical-empirical approach. Recent advances in our knowledge regarding the general behaviour of elements in aqueous systems, application of stable isotopes of such light elements as O, S, C and H to discriminate among marine, meteoric, juvenile, evolved connate or metamorphic waters, role of thermal gradients, osmotic pumping, deformation, mixing of fluids of different sources ranging from high temperature, acid and reducing to cool, neutral or alkaline systems etc. have all to be utilised in the search for concealed, deeper seated orebodies on the basis of ore deposit modelling.

Geochemical modelling of fluid compositions and their host mineral assemblages including alteration profiles, e.g. change in oxygen or strontium isotopes of the minerals caused by fluid infiltration can be used to set limits to possible types of epigenetic mineralisation. For example, in an acidic melt, undergoing progressive crystallisation H_2O and CO_2 are largely excluded from growing crystals. During isobaric closed system crystallisation, the total mass fraction of exsolved gas in a gas-saturated magma thus increases progressively. Since CO_2 is much less soluble than H_2O in silicate liquids, the concentration of CO_2 in glass inclusions at different stages of crystallisation would indicate the trend of evolution of co-existing magmatic gases. Analysis of glass inclusions in quartz phenocrysts from acidic rocks by infra-red spectroscopy (for H_2O, OH and CO_2) and ion microprobe (for trace elements like Ca, Mg, La, Ce, Yb, U etc.) would reveal the pre-existing gas content of the melt, assuming fractional crystallisation and closed system behaviour without any gain or loss. Such an ideal condition is never realised; there are density stratifications within the magma body and gas migrates vertically from lower levels and accumulates near the roof zone. As a result, the computations are approximations.

The following mass balance equations are used for calculating the exsolved gas contents:

$$M_{gas} = \frac{M_{CO_2}^{bulk}\,(1 + F) - M_{CO_2}^{liquid}}{(1 - M_{CO_2}^{gas})\,(1 + F) - M_{CO_2}^{liquid}}$$

where M_{gas} is the total mass of exsolved gas in the system, corresonding to the particular value of *F*, which is the mass ratio of crystal to melt and *M* is the mass fraction of the subscripted component in the superscript phase. In case of H_2O, replace CO_2 in the subscript by H_2O. P. J. Wallace et al. *(Nature*, 377, 1995, 612–16) have thus demonstrated for the 0.76 Ma Bishop rhyolitic tuff in eastern California that the pre-eruptive gradient in exsolved gases varied from less than 2% in the deeper regions to nearly 6% near the top—a favourable milieu for the formation of hydrothermal ore deposits.

H.P. Eugster *(Mineralog. Mag.* 49, 1985, 7–23) developed a geochemical framework for ore forming elements associated with granites, essentially on the basis of their behaviour in Cl^- dominated aqueous systems. Elements comparable to bivalent octahedral cations, which include most of the metals (e.g. Cu, Fe, Zn, Co, Ni) enriched in massive sulphide and porphyry copper deposits are moderately mobilised in hydrothermal systems in contrast to those elements which are comparable in behaviour to alkaline elements (e.g. Ag, Pb, Hg, etc.) in effective ionic radius and ionic charge. Large, highly charged cations (like PGE, Sn, W, Mo, REE, Y, Ti, Sc, V etc.) are the least mobile in Cl^- dominated solutions.

At the other end of magmatic evolution, geochemical modelling can be useful in analysing the trend of evolution of fluid chemistry in mafic-ultramafic assemblages of ophiolitic affinity. High temperature (greater than 350°C) 'black smoker' fluids in the TAG area of the Mid-Atlantic Ridge were found to be Cu-rich, whereas 70 m to the southeast, white smoker zinc-rich fluids were venting at 260°–300°C. M.K. Tivey et al. *(Jour. Geoph. Res.* 100, 1995, 12527–55) have demonstrated that the fluid composition of white smokers could be derived from the black smokers by a combination of conductive cooling, mixing with sea water and precipitation of sulphides and anhydrite. These reactions decrease the pH to less than 3, which favours dissolution of sphalerite precipitated earlier, leading to an enrichment of Zn concentration in the fluid from 46 micromol per litre to 300–400 micromol per litre. This is again reprecipitated by mixing with low-temperature fluids.

Specialised chemistry of the fluids in a dynamic hydrostatic gradient also controls much of sedimentary ore deposition. The Pennine orefields, a fluorite-rich variant of the Mississippi Valley type ore, owed much of its specialisation to the Dinantian-Namurian sedimentary basins in the north and east of England. Rapid subsidence of such basins during late orogenic cycles limit the oxidation and fermentation of organic detritus enriched in U, Pb, Zn, P etc. Ore fluids from such basins generate many of the unusual features like the J-type lead-isotope ages of the deposits, methane and other hydrocarbons in the fluid inclusions, etc.

Such geochemical modelling rests on advanced analytical tools, clear understanding of the trend of evolution of the rock associations and non-linear variations at different steps through partial open system behaviour. Models incorporating advection with diffusion have analytical solutions (cf. J. Baker and M. Spiegelman, *E.P.S.L.*, 136, 1995, 88–96). The NABRE project of the Australian Geological Survey Organisation to develop a time series predictive framework for Paleo- and Mesoproterozoic basin evolution and to provide fluid flow models for these basins is one such example, where varieties of geophysical tools (seismic, well log and borehole cores together with SHRIMP studies—Sensitive High Resolution Ion Microprobe—to provide chronostratigraphic controls) are being combined with isotope and major/trace element geochemical studies to define targets of deep-seated orebodies. Future search for concealed deposits will benefit from such combined forward modelling programs, once refinement is attained in the following aspects:

1. Geometry of the body having fluid-rock interaction. One dimensional model defining progress of reaction as a function of integrated fluid flux along a path through a chemically reactive rock is too simplistic. In actual conditions the temporal and spatial dimensions of the channels through which the fluids flow are non-uniform.
2. The balance between metal transfer through fluids and wall rock—fluid interaction (for extraction and precipitation of metals) is variable. This determines the efficiency of the system.
3. Extent and quality of thermodynamic data used for predicting mass balance in complex fluid-silicate-sulphide systems is uneven. Internal consistency of

multi-component data sets is rarely achieved even by simultaneous fitting of multiple thermodynamic and equilibrium measurements (Heinrich et al., *Ore Geology Reviews,* 10(3–6), 1996, 319–38).

Lithogeochemical prospecting has been used in some mica pegmatites of Hazaribagh and Bhilwara more as orientation programs than for new discoveries. In fact, except for Russia, lithogeochemical prospecting has been very rarely used as a tool for locating unknown ore bodies, not because it is ineffective but on account of a negative mind-set in many parts of the world to rely more on drilling holes than on spending the same amount for a proper mineral deposit modelling using fundamental scientific skills and available knowledge of hydrothermal systems, stable isotopes and fluid inclusions. Such use of isotopes as a discriminator in mineral exploration is based on a detailed understanding of the relationship between isotopic signatures and the nature of the mineralising events. A series of measurements are needed, not just a few samples drawn at random. This is worth emphasizing. Some of the potential isotopes are as follows.

Parent nuclide	Daughter nuclide	Half life in 10^9 yrs.	Tracer ratio (radiogenic/nonradiogenic)
^{238}U	^{206}Pb	4.468	$^{206}Pb/^{204}Pb$
^{235}U	^{207}Pb	0.738	$^{207}Pb/^{204}Pb$
^{232}Th	^{208}Pb	14.01	$^{208}Pb/^{204}Pb$
^{187}Re	^{187}Os	45.6	$^{187}Os/^{188}Os$
^{87}Rb	^{87}Sr	48.8	$^{87}Sr/^{86}Sr$

Radiogenic isotopes have been used in mineral exploration for more than two decades in Australia, Canada, U.S.A. etc. In Precambrian base and precious metal deposits, $^{206}Pb/^{204}Pb$ and $^{208}Pb/^{204}Pb$ have been used to discriminate between mineralised and barren assemblages. Diagnostic $^{206}Pb/^{204}Pb$ ratios have been reported from pre-Tertiary uranium depositis; variations in carbon and oxygen isotope typically associated with MVT deposits, oxygen and hydrogen isotope patterns associated with Vein deposits in plutons and volcanogenic massive sulphide orebodies and sulphur isotope variations in sandstone type uranium deposits are illustrative of the efficacy of stable isotope geochemistry.

HYDROGEOCHEMICAL PROSPECTING

Water sampling is best suited for elements which are easily mobile under near-surface environments, e.g. U, Cu, Pb, Zn, Mo, S (as SO_4). Other elements like As, Be, Co, Ni, Sn, W, Ag, V, Cr etc. are also mobile under special circumstances. The movement is either in groundwater or surface water. For groundwater sampling, dug wells, springs, boreholes etc. are targetted. For surface water, streams are sampled, preferably discharge from lower order streams unless the objective is measurement of pollution.

A special type of problem is faced in hydrogeochemical survey of uranium deposits. Many of these occurrences are not easily detected by conventional water samples due to high mobility of U in the secondary environment and the effect of Fe, Mn and organic matter in such an environment.

A water sample contains some suspended solids. The sample must be filtered through 0.45 μ filter to separate the suspensions from the solution, which contains a number of anions. Since solubility of metal reduces as pH increases from 4 to 7, it is vital to determine the pH of the water *on the spot* with a good pH meter as well as specific conductance, sulphate, chloride, carbonate and fluoride contents. Never use pH papers. When you compare the concentration of an element like Cu from two water samples, their pH must be known. For example, 10 ppb of Cu in water of pH 4 could signify an anomaly comparable to 2 ppb of Cu in water of pH 6. Careful determination of Eh is also required generally by calculating from the content of dissolved Fe, assuming equilibrium with iron oxides.

Hydrogeochemical prospecting is neither useful in semi-arid (less than 20 cm per year) nor in high rainfall (greater than 100 cm per year) areas. Another problem is proper storage of the samples in the field and transport of large samples (1 or 2 litre bottles) to the laboratory, particularly in countries of the tropical belt. The dissolved cation content[5] can be stabilised after filtration by the addition of reagent grade HNO_3 to the water sample to bring down pH to less than 2. Hydrogeochemical prospecting for uranium deposits can be worthwhile if facilities exist for determining the lead isotopes and $^{234}U/^{238}U$ activity ratios. In mildly reducing environments, where uranium anomalies may not be identifiable from total U content, anomalous content of ^{206}Pb in groundwater can reveal the proximity of uranium mineralisation, e.g. the 1300 Ma Old Cigar Lake U deposit in Canada, the biggest ever discovered

[5]Reliable determinations at such low levels of concentration require; (1) Flame AAS for Na, Mg, K, Ca, Li, Si; (2) Flameless AAS for Cu, Zn, Mo, As, Fe, Mn, Al; and (3) Ion Chromatograph for SO_4, Cl, F.

in the world with 14% U_3O_8(av) and lying 450 m below ground! (P. Toulhoat and C. Beaucaire, *Jour. Geochem. Exploration*, 41, 1991, 181–96). ^{234}U may also be used for detection of anomalous uranium concentration, because it is preferentially expelled from U-bearing mineral surfaces in contact with groundwater.

In the Umra-Udaisagar-Debari tract of Rajasthan, where uraninite, gummite and other secondary minerals occur in carbonaceous phyllites, well water samples were found to be unusually high in U with the background value of 8.5 ppb and the highest concentration reaching 80–85 ppb (R. Kaul and S.P. Balakrishnan, *Exploration and Research for Atomic Minerals*, 4, 1991, 117–29).

Hydrogeochemical signals are also recognisable for Au in thickly forested areas. High concentration of organic acids (by dense rotting vegetation) helps in gold speciation. The root systems of many plants contain complexing agents like thiosulphate, cyanide and thiocyanate, which can form stable soluble complexes with Au even at low concentration. Anomalies up to 130 ppt (ng l^{-1}) of Au in water, freed from particulate Au through a 1.27 μ filter, have been reported from some gold fields of New South Wales, Australia.

The size and intensity of an aqueous signal or halo depend on: (1) morphology and composition of the primary minerals and of the primary haloes; (2) porosity and permeability of the surrounding rocks; (3) intensity and duration of present and past weathering milieu; and (4) landscape geochemical conditions and migration characteristics of the ore elements.

In the hot springs of India, various elements occur either in dissolved state (e.g. B, Sr, Li in Subansiri springs) or in vapour phase (He in Rajgir springs). On the west coast, Hg has also been found as intermittent discharge from the neighbourhood of hot springs, although high temperature geothermal springs, characterised by more than 9000 p.p.m. of Total Dissolved Solids (TDS), high NaCl, some Ag and Au as well as Hg and As, have not yet been located.

The use of hydrochemistry is assuming greater importance these days in developing benchmark information on natural dispersion of toxic elements and for identifying pollution. Whenever you are checking for indications of pollution in the hydrosphere, do not forget to check the concentration of the toxic elements (F, S, Pb, Hg, Cd, Cr, Ni, Cu, Zn etc.) in associated clay. The capacity of clay minerals for fixing metals in cold extractable state (cxM) decreases in the sequence:

montmorillonite > beidellite > illite > kaolinite.

Therefore the nature of the clay mineral in suspension should be identified by X-ray diffraction. How much of the toxic metals is sequestered in the sediments can be checked sequentially by adding HNO_3 in the amount of 10, 20, 30, 40, 50, 60 and 70 ml to 10% suspension of bottom sediments. The pH value of the suspension should also be noted after shaking the mixture for 1 hour. Some elements in the food chain are important in trace concentrations for all life forms including human beings. Young immature soils of inland tracts suffer from a variety of deficiencies in some of these elements which lead to a number of diseases (Fig. 4.8). But excess concentration of other metals are also harmful and toxic (Fig. 4.9). From olden times, mining and smelting introduced toxic metals in the environment. The peat beds of Giordano valley in Bristol bear testimony to pollution by Roman smelting operations. Of late, the scale of operations and the rate of increase have become menacing for human health. Between 1850 and 1900, world-wide industrial emissions of Cd, Cu, Pb, Ni and Zn to the atmosphere averaged 380, 1800, 22,000, 240 and 17,000 tonnes per year respectively; between 1900 and 1980, the emission rates increased by 6- to 51- fold respectively. Ice cores from Antarctica document a recent 4-fold increase in Pb concentration.

In tracing local pollution sources, isotopic signatures are helpful for elements like Pb. For example, the isotopic composition of Pb in the surface waters of the Great Lakes of North America is identical with the isotopic signature of the ambient

Deficiency in Se → Muscular degeneration

Se + I → Goitre

Zn → Dwarfism

P → Osteomalaci

Fig. 4.8: Types of malignancy associated with trace element deficiency.

Aluminium factories → Fluorosis

Combustion gases → Acid Rain

Copper Toxication → Death of Sheep (Norway)

Lead → Damage of Liver, Kidney & Bones

Fig. 4.9: Some toxic effects of excess metal intake.

aerosol. With reduction in use of lead in gasoline, there has been a noticeable shift in the isotopic composition of Pb in Lake Erie sediments.

Apparently innocent activities are also adding to the pollution burden. An increase in the Cd content of soil after prolonged application of phosphatic fertilisers, extensive coastal mariculture leading to eutrophication by excess food falls from fish cages and the negative role of pesticides, used for ridding fisheres of parasites, in killing other biota are some examples of harmful interventions across the delicate balance of nature. A perturbation at one end has unforeseen and distant consequences. Acid rain in Japan (rainwater with pH less than 5.6) is suspected to have been caused partly by emissions discharged from the Asian mainland, mainly China!

In fact a new discipline called *Forensic Geochemistry* is emerging to refine analytical and diagnostic techniques for fingerprinting contaminant sources. These include quantitative measurement of heavy metals with recognition of their distinctive ratios and abundances in different types of contaminants, and of stable and radioactive isotopes as well as hydrocarbon and chlorinated organic compounds. Such analytical methods can often be used to uniquely identify the pollutant sources and their relative contributions. For example, large Pb soil anomalies can be easily traced to lead mines or smelters; significant soil enrichment in Cu + Zn + Pb + U around phosphatic fertiliser plants or in cultivated lands with significant fertiliser inputs can be correlated with anthropogenic sources in some cases. Other examples are Hg haloes in air and soil surrounding paper mills and high values of B in small drainage systems polluted by sewage containing disinfectants, preservatives etc.

As a national programme to generate baseline data on hydrogeochemical dispersion, the program of the British Geological Survey deserves mention. Funded by the Department of Trade and Industry, water samples and stream sediments are collected at an average density of one sample/sq. km and up to 28 elements are analysed by a rigorous quality control procedure. The data are made available to users in a variety of hard copy and computer formats, and are also published in the Regional Geochemical Atlas series on 1:250,000 scale.

Further discussions on pollution are available in Chapter 10.

The following is a summary of the advantages and disadvantages of hydrogeochemical prospecting.

Advantages

(1) Samples are usually easy to collect.

(2) In covered or deeply weathered terrains, the water sample provides a direct window to a concealed mineral deposit due to their direct contact.
(3) Since some anions like SO_4^{2N} are useful as pathfinders, information about anions is readily available only from water samples (F^-, Br^-, Cl^-).
(4) Speciation can be determined and the possible state of oxidation of the source and by implication, at least in some cases, about its actual nature, can be suspected, e.g. Cu^+ / Cu^{2+}, U^{4+} / U^{6+}, As^{3+} / As^{5+}, etc. Computer models are available for interpreting speciation, saturation indices and mass transfer.

Disadvantages

(1) Composition of water changes with time and season.
(2) Special methods of preservation and filtration are frequently required to study the pristine nature of the sample.
(3) Special analytical techniques are required where the concentration of the radicals is low.
(4) The sample cannot be preserved over a long time for future cross-check. In fact, it is unwise to keep a sample for more than 48 hours unanalysed.
(5) Extraneous factors like adsorption, osmosis, etc. may modify the water chemistry.
(6) Proper interpretation, particularly where the source is concealed, requires a careful study of flow paths and associated hydrologic systems.

BIOGEOCHEMICAL PROSPECTING

Geochemical prospecting through plants are of two types: *Biogeochemical,* where the plant is chemically analysed for trace metal concentrations; and *Geobotanical,* which depends on identification of *indicator* plants or associations and/or morphological colour changes in some plants during their early growth.

Biogeochemical sampling requires that:
(1) The species should be of wide distribution.
(2) The species should 'accumulate the elements concerned in a reproducible manner and the degree of accumulation should be in direct proportion to the concentration of the element in the soil' (Brooks, 1972).
(3) Plants of the same species and age should be sampled from point to point for proper comparison.

(4) Samples from the same part—root, bark, leaf—should be compared for definition of anomaly.
(5) Samples should be large enough in volume to generate sufficient ash for trace element analysis.
(6) Samples should be carefully washed and cleaned before drying and further treatment.

In hydroponic experiments with *Artemisia tridentata,* which is used as a biogeochemical U indicator in Western U.S.A., (F.E. Diebold and F. Mcgrath, *J. Geochem. Exploration,* 23, 1985, 1–12) it was concluded that the uptake of U is not a function of the concentration of either U or phosphate in the solution until U reaches a certain level, nor is it related to the concentration of any of the specific aqueous uranyl species. Metal uptake in plants is a complex process, depending on: (a) available rather than total metal in the soil; (b) interaction with other metals; (c) pH of the soil etc.

The tree *Curatella americana L.* is reported to be potentially a reliable indicator for epithermal gold-quartz veins in Costa Rica and other Central American countries. Interestingly, highest concentration of Au in the twigs (7.2 ppb) and in the closed pods (2.4 ppb) was found over a soil sample, whose fine size (less than 500 μm) fraction analysed 1000 ppb of Au by INAA—a sure enough lead even in pedogeochemical prospecting. (F.R. Siegel and A.S. Paguaga, *J. Geochem. Exploration,* 41, 1991, 169–80).

Deep-rooted trees such as Mesquite, Acacia and Ironwood have long been used in the arid lands of southwestern U.S.A. and Mexico in biogeochemical surveys for Cu and Mo. *Artemisia* (Sagebrush) is known to accumulate high Cu in British Columbia, Pb, Zn and Ba in Kazakhstan, etc. Sal *(Shorea robusta)* is a common biogeochemical medium in Peninsular India.

One variant of biogeochemical prospecting is the use of aquatic moss. These are passive ion exchangers and therefore accept most metals. Aquatic moss in the Idaho cobalt belt analysed 3.5% Cu and 0.2% Co in its ash. In Zirovski vot, Slovenia, it was found that uranium anomaly zones could be easily picked up by analysis of aquatic moss, which carries ten times the concentration of uranium in associated stream sediments. In fact, *bryogeochemical prospecting* is ideal in karst terrains.

In the Siwalik sandstones of Kango basin, Hamirpur dt., Himachal Pradesh, bryophyte (moss) has been found to be a good indicator of U mineralisation (M.G. Shinde et al., *Exploration and Research for Atomic Minerals,* 1, 1988, 153–64).

Humus biogeochemistry has been found to be successful in Scandinavian countries for W and Sn. It is generally not realised that trees can assimilate W from the substrate specially in the roots; and in thickly forested areas, it is useful to adopt biogeochemistry of roots as an aid to locating concealed tungsten-bearing bodies.

This prospecting technique can be used only as a supplementary tool on account of the many imponderables in metal uptake of a plant species in a new area. Biogeochemical prospecting dates back to 1938.

GEOBOTANICAL PROSPECTING

This is a much older technique. It is based on the presence of indicator plants, which are restricted to the mineralised ground and where competition from other species is slight or absent. The typical flora are the *serpentine, selenium* and *halophytic* types, generally shrubs or ephemerals, which usually contain a large amount of mineral matter, and are generally members of the *Labiaceae. Violaceae,* or *Caryophyllaceae.*

Leucas aspera in the mine dumps of Dariba-Rajpura and *Impatiens balsamia* in the Zawar Pb-Zn field of Rajasthan are location-specific indicator plants.

Sometimes metal toxicity affects the normal growth of plants. For example, over the Kansa nickel deposit, Orissa Sal *(Shorea robusta)* is totally absent, whereas elsewhere within the Damsal Valley, it is abundant.

Such regional or local contrasts have been found in many environments: semi-arid shrub, humid tropical forest and temperate deciduous and coniferous woodland. Discovery of copper deposits in western Botswana and Namibia beneath calcrete and Kalahari sand was aided by the recognition of the Cu indicator plant *Helichrysum leptolepis.* Many of the nineteenth century discoveries of copper deposits in Queensland, Australia were made by prospectors with the help of *Polycarpaea spirostylis*—a small plant. Northwest of the Mount Kelly old mine in Mount Isa polymetallic sulphide district, anomalous communities of *Jacksonia ramosissima,* somewhere accompanied by *P. spirostylis* on some ironstones were pointers leading to a medium-sized copper deposit. In the Khetri copper deposit, Rajasthan, several plants accumulate high doses of Cu in the leaves. *Tephrosia villosa, Aerua tomentosa* and *Bouchea inoribufolia* are good indicators of Cu content of soil (Y.D. Tiari & N.C. Aery, *Jour, Geochem. Exploration*, 26, 1986, 267–274.

Dwarfing of the plants over nickel deposits is observed at both Kansa, Orissa and Pikwe-Selepi, eastern Botswana. This is due to nickel toxicity over serpentinite-saprolite. In the savanna woodlands of Zimbabwe, the surface over the Empress nickel deposit is locally completely barren and oxidised. Elsewhere over the deposit, there is an abundance of small *Dalbergia melanoxylon* in place of other shrubs and many types of grasses.

Carbonatites and kimberlites are usually identifiable by strong geobotanical contrasts with their surroundings, so much so that some are apparent on air photographs and, rarely, on satellite imagery.

PHOTOGEOCHEMICAL PROSPECTING

Abnormal concentrations of metals like Cr, Ni, Cu, Co etc. which create dwarfing or early yellowing of leaves or deformities of other types are utilised in this emerging technique which uses supervised discriminant analysis and unsupervised cluster analysis of multispectral scanner records, mounted on aircrafts flying low and drape style at uniform height above the ground. Matching of the ground and airborne reflectance data is done for proper calibration.

GEOZOOLOGICAL AND MICROBIAL PROSPECTING

Deficiency of Cu in the blood of cattle and death from lead poisoning of cattle and ponies in Derbyshire, U.K. are examples of the role of trace elements in living forms. Even in humans, As in drinking water supplies in W. Bengal, Taiwan and Halifax, Nova Scotia is reported to have caused ailments.

The use of animals in prospecting is recorded by Herodotus (450 B.C.), whose description of marmots (cat sized rodents) from the Dansar plain of the Kashmir Himalaya as mountain ant (from the ancient Persian word) caused considerable confusion among historians for the last 2500 years. "There is found in this desert a kind of ant of greater size—bigger than a fox though not as big as a dog. These creatures as they burrow underground throw up the sand in heaps just as our own ants throw up the earth, and they are very like ours in shape. The sand has rich content of gold, and it is this that the Indians are after when they make their expeditions into the desert." Recent search has revealed that these rodents burrow into a gold-bearing sandy layer at shallow depth and the gold that gets stuck to the rodents fur used to be extracted by local Minaro tribesmen of Kashmir. (*Time*, December 9, 1996, p.55).

In rugged, glaciated terrains of Canada and Finland, Alsatian dogs have been used for sniffing out sulphide shows.

During the last decade, a soil microorganism, *Bacillus cereus*, has been found to grow abundantly over metal (Cu, Au)-rich soils in parts of the northern Rockies, sub-Saharan Africa and Mexico. Three-way correlations were reported between soil-metal content, per cent penicillin resistance in total *Bacillus* species and per cent *B. cereus*. (J.R. Watterson, *Jour. Geochem. Exploration*, 23, 1985, 243–52; N.L. Pardhun, *Jour. Geochem. Exploration*, 41, 1991, 137–49).

ATMOGEOCHEMICAL PROSPECTING

Some mineral deposits are associated with continuous or intermittent flow of either vapour phase components, partly derived from the orebodies or of gases. Four types are well known:

(1) Hg anomalies: These are associated with: (a) concealed, high-temperature geothermal systems; (b) Hg-bearing Pb-Zn sulphide assemblages; and (c) over hydrocarbon gas and oil fields. Normally, Hg in soil gas is collected on extra-pure Ag foils. These are fitted inside the roof of inverted plastic hemispheres, which are placed on the sampling spots at early dawn. The edges of these hemispheres are sunk inside the soil. The hemispheres are collected 2–3 hours later, providing enough time for Hg in the soil gas to form an amalgam with Ag of the foil. The foils are removed and sealed separately in air-tight containers. Analysis by standard mercury analyser in the field itself, far away from sources of industrial pollution, is recommended. A serious problem is the availability of extra-pure Ag foils.

(2) He anomalies: He anomalies are produced from disintegration of ^{235}U and Th and are found over oil reservoirs, in hot springs, and around porphyry copper and uranium deposits. Soils are natural traps. Samples from 0.5 m depth are collected, sealed in aluminium core collectors, and stored in a freezer before analysis of the head space gas by mass spectrometry.

He is abundant in the thermal springs of India, specially Rajgir, Bakreswar, etc.

(3) Hydrocarbon anomalies: Details fall outside the scope of this book. Anomalies of ethane, propane, n- and isobutane are associated with large gas condensate deposits. Hydrocarbon migration from a reservoir to the surface may occur either by diffusion or by effusion—the latter involving a large component of lateral transport. This is a problem. Besides, the anomalies may be ephemeral; collection and storage need care against contamination and a bulky freezer; a gas chromatograph is the best analytical tool at present. Only large organisations can undertake such surveys. A variant of this is the sniffer survey so far undertaken over the continental shelf and slope in some countries. The sniffer consists of a metal 'fish' containing an electric pump and an elaborate sonar system, towed behind the ship, which monitors the 'fish' floating just a few meters above the sea floor. The pump extracts dissolved gases from a rapidly flowing stream of water from the sea bottom. This gas is analysed on board for ethane and higher hydrocarbons.

(4) Nitrogen anomalies: N_2 concentrations increase towards the centre of hydrocarbon-bearing basins.

In arid and semi-arid areas with transported overburden, anomalous levels of CO_2, CS_2 and SO_2 are also found in soil over copper deposits and their wall rocks.

Atmogeochemical monitoring of sources of pollution (Fig. 4.10) is a tricky affair; and suspects usually indulge in bitter scientific battles, unless the tests are diagnostic and thorough. A classic example is the battle of air pollution during the eighties between the Navajo coal-fired power plant, about 50 miles north of Grand Canyon, U.S.A., which was suspected to be causing winter time haze on the spectacular

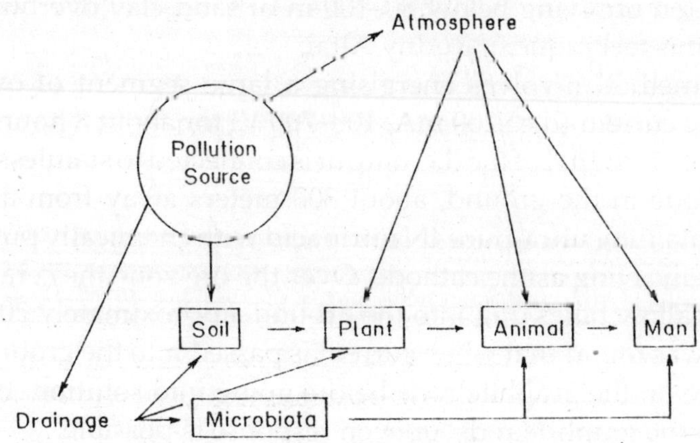

Fig. 4.10: Multiple transfer routes and sinks of pollutant metals.

Grand Canyon vista and the Environmental Protection Agency and the National Park Service of the U.S.A. A 2-million dollar experiment had to be designed by a consortium of government agencies and utility organisations, a battery of monitoring stations set up; and then in 1987, deuterated methane, a rarely-used sulphur tracer that is supposed to mimic the dispersion behaviour of SO_2 was released from one of the Navajo plant's tall stacks over a 6-week period. When the chemical was detected in the Canyonland monitoring stations, it was established that the Navajo plant is the chief contributor of sulphates in the park. Such tracer experiments are critical for bringing the polluter to book.

PEXMEL PROSPECTING

During the late sixties and early seventies, Russian researchers in Leningrad developed an electrochemical method of prospecting for hidden metalliferous deposits. It is reported that they had used this successfully in various localities. This method also known as CHIM 10 was tested by the G.S.I. for Indian conditions in the eighties.

CHIM is the acronym for the Russian words meaning 'partial extraction of metals' but actually it is an electrogeochemical method, initially developed by I.S. Goldberg and Yu. S. Ryss in the early seventies (Goldberg, I.S. et al., USGS Open File Report 90-462, 172 pp, Translated from Russian). There are other methods like MDE, MPF and TMGM (for detials consult S.G. Alekseev et al. *Jour. Geochem. Exploration*, 56, 1996, 79–86, which have been developed over a few decades. Deposits of Pb-Zn ore lying below 80–100 m of sand-clay overburden have been discovered by this technique in Rudny Altai.

Briefly, the method involves energising a large segment of overburden by a constant electric current (d.c.: 200 mA, 100–700 V) for about 8 hours under a stable field. The positive terminal of the d.c. output is connected to stainless steel electrodes used as the anode in the ground, about 300 meters away from a set of ceramic, porous pots containing ultra-pure 4N nitric acid with chemically pure graphite rods immersed therein acting as the cathode. Over the ore zone the ceramic pots are set partly inside shallow holes dug into the ground, approximately 20 m apart. In the trial studies, it was found that when current is passed into the ground, metallic ions first accumulate on the graphite rods before going into solution. If there is undissolved metal in the graphite rods, uneven response is possible.

Chinese researchers (B. Xu et al., *Jour. Geochem. Exploration*, 33, 1989, 99–108) reported that this technique was useful in the Karatungk district Ni-Cu deposits within ophiolite, which lie concealed below more than 200 m of cover rocks made up of folded and faulted argillites and marl. The best response was obtained using currents of 0.38 A to 0.53 A for 72 hours.

This method is still in a trial stage and is not a common prospecting tool.

ANALYTICAL PRECAUTIONS IN GEOCHEMICAL PROSPECTING

Application of geochemical prospecting techniques requires rapidly collectible and dependable analytical data, so that the time lost between reconnaissance and detailed surveys is minimised and results from different campaigns are mutually comparable. Analytical quality control is therefore essential in such work. The checks are designed to measure: (1) within-batch variation; (2) between-batch variation; and (3) overall accuracy. If you are sending samples to the chemist, it is better to send a duplicate sample for every 10th in the batch; and have a set of common samples between your previous batch and the present lot. You can use a different number for the duplicate sample, so that the analyst is not biased. For overall accuracy in determination of trace elements, you must ensure that your samples are being run along with international standards at regular intervals. These are freely available in the market.

During the early years of geochemical prospecting techniques, the focus was on improving speed, simplicity and sensitivity by wet chemical methods. One of the problems was incomplete extraction of the target elements by a particular method of digestion. For example, copper in malachite is more easily leachable than copper in chrysocolla; so also lead in cerussite as against lead in anglesite. There are various options for sample digestion: heating with dilute acid, ammonium citrate extraction, fusion with potassium bisulphate, concentrated sulphuric solid digestion etc. It has been observed that different degrees of digestion of an element are achieved by prolonging/reducing the period of reaction. With some digestants, apparent anomalies can be the result of extraction of a variable percentage (5–90%) of the total metal present. In all methods of digestion, the greatest single source of error is in sample attack.

The second problem is the limited number of sensitive, selective reagents suitable for field laboratories. Dithizone has been used extensively; but its main drawback is the instability of its solutions in carbon tetrachloride, chloroform and other organic solvents particularly at the ambient temperatures prevalent in tropical countries like India, Africa etc.

The third problem is the lack of a universal digestant for a number of elements. Potassium bisulphate fusion is not satisfactory for extraction of tin, beryllium etc.

Speed of operations is also considerably curtailed in procedures which require the preparation of concentrated buffer solutions free from trace metal impurities.

Over the years, different types of fluxes, fusion techniques, mild vs. drastic sample dissolution procedures have been tested; and certain general guidelines have emerged. For example, the cold extraction method is suitable for field use by untrained personnel at low cost and is ideal for locating anomalies of readily-soluble metals in high contrast situations. But it could suffer from high analytical error. As a digestant, hydrofluoric acid attack is the most reliable but the least convenient, followed by nitric-perchloric acid. Dissolution of samples in nitric acid and/or hydrochloric acid is generally safer for routine purposes. In areas with humid climate, sodium or potassium bisulphate is better than a pyrosulphate flux, which readily decomposes to a sulphate. In lateritic samples, best results are obtained with a basic flux.

IMPORTANT INSTRUMENTAL TECHNIQUES

Rapid analytical methods now include: (1) colorimetric analysis; (2) Atomic Absorption Spectrophotometry (AAS); (3) Emission Spectrography (ES); (4) X-ray Fluorescence (XRF); (5) Inductively Coupled Plasma Atomic Emission Spectrometry (ICPAES); and (6) Instrumental Neutron Activation Analysis (INAA). For gold prospecting, bulk leach of extractable gold using dilute cyanide solution has been reported to be successful in picking up signals even 10–15 km downstream. This is a specialised version of analysis of cold extractable metal, which is determined rapidly by colorimetric analysis. Colorimetric analysis is very rarely used today; only in the field for quick and approximate estimation of cold extractable metals (cxM). Emission spectrography is useful for fast, but semi-quantitative determination of a large number of elements at moderate detection limit. AAS and XRF are routinely used for determination of major, minor and trace elements. ICPAES is very useful for rare earth elements and for many other elements in different matrices, although the problem of drift in signal with time and interference in Ca-rich samples is serious. INAA determinations require a source reactor. Precious metals (Platinum Group and gold) are best analysed by fire assay pre-concentration. About 25–30 gm of the rock powder are fire-assayed to concentrate the precious metals in a 2–5 gm NiS button. This is then irradiated along with chemical standards and analysed by radiochemical neutron activation method.

A brief outline of the common instrumental techniques used for geochemical studies is given here to help the geologist choose the right approach.

(1) Atomic Absorption Spectrophotometry (AAS)

The required sample size is very small, about one-hundredth of a gram. The sample is completely dissolved in acids. Then some of the solution is sprayed into a flame through which light of wavelength characteristic of a specific element is shone. For each element and type of instrument, the wavelength, lamp current, spectral band pass and the composition of the flame are fixed. Some of the light emanating from the source is absorbed. This is proportional to the quantity of the element in the solution. Unless total dissolution is achieved, the concentration of the element in the sample may differ from that in the solution and lead to erroneous results. Since measurement has to be made for each element separately using the *same* solution, this destructive analysis in intrinsically slow. However, it is very sensitive even at concentrations as low as 5 p.p.m.

(2) Emission Spectrography (ES)

A small quantity of the sample is mounted on a conducting graphite electrode and excited either by a continuous D.C. arc or by a spark source. The spectrum emitted by the elements in the red to ultraviolet wavelength region is either recorded on a photographic plate or electronically. Due to instability of the arc source, the method is much less dependable than AAS, although it is fast, can provide simultaneous semi-quantitative information on as many as 40 elements and is good for preliminary scanning of a region.

Improved precision is now attainable by inductively coupled plasma spectrometry.

(3) Inductively Coupled Plasma Spectrometry (ICPS)

A sample of about 50 mg is required. Solutions have to be prepared as in AAS. Typically, 10–30 elements can be analysed simultaneously. There are two variants:

atomic emission spectrometers (ICP-AES) use a very high temperature (5,700°–10,000°C) plasma flame to excite the emission lines of elements in the red to UV region of the spectrum; mass spectrometer (ICP-MS) uses the plasma as source but a mass spectrometer as a detector, where individual isotopes of elements can be determined. The precision and accuracy of results from ICP-AES are variable, depending on the laboratory set-up. The high-tech set-up does not automatically ensure highly dependable results. Liquid coolants are also not available easily everywhere.

A relatively new technique is laser ablation ICP-MS. This technique uses a laser beam, preferably in the ultraviolet range, to vapourise a small amount of material from the flat surface of a sample e.g. quenched melt droplets in basalts, hydrothermal fluids trapped within ore deposits, etc. The appropriate choice of external calibration standards remains a major analytical challenge for all such instrumental measurements.

(4) X-ray Fluorescence (XRF)

This is dependable for major and minor elements down to 1% concentration. Liquids or solids can be analysed, powders being held in a suitable container after fusing to form a homogenous pellet. The quantity of the sample required is also low: 0.1–2 g. In contrast to ES and AAS, which affect the outer shell electrons, this method utilises high energy X-ray beams to knock out the inner electrons of the target atom. The X-ray spectra are associated with energy changes in the innermost electron orbits and so the wavelengths are virtually independent of the chemical or physical state of the element. Sealed off X-ray tubes are used to provide a high intensity X-ray beam that excites the sample, which is placed outside the source. Fluorescent X-rays are emitted. These are analysed with a wavelength dispersive spectrometer, a crystal being used as a diffraction grating to disperse the different wavelengths. Unlike normal absorption or emission spectra from outer shell electrons, interference due to overlapping lines is not common, because the spectra consist essentially of two lines of the K-shell electrons and about six of the L-shell. The method is fast and simple and can be utilised to determine up to 25 elements on a fixed schedule.

A variant of this technique is the energy dispersive X-ray analysis (EDAX). The energies of the X-rays (inversely proportional to wavelength) depend upon the elements present in the sample, while the intensities depend upon how much of the elements is present. The spectrometer is used to produce a display of intensity vs. X-ray energy. Energy dispersive analysis commonly attached to scanning electron or transmission ion electron microscope is fast and easy to apply, but has a much lower sensitivity and resolution than the wavelength dispersive analysis of XRF.

In all these analytical procedures, the controlling factor in accuracy and precision is the 'matrix effect'. This depends on the bulk composition of the sample. This may lead both to positive (enhancement) and negative (absorption) deviation from true values. It is therefore advisable for the geologist to determine the mineralogy of the sample *before* chemical analysis and convey the findings from examination under the microscope and X-ray diffraction to the chemist analysing the sample. This point is frequently overlooked by the geologist.

(5) Neutron Activation Analysis (NAA)

When a sample is placed in a dense flux of neutrons, as in a nuclear reactor, the atoms of some elements in the sample capture passing neutrons and are transformed into radioactive isotopes of the corresponding elements. These emit radiation, as the radioactive isotopes decay. After the sample is removed from the reactor and placed in front of a suitable radiation detector, the radioactivity of each element can be measured separately and converted to its relative concentration on the basis of standard materials of known composition, *which have to be irradiated at the same time for calibration purposes.* The quantity required of the sample is about 50 mg. Not all elements produce suitable isotopes for measurement; nor is a reactor available everywhere!

(6) X-ray Diffraction (XRD)

This is useful to determine the mineralogy of very small samples (less than a pin head when using an X-ray camera). All minerals diffract X-rays and produce characteristic patterns, which can be recorded on film using an X-ray camera or on a chart using an X-ray diffractometer (XRD). The peaks in the chart are compared like fingerprints by comparing with rock standards of known mineralogy. Great caution is however required at this step. Computers are no substitute and frequently lead to a list of improbable mineral assemblages.

(7) Scanning/Transmission Electron Microscope (SEM/TEM)

In SEM, a very narrow beam of electrons is generated by heating a wire filament to a high temperature under a strong potential difference. The beam passes down a cylindrical column, about 1 m in length, which is fitted with a series of electromagnetic 'lenses' which allow the beam to be focussed and moved. The sample is kept at the base of the column and the beam is scanned very rapidly back and forth over the sample, which causes some electrons to scatter back from the surface and low energy secondary electrons to be knocked out. These back-scattered and low-energy secondary electrons are converted via electronic signals into images on a TV screen. A very high magnification of the outer forms is achieved under SEM.

While SEM is used to illuminate the surface of the sample, so to speak, like reflected light ore microscopy, the TEM is designed to see through the sample by electrons, like common petrographic microscopes do with visible light. Because electrons are rapidly absorbed, the sample must be prepared as extremely thin sections. Very fine inclusions and even details of atomic structure can be imaged. TEM gives us a picture of the 'real' structure (unlike X-ray and neutron diffraction which 'image' the long range average structure) and has proved very useful in the study of defects in chain and sheet silicates, low temperature alteration reactions in clay minerals, structural damage with increasing dose of radiation in minerals like olivine etc. TEM is also used for the study of shock effects on minerals and their post-shock modification.

The magnification range of TEM overlaps but extends to a much higher range than SEM.

(8) Electron Microprobe and Ion Microprobe

In electron probe, both major and minor elements can be analysed both by wavelength dispersive spectrometer (WDS) and energy dispersive system (EDS). This is one of the non-destructive analytical tools involving specially prepared thin sections of rocks and minerals. Such microfeatures as zoning, exsolution and inclusions become chemically accessible in this technique. Under a beam diameter of around 5 µm, a beam current of around 20 nA and an accelerating voltage of 15 kV, the composition of the different parts of a mineral grain can be determined, both for major elements by EDS and for minor and trace elements by WDS with good precision, except that the oxidation state is not determinable. EDS spectra are collected over 75 seconds whereas WDS peak counting times are generally 20–30 seconds.

(9) Secondary Ion Mass Spectrometers (SIMS)

The elemental composition of the mineral is analysed by bombardment of the sample with primary oxygen ions accelerated through a nominal potential of 10 kV.

A primary ion current of 30–40 nA is focussed on the sample over a spot diameter of 25–35 μm, and sputtered secondary ions therefrom are filtered using an energy window of ± 25 V and sample offset voltages of –105 and –75 V respectively, which effectively offsets the effect of isobaric interferences. Each spot has to be analysed by repeated cycles of peak counting. Absolute concentration of each element is calculated using empirical relationship and daily calibration against standards. This is a very powerful tool, since contaminated mineral separates (so common in destructive analytical techniques, e.g. isotope dilution techniques for sensitive determinations of REE) are avoided by ensuring under large magnification that the probe targets are free from other inclusions and impurities. SIMS is not only an important microprobe technique for both trace and major light lithophile elements (H, Li, Be and B) but is very useful for high (spatial) resolution microprobe dating of zoned minerals using radiogenic isotopes and as a microprobe for stable isotopes.

For further information on quantitative ion microprobe analysis, you may consult N. Shimazu et al., *Geochim. et Cosmochim. Acta,* 42, 1978, 1321–34.

For the geologist, it is important to appreciate that geological samples suffer from a variety of matrix effects. Unless the total composition of the sample is known, suitable corrections cannot be applied to the readings. It is therefore essential to let the analyst know the expected general composition of the samples and maintain a dialogue with the analyst for optimum efficiency. It is important for the analyst to ensure that sample decomposition is complete and that the detection limit (concentration of analyte producing a signal three times the standard deviation of the blank) is quantified. In many developing countries including India, clean laboratories are very rare. Reagents of ultra-pure grade and coolants are not always available. Spares are commonly inadequate for continuous operation. Humidity and heat are additional problems. Problems of spectral and chemical interference are also considerable for some elements and analytical routes. For example, spectral interference, which is produced when absorption of an interfering species overlaps or lies so close to the analyte line that resolution by the monochromator is not possible, is quite serious in emission spectroscopy but much less common in AAS. On the other hand chemical interference, caused by the inability of the analyte to separate as a free atom is common for some elements in AAS using air-acetylene mixtures, where the flame temperature is 2,100–2400°C. One way to solve this is to use nitrous oxide-acetylene mixtures, which reach 2,600°–2,900°C.

For the field geologist, AAS is the most versatile of the instruments. It is necessary to know which elements are best analysed by AAS. The following is a general

Table 4.3: Guide to instrumental determination of elements of interest in geochemical prospecting (after J.A. Plant et al., *Trans, Inst. Min. Metal.* Section B, 97, 1988, B116–B140).

Elements Group	*Instrumental method*		
	ES	XRF	*INAA*
Li, Be, B	S		
Na, Mg, Al, Si, K, Ca	S	S	
Sc, Ti, V, Cr, Mn, Fe, Co, Ni, Cu, Zn	S	S	
Ga, Ge, As, Se		A	S
Rb, Sr	S	S	S
Y, Zr, Nb	A	S	A
Ta, Hf			S
Pd, Ag, In			S
Sn	A	S	
Sb, Te			S
Ba, La	S	S	S
REE		A	S
W, Os, Ir, Pt, Au			S
Pb	A	S	
Th, U		A	S

S: Suitable method
A: Acceptable method but with poor detection limit

guideline (to be followed together with the guideline provided earlier under 'Hydrogeochemical Prospecting').

Easily analysed by AAS	*Moderately complex*	*Most complex for AAS*
Li, Na, Mg, K, Ca, Rb, Sr, V, Cr, Mn, Fe, Co, Cu, Zn, Al, Si	Mo, Ba, Ag, Cd, In, Sn, Sb, Pb, Bi, Tl, Hg, As, Se	Te, Au, Pt

Different elements respond to different instrumental methods with varying success. Table 4.3 illustrates the varying applications, other than AAS.

There has been a proliferation of microbeam techniques ranging from electron microprobe (which is not useful for separate determination of Fe^{3+} and Fe^{2+} as well as of light lithophile elements), ion microprobe (which can determine light lithophile elements also), scanning electron microscope (SEM) with chemical analytical attachment, scanning tunnelling microscope (which produces near-atomic scale resolution of images of the mineral surface), to Atomic Force Microscope (which produces an atomic scale topographic map of the mineral surface both routinely and accurately without the complex coating procedures of SEM). The Transmission Electron Microscope (TEM) has played an important role in unravelling radiation damage in minerals. It has been possible with High Resolution TEM to trace the development of structural damage in high temperature minerals like olivine by 1.5 meV Kr^+ ion irradiation.

Such highly sophisticated facilities need expert maintenance. In many developing countries, this is not very easy. Hence one should aim at a proper mix of classical and instrumental study depending on local situations. For example, a very simple analytical technique of sequential extraction of trace elements, which provides a rough idea about the nature of compounds, and the degree to which the element goes into the hydromorphic regime of the area is not yet routinely adopted for stream sediment and environment geochemical programs in India!

A simple flowsheet, developed by L.H. Filipek and P.K. Theobold in 1981[6] (*Jour. Geochem. Expl.*, 14) is given below:

1. Leach—80-mesh sample with 0.1 M acetic acid at 25°C for 2 hours; solution contains carbonates and exchangeable metals.
2. Centrifuge; leach the residue with 0.1 M $NH_2OH.HCl$ in 0.01 M HNO_3 at 25°C for 2 hours; solution will contain the metal bound with hydrous Mn oxides.
3. Centrifuge again; digest residue with 30% H_2O_2 at 80°C until dry. Extract with 1 M $NH_4C_2H_3O_2$ in 6% HNO_3 at 25°C for 30 minutes (metals bound with organic compounds and sulphides will go into solution).
4. Centrifuge again; leach residue with 0.25 M $NH_2OH.HCl$ with 25% acetic acid at 80°C for 4 hours (metals bound with hydrous Fe oxides will go into solution).
5. Centrifuge; digest residue with HF, HCl and HNO_3 twice for complete dissolution of the silicate bound metals.

Chemical speciation of metals can also be determined as follows:

1. *Exchangeable cations*
   1 M ammonium acetate, pH 7, solid : solution ratio = 1 : 20, 2 h shaking.
2. *Carbonates and easily reducible phases (e.g. Mn oxides)*
   0.1 M hydroxylamine hydrochloride + 0.01 M HNO_3, pH 2, solid: solution ratio = 1 : 100, 2 h shaking.

---

[6] For a complete review of partial dissolution techniques, consult T.T. Chao, *Jour. Geochem. Exploration*, 20, 1984, 101–35.

3. *Moderately reducible phases (e.g. amorphous Fe oxide)*
   0.2 M ammonium oxalate + 0.2 M oxalic acid, pH 3, solid : solution ratio 1 : 100, 24 h shaking.
4. *Organic fraction and sulphides*
   30% H_2O_2 + HNO_3, pH = 2, extracted with 1 M ammonium acetate, solid : solution ratio = 1 : 100, 24 h shaking.
5. *Residual fraction (e.g. silicates) Boiling Concentrated HNO_3*

Note: Determine the total metal content separately by AAS or other suitable instruments; if the sum of metal concentrations determined by sequential extraction differs by more than 10% from the total metal value determined separately, repeat the determinations.

FURTHER READING

A.W. Rose, H.E. Hawkes and J.S. Webb. *Geochemistry in Mineral Exploration,* 2e. Academic Press, London, 1979, 657 pp.

A.A. Levinson. *Introduction to Exploration Geochemistry.* Applied Publishing Ltd., Calgary, Alberta, 1974, 612 pp.

W.K. Fletcher. *Analytical Methods in Geochemical Prospecting: Handbook of Exploration Geochemistry,* Vol. 1, G.J.S. Govett (ed.), Elsevier, Amsterdam, 1981, 255 pp.

A.A. Beus and S.V. Grigorayan. *Geochemical Exploration Methods for Mineral Deposits.* Applied Publishing Ltd., Wilmette, Illinois, 1977, 287 pp.

J.W. Hedenquist and J.B. Lowenstern. The role of magmas in the formation of hydrothermal ore deposits. *Nature* 370, 1994, 519–27.

G.J.S. Govett. *Rock Geochemistry in Mineral Exploration: Handbook of Exploration Geochemistry,* Vol. 3, Elsevier, Amsterdam, 1983, 461 pp.

M. Hale and J.A. Plant. *Drainage Geochemistry: Handbook of Exploration Geochemistry,* Vol. 6, Elsevier, Amsterdam, 1994, 792 pp.

C.R.M. Butt and H. Zeegers. *Regolith Exploration Geochemistry in Tropical and Subtropical Terrains: Handbook of Exploration Geochemistry,* Vol. 4, Elsevier, Amsterdam, 1992, 608 pp.

F.C. Hawthorne. Minerals, Mineralogy and Mineralogists; Past, Present and Future, *Canadian Mineralogist,* 31, 1993, 253–96.

R.R. Brooks. *Geobotany and Biogeochemistry in Mineral Exploration,* Harper and Row, New York, 1972, 303 pp.

K. Rankama, *Bull Commn. Geol. Finl.,* 126, 1940, 90–106.

5

Geophysical Prospecting

Geophysical prospecting requires specialised training in the mathematics of interpretation and in instrumentation. It is not advisable to have the measurements and interpretation undertaken by a geologist not trained in mathematics. It is however essential for a geology student to understand the broad principles of their application. This chapter aims to present this as simply as possible.

Up to the late sixties and early seventies, geophysical exploration technology in the tropical countries remained largely a potential. The discovery rate was low as compared to investment. Airborne magnetic and gravity surveys were of little direct use in mineral discovery; airborne electromagnetic anomalies were far too many, and so frequently caused by surficial wet weathered cover, carbonaceous shales, phyllites and graphite that it was impractical to pursue all the anomalies by ground follow up—the investment being far in excess of the anticipated or demonstrated return. For example, in the Harda region of Madhya Pradesh, 3,000 Aero EM anomalies were recorded over an area of 2,280 sq. km by the multisensor survey of BRGM/CGG of France. Ground Electromagnetic (Turam), Induced Potential and D.C. Resistivity have limited depth penetration and produce too many non-ore anomalies. Mise-a-la-masse becomes useful only after a positive ore intersection has been made. Residual gravity anomaly over a sulphide deposit is only of the order of 1 mGal or less and cannot be modelled accurately even with measured physical rock properties in hand. Magnetic survey over lateritic terrain is so full of noise that it becomes very difficult to isolate the signal related to a sulphide deposit below.

With applied research over the last two decades, introduction of sophisticated mathematical and data processing techniques, extensive application of fast EDP and a progressive realisation of the need to develop location-specific sequential surface and borehole geophysics, exploration programs are now yielding stronger leads to concealed deposits. Advanced instrumentation is gradually transforming geophysical prospecting from a high-cost-low-return technique of the sixties and seventies to a higher-cost-moderate-return technique. Once the new methods are perfected and the exploration approach anchored on more precise geological targets and less on blind, empirical 'hit or miss' mentality, a large number of concealed mineral deposits are likely to be discovered by an optimum interdisciplinary combination of geological, geochemical and geophysical studies and analysis.

Just as geochemical prospecting depends heavily on a sound geological judgement of the evolution of the landscape so that the right sequence of exploration techniques is used, geophysical prospecting depends on a correct understanding of the physical contrasts in the rock body as a result of its mineralogical and lithological make up and structural disposition of the target. The metallogenic potential in terms of possible locales and mineralogic combinations as well as the potential for misleading signals (e.g. graphite in a khondalite terrain where you are searching for sulphides) have to be reviewed and a continuous dialogue and re-interpretation must be ensured among the geologist, the geophysicist and the geochemist. Isolated chambers will no longer make successful case histories of new discoveries. The Indian record of airborne survey exemplifies this.

In India, airborne geophysics has covered a large part of the Peninsular tract under 'Operation Hardrock', BRGM Survey and indigenous efforts by the Geological Survey of India and the National Geophysical Research Institute. Many crores of rupees have been spent. In terms of discovery of new mineral deposits, however, its success has been meagre. The extensive mineralised belt from Turamdih to Badia along the Singhbhum shear zone did not respond to airborne multi-sensor survey under 'Operation Hardrock'. Nor was the NGRI-GSI aeromagnetic survey at 150 m elevation and 500 m interval over the Kimberlite fields of Andhra Pradesh very rewarding. The experience of many other airborne geophysical surveys during the last three decades sponsored by the United Nations in various parts of Africa has been similar; with an average annual expenditure of US dollars 550,000, e.g. Mauritania (1979: airborne magnetics and radiometrics), Tanzania (1980), Cameroon (1981: airborne radiometrics), Rwanda (1982: helicopter magnetics and radiometrics), Malawi (1984–5: helicopter magnetics, radiometrics and EM), Burkina Faso (1987–8: airborne EM) etc. Many of the target areas are covered by tropical rain forest. There is a deep blanket of residual weathering. The areas are difficult to access, with high average rainfall and temperature. Other areas have extensive featureless desert, making navigation and follow-up access very difficult. Support services are not always available locally. The collective experience in the tropical belt is that airborne geophysics by itself does not assure 'mineral deposits flowing down the pipeline', as was touted in the early sixties; and for every new airborne geophysical survey, its potential in relation to other mineral exploration activities must be carefully weighed. (J. Guy-Bray and M. Lewis, *Episodes*, 11(1), 1988, 118–22).

Airborne gravity measurements have the additional limitation of a low signal-to-noise ratio. While the signal across a subduction zone reaches a maximum of 300 mGal, the signal over a sedimentary basin is generally less than 60 mGal. On the other hand the noise can exceed 1,000 mGal due to bumping of the aircraft in slightly turbulent weather. With the advent of the Global Positioning System (G.P.S.) it is now possible to accurately estimate and insert the corrections, particularly the velocity dependent Eotvos correction (R.E. Bell et al. *Geophysics* 56(8), 1991, 1486–93).

Many geophysical exploration programs involve problems of linear imaging. It is essentially model-dependent. Inhomogenous model sampling leads to bias in estimates. To describe the model fully, the set of basis functions (parameterizations) must be complete. In practice, one is limited by finite resolution of the data and limited understanding of the geological set-up—including the range of fluctuation in physical properties and their response to the sensors. Very commonly, the wavelengths chosen lead to unintended bias as a result of undersampling (aliasing) and/or leakage (where the basis functions are not orthogonal with respect to the matrix products). For example, in the determination of regional magnetic anomaly maps, it is common to expand the anomaly field into spherical harmonic degrees 15 to 60. Without any precautions, there is a possibilty of leakage from low frequency (below degree 15) and higher frequency (above degree 60) basis functions.

In fact, all potential field measurements (magnetic and gravity), whether airborne or ground, are subjected to the process of gridding. This is the Achilles' heel involving the use of 2-D algorithms for 3-D space. Mismatches between grid interval and the irregularly spaced natural physical contrast, inadequate algorithms, sampling anisotropy in areas of high topographic relief, etc. are some of the other lacunae. The first stage in the quantitative interpretation of potential field data is to separate the regional from residual component (Fig. 5.1). The smooth regional is often approximated by a low-order polynomial. In mixed terrains of mafic intrusives and metasediments, the curve fitting becomes more a mathematical (Chapter 6) than a mineral discovery task.

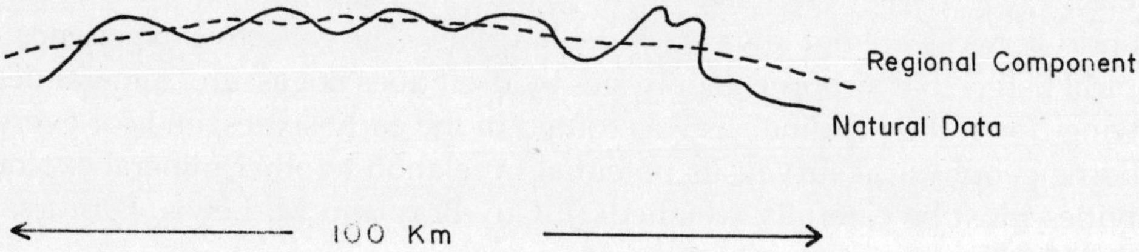

Fig. 5.1: Regional component of potential field values

These limitations of geophysical prospecting do not reduce the importance of this emerging field. The student of geology must realise that geophysics is not a miracle medicine for clarifying ill-understood geological situations. The geologist must at the outset define the mineralogical, lithological and structural milieu of the area correctly and frequently sit down with the geophysicist in the field to exchange notes and refine the search.

The principal methods used in geophysical exploration include:
Magnetic, Magnetotelluric, Electromagnetic, Self Potential, Induced Potential, Resistivity, Gravimetric, Reflection Seismic, Refraction Seismic.

Magnetic, electromagnetic and gravity survey can be both airborne and ground.

Among these different techniques, the most successful for mineral deposits so far are magnetic, electrical and gravity methods arranged in appropriate sequence as shown in Table 5.1.

Different types of mineral deposits respond to different geophysical techniques. These are illustrated in the Table 5.2.

It has been a common practice to combine geophysical prospecting with geochemical survey in different combinations, depending on the local set up. No generalised sequence of operations can be prescribed.

Table 5.1: Examples ore deposits with positive geophysical signals

Type of deposit	*Methods*	*Example*
Massive sulphide deposit	Airborne EM; Ground EM & SP; Ground Gravity.	NW Quebec, Canada
Chromite	Ground Gravity followed by Soil Geochemistry.	Kaliapani, Sukinda, India
Iron Ore	Aeromagnetic survey.	Carajas Province, Brazil
Disseminated sulphide	I.P. and Resistivity.	Kharsawan, Singhbhum, India

Table 5.2: Approprate geophysical methods for some mineral deposits

Geophysical Method	*Type of mineral deposit*
Magnetic	Pyrrhotite-rich sulphide veins and lodes; Fe ore bodies; Magnetite infiltrated wall rocks around hydrothermal sulphide deposits; Chromite deposits (in laterite-free areas).
Magnetotelluric	Deep dislocations which could be related to mineral deposits, e.g. the West Coast hot springs and Hg emissions.
Electromagnetic	Graphite deposits.
Self Potential	Sulphide deposits in veins, lodes and beds; Graphite; Groundwater.
Induced Potential	Sulphide disseminations in large patches; Graphite.
Resistivity	Sulphide deposits; Other metallic orebodies; Saline groundwater front in coastal tracts.
Gravity	Chromite and magnetite deposits; Barite beds; Concealed sedimentary basins; Volcanic plugs e.g. Kimberlite diatremes.
Seismic (Reflection and Refraction)	Concealed hydrocarbon reservoirs and magma chambers; On land and offshore sedimentary basins.

MAGNETIC METHOD

This is the oldest geophysical method dating back to the 17th century. The two parameters measured are the change of direction and intensity of magnetic field. Change of direction in a horizontal plane is a change in declination, whereas change in the vertical plane is a change in inclination. To measure changes in intensity of magnetism the unit is the gamma, or 10^{-5} cgs units. The shape and depth of the source of magnetic anomalies depend on polarities and strength of the induced poles and their distribution over the body producing the anomaly. Where the body parallels the earth's field and has infinite vertical extent, as a narrow dyke in the magnetic meridian or a volcanic pipe paralleling the magnetic resultant, only the magnetic poles induced on top of the body need be considered, since the poles at the lower end of the body are so far away as to have negligible impact on the field. This is represented by an inverse first power function. On the other hand, if the body is low dipping and of finite thickness, so that poles of opposite polarity induced on the upper and lower surfaces both lie at finite distances, the function is an inverse cube. It is important to remember that unless the form of the body is known, correct interpretation is difficult. Magnetic variations sometimes reflect changes in the elevation of the basement. Great care is needed to eliminate false readings. In tropical countries, diurnal variations are often greater than the anomalies due to the influence of the Equatorial Electrojet. A base station is used with a second instrument to filter out the diurnal variation. In ground surveys, it is important to design traverses across the strike of the formations with the stations placed at intervals less than the width of the anomaly sought. Magnetic surveys are extensively used to make qualitative geological interpretations. Combined with conventional petrological studies of the exposed rocks, including the presence, size, alteration and abundance of magnetic minerals and bulk magnetic properties of the rocks, the magnetic anomaly patterns can be analysed and modelled in detail (Fig. 5.2).

The minerals with positive magnetic response are magnetite, ilmenite, pyrrhotite, etc. The magnetometer, a device for measuring magnetism, is essentially a

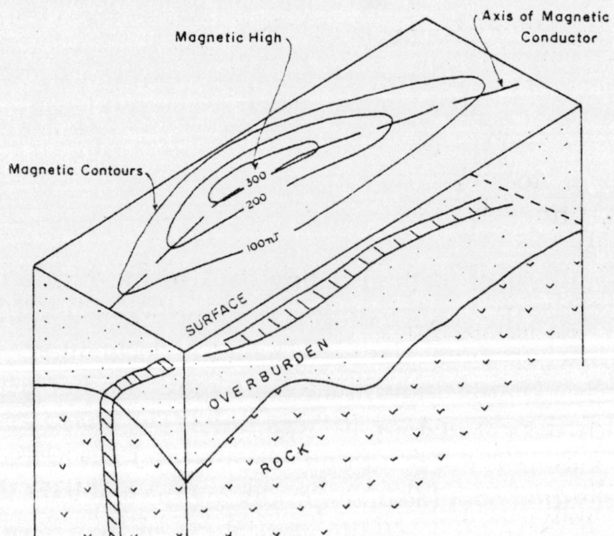

Fig. 5.2: Illustrative sketch of magnetic anomaly induced by a hidden ore body.

refinement of the old dip needle. Following accurate and detailed geological mapping, extended surveys by magnetometer led to the discovery of a number of nickel sulphide deposits in Sudbury, Canada, in the late thirties. The main gold-bearing conglomerate Reef of West Rand, South Africa, associated with ferruginous shales was traced westward under 600 m thick cover of dolomite beds by the combined efforts of a mining geologist and a geophysicist. Nowadays, magnetic survey and observatory readings are most commonly taken with a nuclear precession or proton precession magnetometer. A liquid rich in hydrogen atoms, such as kerosene or water, is used in the canister, which is the sensing device of the proton magnetometer and is surrounded by a coil. The liquid must be checked regularly. The protons in the liquid act as small dipoles, aligned parallel to the geomagnetic field. When a current is passed through the coil in a different direction to generate a magnetic field 50 to 100 times stronger than the geomagnetic field, the protons realign in the new direction. The current is then switched off and the protons return by spiralling or precessing in 1–3 seconds to their original alignment. The instruments provide absolute readings of the total magnetic field, accurate to ± 1 nannotesla (nT) on land and about ± 10 nT in marine surface towed systems. In domains of strong magnetic gradient, aeromagnetic survey with a proton magnetometer suffers from the disadvantage that protons at different parts of the sensor may precess at different rates, thus clouding the signal. Additionally, the 1–3 second time taken by the protons to come back to their original orientation after the current to the coil is switched off may transport the sensor meanwhile by 30–120 m along the survey path. In contrast, the flux gate magnetometer is a continuous reading instrument, comparatively immune to magnetic field gradients. It uses two identical ferromagnetic cores of very high permeability around which primary and secondary coils are wound and an alternating current of 50–1000 Hz is passed through the primary coil generating an alternating magnetic field. The airborne magnetometer, originally under development by the Gulf Oil Company prior to World War II for oil exploration, was perfected during the War as a means of detecting submarines from the air. Modern airborne magnetometers used for mineral prospecting are usually enclosed in a streamlined case and mounted on or towed below the plane.

Aeromagnetic survey for locating mineral deposits should be low level (100–120 m above ground) programs and are best undertaken during periods which are free from both terrestrial and solar storms. The traverse should preferably avoid (or record) metallic objects like railway lines, residential areas, etc; and for both ground and airborne magnetometer surveys, there should be a base-station magnetometer (particularly in tropical countries, affected by Equatorial Electrojet) where readings are to be recorded every 30 minutes for background corrections to the raw data.

Magnetic anomalies caused by shallow structures are more influenced by high wave number components than those resulting from deeper sources. The effect can be quantified by computing the power spectrum of the anomaly.

It has been observed that many ore-bearing granitic plutons can be distinguished from one another by individual aeromagnetic signatures, e.g. the positive anomalies associated with the auriferous pluton in Anchorage, Alaska.

Low level magnetic (flight height 200–250 m above terrain) anomaly maps provide important information about regional geology, especially where rock outcrops are rare or the bedrock is covered by unconsolidated material. Survey line spacing has also to be close. Canada's survey line spacing is 0.8 km; Finland's is 0.2 km; Australia's is being upgraded to 0.4 km. Over large parts of the U.S.A., flight line spacings were 5 km or greater, 'which is too wide to properly characterise isolated sources lying at depths shallower than about 5 km' *(EOS, Trans. A.G.U.* 76(14), 1995, 138). The aeromagnetic survey programme of the G.S.I., under 'Operation Hardrock' and with BRGM collaboration was not properly designed to pick up magnetic anomaly signals of shallow-seated (around 100 m deep) orebodies either.

This is not unusual. Under the usual procedure, signals from shallow sources including those from hidden orebodies are filtered out, as illustrated by the aeromagnetic survey of Northern Algeria. (F. Asfirane and A. Galdeans, *Earth & Planet. Sci. Letters,* 136, 1995, 61–78). The survey was conducted on constant ground clearance of 150 m. Sampling interval along profiles was approximately 50 m. From the recorded magnetic field, the regional field, which corresponds to a polynomial surface of low degree (computed by the Least Square Method), was subtracted to obtain the anomalies. The anomalous field was then interpolated on a regular grid cell of 2 km × 2 km. The anomalies were reduced to the pole to position them on the top of their sources. Furthermore, upward continuation of the potential fields was done. This attenuated the high frequency anomalies.

It is worth emphasizing that downward continuation of the potential fields is very unstable in the presence of proximal sources. Similarly, the reduction of the anomalies to their pole positions necessitates information on their magnetisation direction. While searching for patterns and signals in Precambrian cratons, this becomes an uncertain endeavour, since it is known that the earth's magnetic field before the Eocene was different in direction from the present one.

Unlike its southern neighbours within the tropical belt, airborne geophysical exploration has been successful in China, not only for basic geological mapping and in oil and gas prospecting in the Tarim basin and Daqing and Shengli oil fields, but also in delineating some 460 mineral deposits containing 20 different economic minerals (S. Wang and H. Xia, *EOS, Trans. AGU*, 76 (17), Spring Meet. Suppl., 1995, S 314.

In areas with Mediterranean to polar climate, magnetic survey is a powerful tool for locating mineral deposits concealed below glacial drift. Unfortunately, in the tropical belt, humid weathering (lateritisation) process creates a strong blanket of noise in the ground measurements.

GRAVIMETRIC METHOD

The purpose of such surveys is to measure small local variations (anomalies) in the gravity field, induced by salt domes, dykes, deposits of heavy minerals like chromite, faults and folds, etc. The size of the anomalies is dependent upon two factors: differences in density of the rocks and their geometrical form. Since the geological contrasts are very small as compared to the volume of the earth, the anomalies are correspondingly miniscule. The field unit is gal (after Galileo)—the strength of a gravitational field which will act upon a mass of 1 gram with a force of 1 dyne. The earth's field is equal to about 980 gal, whereas the anomalies are a millionth of this, i.e. 1 milligal. Due to constantly changing tidal and other forces on the earth, the limit of accuracy is 0.1 milligal. One has to determine change of gravity directly from changes measured in the extension of the spring. This requires a specially-constructed spring balance carrying a constant mass. The instrument is known as a gravimeter. Changes in gravity field cause changes in weight and thus the length of the spring, which varies a tiny little bit. The extension of the spring is recorded by suitable optical, mechanical or electronic amplifications.

Gravimetric survey is a cumbersome process. The major corrections required after the raw measurements are as follows:

(1) Instrumental drift: to be monitored by repeated meter readings at base station. This reduces the speed of work significantly. It is due to imperfect elasticity of the spring and/or temperature changes during the working hours.

(2) Latitude correction: This is required because of the non-spherical shape of the earth and because the angular velocity of a point on the earth's surface decreases

from a maximum at the equator to zero at the poles. Precise Pole star observation is needed at every field.

(3) Elevation corrections

(a) *Free Air correction:* Variation in the distance of the point from the center of the earth causes change in gravity.

(b) *Bouguer correction:* needed to compensate for the gravitational effect of the rock present under the observation point, e.g. an ultramafic mass in a granite terrane.

(c) *Terrain correction:* To compensate for the topographic relief in the vicinity of the observation station. Terrain effects are low in flat areas, but are high in steep-sided valleys (as in Damsal valley of the Sukinda ultramafic field, Orissa), at the base or top of cliffs and at the summits of mountains.

(4) Tidal correction: Solid earth tides are no doubt smaller than ocean tides but the observation point may shift from the center of the earth by a few centemeters.

Besides, the density of a large number of samples of the constituent rocks has to be measured (weight of the sample in air divided by the weight of an equal volume of water) for appropriate modelling of the anomalies. Density may be measured in boreholes using a density (gamma-gamma) logger.

In India; gravity surveys have been successful in: (1) locating the extension of the Gondwana sedimentary basin below the Cenozoic cover, east of the Jharia coalfield; (2) delineating the structural environment of the Pench-Kanhan and the Chanda-Wardha valley coalfields; (3) locating medium-sized chromite masses in the north limb of the Sukinda ultramafic field, concealed below thick laterite; and (4) tracing the extension of manganese deposits below soil cover in parts of Madhya Pradesh and Maharashtra (Fig. 5.3). The most spectacular success was in the Odendalsrust gold field, S. Africa where the gold-bearing Witwatersrand Series is capped by about 300 m of Karroo sediments. The thick cover (greater than 1000 m) of basic lavas of the Ventersdrop Series is absent over this area. A survey with a torsion balance about fifty years ago defined the target area on the basis of which more than 100 positive boreholes were later drilled.

The potential field (magnetic and gravity) anomaly of a three dimensional body may be calculated by using the following four steps:

(1) Construction of a reasonable model;

(2) Computation of its gravity or magnetic anomaly;

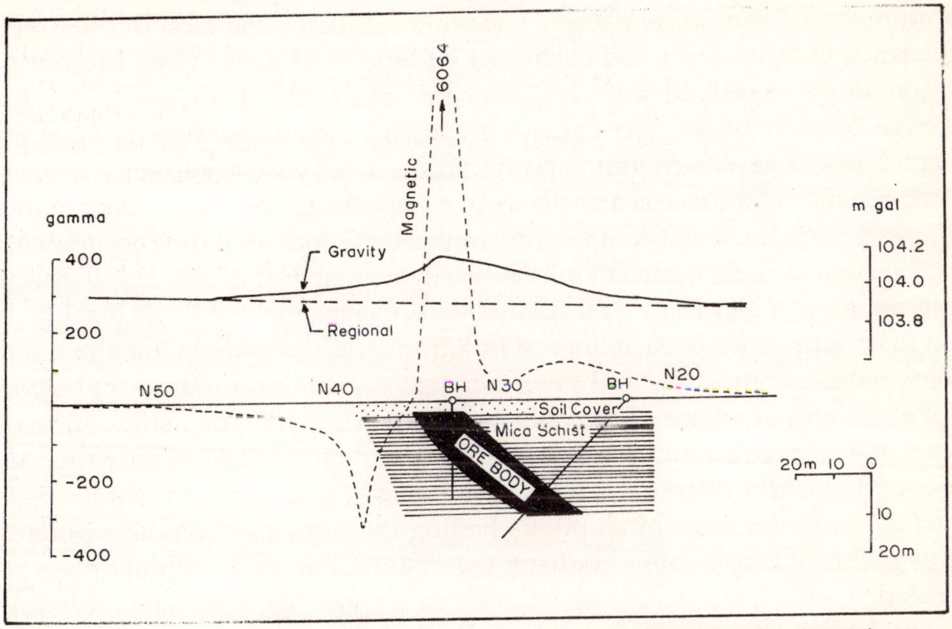

Fig. 5.3: Coincident gravity (Bouguer) and magnetic (V.F.) anomalies over the manganese orebody at Satak mines, Nagpur district, Maharashtra.

(3) Comparison of computed with observed anomaly; and
(4) Alteration of model to improve correspondence of observed and calculated anomalies and return to Step 2.

As emphasized earlier, both magnetic and gravity fields are potential fields. The potential at any point is the work necessary to move a unit mass or pole from an infinite distance to that point through the ambient field. Potential fields obey Laplace's equation, which states that the sum of the rates of change of the field gradient in three orthogonal directions is zero.

GEO-ELECTRICAL METHODS

Geo-electrical methods had their first success in the glaciated tract of northern Sweden, where the country is comparatively flat, and massive sulphide deposits are present below a thin overburden. Such sulphide bodies are highly-conductive, much more than common rock types. Graphite rich beds, common in the Eastern Ghats terraen of India, fractured or altered underground zones with the confined water containing dissolved salts, and, in some cases, clay beds, are also highly conductive. Massive quartz veins are highly resistive to current flow, although the geo-electric response of such thin, resistive sheets is not clearly known.

In understanding the essence of electrical prospecting, you should bear in mind the difference between the flow lines of current and the corresponding equipotential lines. When you introduce current into the earth through two electrodes, connected to the terminals of a generator by insulated wire, electric current flows through the ground in an infinite number of lines of flux from one electrode to the other. If the lithology, physical properties and other ambient conditions are uniform between the two electrodes, the lines of flux will be symmetrically aligned smooth curves. But suppose you have a tabular mass in between with different electrical properties. The lines of flux will be distorted, causing anomalies. If you survey the equipotential lines, which form the locus of all points having the same electromotive potential and thus points of zero current gradient, the distortion over the tabular mass will be revealed.

Electrical prospecting methods are broadly divisible into two categories:

(1) Those which make use of the naturally-occurring electrical fields of the earth.
(2) Those which require introduction of artificially generated currents into the ground using direct currents or low frequency alternating currents.

Since the objectives of geo-electrical methods of prospecting are to define the location and geometry of concealed mineral deposits as correctly as possible to help in subsequent exploration, this field is witnessing a continual refinement in resolution. A general framework of some of the more important techniques is given in the following pages.

Self Potential (S.P) Method

Electrochemical reactions develop within zones of oxidation of a sulphide deposit underground, straddling the water table and forming a gigantic electric battery which sets up electric currents of its own. The currents are usually detected at the surface by measuring the potential drop between pairs of copper electrodes, each of which is placed in a porous pot with saturated $CuSO_4$ solution. These create self-potential anomalies (Fig. 5.4). A pair of electrodes is connected through a high impedance millivoltmeter. One electrode is fixed in barren ground, away from the

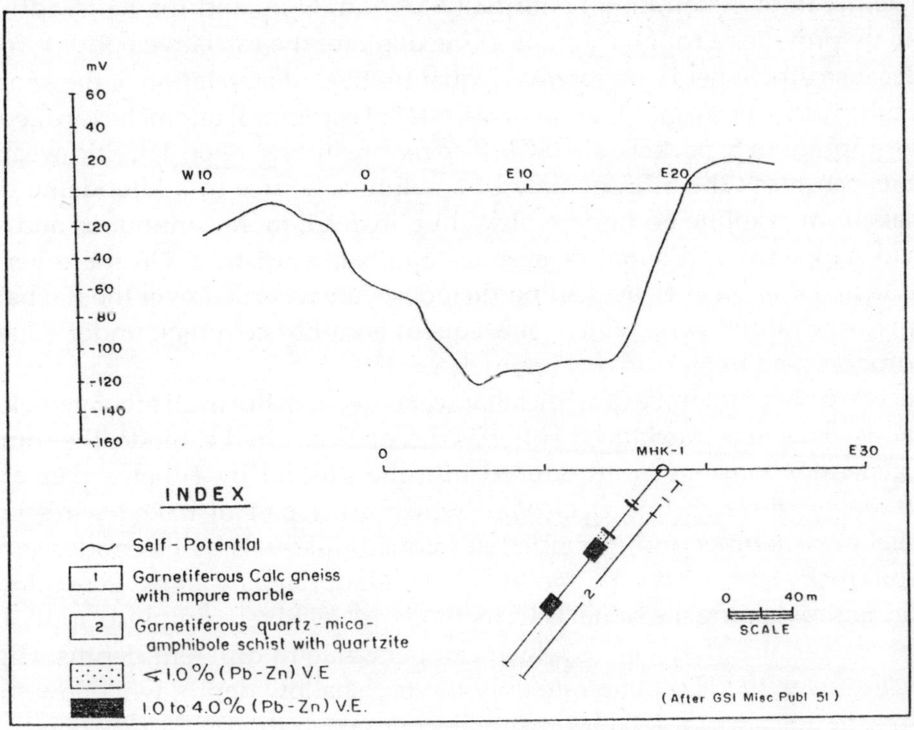

Fig. 5.4: Self-potential anomaly over sulphide zones, Pur Banera lead-zinc-copper sulphide field, Bhilwara district, Rajasthan.

surface trace of the potential target and the other moved in steps across the suspected mineralised zone. Station spacing is normally kept below 30 m. Against normal background fluctuation of up to 50 millivolts, significant anomalies go up to 100–500 millivolts.

There are two methods of field survey: where the terrain is difficult, it is better to have a relatively short distance between the two sets of non-polarising electrodes fixed on the ground. But in flat terrains, it is advantageous to keep one electrode fixed and gradually increase its separation from the other. One uses standard electrical instruments: potentiometer with a range from 1 millivolt to 1 volt, two porous pot ground contacts, wire connectors, tape etc. The method is useful for deposits of sulphides and oxides which have high electrical conductivity. It cannot be used for non-conductors like sphalerite, cinnabar, stibnite, magnetite, etc.

The depth of penetration is normally around 30 m, and the half-width of the anomaly provides a rough estimate of the depth of the causative body.

Because dipole fields are involved, quantitative interpretation of the anomaly is difficult, much like magnetic anomaly. As stated earlier, S.P. anomalies are generated over graphite-rich pockets also. Clay cover, including deep lateritic weathering profile, can mask the S.P. anomaly of a sulphide source in a khondalite terraen. Signals from graphite bodies are picked up instead, more continuous and strong, as had happened at Riamal near Adas, Sambalpur district. On the other hand, consistent S.P. anomalies over sulphide lodes were recorded over the Rakha Mines copper mineralised zone, where subsequent aero-EM coverage under 'Operation Hardrock' failed to pick up any anomaly at all.

In S.P. survey, no source of artificial power is needed. But in all other geo-electrical methods, current is introduced either as d.c. or as a.c. In d.c. mode, the source is a d.c. generator. Current is introduced into the ground by either a pair of point electrodes or through line electrodes, which are a pair of naked wires laid out parallel to each other and grounded at frequent intervals by electrodes sunk into the soil/rocky layer. In the a.c. mode, current is supplied by an a.c. generator, other conditions remaining the same. D.C. methods are relatively simple to apply, but the a.c. offers variable frequencies which can penetrate to different depths. High frequencies (over 10 kHz) penetrate only to very shallow depth, while low to intermediate frequencies (5–100 Hz) ensure deeper penetration.

Resistivity Method

When artificially generated electrical currents are passed into the ground, the resulting potential difference at the surface is measured by this method.

The resistivity of a material is defined as the resistance in ohms between the opposite faces of a unit cube of the material. On the face of it, therefore, a metalliferous mass should be easily differentiated from barren silicate envelopes, which are essentially insulators in compact state. Unfortunately, graphite conducts electricity. The water-charged pore spaces in silicate rocks also conduct electrical current. As a result, massive but fractured rocks with fluid in the open spaces show low resistivity. In terrains of deep weathering, therefore, resistivity probes face complex problems.

In a lithologically and structurally homogeneous tract, the depth of penetration of current is proportional to the separation of the current electrodes. Not so where inhomogenities are present underground. There, resistivity varies with the position of the electrodes.

There are two main types of operation:

(1) Vertical Electrical Sounding; and (2) Constant Separation Traversing.

In Vertical Electrical Sounding, the current and potential electrodes are maintained at the same relative spacing around a central point, which is fixed. The distance from the central point is progressively increased. This method is useful for determining loose overburden thickness over hard rocks and is frequently used in river valley projects.

In Constant Separation Traversing, the current and potential electrodes are kept at a fixed distance but these are progressively shifted along a line at right angles to the strike of the formation. Among the many configurations of current and potential electrodes, designed so far, the most commonly used are the Wenner and Schlumberger configurations, the former keeping the current and potential electrodes at equal spacing whereas the latter keeping the spacing of potential electrodes as a fraction of the separation of the outer current electrodes (Fig. 5.5). Schlumberger configuration places the current electrodes in the ground very far apart and measures the resistivity of the earth near one of the contacts, neglecting the effects of the far electrode. In contrast, Wenner configuration makes equal separation between current and potential electrodes, often with a third potential electrode midway (Lee configuration) which eliminates the surface anomalies.

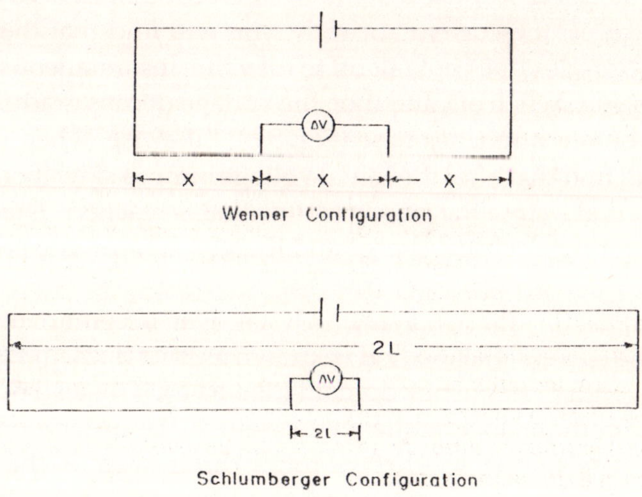

Fig. 5.5: Configuration of current and potential electrodes in Wenner vs Schlumberger arrays.

A recent development is in the field of resistivity tomography, i.e. construction of the resistivity cross-section of a region surrounded by electrodes. Similarly, resistivity plus electrical imaging systems with greater probe depths are being designed with computer controlled, multi-electrode array and switching systems, bringing advanced data processing facilities down to the field level. Most modern resistivity meters employ low frequency a.c. (between 100 Hz for shallow probes to 10 Hz for 100 m penetration) with microprocessor-controlled electronic circuitry. For deeper probes, d.c. must be used, but more complex measures are involved to counter electrolytic polarisation and effects of telluric currents. Additionally, the geoelectric response of deep weathering is quite variable from one area to another and masks the effect of deep-seated contrasts. Like magnetic and gravity survey, the resistivity method utilises a potential field, and suffers from ambiguity in interpretation. Other independent geophysical and geological controls are essential to firm up the interpretations, which are best achieved where the bedrocks have simple structural configuration.

Electrical resistivity technique is also useful for measuring geothermal heat flux, where hot mineralised fluids underground produce anomalous areas of low resistivity.

Induced Polarisation (I.P.) Method

This phenomenon, known from the 1920s and extensively used in prospecting, is not well understood. If you use a standard 4-electrode resistivity spread on a d.c. mode and switch off the current abruptly, you will find that the voltage between the potential electrodes does not fall off to nil value instantaneously; there is a large voltage drop as you switch off, and then the voltage decays gradually at places over many seconds before it touches base (Fig. 5.6). Likewise, when you switch on the current, you will find that after the initial voltage jump, a slow increment takes place over a time interval before the steady state value is reached. Thus the ground acts as a capacitor, storing electrical charge and thereby *induced* into electrically *polarised* state.

When you measure the decaying voltage over a certain time interval, after switching off the current, the method is known as time domain I.P. survey. Alternatively, you can conduct frequency domain I.P. survey, if instead of a d.c. source, you use a variable (2 or more) low frequency a.c. source. It is observed that the measured apparent resistivity of the subsurface rocks diminishes as the a.c. frequency is

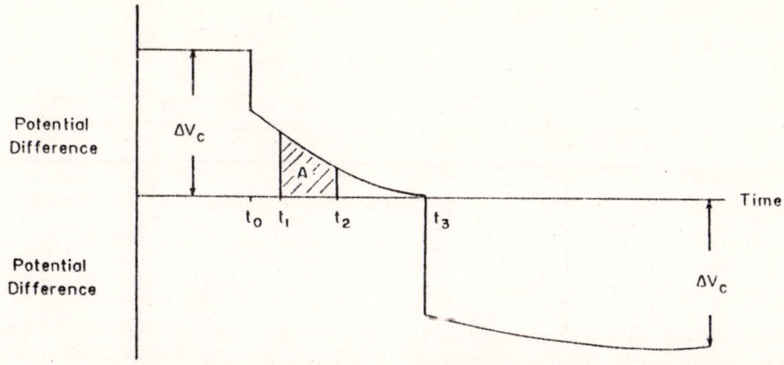

Fig. 5.6: At t_0, current is switched off; at t_3, current is switched on. *A* represents the area under the decay period from t_1 to t_2.

increased in contrast to the passage of d.c. which is inhibited by the capacitance of the ground.

I.P. survey is normally combined with resistivity probes (Fig. 5.7) and has been successful in picking up signals of blind sulphide deposits even beneath 100 m thick limestone cover, e.g. in the Century Zn-Pb-Ag deposit, N. Queensland, Australia. But one has to take care against various sources of noise, e.g. telluric currents, membrane polarisation, electromagnetic coupling between adjacent wires (if the cables are close to one another), water-filled shear zones, graphite-rich bodies with large differences in texture, sharp changes in conductivity distribution etc.

A potentially useful tool emerging now is spectral I.P. which analyses frequency domain phase spectra. The method is difficult and expensive.

ELECTROMAGNETIC PROSPECTING

When alternating current is passed through a small coil into the ground, secondary electromagnetic fields are generated around a conductor underground. This induces its own alternating current in the receiver coil by electromagnetic induction (Fig. 5.8). In an area of uniform lithology, the primary EM field path from the transmitter to the receiver both on and below the ground is homogeneous, except for a slight fall in amplitude; but suppose there is a conducting body somewhere underground, which may or may not be a metalliferous deposit. The magnetic component of the primary EM field path will induce eddy currents to flow in the

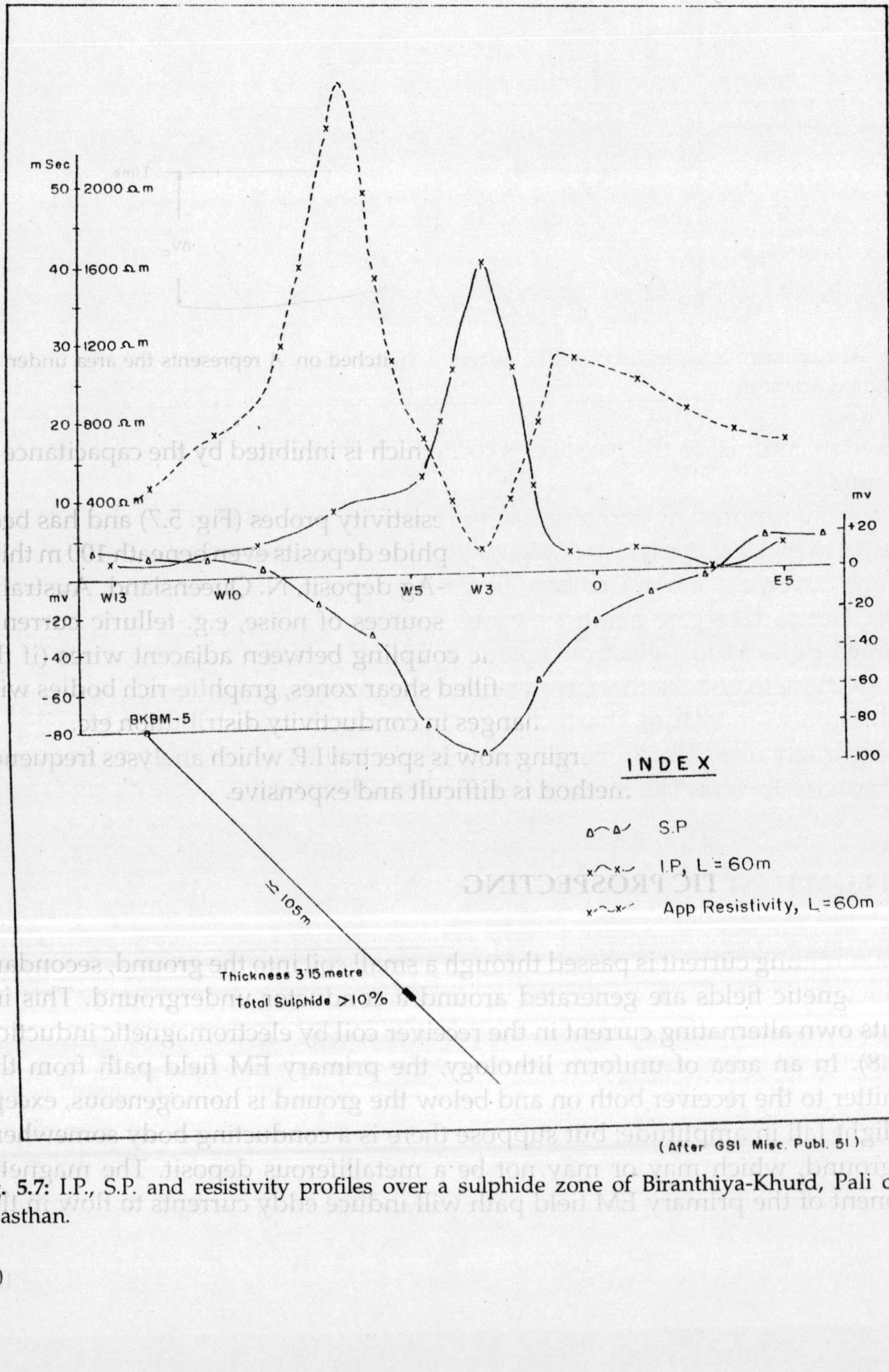

Fig. 5.7: I.P., S.P. and resistivity profiles over a sulphide zone of Biranthiya-Khurd, Pali district, Rajasthan.

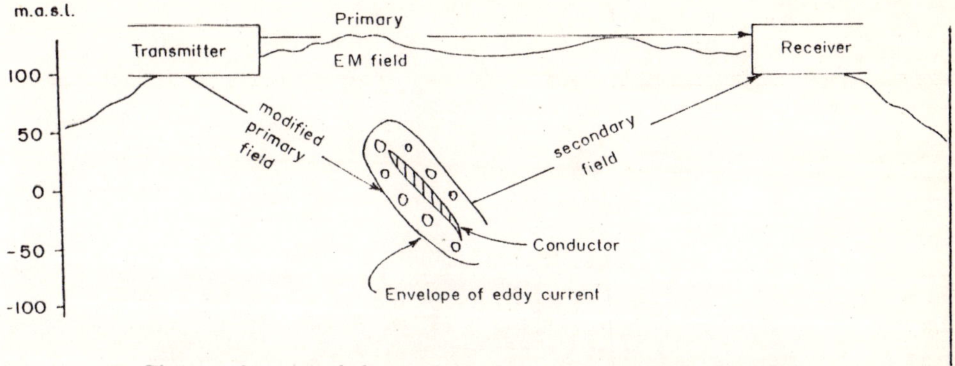

Fig. 5.8: Simplified sketch of generation of secondary EM field.

conductor. This eddy current will create its own secondary EM field in the receiver coil, which will be recorded by differences in both phase and amplitude from the primary field. This method is, potentially, perhaps the most powerful technique for exploration of deep-seated mineral deposits. Here the current in the ground is not measured directly; but the magnetic field is surveyed by means of portable coils, in which it sets up induced currents. By rotating the coil, one can measure both the horizontal and vertical components of the magnetic field.

Sophisticated ground EM surveying systems to measure the phase and amplitude relationship between the primary, secondary and resultant fields include Two-Frame compensator and Turam systems (Fig. 5.9). During field work, the spacing and orientation of the coils is critical. A small error in spacing can produce appreciable error in phase measurement. The orientation of the coil must also be accurate. The TURAM method employs a long, straight conductor laid on the ground, grounded at each end and supplied with a.c. Two coils a fixed distance apart are used to run traverses at right angles to the wire. Changes of phase and amplitude are measured between the induced voltages in each coil.

Since the induced current from such an energised source is essentially generated from the magnetic component of the EM field—which is a potential field—there is no need for physical contact of either the transmitter or the receiver with the ground, unlike S.P. or I.P. or Resistivity surveys. Hence electromagnetic surveys for buried conductive ore bodies can be both ground-based and airborne.

Airborne EM equipment were first developed and used to explore for nickel orebodies in Canada. The general scheme is to transmit strong alternating electrical fields from the airplane and to determine the effect of the earth's conductivity on

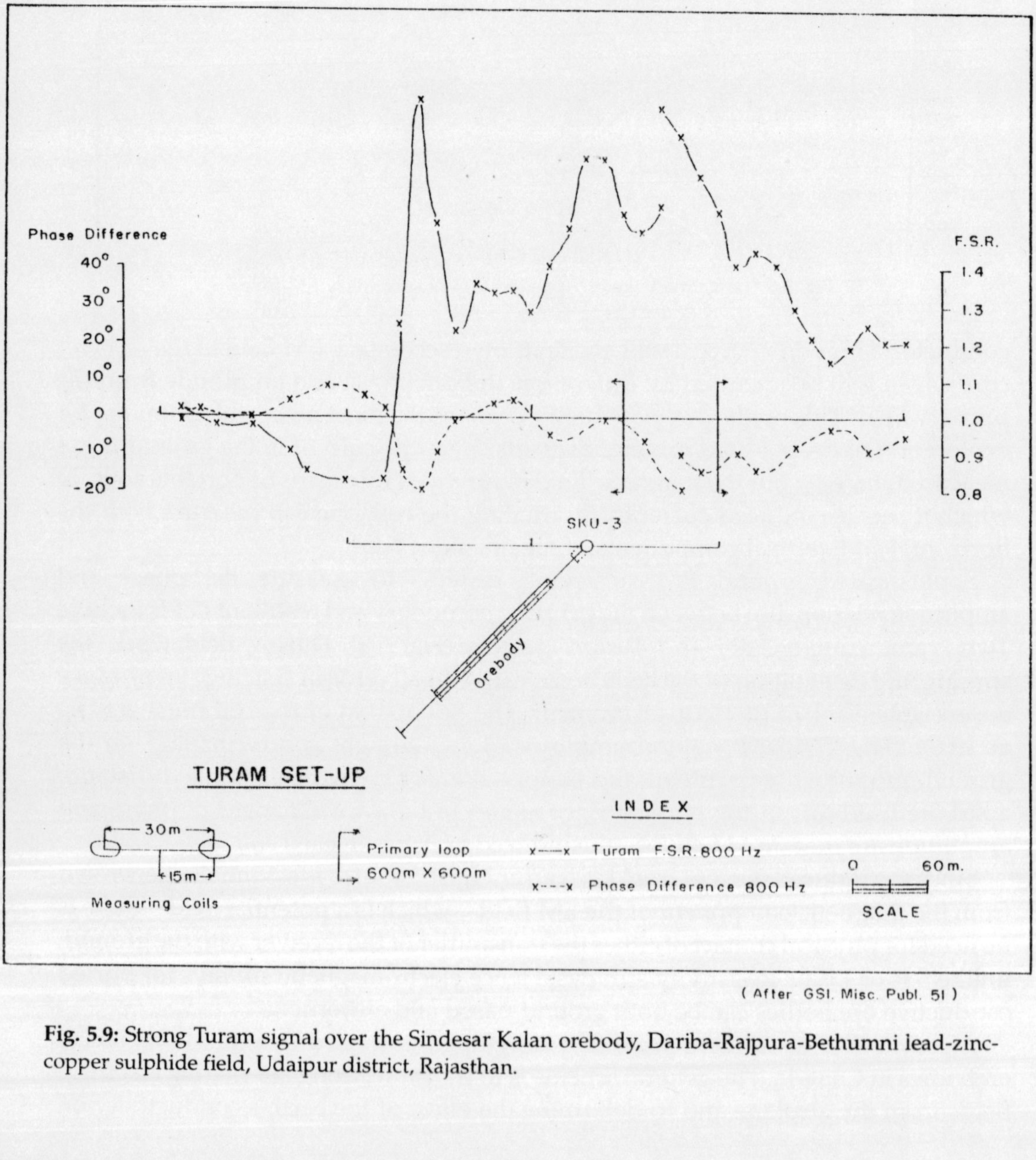

(After GSI. Misc. Publ. 51)

Fig. 5.9: Strong Turam signal over the Sindesar Kalan orebody, Dariba-Rajpura-Bethumni lead-zinc-copper sulphide field, Udaipur district, Rajasthan.

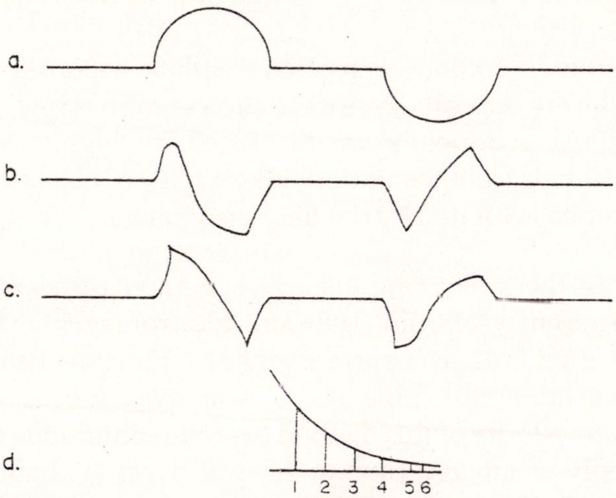

Fig. 5.10: Principle of INPUT system: (a) Primary field; (b) Receiver response to primary field only; (c) Receiver response in the presence of a secondary field; (d) Enlargement of receiver signal during cut-off period of primary field.

these fields. During flight, the detecting device, which is enclosed in a streamlined case, called 'bird', trails along the end of a very long cable, so that the EM effect of the aircraft is minimised when the receiver is on. The Thompson nickel deposit in Manitoba within biotite schist and quartzite was discovered in 1956 by airborne EM, followed by drilling one of many geophysical anomalies in the region.

Present-day airborne EM systems are of two types: passive system, where only the receiver is airborne; and active system, where both transmitter and receiver are airborne. The active system can operate on either fixed separation or quadrature mode. The most commonly used is the INPUT system (Induced Pulsed Transient). The pulse duration is generally 1.5 ms, and the interval between two successive pulses is 2 ms. When the primary field is cut off, the induced current decays exponentially. The receiver is activated when the primary field is absent to record the continuously decaying voltage during the 2 ms interval. The decay curve is sampled at several points, and the signals displayed (Fig. 5.10).

The duration of the induced voltage is directly proportional to the conductivity of the causative source, provided other conditions (flight height, aircraft speed, etc.) remain constant.

Poor conductors produce a rapidly decaying voltage.

The electromagnetic prospecting technique suffers from the following major problems:

(1) anomalies are more commonly caused by graphite, water-filled shear zones etc. than by metallic ore deposits; hence the success ratio is low;
(2) where deep-lying conductors are blanketed by highly conductive water-charged clay, signals from the underlying source are masked by the cover;
(3) the depth of probe is limited by the frequency range.

Notwithstanding these shortcomings, EM method provides a versatile and efficient probe. In recent years, the Transient Electromagnetic Method (TEM) is being increasingly used both as a surface and as a borehole probe. Experimental TEM surveys over kimberlite pipe no. 6 near Wajrakarur, Andhra Pradesh, demonstrated the superiority of this method over the continuous wave EM method in detecting a deeply-weathered pipe under soil cover (V. Babu Rao et al., *Jour. Association Expl. Geoph.* 13(1), 1992, 15–22).

In the discovery of the Eloise Cu-Au deposit in Queensland, Australia below 50–70 m of conducting flat-lying sediments, systematic evaluation of trends with moving loop EM followed by detailed probe of the conductor by fixed loop TEM played a critical role. Downhole TEM surveys are normally used in conjunction with resistivity logging and other physical property measurements. The Transient EM response of a layered structure, where the conductivity is allowed to vary continuously with depth is a relatively poorly understood feature vis-a-vis the galvanic response (allowing for current gathering) of a sulphide deposit, when the ground is excited by a current of the form $I_0H\text{-}(t)$ flowing in a large loop either on the ground or from the air. The time spent in sampling the field and the 'off' time needed, vary on the conductivity contrasts.

Electromagnetic prospecting systems using large stationary transmitter loops have exceptional depth penetration and are therefore useful in the search for conductive mineral deposits at depth. Similarly, correlation of conductive bodies underground, e.g. sulphide intersections in boreholes is considerably helped by EM downhole probes. An example of successful persistence is afforded by the Aguas Tenidas East massive sulphide deposit (27 million tonnes of ore with 1.1% Cu, 2.8% Zn and 0.8% Pb) in the pyrite belt of S.W. Spain. Initial aeromagnetic survey with INPUT (12 channel) system on board flown at a detector height of 150 m and line spacing of 250 m picked up 42 anomalies (EM), mainly over known extensions of abandoned mines. TEM survey along one of the extension zones of a smaller, exhausted mine picked up a strong conductor with a long decay. This was drilled down to the estimated depth of the causative source. It proved barren. But downhole TEM probe here picked up a signal. This led to drilling another hole, which intersected massive sulphides. Subsequent research showed that the error in initial modelling of the TEM data was due to the assumption of only a conductive response, whereas galvanic response was of considerable importance in the area (N. Hungerford, *Exploration Geophysics*, 25, 1994, 1–17).

The moral: modelling of the depth of a causative source is a bugbear in many cases. Various methods of computation are being developed and a variety of software is available. The essential problem is to constrain the choice. Integrating information by trial and error from other geophysical probes, e.g. apparent resistivity, is the age-old approach to solve such situations. Geophysical exploration at the Osborne copper and gold deposit in Mount Isa where mineralisation is associated with ironstone illustrates the uncertainties. Initial interpretation of magnetic data did not take into account the possible effect of demagnetisation; afterwards, this was recognised. A strong conductive zone was also picked up by fixed and moving loop TEM survey. Drill-holes were sunk on the basis of the magnetic anomalies. Downhole TEM probe, together with resistivity logging etc. showed that the physical properties vary both on account of fluctuating magnetic response and sulphide content of the rocks. This caused doubt about the significance of the TEM signals. The approach was then changed. Gravimetric survey was undertaken to pick up zones of ironstone. Borehole magnetic profiling was undertaken to eliminate spurious conductivity signals not related to sulphides. Then radio imaging method was tested as a method of correlation between drill-holes; and it was found that conductivity of mineralisation at 50 kHz is more coherent than in TEM.

No one stopped this work half way on the plea that the findings were not tying up with the orebody, no one condemned the failure, and stopped attempts as useless as some ill-informed geologists do now and then. Geophysical prospecting is much like the general practitioner's art. The patient, in this case the geologist, must extend willing co-operation; and the doctor must communicate his limitations, instead of putting on a poker face.

Among the cheap and rapid tools for obtaining a qualitative response may be mentioned: (1) Very Low Frequency (VLF) method, which uses powerful radio transmitters as used in long range communication and navigational systems; and (2) Audio Frequency Magnetic Field Method (AFMAG) which uses natural EM field induced by thunderstorms and known as Sferics. High frequency radio waves suffer from lack of penetration due to skin effect and absorption of the waves by the rocks.

The VLF receiver is a small hand-held device with two orthogonal aerials, which can be tuned to the particular frequencies of the transmitters. All you need to have is a suitable transmitter with magnetic vector across the geological strike and your VLF receiver. The depth of penetration is low.

The AFMAG method enables a deeper probe into the ground. The sferics propagate around the earth between the ground surface and the ionosphere. This space constitutes an efficient EM waveguide. Thunderstorms anywhere in the world contribute to the field on account of low attenuation.

TELLURIC AND MAGNETOTELLURIC METHODS

Telluric currents are natural alternating electric fields within the earth, induced by low frequency pulsations of the natural magnetic fields within and around the earth, known commonly as magnetotelluric fields.

The telluric currents are used by measuring the potential difference between two points on the ground, spaced 10–20 m apart using non-polarising electrodes or plates made of lead. Corrections for temporal variation in direction and intensity of the currents are provided by simultaneous readings on orthogonal electrode pairs both at the observation station and the base station over a period of 10–60 minutes.

In the basic theory of the telluric current method, it is assumed that the telluric field is a steady state direct current field.

If the ground is non-uniform beneath the base electrodes, the corrections are incomplete.

The telluric method has been used mainly in the exploration of large sedimentary fields and geothermal sites. Some kimberlite diatremes near Wajrakarur and Lattavaram (Andhra Pradesh) showed up in the telluric field picture as 'lows'.

Both VLF and telluric methods suffer from terrain effects, i.e. a distinct correlation between the amplitude of the secondary fields and the topography. VLF fields change over distances of 20–30 km so that data cannot be corrected over the large distances using normal base station monitor. Solar flares also generate a lot of noise.

The magnetotelluric (MT) method utilises the same source field as that needed for the telluric method but in this case both the magnetic and telluric pulsations are recorded. MT essentially aims at deeper probes, e.g. locating faults in the lower crust through imaging the subsurface geoelectric section in terms of 1, 2 or 3-D geometry. The technique cannot eliminate the noise of the local field which produces scatter in the impedance estimate. These techniques are not yet used as stand-alone procedures for prospecting for shallow deposits although some claim that AMT (Audio Magnetotellurics) can be used. The MT method is useful for mapping conductivity distributions to depths of a few tens of km.

Magnetotelluric measurements in combination with reflection seismics and magnetic variation measurements are found to be useful to illuminate crustal structure in zones of convergence, e.g. the Iapetus suture between Scotland and England, lying concealed beneath Carboniferous and younger sediments of the Northumberland trough. Electrically conductive features, which typically map the location of sulphide bodies, or fluids or graphite are revealed on the conductivity section and are correlated with bright reflectors on the seismic profile by extrapolating the latter on to the magnetotelluric image following trends from magnetic variation hypothetical event maps. It is needless to emphasize that the resolution of these images is dependent upon station interval, band width, data quality and interpretative algorithms. It has been found for concealed bodies that a three-step conversion of data is helpful. First, magnetotelluric impedances are estimated as a function of period from measurement of the horizontal components of the electrical and magnetic fields at the earth's surface for each station. Impedances for longer periods provide deeper depth-averaged structures. Next, the horizontal direction in which conductivity has the least variation is estimated from rotations of the impedances for each station. This provides the electrical strike direction. Finally, the impendences are rotated to the strike direction before inversion for two dimensional conductivity structure taking care that the simulated impedances using the conductivity section, the station locations and the inverted periods match the observed impedances within narrow error bars.

REFLECTION AND REFRACTION SEISMIC METHODS

These are the essential tools for hydrocarbon prospecting. All seismic methods involve creation of artificial earthquake waves either by detonating a charge of dynamite or other explosives like compressed air and measuring the reflection or refraction trace of the resultant waves. The velocity of an elastic wave in a homogenous medium, both P wave (dilational or compressional like sound wave) and S wave (transverse or shear wave) depends on a number of factors like its Young's Modulus, Poisson's ratio, coefficient of rigidity, bulk modulus, coefficient of incompressibility etc. The output reflects the variabilities in the path from the point of origin to the destination. Normally in seismic prospecting, the first arrival of the P wave, which is similar to a sound wave and gets reflected and refracted at surfaces of discontinuity is utilised. For reflection, angle of incidence = angle of reflection. In the case of refraction at the border between two adjacent media, sin a/V_1 = sin b/V_2 where a = angle of incidence and b = angle of refraction, V_1 and V_2 being the velocity in the two media. The same formulae are applicable for shear wave. The fundamental difference is that seismic waves carry both compressional and shear stresses at the boundaries of the two media. A compressional seismic wave thus generates not only reflected and refracted compressional waves but also reflected and refracted shear waves. In seismic reflections, a series of waves is thus generated at each surface of discontinuity and internally reflected. This phenomenon is used for contouring deep-seated formations, particularly where beds with greatly differing elasticity are juxtaposed (or superposed). Since the actual velocity of both P and S waves varies from one medium to another, it is necessary to obtain the velocity model of the area by a combination of refraction and wide angle reflection data. In solid mineral deposits, the seismic method is generally used (where thick cover is expected) to determine the depth to bedrock. This is found with the help of shallow seismic reflection survey, assuming standard velocity contrasts for such rocks. One can economise on boreholes to determine bedrock depth and relief beneath alluvial cover using either P or S waves. Even under conditions of shallow water table and thick alluvium over altered bedrock, where only the upper few metres of alluvium are dry, and vertical Electrical Sounding yields misleading information, S waves provide a better contrast than P waves for imaging the bedrock.

The probe capability of conventional geophysical techniques is limited to 100–300 m in crystalline rocks, although mineral deposits having physical contrasts with their wall rocks are found down to depths in excess of 2,000 m; some of these are minable. There lies the present problem. A potential remedy has recently been tested with positive results. This is reflection seismic imaging for exploration of massive sulphide depsits in the Sudbury igneous complex, Canada. Well-tailored and advanced techniques of data acquisition and processing and use of small explosive charges (150–200 gm) placed in water-logged pits for vertical seismic profiling leading to successful extrapolating of subsurface contacts updip from borehole intersections are some of the special features of this experiment (B. Milkereit et al., *Econ. Geol.*, 91, 1996, 829–34; D. Eaton et al., *Econ. Geol.*, 91, 1996, 835–40).

Another emerging geophysical technique is the ground penetrating radar, which can image the subsurface to depths of 15–20 m with a resolution of tens of cm. Such GPR data systems normally use 25, 50, 100 and 200 MHz antennae. These are useful for geochemical and geoenvironmental studies of high definition, e.g. test cells for controlled release of radioactive contaminants.

A recent development is the use of radar for outlining hydraulically conductive fracture zones in hard rocks. The system operates in the frequency range of 20–60 MHz with a resolution of 1–3 m. Downhole use is in three modes: (1) single hole; (2) cross hole reflection; and (3) cross hole tomography. The range of search is approximately 100 m in the single hole mode and 200–300 m in cross hole mode. Cross hole tomography fields outline, just like seismic tomography, radar velocity and attenuation; and agree with seismic cross hole data in targetting shape and location of fracture zones in space. This technology is becoming very important for outlining hard rock zones free from fractures for safe disposal of nuclear waste.

RADIOACTIVE METHOD

Ores of uranium and radium can be located by ground traverses using a Geiger-Muller counter, equipped with meter and earphone, which can simultaneously measure and inform the geologist when he is in proximity of a gamma ray source. Following the Canadian success in the forties, this was used extensively by prospectors in India in the fifties and sixties. Nowadays, airborne gamma ray spectrometry is widely used in reconnaissance of radioactive mineral deposits after suitable calibration and filtering of the aircraft and cosmic components in 3–6 MeV channel. Multichannel logs of the spectra are used to filter out the atmospheric radiation, since it is known that for atmospheric radiation gamma ray counts above the Compton continuance in the low energy ^{214}Bi peak at 0.609 MeV suffers much less attenuation than the ^{214}Bi peak at 176 MeV as compared to radiation from uranium on ground.

No doubt radioactivity can be blanketed by a few metres of solid rock. But in nature, radioactive elements travel from the source both by aqueous transport in solution and by diffusion in gaseous state (radon), resulting in secondary haloes. This is more pronounced along faults and fracture zones. In the Great Bear Lake, Canada, gamma ray count increased so much over a deposit, lying 20 m below the surface, as to endanger the GM counter!

BOREHOLE GEOPHYSICS

Various types of downhole probes have been in use utilising different techniques, e.g. resistivity logging, gamma ray logging, TEM and Pulsed EM surveys, magnetic profiling, etc. In many instances, these have been extremely useful in locating deep-seated ore deposits, e.g. TEM probe in Iberia, Pulse EM probe in the Falconbridge-Lindsley discovery in Sudbury, etc. Special gamma-gamma ratio log (SGG ratio) has been reported to be useful for characterising disseminated lead sulphide deposits at Nova Scotia.

Spontaneous potential (S.P) and resistivity logs can be used as indicators of textural fingerprints among different rock formations intersected in a borehole, Gamma ray logs are useful not only to pick up zones with radioactive material but also phosphatic zones, organic carbon rich layers and weathered zones enriched in hyroxyl-interlayered clay minerals.

Electrical logging is used to determine the resistivity and porosity of the formations through which boreholes are drilled. The conductivity of rocks is not independent of its S planes particularly mineralogical layering. If an electrical current flows into a layered sequence, the surfaces of propagation are not spherical but ellipsoidal, with their axis of revolution lying at right angles to the S-plane. From this asymmetry the direction of dip of the formations can be determined. Borehole surveying is a very powerful tool and was used extensively by the Geological Survey of India for exploration of coal seams and groundwater zones in the sixties. Its potential for defining other types of mineral deposits has remained underutilised in India. Besides electrical conductivity, gamma ray scattering, neutron scattering, natural gamma ray spectroscopy as well as sonic wave propagation have been used to determine the location and type of contrasts within a borehole. The latest technique is nuclear magnetic resonance (NMR), which is usually considered a probe of molecular structure but can also measure the pore geometry in a porous medium, an index of permeability (R.L. Kleinberg, *The Industrial Physicist*, 2(2), 1996, 18–21). The easiest NMR measurement target is hydrogen, since it has the best detectability of any nuclear species at its natural abundance. To make an NMR measurement, protons in fluid are first aligned parallel to a large, steady magnetic field (B_0); then a short pulse of radiofrequency magnetic field turns the protons (H^+) 90° around to the plane orthogonal to B_0. At first, the spins precess in phase in the orthogonal plane, generating a signal of amplitude M_0. As phase coherence is lost, a decay of transverse magnetisation $M(t)$ is observed.

Borehole loggers have to survive under harsh handling and environment. The loggers are generally lowered by stringing several measuring devices, so that the multiple responses can be integrated into a geologically compatible pattern.

GEOTHERMAL METHOD

This is used for delineation of deep-seated (greater than 500 m below) salt domes and other geological bodies with high thermal conductivity. There are two types of measurement: where a borehole has reached thermal equilibrium; and where a temperature transient (due to the presence of formations differing greatly in their ability to transfer heat) is to be defined. The measurements are made either by Maximum Thermometers or Electrical Resistance Thermometers. The well should be probed only after a lapse of a few days after drilling stopped, to allow the heat generated by drilling to dissipate.

The vital questions confronting mineral exploration intropical belt today have been ably summarised by R.E. Smith (*Jour. Geochem. Exploration*, 57, 1996, 159–173, as follows:

(1) What is the geochemical (and other) fingerprint of a concealed ore deposit in deeply weathered terrain? How reliable is this? What media should be sampled? In gold exploration, can the presence of a gold depletion zone in the upper regolith be predicted?

(2) Do ore deposits buried under transported overburden have a surface or near surface geological, geophysical or geochemical expression?

(3) What methods can be used in exploring through younger basin cover?

(4) Can large ore fields (concealed) be distinguished from minor occurrences at the prospecting stage?

In brief, from its early days in the thirties to its explosive growth between the sixties and the eighties, geophysical prospecting has been useful: its promise is all too frequently belied due to inadequate understanding, wrong sequencing of techniques, lack of integration with ground geological and physical features and reliance on mechanical/black box response. Geophysics is a very useful tool in prospecting if it is applied with awareness about possible geological alternatives; it is not a substitute for correct geological studies. This is often forgotten.

FURTHER READING

P. Kearney and M. Brooks. *An Introduction to Geophysical Exploration*, Blackwell Publications, Oxford, 1984, 296pp.

P.V. Sharma. *Geophysical Methods in Geology*. Elsevier, Amsterdam, 1975, 428pp.

M.S. Zhdanov and G.V. Keller. *The Geoelectrical Methods in Geophysical Exploration*. Elsevier, N.Y., 1994, 884pp.

J.C. D'Arnaud Gerkens. *Foundation of Exploration Geophysics*. Elsevier, N.Y., 1989, 668pp.

6

Some Elementary Geostatistical Techniques

Mineral deposits and their host rocks are heterogenous in composition on different scales. When a sample is drawn and analysed or a point observation of a physical property is made, the implicit assumption is that each value is representative of a discrete volume. If the variation of the measured properties from point to point is chaotic, such an assumption becomes invalid. In rock and mineral deposits, chemical and physical variations are non-linear, resulting from superposition of many independent processes. Chemical variation in mineral deposits and their derivatives is found to be scale dependent: the degree of variation is determined, within limits, by the size of the sample drawn. The objective of sampling, be it geochemical prospecting or quality control of the run-of-mine ore or estimation of *in situ* grade of a mineral deposit, is to make observations at selected and suitably spaced locations, so that data will be sufficient to characterise a property at the target location with enough accuracy and reproducibility for the needs of the enquiry. Similar is the implied expectation from a point observation of the value of a geophysical potential field parameter.

It is therefore of utmost importance to understand that such a sampling operation involves four levels of judgement:

1. Selection of site (and volume of sample);
2. Physical preparation of the sample and choice of instruments;
3. Accuracy and precision of the measurements;
4. Extrapolation over a given volume/area of influence (or inversion of data for source characters).

Error at any level distorts the output. Very few campaigns can eliminate the uncertainties inherent in the act of sampling and analysis. Unfortunately, a step-wise presentation of the range of uncertainty is uncommon.

A few illustrations will help comprehension. When a sample is collected or an observation is made on an outcrop or a mine face or a stream bed, it is all but impossible that the chosen sample or site corresponds exactly with all other possible spots available for measurement. It is important to recognise the critical role played by sampling design. If the sampling stations are placed too far apart, the probability of missing a signal or making wrong estimates becomes stronger (Fig. 6.1).

A general precaution is to carry out all sampling and other observations on a regular grid, so aligned that its major dimension follows the strike of the formations with closer measurements across strike. Thus in pedogeochemical sampling over base metal deposits of India, soil samples are collected on lines spaced 10/30/50 m apart with the sample interval at 3/5/10 m along the line.

Deviations from uniformity in a single set comprise a form of 'error'. The larger the volume of the sample, the smaller is the probability of 'error'. But as the sample size increases, so does the operational cost and the added uncertainties of probabilistic sub-samplings (for details vide C.O. Swanson, *Trans. Can. Inst. Min. Met.* 48, 1945, 323–50). The next stage of processing the sample is equally liable to 'errors'. Suppose a 36 kg sample which contains a single 3-mesh (ASTM) grain of molybdenite has been collected in the field, and then powdered. A 2 kg split is then taken out of that lot in the laboratory. It may have no molybdenite or analyse as much as

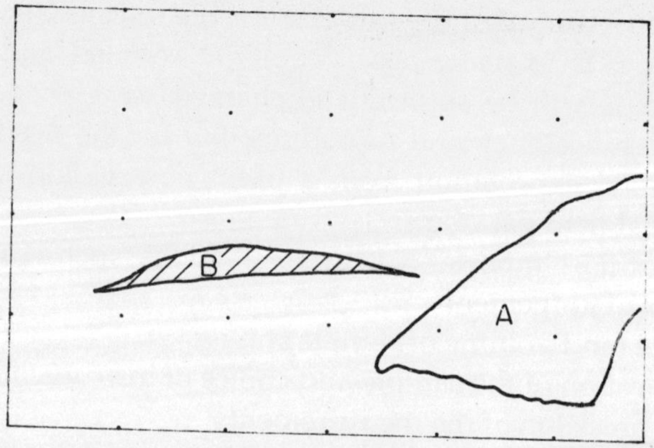

Fig. 6.1: Sampling stations (points) vis-a-vis the size and orientation of the target anomaly. Anomaly B will be missed here. For further details, consult I.D. Savinskii, *Probability Tables for Locating Elliptical Underground Masses with a Rectangular Grid*, Consultants Bureau, N.Y., 1965, 110 p.

400 p.p.m. of Mo (C.O. Ingamells, *Talanta,* 21(2), 1974, 141–55). Even transport of crushed powder in polythene bottles by road/rail from the field to the laboratory creates gravity separation by shaking, if there are heavy and light minerals together and the analyst picks a small sub-sample from the top of the bottle! In fact, a major source of error is the sampling error introduced by the analyst, when he picks up a small portion of the field sample for assay. For example, a 30 gm sample taken for fire assay from a 500 gm crushed field sample, or a 2–3 gm sub-sample taken for X-ray Fluorescence analysis, or a 200 mg sample for Atomic Absorption analysis, or a 5–10 mg sample for Emission Spectrographic analysis from a multi-component, heterogenous (on a microscopic scale) powder, has all the potential for errors. To cite one more example, suppose a 2 kg sample, which has 20 particles of gold, each weighing 0.1 mg, has been collected for gold assay. The correct assay value should be 1 part per million. Suppose the analyst takes a 10 gm sub-sample from this lot from among 200 hypothetical identical looking sample splits. 180 splits will not carry any gold particle; the remaining 20 splits may carry one particle of gold weighing 0.1 mg; or worse, some splits may carry more of it; others none. There is a 90% chance that the analyst will report no gold and 10% chance that the analysis will show 10 p.p.m. of Au! Both results are wrong.

Next in the list is the operational necessity of treating mixed data sets, i.e. combining results for more than one study. The equivalence of chemical analyses and physical measurements obtained with different techniques or from different laboratories using the same techniques is suspect, particularly in the case of trace elements and for low levels of physical contrast. Even in laboratories using geochemical standards, which are very few in the tropical countries of the world, the operational schedules are not consistent.

Geostatistics can not neutralise these 'errors'. What geostatistics can do is to measure the variation within the data set and underline the uncertainty of quantitative estimates.

The aim of geostatistics is to extract the maximum amount of information from the data, using mathematical models for describing the attributes of a population (means, standard deviation), classifying data into similar groups or clusters, exploring the degree of correlation among many variables, and separating signal (non-random) from noise (random). Geostatistical techniques are not a substitute for proper geological, chemical or physical analysis; nor should their mathematical constructs be transposed to support a geological or geophysical model. Geostatistics is today extensively used in the mining industry also.

Shorn of detailed discussions and formulae, we confine our discussion here to elementary applications with very little mathematics, to present the subject to a non-mathematical reader in a general way.

The focus of geostatistics as a predictive tool during geochemical prospecting is somewhat different from its application in sampling and assessment of mineral deposits. In the case of geochemical prospecting, the total variance (S^2) of a set of results is the sum of variance due to:

- sampling error +
- analytical error +
- geological variation +
- secondary processes +
- mineralisation.

One can estimate: (i) the sampling error by study of replicate field samples, (ii) the analytical error by replicate determinations in the laboratory with international standards of similar composition as a reference frame, (iii) the geological variance by determining the background trend across various rock types, and (iv) variance due to secondary processes by comparing between a set of fresh rocks and their residual weathered products; whatever variance is left behind can be attributed to mineralisation. Since the objective is to pick up the signal related to the mineral deposit as against the noise of variance from other sources, appropriate filtering of the data by suitable geostatistical sub-programs enhances the signal.

In contrast, during assessment of the grade of an ore block, the objective is to estimate the nature of distribution of the elements of interest and eliminate:

- sampling error
- analytical error

so that the computations prove reliable.

In the case of orebodies having normal distribution of the ore element(s) with a mean grade and falling percentage of extreme values disposed more or less symmetrically on both the lower and higher ends of the scale, conventional parametric statistics (discussed later) may be used for ore reserve estimation. But deposits of precious metals, tin, tungsten etc., have strongly skewed distribution patterns, where rich zones are many times richer than the lean zones and variation in grade is larger in better-grade zones. Parametric statistics is not the best tool in such cases because of the erratic high values (discussed in Chapter 7).

This distinction among different types of population distribution (Fig. 6.2) is worth remembering for identifying an appropriate geostatistical tool.

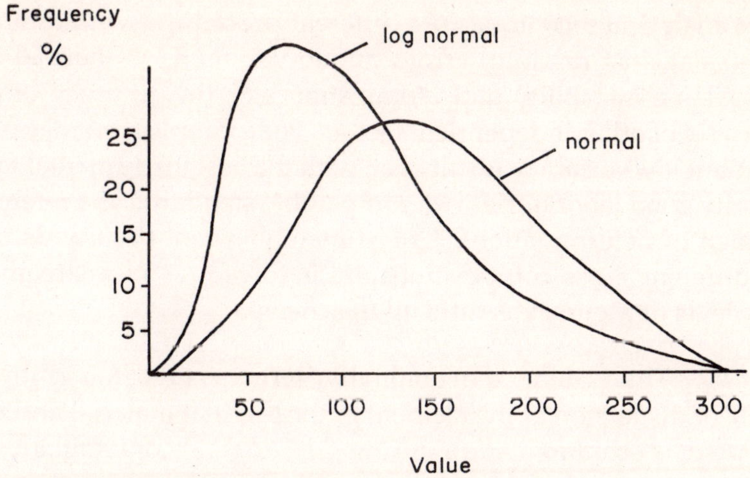

Fig. 6.2: Population distribution curves.

Another aspect which needs careful consideration and reporting in every geostatistical program as well as in all programs of prospecting is the reliability of the values. This is measured by the following three parameters:

(a) Precision: This can be defined as the repeatability of the readings. For example, if the sample is not completely digested, and the concentration of the element is determined by, say Emission Spectrographic technique, the analytical result of the same sample may be different in different runs. The relative precision will also be different for different levels of concentration of the element (A.A. Smales and L.R. Wager (Ed.), *Methods in Geochemistry,* Interscience, N.Y., 1960, 464 pp).

Precision is measured by estimating the coefficients of variation (C.V.) of replicate determinations from the same sample. Plots of C.V. against concentration yield the value of precision, which is expressed as per cent deviation from the mean value. The following formula is used:

$$S = \sqrt{\Sigma(x_o - x_d)^2/2N}$$

where x_o = original result; x_d = duplicate result, N = number of samples.

(b) Accuracy: This is defined as the relation of analytical result for the sample to the true result. The true result is rarely known, but can be estimated with reference to the nominated values of international standards of comparable bulk composition.

Since different analytical techniques use different procedures with different levels of systematic (as against random) errors due to variations in thermal excitation, matrix effects, flame instability and atomization etc., the accuracy of a value is dependent on a set of other independent factors. For example, you may have a very high-precision but low-accuracy result even with the best instrumental facility; this is the reason why good laboratories run comparable standards as a reference frame with every batch of determinations. Unfortunately, where thousands of samples drawn from different gross compositions are involved, as in a stream sediment survey, a high level of accuracy is difficult to achieve.

(c) Reproducibility: This is defined in qualitative terms as high, fair or low, depending on: (1) state of dispersion of the element in the original material and the type of sampling adopted; (2) contamination during grinding; (3) contamination from the reagents used, etc. Factors 2 and 3 vary from one laboratory to another, even if the method of analysis is identical. In large-scale programs involving many laboratories, the difference in analytical results of the same sample from the different sources gives an idea of the reproducibility factor.

Two other important factors of geostatistical relevance are the sensitivity of the technique and the detection limits (both upper and lower). For example, in semi-quantitative, multi-element, Emission Spectrographic technique, the sensitivity of the determination is low as compared to Atomic Absorption techniques due to the fact that variations in particle size and in the chemical and mineralogical composition of the samples play a significant part in the values recorded. The detection limits for many elements of interest in geochemical prospecting are not very satisfactory in standard Emission Spectrographic technique.

SIGNAL RECOGNITION

A geochemical *anomaly* is defined as the value which exceeds the *background* (mean) by 2 standard deviation at the 95 per cent confidence level or 3 standard deviation at the 99 per cent confidence level. Thus the value of $\overline{X} + 2S$, where $\overline{X}$ = regional background and S = standard deviation, will be exceeded by chance 23 times for every 1000 values. A clustering of analytical values exceeding this *threshold* can be considered anomalous.

In their textbook *Geochemistry in Mineral Exploration* (1979, 2/e), Rose, Hawkes and Webb defined a threshold as the concentration value of an indicator element above which a measurement is considered anomalous. In the simplest situation, it is equal to the upper limit of normal background fluctuations. But even there, it is now recognised that anomalous and background data are each characterised by their own probability density functions (A.J. Sinclair, *Jour. Geochem. Expl.* 41, 1991, 1–22).

The concept of a single threshold concentration and a single background value is unreal in field situations; there is a range of background values and of anomalous values for different geological and physiographic sub-domains. The concept of threshold is no longer used in practice, since the interpretative procedure involves multi-parameter pattern recognition.

The fluctuations in space of such geochemical values resemble fractals and multifractals in that on the average, the variability in space of the element under study is independent of scale. Whether you treat the dispersion pattern on microscopic scale or on the scale of metres or kilometres, the property of self-similarity in fluctuation is retained. Fractal models commonly result in power law relations between variables of interest. Such relations plot as straight lines on log-log paper.

The application of the concept of fractals for separation of geochemical anomalies from background values has recently been introduced by Cheng et al. (Q. Cheng, F.P. Agterberg and S.B. Ballantyne, *Jour. Geochem. Exploration,* 51, 1994, 109–30).

Since trace elements are approximately log normal in their distribution, the individual analyses have to be transformed into their $\log_{10}$ values to calculate the background (total sum divided by number of samples) and standard deviation from the $\log_{10}$ transformed values; and these are to be reconverted by anti-log transformation to define the anomalous zones.

By this operation, the non-Gaussian population distribution of trace elements is transformed into a unimodal distribution suitable for parametric tests.

Where calculators and computers are not easily accessible (e.g. in many field camps in developing countries), one can test the distribution pattern by plotting the cumulative frequency on probability paper. The abscissa of the probability paper is on a logarithmic scale where you plot the concentration of the element (col. 1 of Table 6.1) On the ordinate, which is also on a probability scale, you plot the cumulative frequency in per cent (col. 1.6 of Table 6.1). If the plotted line connecting the different points is straight, you have a log normal distribution of the element. The data in Table 6.1 are illustrative.

You can take the value where the line intersects 50% cumulative frequency as average (background), in this case 25 p.p.m. and compute threshold by the intercept

Table 6.1: Calculation of cumulative frequency (Ko, Ko, UNESCO Mineral Resource Dev. Ser. United Nations, New York, 38, 1970, 309–13)

Metal concentration (in p.p.m.)	*Class intervals (in p.p.m.)*	*Number of samples having metal content within this range*	*Frequency %*	*Half frequency %*	*Cumulative frequency*
10	6–15	7	4.8	2.4 2.4	2.4
20	16–25	78	53.4	26.7 26.7	31.5
30	26–35	39	26.7	13.4 13.3	71.6
40	36–45	17	11.7	5.9 5.8	90.8
50	46–55	1	0.7	0.4 0.3	97.0
60	56–65	4	2.7	1.4 1.3	98.7
Total		146	100		100

Table 6.2: Example of arithmetic versus log transformed statistics

	Arithmetic data (p.p.m.)	*Transformed data*	
		Log, p.p.m.	*Antilog, p.p.m.*
Average ($\overline{X}$)	95	1.943	88
Standard Deviation (s)	50	0.204	16
$\overline{X} + 3s$	245	2.555	359

at 84% cumulative frequency, in this case 37 p.p.m. All the higher values are anomalous.

If one ignores the population distribution pattern and computes the mean, standard deviation etc. from the raw data, one may get lost in non-significant values as anomaly targets. This is illustrated in Table 6.2 from F.F. Langford (*Econ. Geol.*, 60, 1965, 360–72).

In this instance, one has to look for anomalies where the concentration is above 359 p.p.m. and *not* where the values are greater than 245 p.p.m. In operational situations, the importance of this essential feature commonly gets overlooked.

PARAMETRIC AND NON-PARAMETRIC TESTS

According to the type of data, statistical methods are divided into two broad types: parametric and non-parametric. Parametric tests assume independent observations from normally distributed populations of similar variance. These are more powerful in their predictive power at any given confidence level; but the snag is that minor and trace elements of a rock body are usually distributed in log normal pattern, because all the constituent minerals in the rock body do not accomodate equal amounts of the target element in their crystal structure.

Non-parametric tests are more relevant to mineral prospecting, since the validity of the tests is not conditional upon an assumption of normal distribution; in fact, in non-parametric tests the form of the distribution need not be known at all.

In geochemical prospecting, the most frequently used tests are parametric univariate and multivariate. Univariate tests are single element programs; multivariate tests examine relationships among several variables at a time. Hence the latter are much more popular in geochemical studies. But in areas without easy access to sophisticated laboratories, even non-parametric multivariate tests like Spearman Rank Correlation Coefficient on mixed parametric and non-parametric data are useful, as illustrated in Table 6.3 for a small, partly chloritised volcanic body, sampled for cold extractable Cu in the field. The first step is to rank the degree of chloritisation in classes 1–5 as follows:

Table 6.3: Classification of Cu content and chloritisation

Chloritisation rank	*Cu p.p.m.*	*Cu rank*	*Rank difference*	*(Difference)^2*
1	20	1	0	0
1	40	3	–2	4
3	30	2	1	1
4	25	1	3	9
5	50	4	1	1
				Total: 15 (Σd_i^2)

rank 1 = free from chlorite;
rank 2 = slightly chloritised;
rank 3 = 30% chloritised;
rank 4 = 50% chloritised;
rank 5 = 100% chloritised.

The boundaries between the classes is subjective.

In its simplest form, the Spearman rank correlation coefficient is given by

$$r_s = 1 \frac{-6\sum_{i=1}^{N} d_i^2}{N^3 - N} = 1 - \frac{6 \times 15}{125 - 5} = 1 - \frac{90}{120} = 0.925$$

Reference to statistical tables would show that a correlation of 0.9 is significant at 95% confidence level for $N = 5$ (p less than 0.05). Since the observed value is higher than this, we can be reasonably confident in expecting a correlation between Cu content in the rock and the degree of chloritisation.

Table 6.3 illustrates how computation is done between qualitative and quantitative observations. One should however avoid making any generalisation if the number of observations is less than 30. Instead of Cu p.p.m., substitute any other parameter, e.g. residual gravity or magnetic anomaly value corresponding to that spot. The only precaution is to ensure that the sampled population (in this case 5) is representative of the target population (infinite number of sub-sets comprising the rock mass). Such scanning type tests are easy to execute, do not require much mathematical prowess and give the prospector a feel of the project area before he gets down to more rigorous parametric tests.

The usefulness of such mixed parametric and non-parametric tests has been largely overlooked. On the other hand, in many modern geochemical survey programs which have easy access to advanced laboratory facilities and computers, an enormous amount of data is collected and processed in a short time.

It is observed that mathematical and statistical processing of a large population of multi-element data have had limited success in locating new orebodies in virgin areas. In contrast, careful processing of precise, diagnostic, bi- or tri-element (mobile-immobile) combinations with back up fingerprinting from fluid inclusions, isotopes etc. have yielded more leads to orebodies. For example, many porphyry copper ore deposits were discovered through strong Cu-Mo association in stream sediments. Not that univariate and multivariate parametric statistics are useless in prospecting. But their essential requirements of unimodal, Gaussian distribution must be satisfied *a priori*.

UNIVARIATE TESTS

Some of the formulae used in univariate tests are given in this section.

(A) Mean

$$\bar{x} = \frac{1}{n} \sum_{i=1}^{n} x_i$$

where x_i are values and n = number of samples.
$n - 1$ = degrees of freedom.

Mean is different from the *median* which separates the upper 50% of a data set. *Mode* is the most abundant value.

(B) Variance

$$s^2 = \frac{1}{n-1} \sum_{i=1}^{n} (x_i - \bar{x})^2$$

Variance is scale-dependent, particularly in ore reserve estimation. The variance of grade from a set of 50 NX sized diamond drill cores of a disseminated sulphide deposit could be appreciably different from grade variance of an equal number of bulk samples, since the volumes of the two sets are different. But once the minimum volume for that type of deposit is exceeded, the variance remains constant (Fig. 6.3). In order to produce estimates with low variance, a common method is to use moving averages, which is an extension of data smoothing. This is done by putting all values of a particular ore zone within a grid (either square or circle), to re-compute the value at the centre of the zone (Fig. 6.4). The count is shifted from one grid to the next till the whole area is covered.

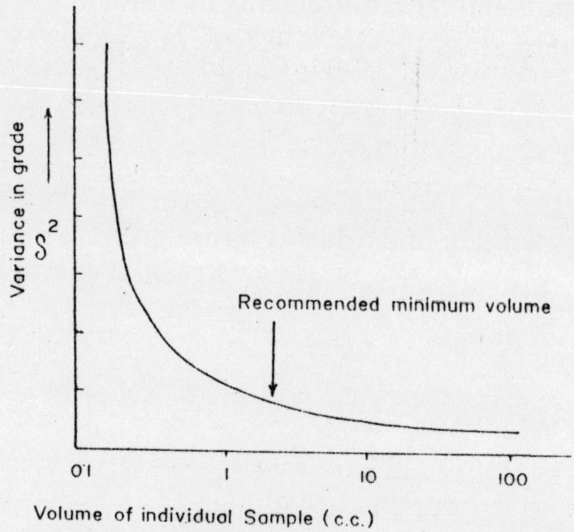

Fig. 6.3: Volume-dependent variance.

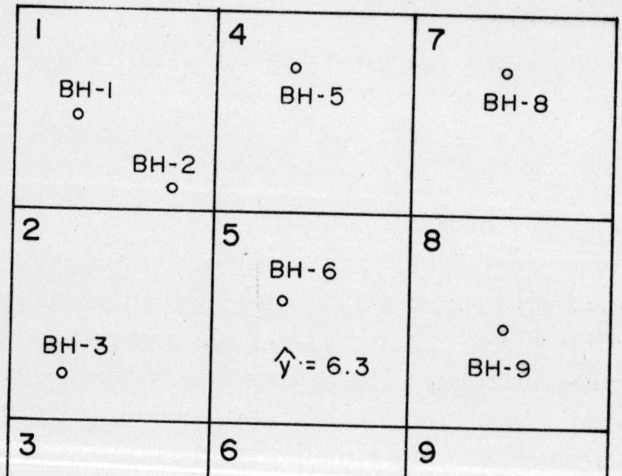

Borehole No	Av. grade (%)
1	9
2	5
3	6
4	2
5	7
6	2
7	8
8	4
9	5
10	9

Fig. 6.4: Moving average method of computation of a variable like the grade of an orebody interesected in irregularly spaced boreholes.

(C) Standard Deviation

$$s = \sqrt{s^2} = \left(\sum_{i=1}^{n} (x_i - \overline{x})^2 / n - 1 \right)^{1/2}$$

(D) Standard Error

The distribution around $\overline{x}$ can be shown to be normal with a dispersion S_e, called the Standard Error, calculated by the formula

$$S_e = \left(\frac{s^2}{n} \right)^{1/2}.$$

(E) F- and t-tests

Whether two sets of data are drawn from the same population or whether these reflect different populations can be found out by using the F-test and the t-test. The F-test measures the divergence in variance.

$F = \frac{s_1^2}{s_2^2}$ s_1^2 being greater than s_2^2; s_1^2 and s_2^2 being the statistical estimates of the variance of the two sets of data, n and m. Their degrees of freedom are $n-1$ and $m-1$. Critical values of F distribution (F_c) for the appropriate degrees of freedom at 95 per cent confidence level are available in standard statistical tables.

For example, suppose samples have been drawn from two plots. 30 samples from plot 1 yield $s^2 = 0.66$, whereas 65 samples from plot 2 yield $s^2 = 0.896$; since s^2 for plot 2 is greater than that of plot 1, one has to put 0.896 as numerator and 0.66 as denominator; the F value becomes $0.896/0.66 = 1.356$. Now look up the Table for F_c for a 5% significance level in a standard statistical table for 64 degrees of freedom of the numerator and 29 degrees of freedom of the denominator to find out whether the value of 1.356 is less than the prescribed F_c. If it is, the two data sets come from the same population.

After it is established that the variances of the two populations are equal, they may still belong to different populations if their means are different beyond a limit. The Student t-test is carried out to check this point.

For log normal distributions:

$$t = \frac{\overline{\log x} - \overline{\log y}}{\left(\dfrac{s_x^2}{n_1} + \dfrac{s_y^2}{n_2}\right)^{1/2}}$$

where $\overline{\log x}$ and $\overline{\log y}$ are the arithmetic means of the logarithms of the values for populations x and y, s_x^2 and s_y^2 are the variances of the two populations and the degrees of freedom are $n_1 + n_2 - 2$.

Consult the statistical table for Student t-test for 95 per cent confidence level and the appropriate number of degrees of freedom for verification or rejection of the 'null hypothesis'.

(F) Class Intervals in Histograms

These should generally be in the range of one fourth to half of standard deviation(s) and should include the mean ($\overline{x}$) value as a limiting value of one of the class intervals. Therefore the best way to prepare the class intervals is to adopt the following procedure:

$\overline{x} - 1/2s$ to $\overline{x} - 1/4s$, $\overline{x} - 1/4s$ to $\overline{x}$, $\overline{x}$ to $\overline{x} + 1/4s$ and so on.

(G) Confidence Limits

These are calculated from the product S_e multiplied by $t_{0\cdot05}\,(n-1)$ at 95% confidence level. Consult the standard t tables for the corresponding value. For example, in a set of 202 values, whose $\overline{x}$ is 105 and s = 125, the confidence limit is 105 ± $\sqrt{125^2/202}$ multiplied by $t_{0\cdot05}(202-1) = 105 \pm 8.8 \times 1.96 = 105 \pm 17.3$.

Therefore at 95% confidence level, the limiting values are 97.7 and 122.3.

In all measurements, e.g. computation of grade of an orebody, the confidence limit of the estimate should be clearly stated.

(H) Co-variance

In any data set, be it magnetic or gravity values, stream sediment analysis, channel sample compositions from an orebody or offshore wave spectra, a part of the variables is dependent on local patterns and the other part on larger regional patterns. In a spatial context, this can be portrayed as a co-variogram.

The formula is as follows:

$$C\,(x_i\,,\, x_i + jk) = \frac{1}{P-1} \sum_{i=1}^{n} (x_i - \overline{x})\,(x_{i+jk} - \overline{x})$$

where n = number of samples/observations/values

x_i = i th data

k = sample interval in space

j = 1,2,3...n

P = number of pairs used in the summation.

A special use of this study is that effects of local (s_e^2) and regional (s_r^2) variance at the sample site can be estimated; thus the impact of the local vs the regional pattern becomes clear.

Kriging

In the course of exploration by drilling, a commonly used technique to ascertain the adequacy or otherwise of sampling points is kriging—named after the noted S. African mining geologist D.G. Krige—who used the theory of regionalised variables. Briefly, the general argument runs somewhat like this: There are some variables like topographic surface, grade of an orebody etc., which change from one place to another in such a way that the value at any given point is related to the value at points some distance away in such a manner that the influence of nearby points is stronger than of points located at greater distance. This apparent continuity

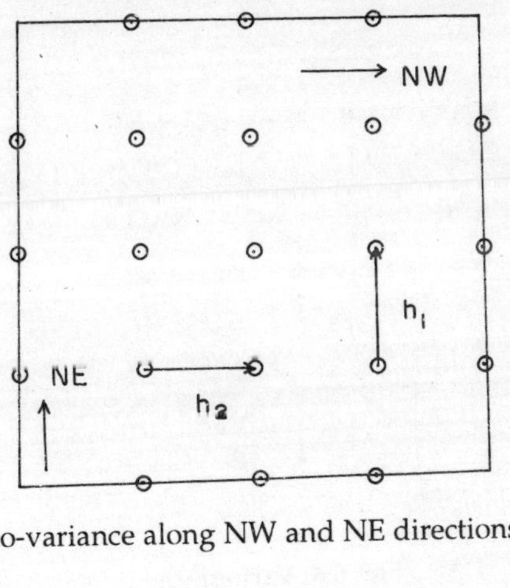

Fig. 6.5: Variable measure of co-variance along NW and NE directions in a bauxite deposit (h = drill interval; h_1 and h_2 are vectors).

cannot however be represented by an ordinary function. The relationship can be defined as a vector of distance h with specific orientation in space. Thus h in a NE-SW direction may not have the same value as h in the NW-SE direction (Fig. 6.5). The degree of relationship between points a fixed distance apart along the stated direction is expressed as a measure of covariance. For example, if ten boreholes have been drilled 50 m apart, and the thickness × grade is constant, then $K_h = s_y^2$, where y = thickness × grade and h = 50 m. As the vector distance h becomes infinitesimally short, the variance s_y^2 and covariance K_h are defined by essentially the same points.

Conversely, as the vector distance h becomes larger, K_h will decrease because of greater independence between points farther apart. These relationships are shown in a variogram (Fig. 6.6).

With the help of variograms, the range of influence from point intersections can be computed; and reserves can be calculated by Block Kriging. In the Hutti Mines, variogram parameters of the strike auriferous reef show that the optimum influence in a line of samples is about 44 m (R.N. Mishra, *Rec. Geol. Surv. Ind.*, 120 (2–8), 1995, 100–108).

In the case of variograms, the mean $(\bar{x})$, standard deviation $(\bar{S})$ and relative standard deviation $(S/\bar{x})$ are computed for a variable for varying density of observations, like the data set given in Table 6.4.

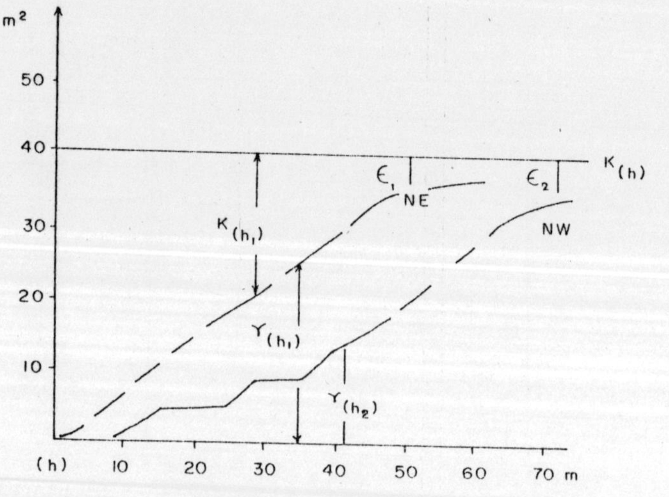

Fig. 6.6: Variogram.

Table 6.4: Grids of increasing density (after Bardossy and Bardossy 1984)

Bauxite Deposit No. II		*No. of observation points*	*Mean* ($\bar{x}$)	*Standard deviation* (*S*)	*Relative Standard Dev.* ($S/\bar{x}$)
	A. Hanging Wall Elevation above mean sea level (in m)	33	349.0	7.6	0.022
		125	348.9	7.7	0.022
		319	347.7	7.9	0.023
	B. Thickness of the deposit	33	16.9	11.8	0.698
		125	17.4	13.3	0.764
		319	19.7	12.5	0.635

It will be noted that the relative standard deviation for the hanging wall elevation is quite small suggesting a broad regularity in its position in space. But an extremely high relative standard deviation for the thickness in Table 6.4 is an unfavourable factor hinting at a large uncertainty in the reserve calculation.

MULTIVARIATE TESTS

Univariate methods miss anomalous zones where interaction among several variables is the distinctive feature of the signal. For such situations, multivariate tests are recommended.

(A) Element Associations and Ratios

This is the best technique for enhancing latent patterns of mineralisation and has already been discussed in the Chapter on Geochemical Prospecting. A Ni/Cu plot may point clearly to zones of sulphide mineralisation whereas a Ni + Cr + Co plot over a flat, soil-covered area may clearly delimit the underlying ultramafic body.

(B) Correlation Coefficient

This is given by the statistics r_{xy}, where r measures the degree of correlation between variables x and y. It measures the overall constancy of element ratios in a population. In actual practice, many variables can be studied together; and computer algorithms are available for generating such matrices.

Even where access to computers is not possible, the correlation coefficient between 2 elements can be manually estimated by the following formula:

$$r_{xy} = \frac{1}{(n - 1)\ s_x\ s_y} \sum_{i=1}^{n} (x_i - \bar{x})\ (y_i - \bar{y})$$

where n = number of samples, s = standard deviation and $\bar{x}$ and $\bar{y}$ are means of log transformed values.

The significance of the value is tested by the Student t criterion

$$t_{xy} = \frac{(r_{xy})\ \sqrt{n-2}}{(1 - r_{xy}^2)^{1/2}} \text{ for } n - 2 \text{ degrees of freedom.}$$

The values of correlation coefficient are seriously affected by: (1) erroneous or anomalous data values, both too high and too low; (2) multiple population mixture in the data set; (3) a low number of determinations; and (4) log transformation. The elements should be normally distributed; and the number of samples should at least be 10 times the number of elements/variables.

A strong correlation between pathfinder element pairs like Cu and Ni or Pb and Mn may be a pointer to mineralised zones.

(C) Regression Equation

The simplest application of regression equation is to describe the relationship between two linearly correlated variables, like Ni and Co in an ultramafic saprolite by the equation of the form $y = a + b.x$ where a is the intercept and b the tangent of the slope making an angle θ (Fig. 6.7). In actual fact, there is always an error term e,

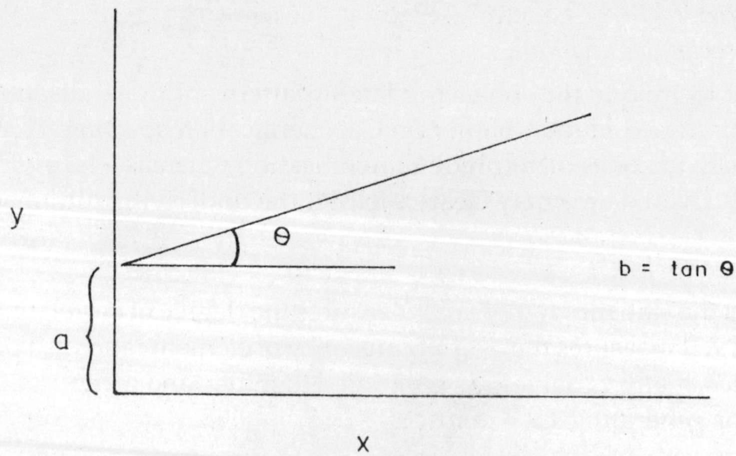

Fig. 6.7: Line of best fit.

so the equation becomes $y = a + b.x + e$. Computer algorithms are easily avilable for applying the standard technique of 'least squares fitting', whereby the line of best fit is drawn through the scattered data points in such a way that the sum of the squares of the deviations of all the data points from the line is a minimum.

The uncertainty of the correlation by regression equation can be represented by calculating the Standard Error of Estimate

$$S_y = s_y \sqrt{1 - r^2}$$

$$S_x = s_x \sqrt{1 - r^2}$$

where r is the correlation coefficient.

Unlike simple correlation between two variables like Ni and Co in a saprolite, there may be situations where the variables cannot be fitted by a straight line. In such cases, a quadratic polynomial of the form $y = a + b_1x + b_2 x^2 + e_2$ or a cubic polynomial $y = a + b_1x + b_2x^2 + b_3x_3 + e_3$ may show the best fit.

(D) Trend Surface Analysis

When one wants to find out whether the distribution of a variable in space is that of a plane or approximates a more complex mathematical surface, so that the trend of the data is unravelled, one utilises the technique of trend surface analysis. Curve fitting for regional and residual components in a potential field data set exemplifies the practical utility of this technique. The basic approach is again to use the least squares method for finding the coefficients of the polynomial.

$$X = a + bx + cy + dxy + ex^2 + fy^2 + gxy^2 + hx^2y + \ldots$$

where X is the dependent variable and x and y are the coordinates in the map frame. A computer is needed for this type of work. It should also be borne in mind that trend surfaces are mathematical constructs whose relevance depends upon assumptions that: (a) the geological set up can be described by a polynomial function, and (b) the data are unimodal and Gaussian in distribution. Where more than one type of rock or sediment are involved, this method is inappropriate. The trend model is rigid; to choose the right polynomial is difficult.

A much simpler method is to use the Moving Average Analysis. This is useful for smoothening the data and observing the regional variation across an area. The method is similar to contouring an equal area hemisphere projection of structural data. A search area of a given size (in the form of a square or rectangle) is moved across the map and the mean $\bar{x}$ of the values falling within the block is plotted at the centre. Before the popularisation of computer plots, this was a favourite tool among geochemists. The values along the edges of the map are not counted. The raw data have to be converted by log transform before computing $\bar{x}$ for each block.

(E) Discriminant Function Analysis

This technique is useful to discriminate between two sets of similar looking samples which have contrasting geochemical attributes; for example, if you come across a set of outcrops looking like gossan over an ultramafic suite carrying sulphide lodes, which could alternatively be pseudo-gossan, you can use this technique by using a discriminant function of the form:

$$D = a\,\mathrm{Cu} + b\,\mathrm{Co} + c\,\mathrm{Ni} + d\,\mathrm{Zn} + e\,\mathrm{MgO} + f\,\mathrm{CaO}$$

where the element values (Cu, Co, Ni) are the variables and the co-efficients are the weights (*a*, *b*, *c*) assigned to each variable. A simple way would be to conduct an F-test first to eliminate the non-significant variables and then carry out the discriminant function analysis on the significant variables only.

Here again a computer is needed to carry out the complex mathematical calculations on a large set of analytical data. *D* scores forming each population will have a minimum spread, i.e. variance and a maximum separation of means (Fig. 6.8).

(F) Cluster Analysis

This is a technique used for taxonomic classification. There are two methods:

(1) data correlated by comparing samples (termed the Q mode);

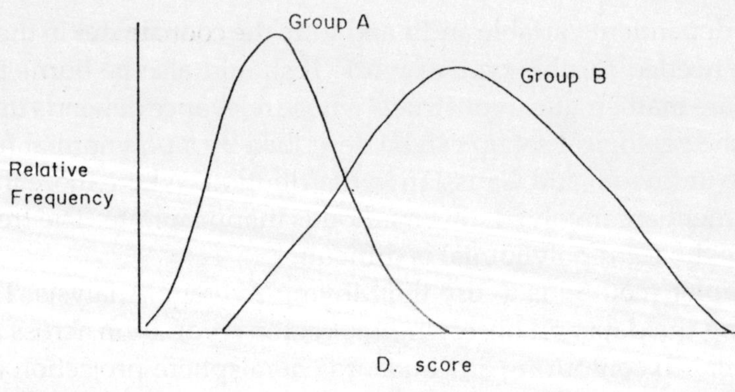

Fig. 6.8: Discriminant Function Analysis for separation between two sets of samples belonging to different populations.

(2) data correlated by comparing variables (R mode).

Many of the classical multivariate procedures require population homogenity, and often the data have to be multivatiate-normally distributed. If the data structure is not known *a priori*, cluster analysis can be used to evaluate the data. Two types of clustering are used: (1) Hierarchical techniques for taxonomic studies; and (2). Ititerative partitioning techniques to group the data into a number of clusters. K-means clustering is the technique commonly adopted. But such hard cluster methods are inapplicable for stream sediment or partly residual soil aggregates where the samples represent a mixture of components derived from different geological milieux. In such cases, Fuzzy-c-means (FCM) clustering is preferable. Suitable algorithms are available in C.J. Bezdek et al., (*Computer Geoscience*, 10, 1984, 191–203).

Q-mode analysis is used in sedimentary facies studies; its use in geochemical prospecting is constrained by the fact that it can handle a limited number of samples using qualitative attributes on a binary nominal scale (present, absent). Dendrograms showing the main groupings and their inter-relationship against a scale of levels of association (Fig. 6.9) could bring out distinction between mineralised and barren samples if the distinctions on the basis of nominal attributes (e.g. colour, iron staining, etc.) are significant as shown in Table 6.5. But generally a good field geologist can and does implicitly (and subjectively) separate two groups of samples on such a nominal basis, when he maps a prospect. This technique is widely used in behavioural sciences.

Where quantitative data (e.g. chemical analysis of elements) are involved, R-mode clustering procedure is used with a large number of multi-element data. Data are first transformed to normal distribution, and the relationship between variables is expressed in a number of factors, which is less than the number of variables, each factor successively accounting for a diminishing per cent of the total variance of the data.

One needs a computer for this calculation. Programs are available in many formats. The characteristic roots (known as eigenvalues) of the correlation matrix are computed by the standard method of matrix algebra. The sum of the eigenvalues equals the number of variables. The number of non-zero eigenvalues determines the number of factors in the multi-element data set. A mathematical process known as Varimax rotation is then applied. This rotates the orthogonal axes about the origin so that the variance of the loadings on each factor is a minimum, while the variance between factors is at their maximum. This is then followed by Promax oblique

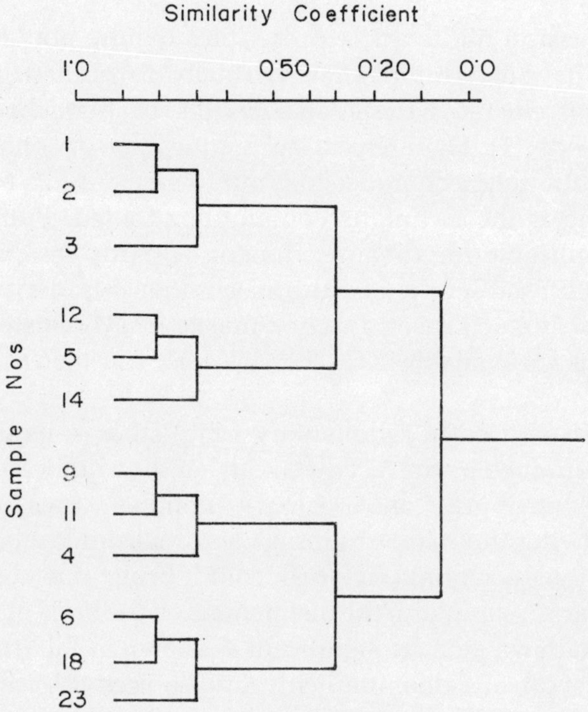

Fig. 6.9: Dendrogram.

rotation to get a matrix of Promax factor loadings of each element vs. factor. The last step involves computation of factor scores for each sample.

Factor analysis places variables (elements) of similar distribution into groups. R-mode factor analysis is used extensively in stream sediment survey. At the reconnaissance stage where the sample number is large and multi-element (30) determinations for such samples are routine, a large data set is generated. Normally a single site would yield one sediment and one heavy mineral sample; in turn the sediment sample would be split into different size fractions depending on the set up and the heavy mineral concentrate would yield 3 sub-samples representing strongly magnetic, poorly magnetic and non-magnetic fractions. Strictly speaking, this process itself creates a multiple population assemblage in both the groups. The data have to be normalised by log transformation. Another problem is poor precision and undefined values in semi-quantitative determination of many ele-

Table 6.5: Q-mode cluster analysis of visible attributes of mineralised vs. barren quartzites in Rakha Mines, Bihar

	Shearing	*Malachite stain*	*Tourmaline*	*Quartz veins*	*Kyanite*	*Fossils*	*Weathering*
Sample 1	1	1	1	1	0	0	1
Sample 2	1	0	0	1	1	0	0
Match	p	m	m	p	m	n	m

Positive matches (p) are (1,1)
Negative matches (n) are (0,0)
Mismatches (m) are (0,1)

ments by optical emission spectrograph. A large number of determinations fall either below or beyond the limits of detection. This happens commonly for many pathfinder elements (e.g. Sn, W, As, Ag).

In areas with thick overburden, factor analysis of stream sediments has been reported to be useful. For example, where there are very high (greater than 0.50) positive factor loadings among Ba, Be, La, Pb, Sr, Y and Zr, one can suspect a source granitic association. Likewise, high factor loadings among Fe, Mg, Ti, Co, Cr, Cu, Ni, Sc and V would indicate mafic association. A problem is faced where associations are ambiguous. For example, where there are high positive loadings for Mn, Co, Y and Zn, these could mean either a disseminated sulphide deposit signal or simply a barren but high Mn background area in which Co and Zn are adsorbed on the surfaces of sediment grains. Factor analysis of heavy mineral concentrates is more revealing and unambiguous. For example, a factor with high positive loading for Fe, Co, Cu and Ni indicates, in suitable cases, the presence of pyrite and chalcopyrite possibly with some pyrrhotite/pentlandite in the samples.

DATA HANDLING AND PRESENTATION

In both geochemical and geophysical surveys, a vast mass of data is normally generated. The need for computers in data management and storage has been long recognised. Large grid areas can be plotted on maps typically with thousands of point data. Options for computer contouring are available. Various types of frequency histograms can be generated for critical scanning. Besides point symbol plots, grey scale methods, coloured cell techniques etc. can be adopted. Plots based on moving average or universal kriging methods, which help in the study of local geochemical peculiarities in detail in the context of regional attributes, can be generated. Moreover, the use of advanced computer graphics techniques, such as image analysis systems makes it possible to analyse and integrate different parameters of a system interactively, combining geochemical, geophysical and other data output (P.M. Green, *Jour. Geol. Soc. Lond.*, 141, 1984, 941–9). The Hunting Geology and Geophysics Limited *(Computer Correlation of Geological, Geochemical and Geophysical Prospecting Data with Enhanced Satellite Imagery for the North and South Pennine Orefields, U.K.*, 2 vols, Elstree, Hertz, 1983, 345pp.) used this combined approach very successfully in the east Midlands of England to generate maps for locating buried epigenetic, MVT Pb-F-Zn-Ba deposits. Negative Bouguer gravity and heat flow anomalies (indicative of concealed granite), seismic refraction and borehole data (to identify sedimentary basins and limestone cover over basement blocks), shadow plots of aeromagnetic data and second derivative gravity maps (to pick up basement and shallow lineament systems) and geochemical data (indicative of shales with trace element rich organic carbonate) were merged in the way oil companies search for hydrocarbon pools. It was found that the integrated approach provided a much more forceful exploration lead than simple indicators based on primary data statistic.

With the availability of low cost, microcomputer-based image analysis systems and various types of computer graphics, it is likely that future discoveries will come largely from such integrated models, where the framework of mineral deposit models and their special features are structured into the composite images.

Models that spell out the appropriate host rock and structural milieu, favourable rock-fluid interaction indicators, optimum environment of dispersion of the target elements in different sampling media, diagnostic types of geophysical response, surface geomorphological habitat etc. will provide the input for such multi-parametric groupings. Image analysis systems will progressively come into their own as the isolated accidents of ore discovery become more and more rare in the decades ahead. The recognition of possible exploration targets will increasingly require combining and screening large numbers of geological, geochemical and geophysical indicators according to different metallogenic models.

A tentative attempt was initiated in the Geological Survey of India in the early seventies but was discontinued within a decade.

In all such approaches, it is essential to bear in mind that point values in space, whether geochemical or geophysical, include a signal and a noise. If the precision and accuracy of the values are poor, no amount of processing will clear the noise.

Similarly, if the interval between two points of measurement exceeds the boundary of domain homogeneity, contouring will be misleading. It would be like drawing a straight contour connecting one hill slope with its counterpart on the other side ignoring a steep valley in between! Limits and error margins of extrapolations should be kept in view.

FURTHER READING

John C. Davis, *Statistics and Data Analysis in Geology*, John Wiley & Sons, New York, 1973, 550 pp.

G.S. Koch, Jr. and R.F. Link, *Statistical Analysis in the Geological Sciences*, John Wiley & Sons, New York, 1971, 483 pp.

I. Nichol, R.G. Garrett and J.S. Webb, The role of some statistical and mathematical methods in the interpretation of regional geochemical data, *Economic Geology*, 64, 1969, 204–20.

S. Siegel, *Nonparameteric Statistics for the Behavioural Sciences*, McGraw-Hill, Tokyo, International Student Edition, 1956, 312 pp.

S.L. Bolivar, K. Campbell and G.W. Wecksung, R-mode factor analysis applied to uranium exploration in the Montrose quadrangle, Colorado, *Jour. Geochem. Exploration*, 19, 1983, 723–43.

R.J. Howarth (Ed.), *Statistics and Data Analysis in Geochemical Prospecting: Handbook of Exploration Geochemistry*, Vol. 2, G.J.S. Govett (Ed.), Elsevier, Amsterdam, 1983, 438 pp.

A. Bardossy and Gy. Bardossy, Comparison of geostatistical calculations with the results of open pit mining at the Iharkut Bauxite District, Hungary: A case study, *Mathematical Geology*, 16, no. 2, 1984, 173–91.

A.G. Journel and Ch. J. Huijbregts, *Mining Geostatistics*, Academic Press, London, 1978, 600 pp.

M. David, *Handbook of Applied Advanced Geostatistical Ore Reserve Estimation*, Developments in Geo-Mathematics, Vol. 6, Elsevier, New York, 1988, 232 pp.

7

Preliminary Exploration

There is an informal distinction between prospecting and exploration. Prospecting is the stage of search for a mineral deposit; exploration is the stage of its appraisal by systematic measurements. Usually, the two stages follow each other with some overlap. But there are many instances where prospecting is immediately followed by exploitation. This can happen under a variety of situations e.g. where a mineral deposit cannot be evaluated by systematic measurements in advance of actual mining. D.H. McLaughlin (*Econ. Geol.*, 34, 1939, 589–621) had proposed classification of mineral deposits into three types: Plenemensurate, Partimensurate and Extramensurate 'according to the assurance of ore supply that they are ordinarily capable of providing with the amount of exploration that is customary in good current practice'.

Plenemensurate deposits are those which are amenable to full measurements regarding grade and tonnage at an early stage of the operations.

Partimensurate deposits are those which remain partly indeterminate until the later stage of the mines.

Extramensurate deposits are those whose grade and tonnage cannot be measured much in advance of mining and in which the value of the deposit in the ground based on geological judgement exceeds the value of proved reserves throughout most of the life of the workings.

Plenemensurate deposits have well defined lateral extent, thickness and grade variations and top and bottom configuration. A stratiform sulphide deposit like the Amjhore Pyrites bed within the Bijaigarh Shale of the Proterozoic Vindhyan System in Sahabad district, Bihar is a good example.

Fig. 7.1: Relicts of an uplifted planation surface, Saladipura, Rajasthan.

Partimensurate deposits form the most common type. The deposit is likely to extend much farther or deeper than the limit of the openings available at the stage of early development or is likely to be associated with new deposits, which might lie concealed or unexplored (Fig. 7.1). Such expectations must be based on sound geological arguments. For example, the Sukinda chromite deposits in Cuttack and Dhenkanal districts, Orissa are mostly exposed and developed along the south limb of the westerly plunging synform. The orebodies in the north limb lying concealed beneath laterite and colluvium have only been partly opened up.

Extramensurate deposits are the most difficult to evaluate. Depending on market conditions or underground indications, the spectre of mining activity coming to a close haunts the investor now and then, although some of these mines may enjoy a long productive life with new discoveries of other economic minerals. For example, the Bihar mica field has been producing ruby block mica for more than a century, since the founding of thc Chrestien Mining Company in the Kodarma Reserve Forest in 1870. Workings at some places, e.g. Setwa, have reached more than 120 m in vertical depth. But neither Raj Krishna Sahana, one of the Indian pioneers of mica mining in 1880, nor his descendants had the benefit of proven reserve underpinning their investment at any time. The recent discovery of gemstones gives a new lease of life to mining activity in this field.

At an early stage of prospecting, you should attempt to pigeon-hole the deposit in the McLaughlin scheme so that the scale of investment in mine development can be tuned to the confidence level of the estimate. No corporate manager will spend more than 1% of the ground value of a deposit to find out its *in situ* grade and tonnage. If the deposit is such that it cannot be measured with an acceptable level of reliability (see Chapter 6) before mine development, this must be explained to the management.

There are situations or circumstances where exploration and mine development have to overlap. These include:

(a) High grade extramensurate deposits of strategic and critical minerals.

(b) Deposits in areas where the political situation is so volatile that no long-term investment is wise; quick mine development and mineral extraction is the only option.

(c) Cases where funds are very limited, but markets for the mineral are buoyant.

Under such conditions, it is common to merge exploration with exploitation of the deposit during the early stages. The geological framework of the deposit, i.e., its strike and dip, extent, wall rock and faults should be delineated as far as possible by surface studies. For example, if the dip of a deposit is towards the south and if open cast operations are planned here, the dump of wall rock must be placed far away (Fig 7.2) so that you need not move it again with deepening of the pit. If you pile up the dump on the hanging wall side to the south, you will have to spend extra money to remove it when you deepen the pit. A clear delineation of the major structure of the deposit and the position of hanging wall and footwall are essential before excavating a mineral deposit. There is no substitute for correct measurement of strike and dip of a mineral deposit. The mining geologist who ignores this simple rule, lands not only himself but his company into trouble.

(d) Instances where short-term gains prompt exploitation without proper appraisal.

This happened in India and many other countries before their independence and may happen again under the glib garb of globalisation. Many better grade and shallow deposits have been selectively mined out, leaving large blocks of lower grade material untapped and making their extraction at a later date more problematic (Fig. 7.3).

Under normal circumstances, the amount of money spent on prospecting and exploration should not exceed one per cent of the present value of the deposit (see

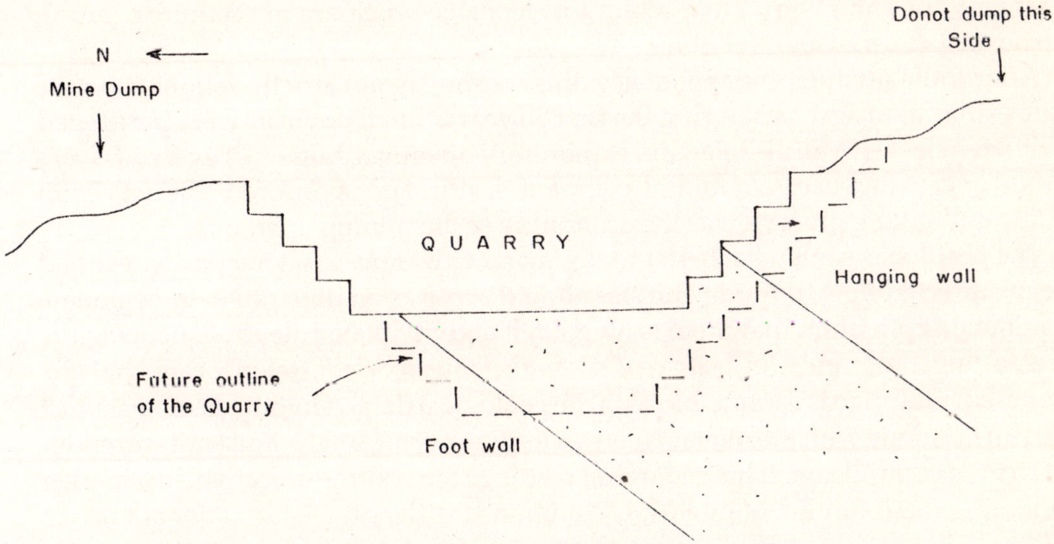

Fig. 7.2: Cross-sectional view of a quarry.

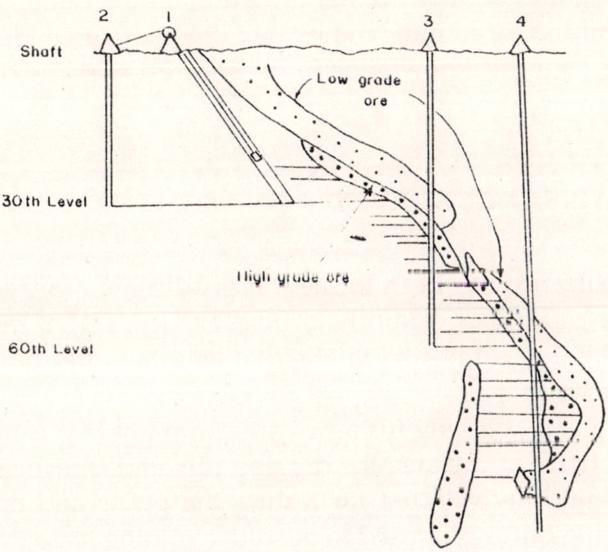

Fig. 7.3: Consequential problems of selective mining of high-grade ore. Once the mine is abandoned, the large low-grade orebodies on the hanging wall side become technically and financially unattractive.

Chapter 9 for valuation). Prospecting for deposits which are not required during the next 30 years is not advisable.

After India attained Independence, this norm was not strictly followed by the state exploration agencies during the first 30 years. Small deposits were perforated at different levels by drill-holes and exploratory openings; huge cost overruns were passed over to the successor mining companies, also state-sponsored. The net victim of this unthinking practice was the economics of the mining operation.

The position is somewhat better today, market awareness having partly rectified the misdirected flow of funds. But this should serve as an illustration to beginners in mineral exploration that there is no golden and inviolate rule of sequencing the prospecting program. *Cut your coat according to your cloth,* taking care that the proposed mine plan is compatible with the geological data. A mining geologist must work in harmony with the management as long as he can; but he must not surrender to forces of compulsion, if his geological readings are contra-indicative. In a market economy, where conflict of interest is common at different levels: national interest vs corporate interest or corporate interest vs group interest, or group interest vs individual interest, it is difficult to formulate a general rule of conduct for all. But the exploration geologist should continuously communicate to the management the imperative need for gathering essential information on the mineral deposit before a large sum is committed for mining and related downstream endeavours.

How should one gain this knowledge in the shortest possible time and at least cost?

STEP 1: RECONNAISSANCE SURVEY

Once a mineral occurrence has been located, it is advisable to trace its extent on ground along strike and dip as carefully as possible. In most of the cases, neither the total width of the deposit nor its total strike length would be visible without some pitting or trenching.

Where the geologist is working for a private company, it is essential to have a prospecting licence (P.L.) of the area for digging pits and trenches, so that representative samples could be collected for testing the grade and other characters; where the material dug out is proposed to be sold, a mining lease (M.L.) of the area is necessary. Similarly, if preliminary exploration requires pits deeper than 6 meters, a qualified mining engineer/overseer is needed, according to Indian law, to help in the operation. Read the updated MMRD Act, the labour laws, etc. including the fine

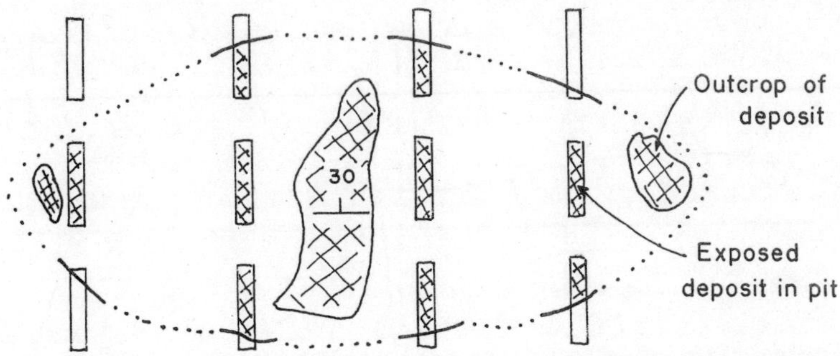

Fig. 7.4: Design of small trenches across a shallow deposit for proper definition of outline and grade.

print. If accidents, like wall collapse or physical injuries take place in the course of digging, the management is held accountable. It is not advisable to overstep or short-circuit the operations for limited gains—a common enough practice among small mine operators.

The other point to check at the beginning is environmental and security clearance (for storing explosives in properly constructed magazines). Sanctions from state governments have to be arranged for felling trees, making access roads (wherever required) and for other essentials like tapping water sources, police pickets for protecting the camps from hostile groups etc. It is better to evaluate possible problems at the reconnaissance stage itself.

For defining the sub-outcropping extension of a deposit, it is cheaper to sink small pits end-on at intervals across the strike of the deposit in the covered areas (Fig. 7.4). On the other hand, where a complete evaluation of grade and minable width is needed, a number of trenches may be dug across the strike from the hanging wall to the footwall of the deposit and as far down as necessary to expose completely fresh material. It is advisable to draw channel samples of appropriate width from the side walls of the trenches. Where the deposit shows pinch and swell, channel sampling should be done on both the walls separately. The uniformity or disparity would provide a rapid glimpse into the extent of grade fluctuation of the deposit. If the width and grade of the deposit on opposite walls do not match in many of the pits, this may suggest an extramensurate or partimensurate deposit. The reverse is not always true, unless a large number of pits covering the whole deposit have been dug, sampled and analysed.

It is essential to prepare detailed sketches of the walls of the excavations on 1:100 scale with special reference to the disposition of the mineralised patches, the dip of the wall rocks, the depth of weathering (or soil cover) and other significant features as well as the locations of the samples.

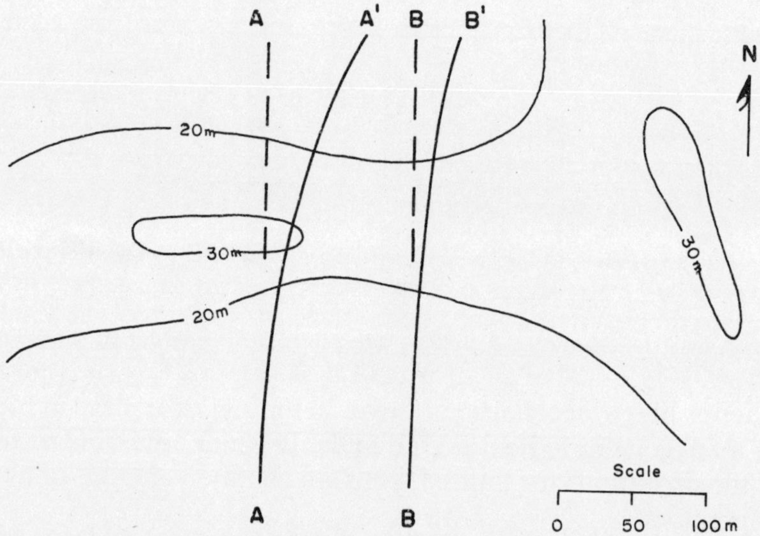

Fig. 7.5: Illustrative errors in open-ended survey by prismatic compass and tape. Due to thick forest cover in an undulating terrain, lines A-A and B-B actually veered into lines A–A′ and B-B′. The errors would have escaped notice but for a subsequent closed traverse triangulation.

STEP 2: LARGE-SCALE MAPPING

If initial findings from pitting are promising it may be necessary to take up large-scale survey of the exposed mineral deposit within the leasehold. This is done normally on scale 1:1000 to 1:2000 with a plane table, stadia, ranging rods and a telescopic alidade or theodolite. Detailed procedures for such a survey are given in Lahee's text book on *Field Geology* (1961). For quick operation over a small undulating prospect, pace and compass or tape and prismatic compass survey provides a first approximation; but without prior triangulation of the end points, open lines laid with prismatic compass get slightly curved on uneven ground (Fig. 7.5).

The Survey of India topographic sheet is very useful to locate a benchmark and other identifiable points near the prospect. In India, many of the topo-sheets are still restricted documents. The best course in such a situation is to draw the level from the nearest benchmark and prepare a topographic map of the prospect on a 1:1000 scale by triangulation. Exposures of the wall rocks and the mineral deposit should be plotted as carefully as possible on this sheet. An error in the plot by a meter or two could prove very serious where steep dipping, thin mineral bodies are to be drilled. For plane table mapping, thick, cloth-mounted drawing sheets and 3H pencils are recommended.

At the end of the survey, a few permanent pillars with suitable identification marks may be erected. These might be required later for further exploration. At least three pillars are necessary within a clear line of sight.

Thickly forested and steeply sloping tracts are unsuitable for rapid triangulation by plane table–telescopic alidade/theodolite. In such fields, traverse lines at right angles to the strike of the bedrock may be laid at intervals of 10/20/50/100 m and numbered pegs hammered into the ground at 5 m/10 m intervals along each traverse. The outcrops are plotted with the help of the numbered pegs, the distance being measured by taping or pacing. On sloping ground, pacing can be wrong by more than 100%.

STEP 3: SAMPLING

Sampling is the process of obtaining *more or less* representative samples of the mineral deposit which would enable computation of the average bulk composition. It is at best an approximation, and is usually confined to collecting representative samples from the *accessible* parts of the deposit as far as circumstances would permit and costs justify.

A mineral deposit is a mixture of economic plus gangue minerals, occurring in different ratios in different parts of the deposit. Ideally, if the ratio of economic to gangue minerals is constant all over, a single sample would be enough to estimate the grade. If the ratio varies randomly, or in other words, if the economic element(s) is randomly concentrated, e.g. in a gold-quartz vein, a large number of bulk samples will be needed for specific estimate of average grade. If there is a lateral change in the ratio, and if the rate of change is known, sampling at suitable intervals would reflect the pattern of variation. But if the frequency of change is not known, and if sampling is done at intervals exceeding the frequency limit, the estimate of grade will be wrong. Thus the accuracy of an estimate depends on the type and interval of sampling vis-a-vis the type of natural grade variation of the mineral deposit. A careful, visual classification of the exposures on the basis of grain size, colour, alteration etc. may help in ensuring that the gross variations are not missed in sampling. Adequate representation is essential from both the rich and the lean parts of the deposit in proportion to their volumetric abundance (Fig. 7.6).

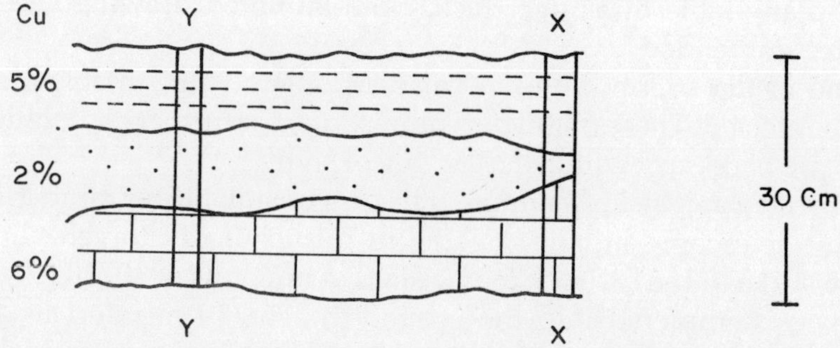

Fig. 7.6: Channel sampling site X-X: wrong; Y-Y: representiative.

There are various types of sampling depending on the stage of enquiry and the funds and time available for the job. These range from grab sampling to drill-hole sampling.

Grab Sampling

This is done at the very beginning of prospecting. Hand specimen size or smaller pieces of the mineral deposit showing differences in granularity, colour, alteration, host rock association, fabric and any other distinctive feature are collected from the outcrops/openings, aggregated and analysed to obtain a first approximation of the grade and other characteristics of the deposit. Collection of loose pieces from the ground should be avoided.

Chip Sampling

This is done by chipping off fragments of the deposit regularly along traverses at right angles to its strike. Rock chips are aggregated over each homogeneous section across the width of the deposit. For example, in a limestone deposit, chip sampling across its whole width at regular intervals may provide quick preliminary evaluation whether the material is cement/steel melting grade. It can never be used as a substitute for channel sampling, unless the deposit is nearly uniform.

Channel Sampling

This involves cleaning and smoothening the faces of the outcrops or exposures in pits/mines, marking two parallel lines 10–30 cm apart on the rock face with chalk or other suitable marker, cutting the channel with a sharp chisel and hammer, and collecting all the fragments and powder in a strong canvas bag. Care must be exercised to ensure that the width and the depth of the channel are constant, generally from 4 to 10 cm. The coarser the mineral body or the greater the variation in texture and grain size, the larger is the volume of the channel needed for a proper estimate of average grade. If a deposit is more than a meter thick, it is advisable to subdivide the channel in such a way that no individual sample represents a width of more than a meter. The advantage of such careful work is that the rich and the lean layers/bands are delimited early in exploration; and boundaries of sub-economic material broadly outlined at relatively less expense.

The width recorded in the notebook should be the true width. In steep dipping mineral deposits, one may also note the horizontal width besides the true width; the volume of the mineral deposit can be calculated either by multiplying the total area in a horizontal section by the vertical distance between the top and the bottom of the deposit or by multiplying the area of the deposit along its dip by the true width, i.e. the width measured perpendicular to the true dip of the deposit. Otherwise, estimates of the average grade and width will be wrong.

Channel samples across a deposit are normally spaced at regular intervals ranging from tens of meters, as on the scarp face of a bauxite deposit, to 1–2 meters, as along a sulphide vein in an underground drift. When sampling is done in an old working, it is easier to collect channel samples from the walls than from the back (i.e. roof). *Floor samples are always to be avoided*, because these are almost always contaminated.

After the fragments and powder are collected in a canvas bag, it is necessary to reduce the weight of the sample by coning and quartering before chemical assay. Coning consists of piling up the aggregate sample into a conical heap and then spreading it into a flat, disc-shaped pile. Quartering consists of dividing the disc into four equal parts radially, then combining two opposite quarters to make a sub sample and discarding the other two quarters. This process is repeated hand in hand with progressive reduction in the size of the largest pieces. It is important to remember that such sequential volume and size reduction is a very important step in ensuring representativeness of the sample. For example, if only the coarse fragments are picked up discarding the powder, where the coarse, harder fragments are compositionally different from the softer mass, there will be a bias in the average grade. Ideally, all the bulk has to be crushed to –230 mesh and mixed completely before drawing a representative volume (say 50–100 gm) for chemical analysis. But this is both time-consuming and costly. Hence one follows the time-honoured practice of sequential size and volume reduction. Many follow R.H. Richard's Table

(*E. & M.J.*, 2, 1903, 852). The job can be done very quickly and thoroughly with the help of a Jones Riffle sampler and a small crusher. These are normally used in large survey programs or in areas where labour is scarce or costly.

The size reduction may follow the norm given in Table 7.1

Table 7.1

Weight of sample (kg)	*Size of largest fragment (cm)*
500	4
100	2
20	1.3
5	0.7
1	40 mesh (ASTM)

After the weight is brought down to 1 kg and the size of the largest piece to –40 mesh it is advisable to crush the whole sample to –120 mesh. The powdered sample should be coned and quartered, and one half crushed further to –230 mesh, retaining the other half (500 gm) as a reference sample for future replicate measurements or compositing. Half of the sample, crushed to –230 mesh, should be preserved in a sealed bottle. The other 250 gm may be used for various tests.

Special care is needed while sampling spotted ore or gold/tin-tungsten ores. The initial weight of the channel sample should be around 500 kg. This means that for 1 m-long channels, one has to dig at 10 sites, each excavation measuring approximately 30 cm wide and 10 cm deep.

For metallurgical tests, a composite sample is to be prepared from different parts of a deposit. The duplicate sample (previously retained after crushing to –120 mesh) from each sector has to be mixed in such proportions by weight that each part is proportional to the total sample width or to the fraction of the mineral body it represents in bulk tonnage.

If there are nine samples, say N1 to N9 where each represents variable width/tonnage, the fraction of N1 which has to be taken for the composite sample will be proportional to the tonnage, represented by the sample (Fig. 7.7). The composite sample so gathered should be prepared carefully according to the specification indicated by the metallurgical laboratory. For metallurgical tests on bench scale, it is advisable to draw samples from cross cuts.

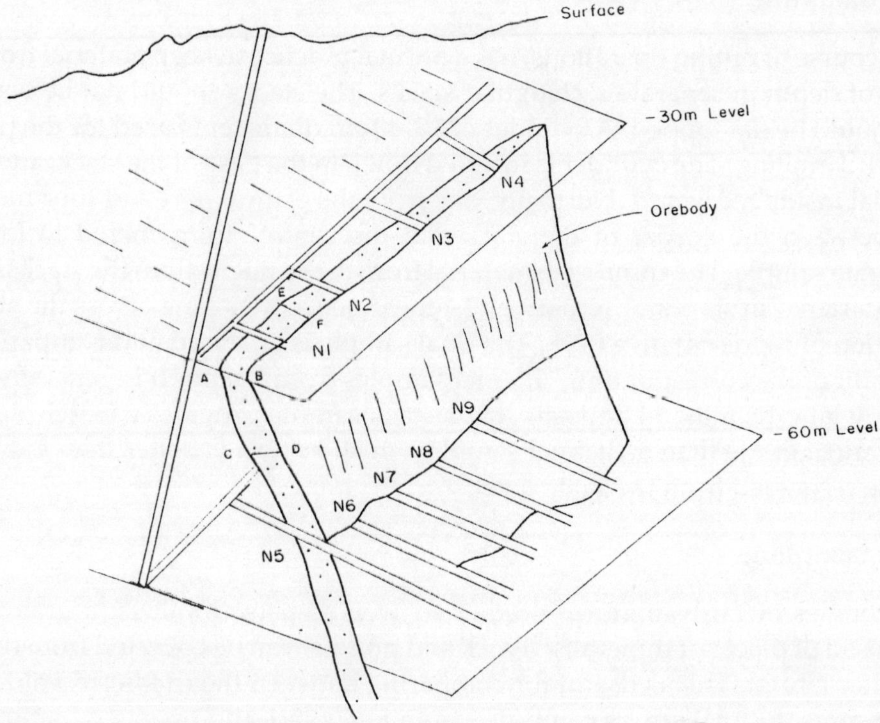

Fig. 7.7: Composite sample for beneficiation tests from cross-cuts N1 to N9 should be proportionate to the volume of ore around; thus volume of sample to be drawn from cross-cut No. N2 is not equal to volume of sample from N4.

Even in finely crushed powders, the maximum dimension of particles is approximately 75 μm. If the economic minerals/metals occur in finer size within the parent rock, as in Au, Ir, Pt, Pd etc., typical grinding procedures are incapable of homogenising the dispersion of these elements to an extent that would ensure a representative sample. Even if replicate splits from such powders are indistinguishable analytically at $\bar{x}+2s$ level, one is still not sure, since both the splits may be devoid of the target element. Failure to detect the target element in such cases may also result from problems of obtaining representative samples in splits of a few milligrams. In all such cases, it is useful to examine samples and sections concurrently by chemical and mineralogical techniques. Scanning Electron Microscope with EDS X-ray scanning of the suspect zones in thin section may in such cases reveal hidden mineralisation.

Stack Sampling

In the course of pitting operations, it is a normal practice to keep material from each meter of depth in separate rectangular stacks. The stacks should not be very high and should be flat topped. A cylinder of 15–40 cm diameter is used for the purpose of stack sampling. The cylinder is inserted down to the base of the stack, and all the material inside recovered. Normally, one from the central part and four more half way between the border of the stack and the centre, are gathered to form the aggregate sample. The composite material from the 5 spots within the stack is coned and quartered in stages. Alternatively, some practice trenching across the stack for collection of representative bulk. The final sample is analysed and compared with the result of the corresponding channel samples from the pit. It is generally found in many lateritic mineral deposits that a stack sample provides a better picture of the average grade than a channel sample, which in turn is better than a drill core sample recovered from the same level.

Muck Sampling

In orebodies of fairly uniform grade and well-dispersed values, a grab sample composed of pieces of mineralised rock and powder can be collected from the mine face after a blast. This is useful for comparing between the predicted value of the run-of-mine (R.O.M) ore, as computed from pneumatically-operated hammer drill cuttings, and the actual raising from the mine face. It is normally seen that the values do not match in detail, not because of mistake in sampling but due to inherent dilution in course of mining.

Car Sampling

This provides an estimate of the run-of-mine (R.O.M.) grade. A handful of ore pieces is taken out (a shovel is recommended to avoid bias in selection of pieces) from every 2nd/4th/8th car as it comes out from the mine loaded with the mineral. In some mines where smelter/ beneficiation plant is integrated with the mine, daily averages of car samples are compared with the mill head samples for grade control.

DRILLING

Drill-holes are sunk at various stages:

(i) during the early exploration phase to find new ore or to obtain critical geological information; (ii) during the stage of systematic evaluation from the surface; and (iii) for quality control in mine production from different blocks, so that the raisings do not show extreme grade variations from one month to another. In the first case, a non-coring churn drill is normally adequate. Banka drills are used for placer tin in Malaysia. In the second instance, wet or dry rotary drilling with tungsten carbide or diamond bits is used; while the third type of operation uses pneumatically-operated hammer drills.

The techniques of drilling operation are available in many standard text books, and are not given in detail here.

There are esentially two methods of drilling: rotary and percussion. Rotary methods include auger drilling, diamond drilling, and calyx drilling. Percussion drilling or churn drilling is less commonly used these days.

Auger drilling uses a hand-operated or machine-driven auger for cutting through soft layers. Although it produces a disturbed sample, it is very useful for penetration through saprolite zones of laterite-covered areas and was extensively used in the Sukinda nickel investigation in the sixties. Once the hard carapace is dug out manually over a 2 m × 2 m sized pit, the auger drill can be placed on its floor to recover samples of the underlying soft layers for geochemical and mineralogical studies, if the grain size of the material is clayey. It is cheap, easily transportable in interior areas and fast.

A modified version of diamond drilling is the calyx drill, used for boring mine ventilating shafts and chutes for ore and waste. The bit is rotated by hollow rods driven by an engine and gear on the surface. Small chilled steel shot are used as the abrasive medium. The shot fed into the rods with the wash water pass to the inner side of the core barrel and bit and some of these are rolled under. The sludge collects in a hollow cylinder, called calyx, above the core barrel and open at the top. The calyx drill can bore holes from a few cm to greater than 1.8 m in diameter.

The choice of drilling technique depends on: (1) depth of the holes required; (2) speed of drilling; (3) operating cost; (4) nature of ground; (5) nature of rock formations; (6) convenience of transport; and (7) available expertise. The choice of drill sites depends on the nature of work and the degree of detail. Initial drilling is aimed at: (a) defining the presence and general layout of the subjacent part of the deposit; and (b) obtaining a broad idea about the physical and chemical characters of the deposit. For flat and massive deposits, drill-holes are normally sunk vertically. For steeply dipping deposits cut up by a number of strike faults, as the Michigan copper deposit, drilling is undertaken in the form of overlapping holes perpendicular to the strike. For steep dipping deposits, the plan should be to intersect the body at as high an angle as possible, although drill-holes at angles of less than 30° are liable to deviate substantially from the target. Where the deposit is characterised by erratic distribution of metal values, drill-holes are not expected to yield representative samples for estimation of grade. Where overburden is thick, bouldery and difficult to penetrate, it is better to align the holes at steep angles even if the mineral deposit is not low dipping. No doubt the intersections will be at low angles to the deposit; but this problem is more than compensated for by the shorter distance of drilling through overburden. Where ore zones are diversely oriented along fissures and bedding planes, inclined holes oblique to both the fissures and bedding planes are planned since these are most economical for simultaneous evaluation of both the types of structural control.

A thumb rule for reconnaissance drilling is as follows: where nothing is known about the dip of the formations or about lie of the orebody, plan for vertical holes. Where the formation dips more than 30°, plan for inclined holes.

For systematic drilling, the spacing between holes is a matter of judgement. From the angle of cost control, holes should be as far apart as possible, but reliability of estimate demands that the interval should be less than the maximum distance over which the orebody is expected to maintain its thickness and grade—a fact which cannot be known before the orebody is opened up. We come back to this question again later in the chapter.

Drilling is not the best method for exploring narrow, steeply-dipping veins, small and irregular orebodies like those of Au, Sn, W, etc. or high grade but spotty deposits. One should rely more on deep pitting and exploratory mining down to 20 m. Unfortunately, the trend so far in our country, specially in state-funded organisations, has been to ignore this basic consideration and sink time and money in 'deploying' drill machines. Because of small diameter, a drill-hole may either miss an orebody where it has locally pinched out or present an abnormally rosy picture if it intersects a swollen part. In Cobalt, Ontario, Canada, diamond drilling in the early years failed to discover a rich vein system, subsequently found by underground work.

Briefly, the two most common types of drilling employed at the initial stage of non-fuel mineral exploration are churn drilling and diamond drilling. Hammer drills, shot drills etc. are used in underground operations.

The churn drill can only drill a vertical hole and yields cuttings by churning motion of the bit, hung on a cable. The cuttings are recovered from the hole at regular intervals. Before World War II, churn drilling was very popular for placer exploration as well as for different types of sulphide deposits. Some churn drill-holes, particularly in porphyry copper fields, reached down to depths of nearly 500 m. Tools are dropped 30–60 times a minute; for deep holes, casing is essential. A hole of 70 cm diameter at the collar becomes progressively reduced to 10 cm diameter at 450 m depth at the bottom.

A large, level area is needed for churn drilling. The drill rig is either self-propelled or truck-mounted. The drilling cycle begins with lowering the bit to the bottom of the hole, dumping water there through a bailer (not to be poured from the collar) and pounding the bottom by rhythmic raising and lowering of the bit.

After every two meters of penetration, the bit is raised above the collar and the bailer is lowered; this gets filled with drill cuttings and water. The end of the cycle involves hoisting the bailer and collection of the cuttings. The bailer is lowered and hoisted repeatedly until all the sludge is removed from the bottom of the hole.

Casings consisting of iron or steel pipes are lowered down to the bottom of the hole.

The cost and speed of drilling depend upon hardness of the rocks, degree of fracturing, extent of casing needed, speed of bailing and the diameter and depth of the hole. For shallow holes, this technique gives a satisfactory result in some fields. But essential structural features like dip of banding within the deposit etc. are missed. Estimation of grade of a deposit by this technique is crude and approximate.

Although churn drill cuttings cannot provide a correct estimate of the grade of a non-uniform mineral deposit, it is essential to preserve the following log for every hole: location of the hole; height of borehole collar; depth of hole; date of drilling; depth where loss of return water was noted; amount and colour of sludge; diameter of the hole; chemical analytical results; thin section description of rock fragments; and unusual features, e.g. caving of the hole, depth of groundwater standing in the hole, sharp variations, if any, in drilling time from one section to the next.

In India, diamond drilling is more common for mineral exploration (Fig. 7.8a). Types of drills range from portable hand-operated machines to heavy duty, engine-driven types. Diamond drills are generally powered by gasoline or diesel or electric motor or compressed air, the last two types for underground drilling. Basically, a bit armed/impregnated with tungsten carbide or industrial grade diamond pieces rotates and cuts out a cylindrical core from the rock body. The back of the bit is threaded on to a core barrel—a cylindrical chamber. Its other end is screwed on to drill rods of standard lengths. As the hole becomes deeper, more and more rods are added. The casing of the wall is required where there are risks of caving, i.e. collapse of the hole. Rotation of the drill string is effected by the drill machine at variable

Fig. 7.8a: Diamond drill (Model: Voltas Joy 12 B) at South Andaman island. (Photo: D. Halder, G.S.I.)

speed and pressure, depending on the nature of the rock being penetrated. Water circulates through the rods and flushes out of the collar of the hole carrying sludge and fine cuttings. Loss of return water implies a highly permeable, possibly crushed zone. Various types of core barrel are used. For ensuring better core recovery from fractured/broken rocks, double tube core barrels are used.

The success of a diamond drilling operation depends to a large degree on the type of equipment used and the skill of the operator. The core is cut by a bit into which are set either industrial diamonds or tungsten carbide fragments. The core passes up into the core barrel from which it is removed when the length drilled reaches more than half the length of the core barrel (at shallow levels) or nearly the full length of the core barrel (in deeper holes) in the case of homogenous, undisturbed strata. If the rocks are broken, short runs are preferred to ensure better core recovery. As mentioned earlier, the type of core barrel used is important. Single tube core barrels, which consist of a single steel tube, should not normally be used, since

Fig. 7.8b: Core box with drill core samples arranged one below the other in proper sequence in four columns separated by wooden partitions. Markers in between runs provide the details of depth. Drill-hole collar behind the box, with a drill rod jutting out. Karjaji, Dharwad district, Karnataka. (Photo: P.K. Basu, G.S.I.)

core recovery will be poor due to vibration and rotation of the drill string and barrel and scouring by drill fluid.

The most-preferred type of core barrel is the M-series triple tube variety with split innermost tube.

The choice of the bit size is also important for ensuring high core recovery. But this has to be balanced against the volume essential for mineralogical and geotechnical/geochemical analysis. The standard sizes are EX (18 mm diameter), AX (30 mm diameter), BX (41 mm diameter) and NX (54 mm diameter).

Of course, the diameter of the actual core recovered will be slightly lower, e.g. an NX core has a diameter of 47 mm. This is important while computing the volume of the material for specific gravity and other determinations.

The speed of drilling depends on the nature of the rock, depth and direction of the hole, type of drill, fittings and accessory outfit, labour, climate, number of shifts per day, specific requirement of core recovery and core length etc. The rate of advance is better in hard, uniform rocks than in alternating hard and soft strata and is very poor in broken zones. Contract drilling is generally faster than departmental drilling provided you take care to insert a penalty clause against less than 90% core recovery. In rocks which core well, the longer the core barrel, the faster is the drilling.

Drill-Hole Sampling and Core Logging

It is advisable for the geologist to be present at the drill site whenever a core is removed from the core barrel, not only to ensure full collection in proper sequence (bits and pieces of the core tend to be kept in the core box jumbled together by an untrained drill-man) but also to discourage mischief. In one instance, the resident geologist of a government department used to visit the drill site once every day; a drill-man had deliberately put a BHJ core sample from another hole in the corebox after a few runs through iron ore, so that the geologist would close the hole! The site was tough, and the drill-man wanted to shift!

Each length of core should be split longitudinally; half of it should be preserved in the core box (which is normally a 1 m × 0.5 m sized flat wooden or aluminium box with partitions fitted lengthwise, so that the cores could be kept end on; the core recovered and the length drilled are marked with black paint on small wooden blocks placed in between the runs) (Fig. 7.8b). Each core box is numbered and preserved for future reference. However, in organisations which drill thousands of meters every year, it becomes physically impossible to preserve all the cores all the time. Skeletonisation of cores is done, and typical sections are preserved.

The core is first studied by the geologist and a detailed log is entered in the field note book, covering the following points: name of rock; angle between the layering and the axis of the core; percentage of core recovery [(total length of the cores recovered arranged end on divided by the total run) multiplied by 100]; grain size and colour; alignment of economic minerals with respect to the planar surfaces in the core; other easily recognisable minerals like garnet, etc.; angle between veinlets and the axis of the core (Fig. 7.9); alignment of slickensides or crush zones; other special features.

The core is thereafter split longitudinally by a core splitter and the fresh surface is re-logged against the above checklist after wetting it. This is very useful for bringing out latent textural contrasts. One half of the split core is left in the core box for future reference; the other half is processed according to its type. Barren parts need not be crushed and sampled in the first instance. Feebly mineralised,

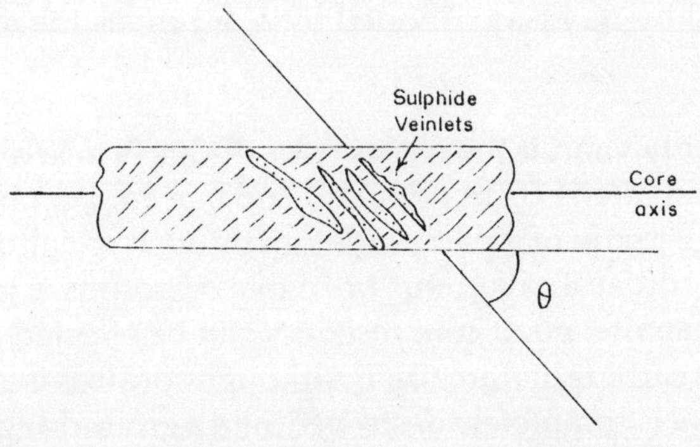

Fig. 7.9: Sketch of a borehole core with the mineralised zone aligned obliquely to the drillhole. Without this information, proper correction cannot be applied for computation of true/horizontal width.

moderately mineralised and strongly mineralised parts are to be sampled as closely as possible, the sampling interval depending on changes in type and intensity of mineralisation, host rock composition etc. For sulphide deposits, each core sample should represent a length of 10–50 cm, depending on uniformity of mineralisation. For chromite, a sample length of 1 meter is acceptable, provided there are no silicate partings in between; for gold-quartz veins, a sample length of 10 cm should be the maximum; and so on.

Basically, the idea behind close interval sampling is to ensure computation of tonnage on variable cut off, where the contact between the mineralised zone and the wall rock is diffuse and the limit of the mine has to be decided on the basis of *cut off boundary* which defines the lower limit of grade which would yield R.O.M. material suitable for economic exploitation.

The sample is crushed to –230 mesh, and an adequate number of replicates preserved. This helps to cross-check later.

Where core recovery [(aggregate length of core recovered ÷ length drilled in a run) × 100] in wet rotary drilling is less than 90%, it is necessary to collect the sludge separately for every run from return water as it pours through the collar of the hole in three-tiered boxes placed end on. You have to sample the sludge for both chemical and mineralogical analysis. The grade of material corresponding to the total run can be calculated approximately by combining the assay from the core and the sludge, as follows:

Step 1: Calculate the theoretical volume of the hole ($V - 1$).
Step 2: Measure the actual volume of the core(s) recovered ($V - 2$).
Step 3: $V - 1$ minus $V - 2$ is the volume of material now recovered as sludge.

Step 4: ($V-2$ multiplied by the assay of the core sample + the volume of the sludge multiplied by its assay) divided by $V-1$ gives the average grade of the run.

This method is only valid if the recovery of sludge is nearly complete.

Where a single run intersects mineralised and barren sections, it is impossible to compute the average grade of a part of the run by such weighting procedure.

Where the ore is soft and cavernous or friable or porous, e.g. nickel saprolite or cavernous laterite-bauxite, good core recovery can be effected by dry drilling. For such rocks, tungsten carbide bits are used. Although core loss is avoided, the internal texture of the material is completely destroyed, and a ground aggregate is recovered. There is also a risk of loss of bound water and consequently an apparent improvement in grade; sub-sampling on the basis of variations in colour, texture and granularity can not be done. Run-wise sampling and dry drilling both require short runs to be drilled.

In the case of air drilling, a canvas bag is held around the mouth of the hole to collect the cuttings. The drill steel is passed through the base of the bag. The hole in the bag is made tight with the help of a rubber gasket or other suitable lining, so that the cuttings do not escape. Hammer drill-hole samples are generally as good as channel samples, provided care is taken against loss of the finer particles.

Deep holes by air drilling are drilled wet. Pans instead of bags are held at the collar of the hole. An auxiliary hole is drilled below the proposed main hole in the same vertical plane at a lower angle, so that this hole meets the main hole at a distance of 10–20 cm from the collar. A pipe is passed into the auxiliary hole, through which the return water is fed directly into the pan. In downward-going holes, however, the cuttings are recovered by injecting air and water alternately through the hollow steel.

Whatever technique is used, it is necessary to ensure complete recovery of the cuttings for preparation of a representative sample. Only then will the assay data be correct.

The geologist guiding a drilling program has a number of responsibilities. He has to site the holes, indicate the angle and depth of the holes required for his interpretation, prepare alternate cross-sections along the profile based on his ground data and the limits of uncertainty in structural extrapolation, log the cores, collect and process sludge and core samples for analysis, measure the angle of deviation of the holes and the depth actually drilled, and then prepare the final borehole sections on a suitable scale so that the special features of the holes are depicted properly.

Drill-hole Spacing

For siting the holes from the surface, there are two ways: one geometrical, followed by many mining geologists and the other to feel your way along, where the surface indications of the orebody are poor (laterite cover is frequently a problem as at Adas, Orissa).

The geometrical approach requires, as some wag once said, a ruler and a pencil. But such preconceived programs have some advantage, where a large number of holes are to be drilled; it is easier to prepare regular cross-sections without extrapolations; it is also possible to deploy a cluster of machines to the maximum advantage, shallow machines for the shallow holes, and heavy duty machines for the deep holes, reducing the cost of maintenance, operational overhead, period of exploration and ensuring a standard procedure throughout the campaign.

On the other hand, the method of feeling your way gives scope to using geological judgement at every step, getting the lie of the deposit with minimum amount of drilling, initiating exploratory mining as soon as the holes indicate enough potential for development or stopping exploration of a sub-marginal orebody at an early enough stage.

The spacing between two holes is a matter of judgement, depending on the continuity of the exposures, the general habit of the mineral deposit, the lie of the land, the time and money available for the campaign and so on. But if the boreholes are spaced far apart, say 200 m along strike for a 2 m wide vein which pinches and swells every 50–100 m, problems are bound to crop up when the mine opens. Similarly, if one intersects an orebody at 30 m vertical depth and then plans directly for intersection at 300 m vertical depth (as had happened at Sargipalli Cu-Pb deposit, Orissa during the early seventies), not knowing that a granite is lurking below at 150 m depth, wasteful expenditure cannot be avoided. Level-wise exploration is the only route for concealed orebodies. But for simple campaigns like proving an orebody of regular, flat-lying habit, e.g. deposits of residual weathering, or a shallow and large deposit like porphyry Cu, drilling programs by vertical holes are best undertaken on a geometric grid for maximum definition. The grid interval should be anywhere between 15 m and 50 m. There are certain essential precautions to be followed:

(1) Computation of grade of a deposit from drill-hole intersections is at best approximate and at worst misleading. A few properly-sited bulk samples provide a better picture of the grade, e.g. a cross-cut sample from an under-

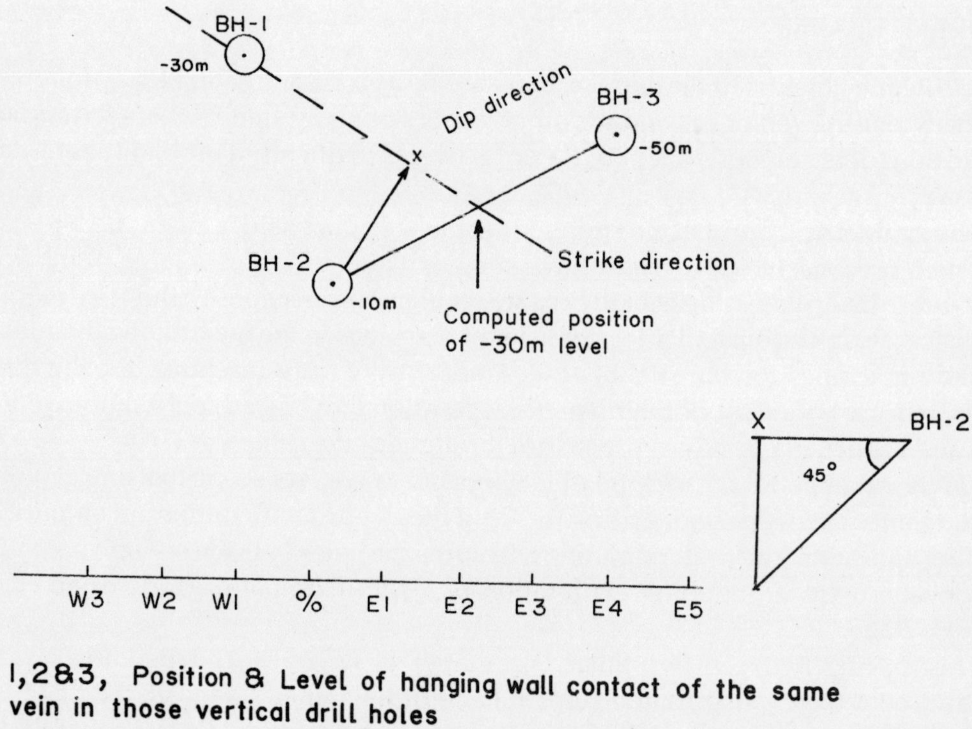

Fig. 7.10: Three-point method for determination of strike and dip of a horizon from borehole intersections.

ground working or bulk samples from pits and trenches. The geologist must guard against over-interpretation from borehole chemical data.

(2) In deposits like Au- or Sn- or W-bearing quartz veins, computation of the grade on the basis of drill-hole intersections is not recommended. Bulk sampling at an early stage of exploration is the safest approach.

(3) In inclined holes, the apparent width of a vein may be 10 times larger than its true width, depending on the angle between the drill-hole and the disposition of the vein. Careful measurement of the angle(s) between the vein and the axis of the hole from drill cores would provide a first approximation of the dip of the vein. Where there is convincing evidence that the same vein has been intersected in 3 boreholes at different depths, one can compute the strike and dip of the body following the three point method (Fig. 7.10).

(4) In inclined holes, the extent of borehole deviation must always be measured. Few drill-holes exceding 100 m in length are straight. Deviation is least in

near-vertical holes; horizontal holes bend both upward and downward. Deflection generally varies inversely with the length of the core barrel. There is a greater possibility of deflection if worn or short core barrels, or light drill rods, or excessive hydraulic pressure on the bit are used. There are various instruments to measure deflection: (1) *Photo-magnetic instruments* record on sensitised paper disks the drift angle (by a delicate plumb bob) and the compass bearing. Inside casings the bearing data are unreliable; so it has to be lowered 2–3 m below the lowest casing. There are two types: single shot and multishot instruments. A single shot instrument is loaded in daylight from a clip of sensitised disk. The time of lowering is pre-set on the instrument watch which closes and establishes electrical contact at the desired moment. A synchronised watch on the surface will keep track of the level reached. (2) *Gyroscopic clinograph* maintains a fixed, pre-set bearing and carries a non-magnetic watch, compass dial and thermometer. An electrically-operated camera with double lenses and timing contact records temperature, inclination and time in seconds. It is a very heavy instrument, generally used for oil wells. (3) *Hydrofluoric acid method* is the simplest technique. A test tube partly filled with HF is lowered into the hole after enclosing it in a steel case and left undisturbed for 10–15 minutes. It is then pulled out and the acid is discarded immediately. The angle of inclination between the etched line on the test tube and the axis of the tube is the dip of the hole. In a vertical hole, the etch mark is at right angles to the wall. As the hole becomes less steep so does the angle of the etch mark. The measurement is repeated for every 10 m interval along a borehole down to its bottom.

The hole may also deviate from its bearing particularly along the contact between hard and soft rock formations. Such deviation may be substantial. This can be measured by the Borehole Compass. It is a difficult operation at the best of times. In place of compass, which consists of a small magnetic needle on a pivot, attached to a cork floating in gelatine, borehole cameras are also used. This has two disadvantages. The photographs may not reveal how far the azimuth of the hole has changed, unless very thinly banded units with sufficient colour contrast are exposed on the walls. If the camera is stuck inside the hole due to mishandling, a costly instrument could be lost. As a result, neither the borehole compass nor the camera are very popular.

There are some geologists who press the driller for faster progress. Where the formation is broken, fast drilling results in poor core recovery, and the purpose of the work is defeated. There is no substitute for careful drilling by an expert driller.

At the preliminary stage of prospecting and exploration, drilling is aimed at establishing a minimum acceptable dimension of the deposit of required grade to ensure profitability. Once the dimension is broadly conjectured, the cost of any additional probe drilling has to be balanced against the anticipated saving in developmental expenditure. Where the cost of such drilling is excessive or the campaign of exploration is prolonged, a marginal deposit could turn into sub-marginal, once the investment on exploration is taken into the costing. For state-run endeavours in India during the previous decades, it was not uncommon to have a long delay in mine development after exploration. The computed interest on the funds invested in exploration over, say, a decade of indecision could exceed the total cost of exploration. P.P. Kala et al. (*Jour. Mines, Metals & Fuels*, 1994: 163–70) used the concept of *Economic Sampling Limit* to estimate that 35 boreholes are optimum for maximising profitability and minimising risk in respect of the Bamnia Kalan Pb-Zn prospect, 10 km north of the Rajpura-Dariba mine of Hindusthan Zinc Limited.

DISTRIBUTION OF VALUES

Mineral deposits show three types of distribution of values.

(1) *Bodies of regular shape with values distributed normally around a mean grade, e.g. a chromite seam within dunite.* Grades of individual samples are distributed more or less symmetrically about the mean with falling percentage of extreme values. In such cases, the computed average grade, based on channel or drill core samples corresponds closely with the actual grade, *once the minimum required volume of the sample is exceeded.* For instance, the variance of ore grade (vide Chapter 6) will be less, if one uses NX diameter drill core samples of 50 cm length instead of AX diameter drill core samples of say 5 cm length. The *minimum volume* of the sample required varies according to the extent of heterogeneity in distribution of target elements and gangue material. This can be evaluated by thin and/or polished section studies. Thus the minimum volume of the sample for a chromite seam is proportional to the abundance of silicate gangue and nature and intensity of alteration of the chromite grains.

(2) *Bodies of regular shape with element values intermediate between truly random and completely deterministic variable.* The minimum volume of the sample for, say, a vanadiferous magnetite seam where vanadium is distributed in different minerals,

as in the Mayurbhanj occurrences, is related to the abundance of magnetite-ilmenite intergrowths (which host vanadium) and the associated haematite, chlorite, plagioclase and pyroxene. Variable fugacity of oxygen prevailed in the crystallisation chamber as the threshold of solidus was reached and generated complex partitioning and non-homogeneity in Ti and V within the titanomagnetite masses themselves. As a result, borehole samples show erratic fluctuations from 0.16% to 3% V_2O_5 even where magnetite content remains constant. The kernels of larger orebodies are richer and more uniform in V than their fringes.

Thus the pattern of distribution of V in the Mayurbhanj orebodies is more complex than that of Cr in chromite of the Nausahi ultramafic complex, although chromite composition is variable from one seam to another. As a result the minimum volume of sample for computation of grade of such a vanadiferous magnetite deposit has to be larger than that for chromite. One can generate estimates with less variance by using the moving average technique for the drill core values. This is an extension of data smoothing technique. The grade is estimated by weighting all analytical values within a gridded frame to re-compute the average value at the central point of the target sub-zone (see Chapter 6 and Fig. 6.4). The count is then shifted to the next grid point and the process is repeated. Another way to tackle this problem is to compute the semi-variance (see Chapter 6), which is a measure of the degree of spatial dependence between samples of identical nature like drill core, etc. If the spacing between samples along a line is the distance *d*, the semivariance can be estimated for distances that are multiples of *d*. If the semi-variance between AX-sized drill core samples of one block and channel samples from the same block shows large difference, all other conditions remaining identical, the estimation of bulk grade on the basis of such drill core samples is suspect. The fact that samples of both the sets are collected from the same deposit at neighbouring locations does not eliminate the innate difference between the two sets of original samples, one a few cubic centimetres and the other a few cubic decimetres in volume at the stage of initial collection and the resultant differences in their average grade.

This is a fundamental aspect to be checked at the stage of initial sampling. The estimation of the value of a critical variable like grade at a localised point of observation and extrapolating it over a larger area or volume requires initial statistical tests about the distribution pattern of the target value and choice of appropriate sampling volume.

(3) *Deposits with erratic high values like Au, PGE, Sn, W etc.* do not show a Gaussian distribution pattern, when a large number of values from drill cores or drift samples

are plotted. The spatial distribution is marked by erratic high values of target elements. These do not satisfy the essential needs of parametric statistics (Chapter 6). It is observed in such ore deposits that the rich zones are many times richer than the lean zones, and also that the variation in grade is larger in rich zones. In such cases, the values should first be averaged block-wise by logarithmic transformation of the raw data and then the averaged log values reverted to their original set by anti-log transformation. One must take care to delimit the lean and the rich zones separately into discrete blocks on the basis of adequate geological controls before carrying out such logarithmic transformation; otherwise application of statistics may prove to be unrewarding.

Once the distribution pattern of metal values is understood, the appropriate sampling technique is identified and acceptable minimum volume of sample for computation of average grade of each sub-block of the deposit is defined, one can proceed with the task of systematic sampling for ore grade evaluation.

The importance of orientation geostatistical tests at an early stage of the sampling program can never be over-emphasised. Thus, in the Kansa limonitic nickel deposit of Sukinda, Orissa, it was found in 1965 that the grade of ore, as computed from NX-sized drill core samples, aggregated for every 50 cm of run, shows erratic fluctuation in contrast to stack samples for corresponding depths from an adjacent deep pit only 3 m away, collected almost concurrently and analysed in the same laboratory. It was therefore recognised that stack samples from deep pits would provide a better average picture of nickel values in limonite saprolite of Kansa than drill core values. Without this initial orientation, limitations of drill core sampling in this field would not have been recognised.

Calculation of Average Width and Grade (Uniform Specific Gravity)

The analysis of various samples drawn from a mineral deposit are aggregated together to calculate the average grade. Examples of different situations are given.

A1: Where each sample represents the complete width of the deposit at equal distance from one another (Fig. 7.11), width being constant.

Average grade = arithmetical average of the assays.

A2: Where the width is variable, but sampling interval is constant (Fig. 7.12 and Table 7.2).

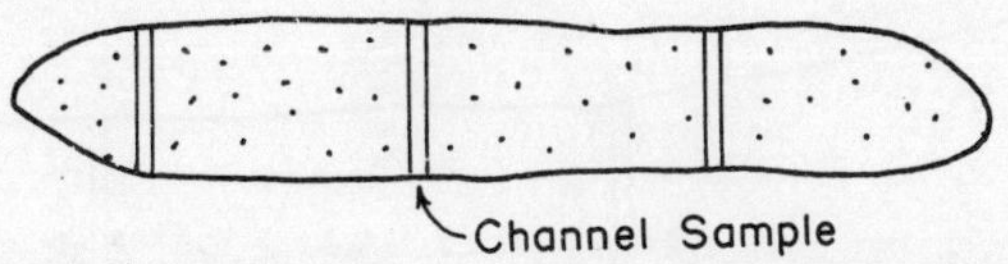

Fig. 7.11: Constant separation channel sampling where width of the target zone is constant.

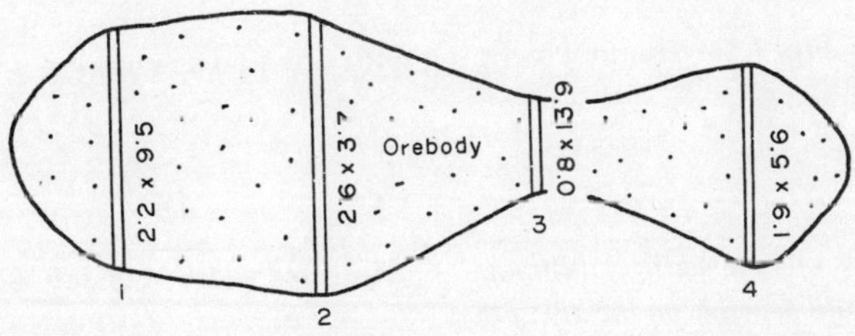

Fig. 7.12: Constant separation channel sampling where width of target zone is variable.

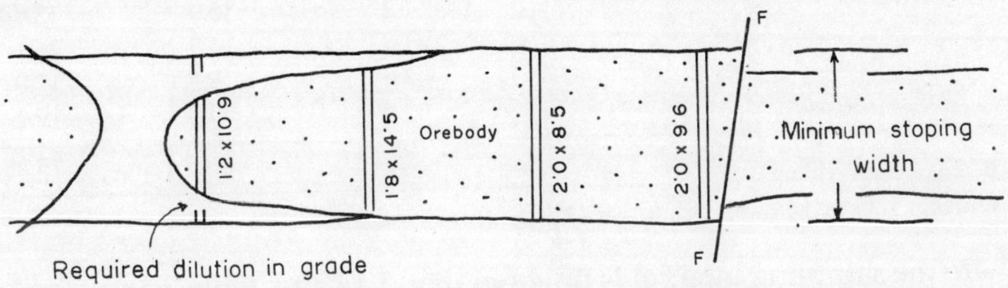

Fig. 7.13: Constant separation channel sampling across a mineralised zone which is intermittently thinner than the minimum stoping width for an underground mine.

Table 7.2

Sample	*Width (m)*	*Assay (Zn%)*	*Width × Assay*
1	2.2	9.5	20.50
2	2.6	3.7	5.92
3	0.8	13.9	11.12
4	1.9	5.6	10.64
Total	6.5(*a*)		48.18 (*b*)

Average width = 1.625 m; average grade = 7.41% (*b*/*a*)

A3: Where the minimum minable width is larger than the width of the deposit, causing dilution of grade; channel sampling interval constant (Fig. 7.13 and Table 7.3).

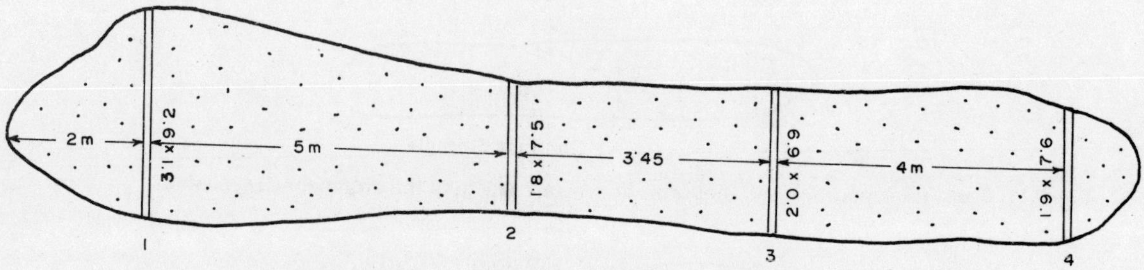

Fig. 7.14: Channel samping with unequal spacing.

Table 7.3

Sample No.	*Minimum minable width (minimum minable width depends on the dip of the deposit, the design of stoping etc.) (a)*	*Measured width (b)*	*Assay % Zn*	*Width × Assay (b)*
1	2.0	1.2	10.9	13.08
2	2.0	1.8	14.5	26.1
3	2.0	2.0	8.5	17.0
4	2.0	2.0	9.6	19.2
Total	8.0 (*a*)	7.0	48.5	75.38 (*b*)

Average width = 1.75 m; Minable grade = 9.42% (*b*/*a*)

B1: Where the sampling interval is unequal (Fig. 7.14 and Table 7.4).

Table 7.4

Sample No.	*Interval (m)*	*Width (m)*	*Width × interval*	*Assay (Zn%)*	*Width × Assay × interval*
1	2.0	3.1	6.2	9.2	57.04
2	5.0	1.8	7.5	8.9	66.75
3	3.45	2.0	6.9	7.8	53.82
4	4.0	1.9	7.6	8.7	66.12
Total		8.8 (*c*)	28.2 (*d*)		243.73 (*e*)

Average width = 2.01 m (*d*/*c*); Average grade = 8.64% ((*e*/*d*)

B2: Computation of average grade of a mining block, sampled on all four sides (Fig. 7.15 and Table 7.5).

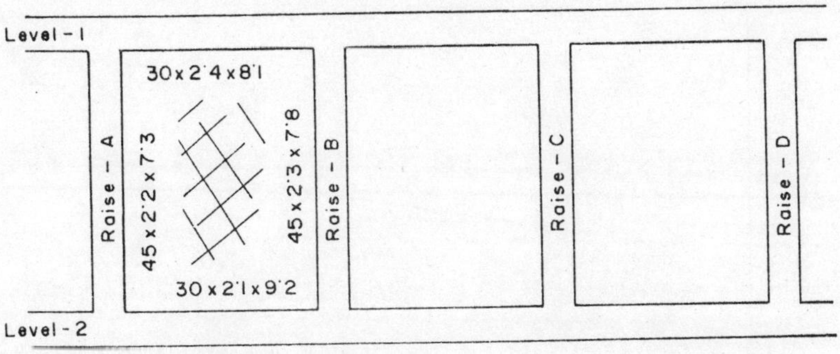

Fig. 7.15: A mining block (Proved Reserve) sampled on all sides.

Table 7.5

	Length (m)	*Width (m)*	*L × W*	*Assay %*	*L × W × A*
Level 1	30	2.4	72	8.1	583.20
Level 2	30	2.1	63	9.2	579.60
Raise A	45	2.2	99	7.3	722.70
Raise B	45	2.3	108.1	7.8	843.18
Total			342.10		2728.68

Average width = 2.25 m; Average assay = 7.97%

If there are wide differences in grade and/or width of the deposit on four sides of a block, it is advisable to further sub-divide the block into smaller units of near uniform behaviour.

B.C. Sarkar et al. (*Jour. Geol. Soc. India*, 46, 1995, 139–47) have shown that in deposits where the values are distributed in different host rocks and show a log normal pattern, it is incorrect to compute average grade on the basis of conventional cross-sectional methods. A difference of nearly 1% in P_2O_5 content of the average grade of phosphorite in the Khatamba block, Jhabua district, Madhya Pradesh, resulted in substantial underestimation of total recovery potential by the conventional method. As a general rule, it is necessary to compute the grade for each lithofacies separately with the help of a simple computer programme instead of sticking to the blind geometrical approach.

Calculation of Average Grade (Variable Specific Gravity)

The foregoing calculations of average grade do not take into account the changes in specific gravity of a deposit from point to point depending on variation in grade.

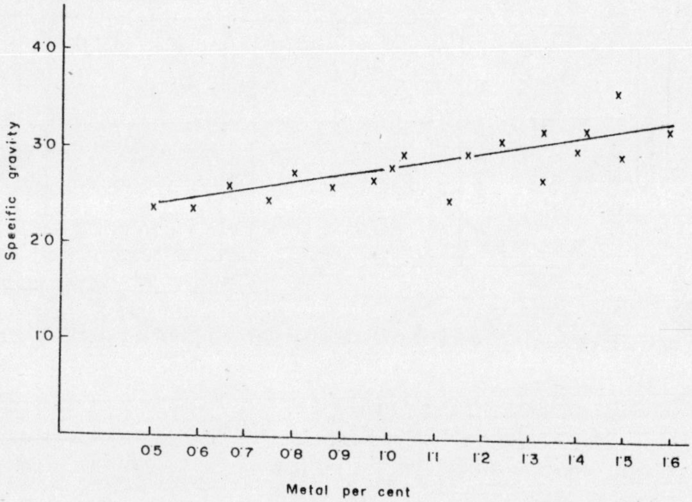

Fig. 7.16: Line of best fit between sp. gravity and metal per cent for extrapolation of sp. gravity from metal values, *in a known field*. Note: Blind extrapolations are inadvisable.

Specific gravity does not usually vary so much that this has to be weighted into the calculations. But in extreme cases, like a lead sulphide deposit, it is necessary to multiply every assay with the corresponding specific gravity and then compute the average grade as follows:

$$\text{Average grade} = \frac{\Sigma \text{ width} \times \text{interval} \times \text{assay} \times \text{sp.gr.}}{\Sigma \text{ width} \times \text{interval} \times \text{sp.gr.}}$$

It is not necessary to determine the specific gravity of each core sample or channel sample. On the basis of 100–150 determinations of specific gravity of samples covering the whole range of assay, a curve of best fit is constructed showing the correlation (Fig. 7.16). Specific gravity for each sample can be read off this curve against the corresponding chemical analysis.

Erratic High Values

Whenever one comes across unusually rich values at random in a series of chemical analyses, one must check for the following possibilities:

(1) Error in sampling;
(2) Error in chemical analysis;
(3) Erratic distribution of high values in the orebody.

Re-sampling the section which yielded such high values and re-analysing the sample in a different standard laboratory might give a clear idea whether the departures are due to the first and second alternatives. But in case of sampling of gold/tin/tungsten lodes, such departures are to be expected as genuine (Chapter 6).

In such cases, if the high values are ignored one will miss the indications of a deposit. On the other hand, if it is assumed wrongly that the erratic values represent the average grade over the sampled width and interval, one will be led into an overestimate. To avoid such pitfalls, there are many statistical techniques to ensure an objective appraisal. A simple technique is to estimate the grade of a block by weighting the metal values by their relative frequency. A curve is then drawn with frequency plotted on ordinate and the metal values on abscissa. The average grade can be computed by the following formula:

$$\text{Average grade} = \frac{\Sigma\ (\text{width} \times \text{frequency} \times \text{assay})}{\Sigma\ (\text{width} \times \text{frequency})}$$

Real erratic high values, which might constitute an important component of the ore deposit will thus neither be eliminated from the reserve calculation nor will they enjoy a predominance in the computation of average grade.

If an erratic high value is noticed in a sample, it is always necessary to re-cut the channel not only to confirm the presence of rich material but also to have a closer look at the possible presence of rich portions in small shoots, which might have been overlooked in the first sampling campaign. A few additional channel samples at shorter intervals may also be drawn around such anomalous spots. The additional values so generated should then be included in the assay-frequency curve; and the grade recomputed by substitution of the initial value by the set of new values, suitably averaged.

FURTHER READING

F.H. Lahee, *Field Geology*, 6/e, McGraw-Hill, New York, 1961, 762 pp.

J.H. Reedman, *Techniques in Mineral Exploration*. Applied Science Publishers Ltd., London, 1979, 533 pp.

J. G. DeGeoffroy and T.K. Wignall, *Designing Optimal Strategies for Mineral Exploration*, Plenum Press, New York, 1985, 364 pp.

R.N.P. Arogyaswamy, *Courses in Mining Geology*, Oxford & IBH, New Delhi, 1980, 927 pp.

8

Mineral Reserves and Resources

The term 'mineral resource' includes only such naturally-occuring, non-renewable material of the earth, which is amenable to industrial utilization now or in the forseeable future *economically*. It is a means to maximise the Net Present Value (NPV) for the country or for the shareholders of the company. It is, therefore, desirable to reach an agreed definition of Mineral Resource for universal adoption. But it is not yet available. However precise we might try to be, the accuracy of an estimate can never be confirmed. Technology and market price are never the same. Fluctuations in the distribution of ore material cannot be assessed completely before mining. The term *Reserve* is used only for deposits which have been or are being mined and which have been measured on all its sides. On the other hand, the term *Resource* is all-encompassing for deposits mined, under mining, likely to be mined etc., whose characters may be partly known. Like a prudent pensioner, calculating at intervals what remains to support him in his later years, every state/lessee periodically takes stock of how much mineral it has in the 'bank'. One cannot simply treat the whole as a current account deposit to be tapped as and when needed. Some of this is in 'Fixed Deposit form'. At today's prices much of that might be prohibitively expensive to extract but it could be extremely valuable in the next century. Unlike a pensioner's bank account, one cannot simply consult a ledger. There are innumerable geological uncertainties, technological 'time bombs' and socially controlled parameters which can produce both happy surprises and shocking 'overestimates' at intervals of a few decades. Thus the economist will be well advised not to treat reserve and resource figures like bank accounts. Resources include Reserves but not vice versa. The demand that the term Resource be defined sufficiently accurately to convince the lending institutions to provide 70–80% of the capital expenditure for mine development is unreal. Although efforts for reaching a consensus definition are made now and then, the infinite variability of mineral deposits can hardly be ignored or solved by recourse to statistical treatment of exploration data. For example, the Broken Hill sulphide deposit has yielded ore worth some 70 billion Australian dollars since its discovery in 1883, but at no time in the past could the estimates have reflected the total potential. *Estimates of mineral reserves or resources are therefore, always approximations, not certainties.* The degree of uncertainty in the estimation is qualitatively classified by using different terms for the estimates. It is conventional to accept such categorisations at their face value, although the degree of assurance of the grade and dimension of a mineral deposit, as estimated from limited openings, involves assumptions which are subjective in the ultimate analysis.

There are several classifications of mineral reserves in use in different countries. The oldest classification is as follows.

Positive Reserve or Blocked-out Reserve: Applicable to blocks of orebodies which are mined underground and for those parts only where the deposit is exposed and sampled on all four sides in the levels above and below and by raises and winzes on the sides of the blocks (Fig. 8.1).

Probable Reserve: Deposit exposed and sampled on at least two sides of an underground mine.

Possible Reserve: Deposit exposed on only one side, the other dimensions being conservative estimates partly on the basis of trenches and shallow boreholes.

Some use the term *Proved* in place of *Positive Reserve*, implying that there is practically no risk of error in the grade and tonnage estimate. Similarly, the term *Prospective Reserve* is used in place of *Possible Reserve.*

Another set of terms, more subjective and popular among survey geologists, are *Measured, Indicated* and *Inferred*. But these are applicable to resources, *not* reserves.

Measured resource is estimated from dimensions and grades actually inspected, sampled and measured in outcrops, trenches, workings and drill-holes at such close intervals that the computed grade and tonnage are not different from actual raisings from the block by more than 20 per cent.

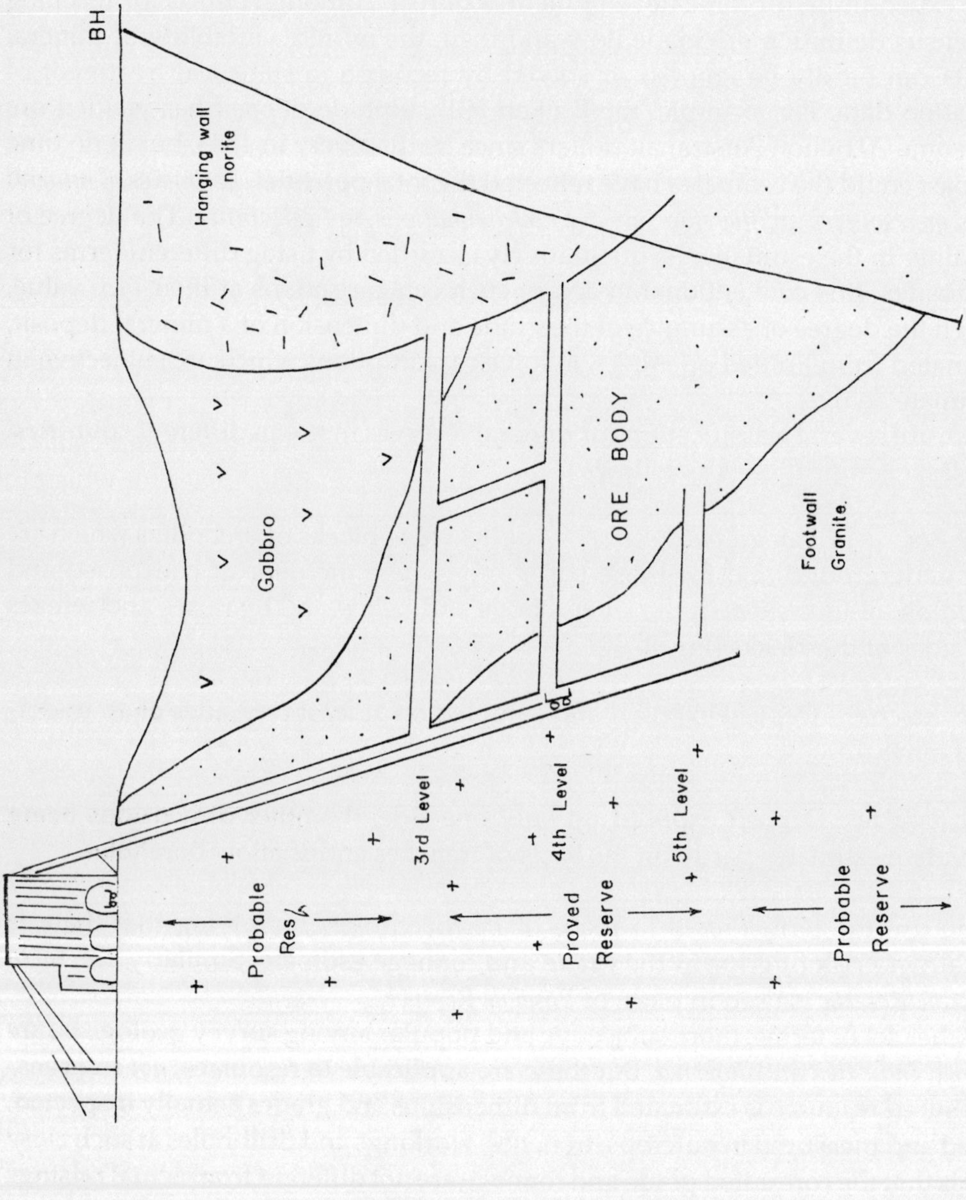

Fig. 8.1: Illustration of Proved and Probable Reserves.

Indicated resource is estimated partly from specific measurements and partly from extrapolation over a reasonable distance on geologic evidence.

Inferred resource is estimated on a handful of samples and measurements; the estimates are based largely on assumed continuity and broad geologic knowledge of deposits of similar type.

It is clear from the foregoing that this terminology is vague and ambiguous. It is useful for regional scale summations and broad overviews but is not adequate for deposit-specific investment decisions of a mining concern.

Many advanced countries have now adopted the Mckelvey Box of the United States Geological Survey which is based on two parameters, namely economic feasibility and certainty of occurrence. Under economic feasibility there are two categories: economic and sub-economic resources, based on their economic viability *at the time of estimation.* Sub-economic resources are termed as *Potential deposits.* Certainty of occurrence includes Identified (Measured, Indicated and Inferred) and Undiscovered (Hypothetical and Speculative) resources. *Measured* and *Indicated* resources are sometimes clubbed together as *Demonstrated* resources for which the quantity and quality are based partly on measurements and partly on extrapolation. *Inferred* resource is actually a half-way house between discovered and undiscovered resources. *Hypothetical* resources are those which may reasonably be expected to exist in a known mineral district under known geological conditions, while *Speculative* resources may occur in known types of favourable geological setting, where no discoveries have yet been made (Fig. 8.2).

For example, suppose there are stratiform ore deposits on both the limbs of a major fold; but only for one of the limbs are there abundant data on the grade and tonnage of ore. Geological indications are available that the strata continue undisturbed into the other limb. One can estimate *Hypothetical* resource of this unexplored limb for deciding on the *economics of future exploration*. Such estimates could be in error by a large margin. On the other hand, consider the case of the Western Belt islands of Santo and Malekula in the New Hebrides, which form part of a chain of Miocene calc-alkaline volcanics with large porphyry copper deposits like Bougainville in Papua New Guinea and Namosi in Fiji. One can estimate speculative resources of copper in these islands, once the appropriate intrusions are located.

The term *Resource Base* is presently used to include both identified and undiscovered resources, actual and potential. Thus the term Resource is used to delimit the known component of the Resource Base, whereas the term Reserve is restricted to the *Demonstrated* tonnage of economic mineral deposits.

	Identified	Undiscovered	
		In known ore districts	In undiscovered ore districts / formations
Economic	Reserves	Hypothetical	Speculative
Sub-economic	Identified Sub-economic Resources	Resources	Resources

Fig. 8.2: Classification of Mineral Reserves and Resources (as per USGS Circular 698, 1974).

A mining concern looks for the estimate of *Reserve*. A State Survey Department attempts estimation of Resource. A Global or Regional Inventory will look for Resource Base. Mineral resource assessment is essentially a multidisciplinary effort involving mineral economics, mining engineering and metallurgy besides local and regional geology. In such a mix, the jargon of different disciplines creates severe problems of communication. This is compounded by undefinable factors like (mis)management, control and labour policies. A classic case history is the Khetri Copper Mine in Rajasthan. The Indian Bureau of Mines had estimated in the fifties a 'proved reserve' of 112 million tonnes of ore averaging 1% Cu comprising a block of about 3000 m in length and 600 m in depth (following geophysical survey and initial drilling by the Geological Survey of India). The estimate was based on 46 boreholes and 1000 m of underground exploration. While the estimate of this *in situ* resource was broadly correct from the viewpoint of a geochemist, factors like *mineable* reserve, recoverable grade and output capability escaped attention, when the investment decision was taken by the Mines Ministry of the Government of India to open up a mine and construct treatment plants with an annual production capacity of 31,000 tonnes of copper wirebars. The options of design of stopes for a 10 meter-wide orebody versus five 2-meter wide orebodies and the attendant dificulties in mine design for the latter were not gone into. Moreover, ore recovery from an underground mine peaks at a slower pace than an open cast mine. This was also not realised in drawing up a development schedule. The result: a long and bitter post mortem to fix the responsibility for the initial teething troubles.

The exploration geologist cannot plead innocence in such a multi-disciplinary endeavour by saying that his *in situ* estimate was correct. *In situ* 'geological resources' are of little consequence in investment decisions. What matter most are the mineable reserve, recoverable grade (instead of *in situ* grade) and the sectoral distribution of reserves and mineral-rich zones vis-a-vis the proposed mine design.

CUT-OFF GRADE

In order to compute the reserve of a deposit, the usual tool of an exploration geologist is to decide upon one or more arbitrary cut-off grades and compute the dimensions of the mineral deposit accordingly. The definition of *cut-off grade* sounds simple—the lowest grade that will meet costs; but who decides the cost? Not the geologist, nor the mining engineer, not even the financial manager of the company. Cost varies with:

- rate of production;
- method of mining;
- natural disposition of mineral matter in the rock body, e.g. high-grade oreshoots with clear boundaries vs. dispersed ore whose values decline gradually or irregularly from the vein into the wall rock;
- metallurgical characters;
- national and international prices;
- cost of labour, equipment and other infrastructure related to mining (like power);
- taxes and royalties.

The appropriate cut-off grade can be decided only in the course of actual test mining and stoping during the initial stages of mine production.

Using current metal prices, reverse cash flow scenarios can be generated for a number of simulated mining, milling and marketing conditions to deduce cut off grade. Thus Kala et al. (*Jour. Mines, Metals & Fuels*, 1994, 163–71) have computed minimum ore reserve vs. grade curves for different types of Pb–Zn deposits of India, close to and far from milling facility, viz. deposits of Pb, deposits of Pb with Ag, deposits of Zn and deposits of Pb + Zn + Ag at the market prices of these metals prevailing in 1994.

In recognition of the complexity of the problem, the present practice of a mining concern is to undertake a feasibility study before taking a major investment decision on a deposit. There are three main areas covered by the feasibility study: (1) the capital account; (2) the summarised operational account; and (3) the tax account. These are estimated on the basis of the given geological facts (details of the orebody outline, grade, distribution, etc.), engineering and metallurgical test reports, and other relevant details from local experience. The profitability of the venture is called the Discounted Cash Flow Rate of Return. Besides, some companies spread the cost of a proposed mine on to the general cost of other mines—a bad practice no doubt, but quite frequent. It is, therefore, unwise for an exploration geologist to pronounce on the profitability of a venture. Technical viability is not synonymous with economic viability. For example, in an open cast operation, the incremental waste: ore ratio from the beginning to the end of the operation is critical for deciding upon the maximum depth of the open cast mine and the final surface outline. Both are technologically measurable; but the choice between open cast at extreme depths vs. underground workings will depend, among other factors, on the capital and operating costs of an open pit vs. a similar capacity underground working.

Inconsistencies in such a feasibility study could come from quite a few sources: some companies include the initial cost of exploration as a sunk cost, while others do not; some include the rate of inflation and the normal delay time for cost escalation factor, some do not; some insist on detailed cross-check of the measurements before preparation of a feasibility report; some use this pretext to improve their own cash balance or get a toehold on the management of the industry later on; and so on. Preparation of a good feasibility report is not always the passport to a successful mining venture. Funds for a mining company have to come from three sources: company reserve fund; equity (from shareholders); and loans (from financial institutions). Loans are to be repaid according to agreed interest rates and repayment periods; shareholders contributing to the equity base expect good dividends. Therefore, the company has to plan for a high rate of return from its early days, otherwise its market reputation will be adversely affected. Should there be a need to raise fresh loans from the market, the company will find itself in difficulty.

It is, therefore, very important for any investor to find out the capital outlay required and the operating cost of a mine for the first ten years. These come under three heads: labour, supplies and equipment. For each cost centre, e.g. cost of drilling or cost of hauling, the direct and indirect costs are to be calculated separately. The whole estimate can be added up to find out the average cost per tonne of ore raised. The most important variables for which cost estimates are to be calibrated are:

- Width of the minable zone(s)
- Hardness and other physical characteristics of the ore
- Cost of drill bits per meter drilled

- Cost of explosive per cubic meter of excavation
- Strength of the wall rocks and need for timbering/roof bolting
- Depth from which the ore is to be hoisted
- Amount of water to be pumped
- Local wage rates
- Power costs
- Cost of transportation of both incoming and outgoing material
- Taxes.

It is also useful to remember that the most economical rate of production is usually determined by the rate at which ore can be developed. Usually, in the first one or two years, it is safer to plan for low output from an underground mine, when the miners go through considerable 'trial and error' during initial development. Since a mining venture is normally more hazardous than, say, an equal investment in agriculture or fishery, the rate of return has to be higher on the capital investment, which consists of: (1) purchase price of property; (2) cost of mine development before regular production; and (3) cost of equipping the mine to produce. It is thus not unusual to find operating private mines changing hands. A critical evaluation is needed on such occasions.

METHODS OF COMPUTATION OF TOTAL IN SITU TONNAGE OF A MINERAL DEPOSIT

The first step in this endeavour is to prepare a detailed outline and cross-sections of the mineral deposit at regular intervals. Such cross-sections are usually drawn on the basis of actual measurement of width and dip of the deposit on the surface and of the intersections underground. Each cross-section must be related to a pre-determined survey grid.

In case of oxidised sulphide deposits, exposures near the surface are rare. One must prepare cross-sections on the basis of drill-hole intersections, which are normally planned at right angles (or as close to it) to the strike and dip of the host rocks *on that profile.* But the vein may dip at a different angle or strike obliquely to the host rock. It is never advisable to assume a regular bedded behaviour for vein-forming mineral deposits before seeing the body underground. Cross-sections of the mineral deposit, in all such cases, are to be treated as models, and alternative cross-sections must be drawn for correlation purposes.

In addition to computing the gross distribution of ore matter in the different surface and borehole intersections, the geologist has to conceptualise the overall shape of the orebody from genetic and structural environment. Thus, in placer deposits, one has to look for the channels and more particularly the portions therein, where the stream velocity had decelerated, e.g. around sharp changes in gradient, around piled-up boulders, in potholes, in a complex succession of channels in an aggrading river, etc. An early magmatic orebody like chromite is essentially tabular, if the host ultramafic body is stratiform, but pod-shaped in ophiolitic masses. Gold values in a quartz reef are in streaks along fold hinges or shear zones. To ignore such fundamental attributes in the distribution of ore elements and adopt a purely geometric approach to reconstruct the shape of an orebody between positive borehole intersections is a common error; the shape of a skarn zone will hardly be identical with that of a porphyry orebody even if the widths of the intersections are the same (Fig. 8.3)!

In all instances other than underground stopes, it is worth remembering that the computation of tonnage of a deposit involves the definition of its boundary; conceptualisation of its margin is always a matter of judgement.

Once the mineral deposit has been delineated in fair detail by surface excavations and drilling, it is advantageous to take up test mining in one or two underground levels, if the deposit is suitable for underground mining or if surface excavations are inadequate and costlier, e.g. in an old, abandoned property with large dumps.

ESTIMATION OF VOLUME OF A MINERAL DEPOSIT

The degree of accuracy of volume estimate of a mineral deposit is variable, depending on the stage of prospecting. At the beginning, after the outcrops of the deposit have been mapped, but before the covered stretches of its assumed extension have been established, estimate of the size of the deposit could be in error by 90%. Suppose a low-dipping limestone band has been traced over more than a kilometre of strike length on the basis of intermittent outcrops in undulating ground and an estimate of the volume has been made on the assumptions that: (1) the band continues down dip to at least 30 m vertical depth; and (2) that the horizontal width of the minable zone is the farthest distance between the outcrops closest to the

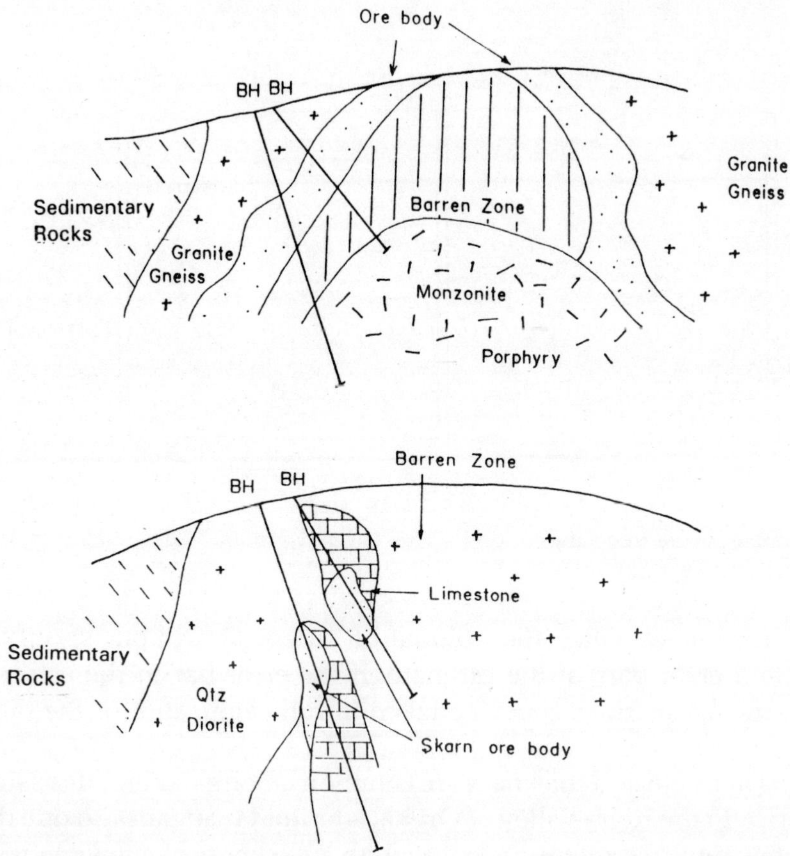

Fig. 8.3: Contrasting forms of extrapolation from borehole intersections of similar widths, depending on the type of deposit.

hanging wall and the footwall of the deposit; the resource estimation on such a basis could be in error by a large margin (Fig. 8.4). The unexposed parts of the limestone could be shale partings; there could be large caverns filled with sand, clay or alluvium inside the limestone terrain; etc. To illustrate another case, suppose a bauxite zone is exposed along the scarp faces of a plateau; and one has computed the resource of bauxite on the basis of the average thickness noted on the scarp faces, without checking whether the central depression of the plateau is bauxite-bearing or completely kaolinised. The volume calculation could be grievously wrong. Such mistakes have actually happened, causing serious problems during mining.

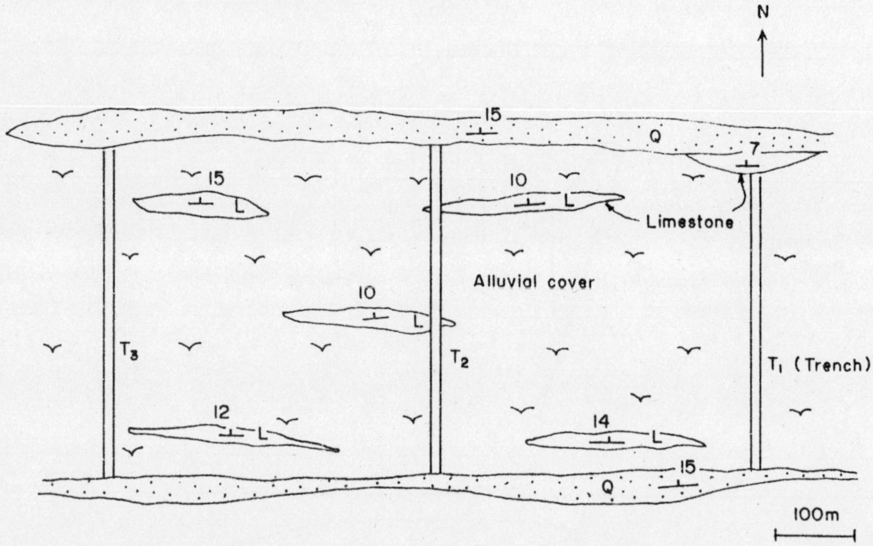

Fig. 8.4: An example where trenching/pitting across covered ground is essential. (L = Limestone outcrop; Q = Quartzite outcrop.)

One should never calculate the volume of a deposit without specifying the assumptions and error bars of the estimate. If the error bar in the estimation is defined, investment decisions could be taken in full cognizance of the margin of uncertainty.

Fluctuations in grade and thickness are common among mineral deposits of the same ore district. In the Koira valley of Orissa, lateritoid manganese oxide deposits range from a few hundred metres in length with a thickness of a few metres to less than a few meters in length and plum-shaped in cross-section. The long and tabular chromite deposit extending from Sukerangi to Saruabil in the Sukinda field is as much a part of the ultramafic complex as the small massive chromite lenses next to the Mahagiri Quartzite at Bhimtangar. The persistent copper lodes extending from Chapri to Tamapahar in the Singhbhum shear zone are only a few kilometres to the northwest of the impersistent streaky ore zones at Kendadih and Surda.

In flat lying or low dipping, tabular or lenticular ore deposits with a Gaussian distribution of metal values, it is advisable to have an orientation survey at an early stage to decide upon the appropriate spacing between the sub-surface intersections. First, divide the surface extent of the deposit into blocks of homogeneous domain on the basis of geological understanding, taking care that faults, host rock facies boundaries, stratigraphic breaks, geomorphologic contrasts etc. are not ignored in outlining the blocks. Within each block, select a test strip, where intersections are made at variable spacing (Fig. 8.5). The thickness × grade values of the intersections are to be analysed by parametric statistics. Such test strips, located at the central part of each block and having intersections on variable spacings ranging from 5 m to 150 m would provide a relatively better estimate of both the natural area of influence for the block and the error bars for the alternate spacings. In extension areas of already-explored sectors, however, such exercises are redundant, if the records of the explored sectors are available. Equally inadvisable are such attempts in the case of steep dipping, thin mineral deposits with zones of oxidation and secondary enrichment and intermittent surface indications. In such fields, it is advisable to space inclined boreholes at 50–100 m spacing along strike and plan the angle of the holes at right angle or so to the dip of the ore zones. Assume the area of influence to be halfway between the boreholes both along strike and dip, except for the outlying intersections, where the area of influence should be confined to the inside boundary of the explored panel (Fig. 8.6). Confirmation of the area of influence can only come from underground drifts. As mentioned in Chapter 7, special care is needed for deposits with erratic distribution of metal values like Au, PGE, Sn, W etc. The volume of the host rock for such deposits—stockwork/quartz vein/skarn/mafic igneous patches—can no doubt be computed by regularly-spaced boreholes; but computation of the average grade on the basis of drill-hole samples is inadvisable.

Area of Influence

A central concept in the estimation of volume of a deposit is the area of influence around the points of intersection. Basically, it involves extrapolation of 1-d information into 2-d space or 2-d information into 3-d space. Imagine a tabular, flat-lying, uniform (in both thickness and grade) mineral deposit whose limits are well defined, say a pyrite seam within carbonaceous shale (e.g. Amjhore pyrite) exposed on all the scarp faces of a small mesa. A single borehole at the central part of the mesa should be enough for checking whether the thickness and grade of the pyrite seam in the hole is identical with the scarp sections. If it is, the area of influence of the borehole for computation of volume is the area of the mesa top (Fig. 8.7).

If, however, the thickness and/or grade in the borehole do not correspond to the scarp data, one has to drill more holes on the mesa top. In all such contingencies, it is better to drill the holes on a regular grid (equilateral triangle/square/rectangle) interval, so that personal bias in borehole site selection is excluded and at the same

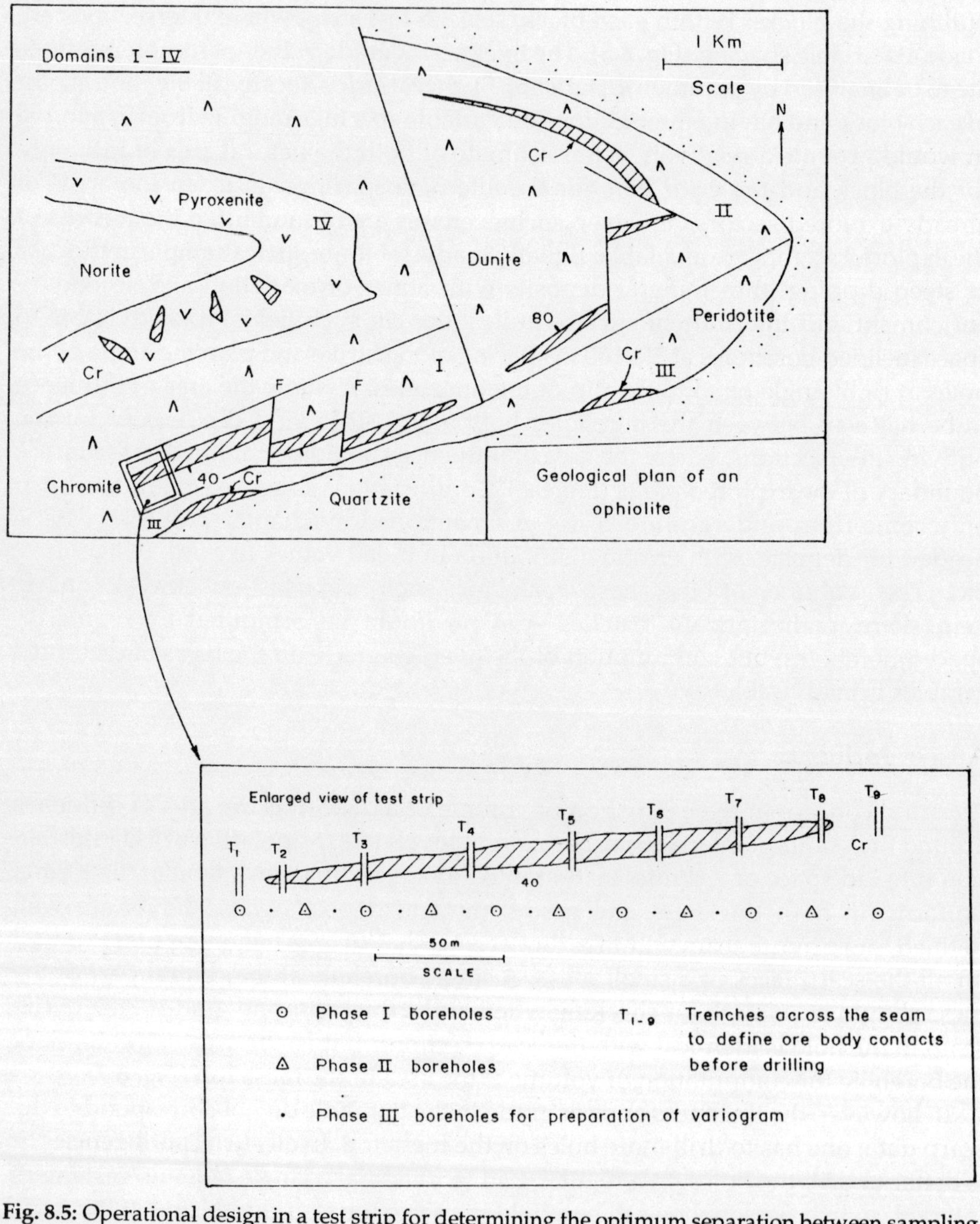

Fig. 8.5: Operational design in a test strip for determining the optimum separation between sampling stations.

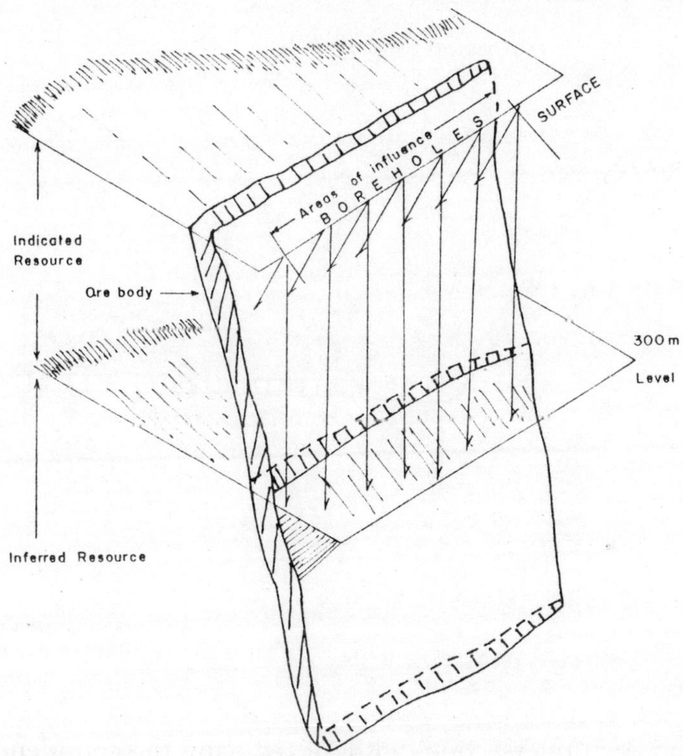

Fig. 8.6: Area of influence around borehole intersections and categorisation of resources. Note that the outlying boreholes are not assigned any area of influence beyond the points of intersection.

time additional controls for preparing cross-sections at regular intervals are generated. Conventionally, each borehole/pit intersection in such a case has an area of influence up to half the distance from the nearest borehole on all sides.

The optimum separation between two intersections is determined by: (1) time and money available for prospecting; (2) nature of the deposit; and (3) type of mining planned. Vertical holes are preferred for deposits suitable for open cast mining, so that level plans for different benches could be prepared easily. For steep dipping, thin veins which require underground mining, drilling is usually by inclined holes as near orthogonal to the veins as possible. The area of influence around any intersection is basically controlled by the geological features of the deposit. Extraneous considerations cannot be used for assigning an inflated area of

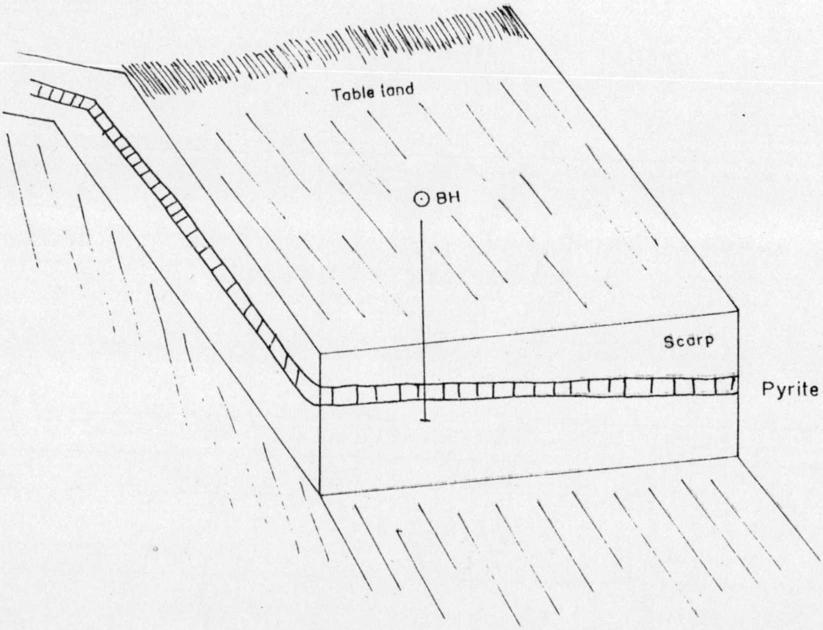

Fig. 8.7: Where a bedded deposit is exposed on the scarp faces as a regular seam, a single borehole is enough for computation of inferred resource.

influence around each intersection, without reducing the confidence level of the estimate.

Where the surface expressions of a mineral deposit are very patchy, pitting/drilling on wide grid intervals of say 150 m/300 m are initially recommended. Around successful boreholes, the ground is drilled at 30 m/ 50 m grid intervals. The grid layout varies from one company to another. For example in the massive sulphide deposits in Cyprus, the drill grid is of equilateral triangles with the boreholes at the apices. The volume estimation of reserves is based on cross-sections at 10 m intervals along one trend, counterchecked by cross-sections at right angles to the previous direction.

On the other hand, in the Namosi district of southeast Viti Levu, large, low-grade, porphyry copper deposits are explored on the basis of 70 m square grid spacings.

In India, the preferred practice in the GSI in the sixties and seventies was to adopt a square or rectangular grid. For moderately to steeply dipping mineral deposits, the spacing between holes was kept at larger intervals for the deeper levels.

The volume of the deposit is calculated as follows:

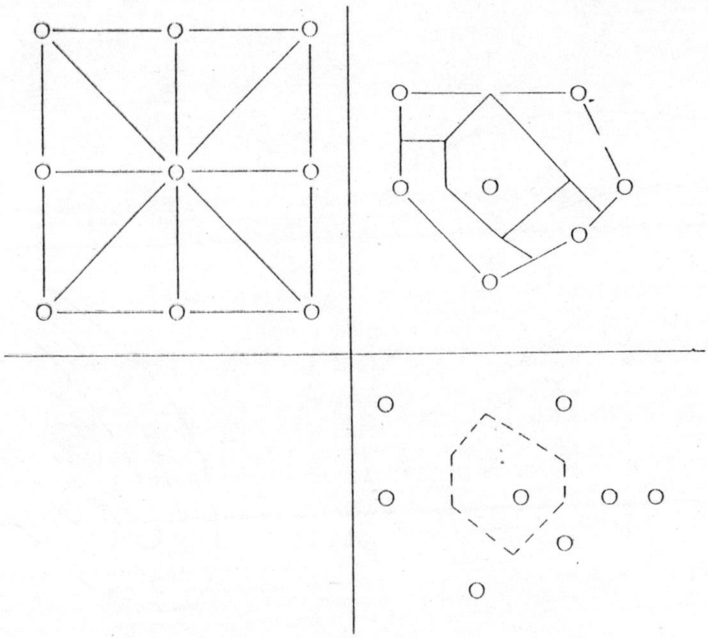

Fig. 8.8: Polygon methods of volume estimation.

(a) Polygon method: Polygons are drawn around each borehole by the perpendicular bisectrix method (Fig. 8.8) and the area of the polygon around each positive intersection is measured by either a planimeter or an overlay of transparent graph sheet. The area in sq. m is multiplied by the thickness (in metres) to get the volume in cubic meters. Multiply this by the appropriate bulk specific gravity of the ore to obtain gross *in situ* tonnage.

(b) Isopach method: For flat lying or low dipping broadly tabular ore deposits varying in thickness and grade from point to point, isopach (connecting points of identical true thickness of the deposit) and isograde maps are prepared for reserve computation.

The areas are measured either by planimeter or by graphical counts. The areas between successive thickness contours are multiplied by the mean value between the lower and upper contour to obtain the total volume of the sector. For computation of grade-wise volume combining isopach and isograde maps, one has to maintain constant interval between the contours to avoid future errors through oversight. The average grade of the deposit is computed by overlaying the isograde map over the isopach, measuring the thickness of individual isograde and isopach

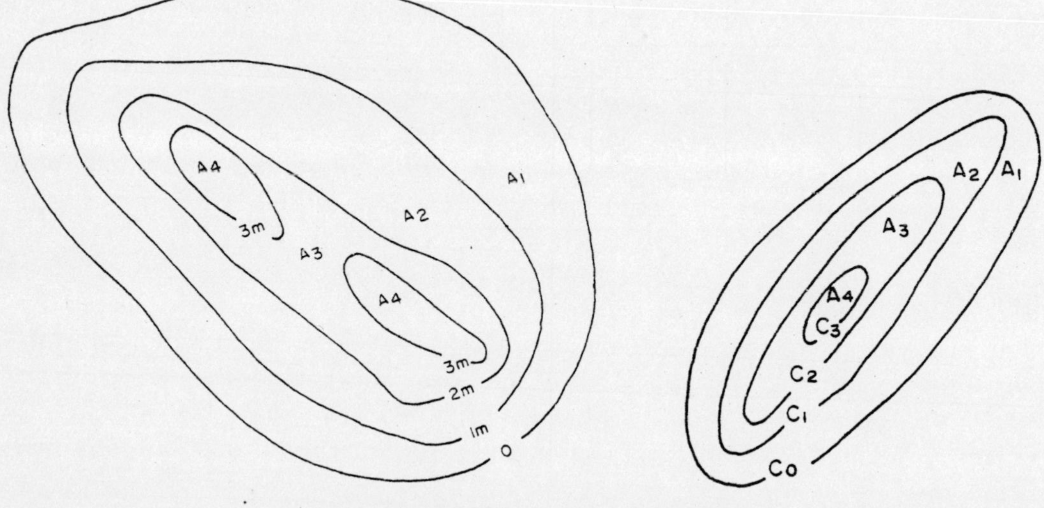

Fig. 8.9: Isopach method of volume estimation.

sub-sectors separately, adding the columns and dividing by the volume of the deposit, computed separately from the isopach map (Fig. 8.9).

(c) Cross-section method: For this purpose, the intersections should preferably be on grids and the distance between two successive cross-sections (D) should be constant. The outline of the deposit on each cross-section should first be drawn on the basis of borehole intersections and surface outcrops (if available) and the sectional area measured with a planimeter or graph paper overlay.

The formula for volume is:

$$V = \frac{A_1 + A_2}{2} .D + \frac{A_2 + A_3}{2} .D + \dots \frac{A_{n-1} + A_n}{2} .D$$

where $A_1, A_2 \dots A_n$ are sectional areas in sq. m from one end of the deposit to the other;

D = constant distance in metres, perpendicular to the cross-section;

V = total volume of the deposit in cubic metres.

Where distances between cross-sections are variable, D_1, D_2...D_n, you have to multiply the average of two adjacent sectional areas by the intervening distance. Thus, the general formula would be:

$$V = \frac{A_1 + A_2}{2} .D_1 + \frac{A_2 + A_3}{2} \cdot D_2 + \ldots \frac{A_{n-1} + A_n}{2} .D_n$$

The cross-section method is very popular for lateritic mineral deposits, like those of Fe, Mn, Al etc. as well as for stratiform sulphide deposits like Amjhore pyrite, no matter how the boreholes are arranged, so long as these are vertical (Fig. 8.10).

(d) Longitudinal Vertical (LV) section method: In the case of moderate to steeply dipping, relatively thin mineral deposits, amenable to underground mining, computation of volume of ore level-wise requires the measurement of horizontal width *and not the true width.*

Thus, in a longitudinal vertical section of the deposit, the volumes are computed panel-wise (Fig. 8. 11).

$V_1 = A_1 \times W_1$ for panel 1,

$V_2 = A_2 \times W_2$ for panel 2 and so on,

$V_{1,2...n}$ being the volume and $A_{1,2...n}$ being the area on the vertical plane around each positive intersection. Such extrapolated area of influence along strike and dip is frequently unreal and excessive. Later mine openings reveal discrepancies leading to a sharp change in tonnage estimates.

For computation of tonnage of ore from LV sections, the following formula is used:

$$(A_1 \times W_1 \times g_1) + (A_2 \times W_2 \times g_2) + \ldots (A_n \times W_n \times g_n)$$

where A_1, A_2... A_n are the sectional areas of the panels 1, 2...n, W_1, W_2...W_n are the aggregated horizontal widths of a lode[1] at each positive borehole and g_1, g_2...g_n are the average grades of the particular lode at each positive intersection.

Each LV section must be supplemented with transverse sections orthogonal to the strike of the deposit, where the boreholes and the ore intersections are plotted true to scale and matching with the levels of the LV section. The volume and tonnage

[1]A composite lode could have a number of partings depending on the cut-off used.

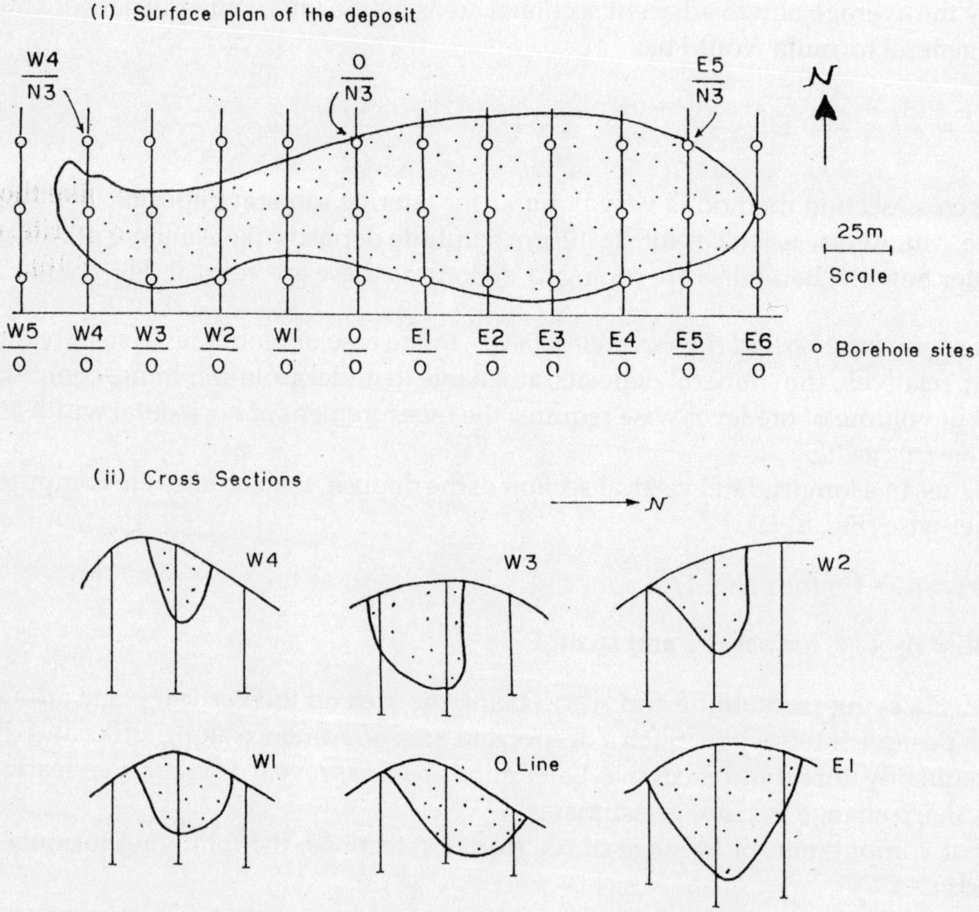

Fig. 8.10: Cross-section method of volume estimation.

computed by the LV section method should be checked by an alternate method to find out the degree of coherence between the estimates, i.e. the precision, although the *accuracy* of the estimate cannot be evaluated by such alternative estimations.

The following steps are needed for construction of a longitudinal vertical section.

Step 1: Prepare a large-scale topographically contoured map (scale 1:1000, contour interval: 1 m) of the mineralised area including the drill-hole sites.

Step 2: Prepare a topographic profile along the projected surface expression and strike of the mineral deposit with closely spaced geographic co-ordinates.[2]

Step 3: Draw cross-sections on the basis of boreholes, and plot the mineralised zones on these sections. Correct for borehole deviations and compute the geographic co-ordinates of the hanging and footwalls of the intersections.

Step 4: Plot the Hanging Wall (HW) and Footwall (FW) of each intersection according to their reduced level and geographic co-ordinates on the LV section.

Where the borehole is oblique to the LV section, the HW and FW points on the LV section lie oblique to each other instead of being vertically aligned; so also the trace of the borehole on the LV section. The borehole numbers have to be plotted both on the transverse and the LV sections for purposes of correlation.

A common error during preparation of cross-sections and LV sections is the mixing of different scales. Whenever you transfer from one scale to another, the relevant factor of enlargement/reduction has to be applied.

LV sections are essential for underground mine planning and reserve estimation.

Step 5: Mark out suitable rectangular panels on the LV section around each positive intersection, number these panels row- and column-wise (corresponding to different levels) and present a panel-wise estimate as a small inset within the plate.

Bulk Specific Gravity

It is important to remember that the bulk specific gravity is different from the specific gravity of a small piece of ore. The porosity of the material in bulk, the specific gravity of the ore and gangue minerals in their variable combinations, the moisture content etc. play important roles in bulk specific gravity.

[2]If the deposit is sinuous in plan, the LV section should be in strips of different trends on discrete vertical planes as close to the sinuosity of the outcrops as possible. The orientation of the sections must be plotted on the topographic map and shown on the sections.

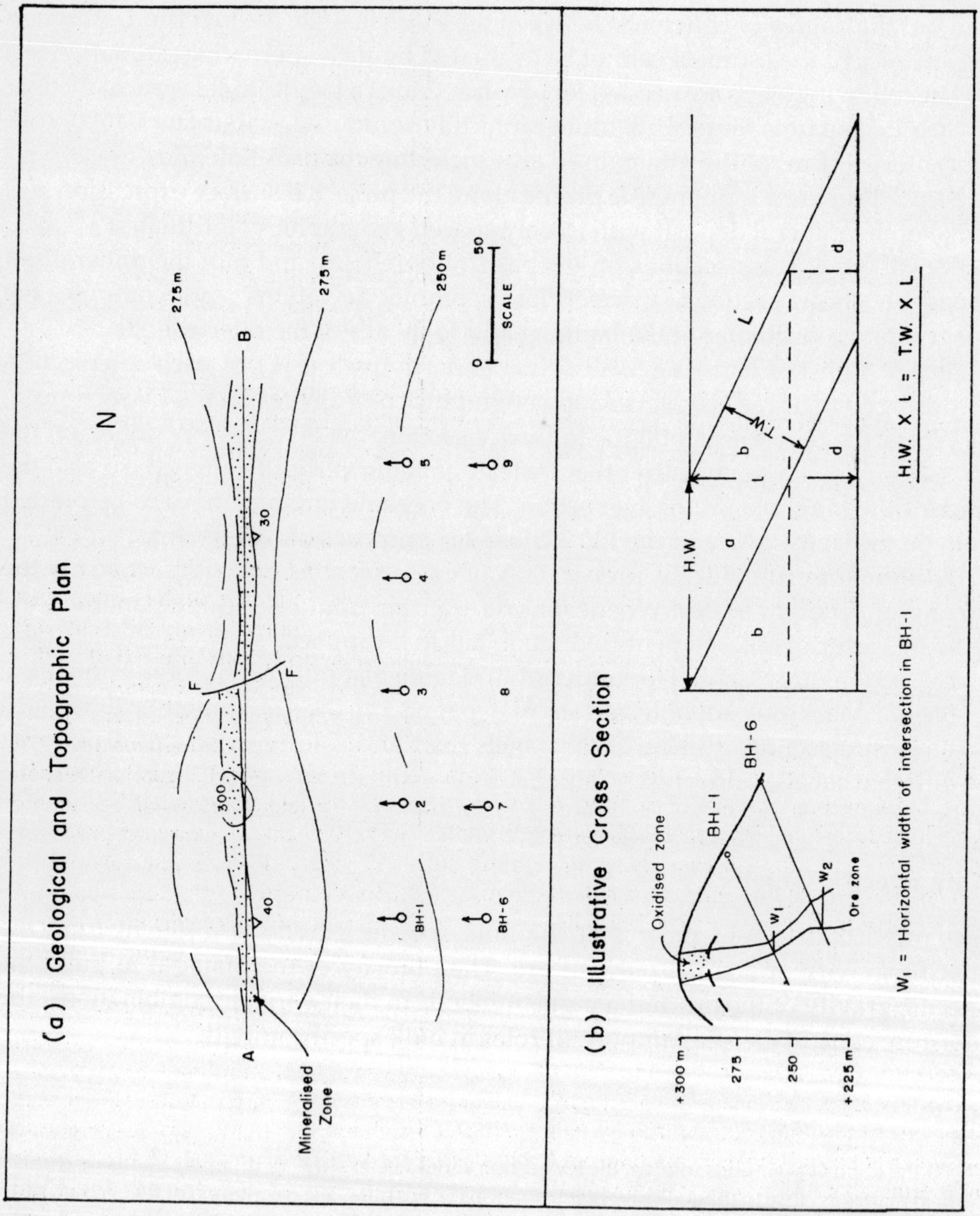
(a) Geological and Topographic Plan
N
275 m
250 m
SCALE
0
50
Mineralised Zone
A
B
F
300
40
30
BH-1
BH-6
(b) Illustrative Cross Section
Oxidised zone
Ore zone
+300 m
275
250
+225 m
H.W
T.W
W_1 = Horizontal width of intersection in BH-1
H.W. X l = T.W. X L

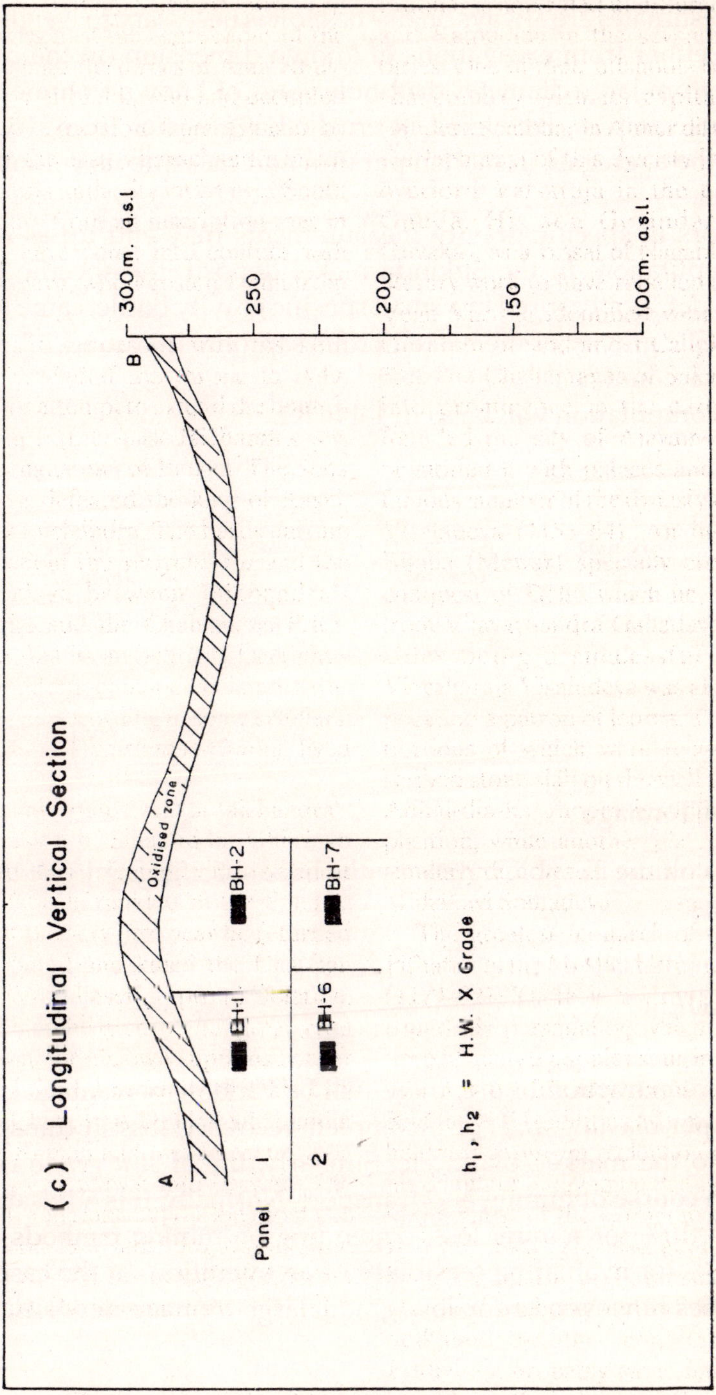

Fig. 8.11: LV section—stages of drawing.

Since ore estimates are always on dry basis, it is necessary to weigh the ore blocks after drying either from excavations of known dimension (in the case of shallow deposits) or from large diameter drill-hole cores of known volume. In the case of highly porous samples, recovered in crushed aggregates from dry drilling, you should coat the aggregate in molten paraffin and measure its volume by displacement of water.

Small errors in specific gravity measurements may end up as large errors in tonnage computation. In the Sukinda nickel deposit, the specific gravity of the goethite powder, as measured in a small specific gravity bottle, came to 2.2, whereas the bulk specific gravity of the nickeliferous saprolite is around 1.2. Porosity must be taken into account.

The final computation will be as in Table 8.1.

Table 8.1

Block	*Volume (m^3)*	*Bulk sp. gr. (average)*	*Grade %*	*In situ ore (tonnes)*	*In situ total metal (tonnes)*
1	825	2.40	6.6	1980	130.68
2	716	2.36	5.9	1690	99.69
3	923	2.42	7.1	2234	158.58
Total				5904	388.95

Estimation of Tonnage

Multiply the volume in cubic metres by the bulk specific gravity of the ore zone to get metric tons.

R.O.M. GRADE

In the course of extraction of ore, there will be variable percentage of mining loss due to improper blasting and/or incomplete recovery, loss in transport from the mining face to the market/plant, etc. Similarly, the *in situ* grade can hardly be maintained in course of mining and transport. Normally, it is advisable to provide a margin of 5–10% for mining loss, depending on mining methods, and a grade dilution of 10% for evaluating feasibility of an operation. In the case of marginal grade orebodies however, or for low-grade, large-tonnage deposits, extracted by open cast method, e.g. porphyry Cu deposits, the run-of-mine (R.O.M.) grade is adjusted by suitable scheduling of extraction from different mine faces, so that the grade of the combined ore comes as close to the desired grade as possible. Such quality control of mine faces is normally done by the resident geologist, who bases his scheduling on the basis of analytical results on samples from pneumatic drill-holes on a close grid (5m × 5m or less) planned ahead of the mine faces.

FURTHER READING

Constantine C. Popoff, Computing reserves of mineral deposit: Principles and conventional methods, US Bureau of Mines Information Circular 8283, 1966, 55 pp.

J.H. Reedman, *Techniques in Mineral Exploration*, Applied Science Publishers, London, 1979, 533 pp.

9

Valuation of a Mine

This is an important aspect of the mining industry. Hard technical data are provided by the exploration group and the viability of the deposit decided by the financial group. A dialogue between the two groups must be based on clear appreciation of mutual needs.

Mine valuations are required for: (1) sale of property; (2) dissolution of partnership; (3) merger; (4) tax appraisal; (5) obtaining loans from financial institutions; (6) litigation; and (7) listing on the stock exchange.

Mining is different from all other industries. Every business venture has an element of risk, but in mining the risks are higher for the following reasons:

(1) The minable reserve may fall short of initial estimates due to errors in sampling.
(2) Unforeseen contingencies (fresh statutory obligations, political or economic changes, natural hazards etc.) may affect the profitability of the operation.
(3) Severe fluctuations in the demand-supply position of the commodity market may render a low grade deposit totally uneconomic.
(4) Introduction of rigid environmental codes may place a working mine within a protected zone.
(5) The deposit may change its grade and shape erratically, particularly in extramensurate bodies, leading to costly and unproductive ventures.

A mine is a wasting asset. Unlike mining, all other major industries are taken to be perpetual for purposes of economic appraisal. The resource underground is progressively exhausted in the course of mining operations. Therefore, from the investor's point of view, it is not enough to earn annual profits. The initial capital invested has also to be recovered during the productive life of the mine. Where additional funds are raised from the market, the normal practice is to make periodical payment of dividend to the investors. As a non-renewable resource, a mineral deposit cannot be equated with other regenerative industries like agriculture. If the monsoon fails one year, one may wait for the next year's crop to recover the loss; not so in a mine. If the deposit is so small that the cost of its development exceeds the earnings out of its sale, all the expenditure goes down the drain (Appendix I).

Mining companies are essentially of two types: (a) those who work a given property and when that is exhusted give up their business; and (2) those who contemplate perpetuating their business and own a cluster of properties or a variety of activities other than mining as well and set aside part of their earnings for other interests or from time to time obtain new capital from the market to provide for purchase of new mines or properties, both within the country and overseas. Some of these latter types are the giant multinational conglomerates. They may mine a mineral in one country, process it in a second country, extract metal from the processed ore in a third country and market the product globally. For such operations, it is not possible to provide a dependable estimate of profitability of a single mine, since the operating cost (expenditure charged to production at the time it is made) and capital accounts (to be written off as depreciation) of individual mines are not always available on operating books separately, and the final cost sheet is a mixture of diverse activities. In a hierarchical order, the mine cost sheet at the lowest rung of the ladder has to include expenditure at the mine for: (1) labour; (2) supplies; (3) mechanical department; (4) electrical department; (5) compressors; (6) power; (7) construction; (8) civil and welfare activities etc. At the top of the ladder in the Head Office, the records include summarized details of: (1) capital stock and dividends (for stockholders); (2) receipts from and payment on bonds (for bondholders); (3) purchases of property; (4) deposits into and cheques on bank accounts; (5) receipts from and payment on loans; (6) amount of investment; (7) dividends from investment; (8) expenditure on administration; and (9) payment to as well as receipts from operating mine office.

A proper valuation of a mine presupposes that the owner is not making a distress sale.

FACTORS IN MINE VALUATION

The natural value of a mine is expressed simply as:

$V = R \times C \times e \times t \times s$; where

V = the value of the mine in Rupees;

R = recoverable reserve of raw material in the mine in tonnes;

C = price of the saleable product per tonne in rupees;

e = per cent recovery during mining;

t = per cent recovery during dressing;

s = per cent recovery during other pre-sale refining.

Additionally, valuation of non-renewable resources like a mine must also incorporate the cost of replacing the resource or for its substitution. This is not yet taken into account either locally or nationally.

Conventional accounting does not provide for depreciation due to loss of the non-renewable resource, as it is mined out. Exploitation and sale of these assets is treated as a free income. This is no longer acceptable. Moreover, the damage to forests, soil, biotic habitat etc. is not recognised as a cost. The loss in long-term value of these resources has to be considered in the total cost-benefit analysis before wild habitats are converted to mines and ancillary industries. An example from an allied activity would illustrate the importance of such a holistic approach in a cost-benefit analysis. Some time ago in Thailand, the cost-benefit analysis of a proposal to convert a mangrove ecosystem into shrimp farms (a common practice in the current globalised market) found that mangrove-dependant fisheries and forest products generate as much wealth as shrimp farms in terms of creation of jobs and sustainable development. Additionally, they protect the shoreline from erosion and other damage. Similar choices will have to be made in future evaluation of agricultural or forest land for potential mine-related uses.

The following factors have to be determined for a valuation.

Annual Profit

The annual profit from the mine is the recoverable value (a) minus the cost of production (b).

(a) *Recoverable Value:* The recoverable value is estimated on the basis of past mining records or by undertaking test mining of a representative part of the deposit.

The relevant parameters are sampled grade within the mine, percentage of recovery in course of mining and where the mine is integrated with a smelter, the total metal recovery per cent. During mining, either some gangue gets mixed with the output or some part of the deposit is left unmined, reducing the total estimated tonnage. Thus the sampled *in situ* grade is usually different from the grade at the pit head; some further dilution is expected during transport of the material to the market/beneficiation plant and smelter. The net effect is that the recoverable grade of a deposit is very rarely close to its *in situ* grade.

(b) *Cost of Production*: This includes both direct and indirect costs. The important variables have already been listed in Chapter 8. In case of an operating mine, past records may help, if correctly and truthfully maintained. Otherwise, general market norms may be adopted from similar deposits in the neighbourhood. The estimate of cost must include the following:

(i) Operating cost, including maintenance of equipment etc.
(ii) Developmental cost to establish new proved reserves equal to the quantity mined out.
(iii) Cost of transport of material raised to market (f.o.r or f.o.b).
(iv) Establishment cost of selling the commodity.
(v) Administrative and other general expenses, commonly clubbed under 'overhead expenses'. This remains constant irrespective of fluctuations in production from time to time. This should be kept as low as possible.

The cost of production in a vertically integrated mine-beneficiation plant-smelter complex can be calculated by Rachkovskii's formula as follows:

$$C = \frac{R_3(C_p + C_{ob})}{f \times i_0 \times i_m \times (1 - q)} + \frac{R_3\ (C_t + C_m)}{R_f \times i_m}$$

where C = production cost of 1 tonne of product; C_{ob} = cost of treatment of 1 tonne of ore; R_3 = content of useful mineral in the final product; C_p = cost of extraction and transport of 1 tonne of ore; f – content of useful mineral in the ore, based on sampling; q = coefficient of ore loss during mining; C_t = transport cost from the dressing to the smelting plant; C_m = cost of smelting 1 tonne of concentrate; R_f = content of useful mineral in the concentrate i_0 & i_m = coefficients of yield of useful mineral in the dressing and smetting plants.

Once the cost figure and the recoverable value per tonne of material sold are available, a general estimate of the margin of profit against the rate of annual production can be prepared subject to inflation corrections.

Productive Period

The second important factor in valuation is the number of productive years for the mine. Suppose there is a deposit close to the limit of its minability; or so near an abandoned mine that a part of the reserve has to be left untapped. For example, in the Sukinda chromite field, a large part of the estimated resource of nearly 120 million tonnes lies below quarriable depth. Underground mining of soft limonite saprolite wall rock will not be easy. Hence the minable reserve is likely to be much less than the estimated resource. These are to be taken into account. The productive life of a mine is not always proportional to the total mineral in ground. The rate of mining vis-a-vis the minable reserve provides an index of the life of a mine.

Simply stated, the life of the mine is

$$L = R / A$$

where

L is the life of the mine in years;

R is the recoverable reserve; and

A is the annual production of raw material from the mine.

A, the rate of mining, is not an absolute, independent parameter. The mining method adopted partly decides how much one can mine in a day. In terms of output per man shift (OMS) an underground mine is handicapped vis-a-vis an open cast operation. Fluctuations in the commodity market may accelerate or reduce the rate of mining. One can never be too sure. This is a speculative game. But it is vital to establish *amortisation tonnage* (the smallest scale of operation that would yield reasonable operating profit on the capital invested with its interest) as the crux of the decision. Where there is a reasonable chance of finding more minable material, the company may progressively build up its production schedule. It is a general practice to carry out development of the extension areas hand in hand with mining, so that proved reserves of about five years are in hand all the time till the mine reaches its last phase.

The maximum annual output can be expressed by the formula

$$O_{max} = A \times D \times s \times r$$

where

O_{max} is the maximum annual raising;

A = the slice of the deposit in sq. m bounded between an upper and a lower surface which can be mined in one year;

D = incremental depth reached after one year of mining, i.e. final depth minus initial depth; and

r = recovery per cent of raw material.

Potential Value in Ground

The third relevant issue is to estimate the present value of the future earnings. Mineral commodities show considerable annual and decadal price fluctuations. It is the general practice to take the average price for the last 25–30 years. The prices are normally governed by laws of supply and demand; but with the collapse of the USSR, opening up of the South African commodity market, globalisation of industries and a preliminary proposal for levying taxes on mining as a 'green fee', the present picture is in a state of flux.

An idea about the prevailing market price of selected commodities is given in Table 9.1 as an illustration of the wide range.

METHODS OF VALUATION

Once the three aforementioned important parameters have been broadly assessed, the value and worth of a mine can be reasonably estimated, given satisfactory information on technical parameters (Appendix II). There are different methods. The simplest is to find out the market value of the mine stock, but a mine is seldom worth the price listed on the stock exchange. The net earnings from a mine can never be correctly computed in advance.

This computation is possible only after the mine is exhausted. One can then compute the net profit by simply adding the annual profits over the years. But this gives a distorted picture. The purchasing power of a rupee today is less than what it was a year ago; and the rupee you earn ten years later may have only 1/10th of today's purchasing power. A rupee for mine investment has therefore to be viewed in much the same way as one would view a potential investment in a National Savings Certificate where the principal amount is recovered after a fixed period;

Table 9.1

Commodity	*Estimated value during 1995–96 (Indian Rs.)*	*Metal*	*Average price in London Metal Exchange during 1994 (U.S. Dollars)*
Bauxite	177/ton	Al	1480/ton
Copper ore	440/ton	Cu	2312/ton
Lead concentrate	9050/ton	Pb	549/ton
Zinc concentrate	5842/ton	Zn	998/ton
Gold	5300/10 g	Ni	6341/ton
Silver bar	7100/kg*	Pd	356/oz**
Iron ore	193/ton	Pt	1196/oz**
Manganese	837/ton		
Chromite	2190/ton		
Tungsten concentrate	185/kg		
Tin concentrate	68/kg		
Phosphorite	1034/ton		
Barytes	498/ton		
Dolomite	189/ton		
Diamond	4379/carat		
Graphite (R.O.M.)	282/ton		
Gypsum	780/ton		
Kyanite	573/ton		
Sillimanite	2356/ton		
Limestone	80/ton		
Magnesite	753/ton		
Mica (crude)	12534/kg		
Pyrites	488/ton		

* Price at the end of 1996. Prices of precious metals are volatile.
** Price in New York Mercantile Exchange in 1990 when free trading in precious metals became a hedge against inflation.
(*Source: Indian Mining Directory*, 1996, 5/e, MGMI, Calcutta and *Metals and Minerals Annual Review*, 1991–1995)

and meanwhile it would either grow into double the original or fetch the investor a fixed return every month or quarter. Mining is a high-risk investment. Therefore the rate of return must be higher than other normal instruments of investment, and one needs to convert future earnings to their present value according to the formula:

$$V_p = \frac{1}{(1 - r)^n}$$

where V_p is the present value of Re 1 due in n years and r is the rate of interest compounded annually.

If interest has to be paid more than once each year, the formula becomes

$$V_p = \frac{1}{(1 + \frac{r}{t})} t_n$$

where t is the number of times a year the interest is compounded.

If you want to avoid converting each instalment payment separately to its present value, you may use the following formula

$$V_p = \frac{(1 + r)^n - 1}{r\,(1 + r)^n}.$$

Another method for estimating the value of a mine is derived from the century-old practice of the British Coal Mining Companies, which floated its shares in the capital market much like the offers of the Unit Trust of India, indicating in effect that the company would pay a dividend to the investor each year and refund the principal amount when the mine is exhausted.

But at the end of mining activities how does the company get so much money? In order to ensure this rather uncertain prospect, the mining company sets aside each year an appropriate amount of its earnings on compound interest, so that when the reserve is exhausted, money for refund of the principal amount is in the kitty. H.D. Hoskold, a British mining engineer, developed a formula for this.

The Hoskold formula for mine valuation is based on the following assumptions:

(a) That the annual income from the mine is a constant amount from year to year;

(b) That the uniform speculative rate of interest 'r' covers both the interest on capital, as well as on the amount needed for redeeming of the capital simultaneously;

(c) That the contribution towards capital earns interest at a rate 'r'.

If V_p is the present value of immediate (non-deferred) redemption annuity, n is the number of years and A is the amount of annual earnings on dividend,

$$\text{then } V_p = \frac{A}{\dfrac{r}{(1+r)^n - 1} + r'}.$$

Example: The annual output of an iron ore mine has been estimated at 200,000 tonnes, the net profit being Re 1 per tonne. Assuming the proved reserve to be 4,000,000 tonnes what will be the present value of he mine, if 7½% C.I. (compound interest) is allowed for repayment of capital and the redemption of capital is provided at 2½% C.I. ?

$A = 200{,}000 \times 1 = \text{Rs } 200{,}000 \text{ p.a.}$

$$n = \frac{4{,}000{,}000}{200{,}000} = 20 \text{ years}$$

$r' = 0.075$

$r = 0.025$

$$V_p = \frac{A}{\dfrac{r}{(1+r)^n - 1} + r'} = \frac{200{,}000}{\dfrac{0.025}{(1.025)^{20} - 1} + 0.75} = \text{Rs } 17{,}52{,}111.$$

If V_p is taken to represent the present value of deferred redemption annuity and if the period of deferment be m years, then the following points need to be taken into consideration.

(i) That the buyer of the annuity will obtain interest on purchase money at a particular rate during the life of the annuity.

(ii) That the rate of interest may either remain the same or change during the deferment period.

(iii) That the overplus dividend for redemption of the capital (simultaneously with the annuity payment) will be paid at another but practicable rate.

Taking the above points into consideration the present value of a deferred redemption annuity can be computed.

If r = safe rate of interest on redemption,

r' = speculative rate of interest on capital investment during the period of annuity payment,

r'' = rate of interest on capital during the deferment period,

V_{bi}= value of annuity at the commencement of its interest earning period. This amount is different from the present worth because of the period of deferment. V_{bi} is discounted to present value at the rate of r'' for the deferred period of m years, and

V_p = present value = value at the beginning of the period, during which the annuity payments are to be made.

$$V_p = \frac{\dfrac{A}{r}}{\dfrac{(1 + r)^n - 1}{(1 + r'')^n}}$$

CASH FLOW PATTERN

(1) Capital: This is required not only for meeting the direct and indirect costs of the mining operation, including purchase of equipment and machinery, labour payment, royalty and other taxes etc. There are associated social and environmental costs as well. Mining and labour laws and regulations specify introduction of welfare measures for the workers like shelter, subsidised food and fuel, drinking water etc. besides creche, first aid centre/hospital and roads. This investment is a social cost. The larger the workforce, the greater is the investment required for setting up such facilities. Since mines are generally located far from townships, development of the area and creation of infrastructure for a proper living style depend on the active support of the mine owners. Where open cast mining is undertaken, present environmental regulations require restitution of the ground after the termination of mining. This also costs money. The day may not be far off when the cost of substitution of the non-renewable resource will also be included.

No wonder therefore that a mine has to provide for a much higher rate of return on investment than any other industry of comparable scale.

(2) Interest rate: A return of 10% on the investment is considered adequate for normal mining ventures. This rate may however be as high as 50%, where the mine is located at a remote place or infested with terrorists or facing very volatile labour problems.

FURTHER READING

M. Kuzvart and M. Bohmer, Prospecting and exploration of mineral deposits, *Developments in Economic Geology* No.21, Elsevier, Amsterdam, 1986, 508 pp.

R.N.P. Arogyaswamy, *Courses in Mining Geology*, Oxford & IBH Publications, New Delhi, 1980, 927 pp.

10

Environmental Impact of Mining

There is nothing magical about a gold mine. Barren and pockmarked; all dirt and no trees, fenced in on all sides, a gold mine resembles a war-torn battlefield. The noise is harsh and ubiquitous; the rasp of shaft-lifts, the jangling power drills, the distant rumble of dynamites....

—Nelson Mandela: *Long Walk to Freedom*, 1994 (Macdonald Purnell)

The emperor of sustainable development has no clothes.

—W. Beckerman: *Small is Stupid*, 1995 (Duckworth)

Be it an underground or a surface working, for precious elements or for road metal, any mining activity affects the environment adversely. But the awareness of its possible impact on mankind can be traced to the International Geophysical Year, 1957–58, which acted as a catalyst for planetary and environmental sciences. The successor projects, including the on-going International Geosphere Biosphere Project (IGBP) and the Brundtland report (1987) which popularised the concepts of 'sustainable development' and 'precautionary principle', are direct consequences. Seemingly unrelated phenomena from local to interplanetary scales were progressively found to be linked. Questions about the history of the earth's climate led gradually to the recognition that glaciation in both the North and South Poles waxed and waned during the last 7 Ma (Leg 152 Shipboard party, *EOS*, 75(35), 1994, 401–6); that CO_2 in the oceans and the atmosphere needs to be budgeted with the plants for checking the 'greenhouse' vs. 'whitehouse' effect; and that the earth constitutes a unified system from the solid core to the outer magnetopause. Change at one place beyond a threshold affects the whole system. We must learn to maintain both species diversity and the global scale circulation patterns within the limits of their natural fluctuations.

Mining activities create considerable environmental changes as a result of excavations into the ground and the chain of downstream development activities generated in their wake. The type of drastic change, not only in land use but also in the fabric of socio-economic set up, is illustrated by the transformation in Papua New Guinea, where during the last few decades, large porphyry Cu deposits (at Bougainville), sulphides with appreciable Au and Ag contents (e.g. at Porgera) and oilfields have been developed. The Porgera deposit alone will yield more than 100 million tonnes of gold ore over the next 20 years. Some years ago the American oil giant Chevron pumped in 1,000 million US dollars in equipment and manpower to tap an oilfield in the Southern Highlands that is believed to contain at least 200 million barrels of hydrocarbon reserve.

This 600-island mountainous archipelago in the western Pacific, hidden under a canopy of rainforests and swamplands and sustaining its inhabitants with yams and pigs for centuries, has turned, as it were overnight, into a country dotted with high-rise buildings and satellite dishes. People who used to fight with bows and arrows and travel by foot now carry automatic weapons and drive Toyota Landcruisers. Displaced farmers have flocked to the towns in search of scarce jobs. Unemployment is rampant. Fast money has led to an increase in crime. Lightning transformation from stone age to electronics has only exacerbated the country's myriad political and social problems.

It is not for the mining geologist to anticipate the diverse environmental ramifications of development. But certain parameters can and should be measured as a baseline information package before mining is set in motion. The environmental impact can be broadly classified under the following categories:

- Physical impact;
- Chemical impact;
- Biological impact;
- Socio-economic impact;
- Cultural impact.

It is relevant to note that in pilot studies by the World Bank, the Net National Product (NNP) in Papua New Guinea has been found to have been reduced by as much as 10% after adjustments for environmental degradation and resource depletion caused by mining.

In Indonesia, from 1971 to 1984, GNP rose by 7.1%. But taking the depletion of natural capital into account, the GNP gets reduced to 4%, which would be further lowered since Indonesia has been investing too little of the profit from the natural capital (ore, timber, etc.) into fabricated capital to guarantee the future income of its growing population.

Similarly, a study in 1990 by the Costa Rican Tropical Science Centre found that the country's GDP growth averaged 4.6% annually from 1970 to 1989. But depreciation over that period in the value of its forests, fisheries and soil was equivalent to a reduction of potential GDP growth to 1.5–2.0%.

In India, large tracts of country in the coalfields, iron ore and other mineral fields where open cast mining is undertaken, have been damaged beyond repair. For example, the Sukinda valley in Orissa, where chrome ore mining is undertaken extensively by quarrying, is now dotted with large dumps of nickel-rich laterite saprolite (a toxic material for plants); timber has been extensively felled and wildlife completely destroyed. The negative impact on the local population has yet to be assessed.

The UN General Assembly Resolution 2994 of 15 December 1972 declared June 5 of every year as 'World Environment Day' and thereafter the United Nations Environment Programme was born. In June 1992 the greatest and boldest protection measures for environment and development were adopted in the Rio Declaration. Since the present US administration is also careful about environmental implications of development, it is expected that by AD 2000, environmental restoration will be an important agenda and cost in all new mining ventures (Appendix III).

As long as mankind cannot do without minerals, rocks and metals for sustenance, mining has to be undertaken on our planet, both on land and under the sea, and the environment of the surrounding area is bound to be affected to varying degrees. The impact fluctuates in both space and time, ranging from temporary micro-environmental perturbations, e.g. around small mica mines in pegmatites of Kodarma, Bihar to large-scale and long-term damage to vegetation, soil and habitat of life forms, e.g. around open-cast mines in chrome-rich ultramafic fields at Baula and Sukinda in Orissa (Fig. 10.1); magnesite mines at Salem, Tamil Nadu, bauxite mines in the Ranchi plateau (Fig. 10.2), iron and manganese ore mines in the Bonai-Koira-Jamda sector of Orissa, etc. Whether the total impact of all land and ocean mining will create irreversible change on a global scale is not yet known. It is however important to recognise that the needs of the present generation cannot be ignored

Fig. 10.1: A chromite quarry at Sukinda, Cuttack district, Orissa.

Fig. 10.2: A bauxite quarry at Bagru, Ranchi district, Bihar.

on the plea of sustainable development. The goal of sustainable development is itself not sustainable across generations in the case of non-renewable resources. Uses and requirements change and new types of resources are discovered. Even 20 years ago, mining activities sought justification and support on the ground that the world needs metals. That argument is likely to be less compelling in the next century, at least for the more common metals, thanks to recycling, substitution and miniaturisation. Support for mining activities in both the developed and the developing countries may come more from its contribution to regional economic development and social progress, particularly for eco-friendly practices.

As far back as AD 1661—during the dawn of modern science and technology—the impact of mining and metallurgical pollution through emission of SO_2 and NO_x and their subsequent oxidation and transfer as H_2SO_4 and HNO_3 to the hydrologic regime were recognised by J. Evelyn in the U.K. Somehow this field was not pursued for centuries till the National Acid Deposition Program (NADP) was initiated in 1976 in the U.S.A. to study the effects of these radicals on surface waters, aquatic organisms, forests, agricultural crops and building materials. In 1990, the US Congress authorised *indefinite* continuation of this study, including installation of a nation-wide network of observation stations.

The impact of any mining activity falls in a space-time frame under the following broad categories:

A_1: Removal of:
- (a) indigenous flora;
- (b) indigenous fauna;
- (c) soil layers from A_1 to C_1

} leading to land degradation

A_2: Planned and potential change of landforms
- (a) by open cast excavation;
- (b) by mine dump;
- (c) by subsidence of land;
- (d) by landslide.

A_3: Impact on cultivated lands and dwellings of the indigenous population.

B: Interference with natural hydrosphere and of geochemical perturbations through:
- (a) intervention across local drainage channels—both minor and major;
- (b) intervention with static pools like lakes or other bodies of water;
- (c) intervention with underground water regime by enhanced drawdown or input of extraneous elements through underground excavations;

(d) mobilisation of toxic elements and material in the ecological system through both hydrosphere and atmosphere;
(e) mobilisation of toxic elements in the marine domain by movement of sediment and water masses.

C: Cost of restitution to near original system.

Before mining begins, the study of an ecosystem and the report on Environmental Impact Assessment (EIA) can be organised under the following heads:

1. Relief and landscape.
2. Existing land use pattern.
3. Overburden and soil characteristics (texture, thickness and composition of the units of soil profiles, measured at a minimum of thirty sites per soil zone).
4. Hydrogeological attributes (catchment and recharge area, surface and groundwater composition, level fluctuations, flow vectors).
5. Climate (monthly temperature range, rainfall and wind patterns—both direction and speed at ground-level and at 100 m elevation above ground).
6. Flora and fauna.
7. Human habitation—nature and density.
8. Public utilities, monuments.
9. Existing level of pollution (noise, dust, air, water, etc.).
10. Existing environmental health problems, if any.
11. Notified area under Water Act 1974 or otherwise.

Mining activities in India can be divided into two periods: Ancient to Moghul period; and the last 150 years (1851 onwards). It is only during the eighties of the present century that environmental awareness has surfaced once again in India's mining sector—and that too mostly in the large mines. We do not have a complete inventory of: (1) mine sites degraded by nearly 5,000 surface and underground workings in the non-fuel sector, (2) the extent of degradation of land around the workings, (3) analysis of heavy metals etc. in the groundwater, rivers and lakes around the mines, (4) qualitative and quantitative analysis of polluting particles in the aerosol around the workings, (5) data on subsoil permeability around the mining area, and (6) hydrological characteristics of the neighbourhood.

A degree in geology is not adequate for expertise in all the aspects of environmental assessment. But a geology graduate can undertake measurements of the surficial geology. The rocks need to be *mapped* in detail, the soil and regolith types classified, chemically analysed, their vertical and internal continuity measured and the hydrogeological and hydrogeochemical features, both of surface runoff and groundwater (accessible wells, springs, etc.) analysed and documented systematically. Other disciplines like botany and microbiology have to be woven into a cross-disciplinary program. The National Environmental Geoscience Mapping Accord of the Australian Geological Survey organisation has launched upon such surveys recently, planning linkages with other participating agencies.

Such choices are not easily available in our country even today. Some collaborative work has been tried in India between mining companies and environmental agencies.

Environment is still considered a soft science issue without the discipline of conservation equations. We therefore find many charlatans, flag-waving politicos and green activists, gathered for the limelight. The comment of D.A. Brew (Environmental impact analysis: The example of the proposed Trans-Alaska Pipeline, *U.S. Geol. Surv. Circular*, 695, 1974, 16 pp.) is still relevant after two decades:

> It is likely that almost all environmental impact analysis will be conducted in situations which are influenced by external pressures. These pressures lead to the imposition of time constraints and to requirements that the analysis be made without significant amounts of additional information that would normally be required through extensive research. Although the involved scientist will be affected by these pressures, he will not be absolved of the responsibility of conducting the analysis in a rigorous scientific fashion...*The scientist involved in environmental impact analysis should use the same standards and practices that he uses in scientific work. He is not only responsible for using the best available information and using it in the best possible way, but also for making sure that no personal biases enter the analytical procedure.*

In other words, any report on environmental impact assessment (EIA) should clearly state the methods adopted, instruments used, error bars in the estimates, and the assumptions underlying the evaluation, instead of being made up of unsubstantiated and unverifiable pronouncements. One needs the best available instruments and clean laboratories for measuring contamination-related elements at p.p.m./p.p.b. level in soil, hydrosphere and atmosphere, both in organic and inorganic forms, to build up a benchmark information bank. The measurement protocol for environmental geochemical studies differs according to whether the environment is pristine or perturbed by human interventions. Chemical analysis must be coupled with mineralogical determinations for diagnostic attributes and tracer experiments. For example, the correlation between asbestos and carcinogenicity was demonstrated by Malcolm Ross, the first recipient of the Mineralogical Society of America's Distinguished Public Service Medal, after a difficult battle with the asbestos community. In all such environmental investigations, mineralogy, geochemistry, soil science and geohydrology play a co-ordinated role in unravelling the complex interplay of biotic and abiotic forcings (both organic and inorganic).

An environmental geochemist has to be a far better informed multi-disciplinary scientist than an average chemist. The geochemical processes at or near mineral surfaces are influenced by bio-organisms and organic acids (which presumably modify the hydrogen-bond structure of an activated complex). These play an important role in determining the residence time, transport routes and sinks of pollutants. The monitoring system should be able to measure the incremental changes in the geochemical environment, particularly in areas around radioactive deposits and sulphide mines. The required levels of detection being very low, highly accurate analysis is needed. Such facilities are not available at many places.

In environmental measurements where automated analytical systems with long counting times are used for regular monitoring, the three most important parameters one should check in the instrument chosen are resolution, stability and throughput. Where less than ideal electronic compromises are made, ballistic deficit problem degrades the resolution. The precision of the diagnostic peaks fluctuates either in terms of total count or in position. The other problem in most Indian laboratories is the non-standard environment. In specific terms, the EIA report (Appendix IV) should also work out the cost involved to repair the environmental damage and the cost of generating the substitute, once the resource is exhausted.

TYPES OF LAND DEGRADATION

The nature and extent of land degradation depend on the type, rate and extent of mining operation. Open cast mining destroys vegetation, wildlife habitat, farmland and homesteads of the local people and at places diverts and contaminates natural drainage channels on which the local inhabitants depend for their drinking water. Frequently, the abandoned pits are not fenced with permanent barriers, leading to loss of life of cattle, wild animals and occassionally of humans in search of firewood. Open cast mines are broadly of two types: *Area Strip Mining*, and *Contour Strip Mining*.

For area strip mining, the deposit should be flat, near surface and extensive, e.g. Fe ore, bauxite and other lateritic mineral deposits, chromite, limestone etc. After mining is over, the countryside turns into a barren, uneven ground with dumps and water-logged workings. A large part of the affected land is no longer amenable to cultivation or forestry without removing material once again. Present environmental regulations in many countries (like the U.S.A.) require that the mine owner shall recontour the land (landscaping), replace the soil material on the top once again and plant new vegetation in the mined area. At places, such programs have been very successful under enlightened management, e.g. in the Pocos de Caldas bauxite mine in south Brazil. Here the mine maintains a large and varied nursery. The forest cover in the reclaimed area is denser than in the adjacent virgin area. The other type of open cast operation, contour strip mining, is adopted where the relief is strong and mining is undertaken in the valleys between hills. This results in steep cuts along the hill slopes and resultant risk of landslides during the rainy season, e.g. Mahagiri hill slope chromite quarries in the TISCO leasehold of the Sukinda ultramafic field, Orissa.

Another specialised type of surface mining is *hydraulicking and dredging for placer deposits.* Hydraulicking involves the use of high pressure jets of water to break down the placer, separate the heavy minerals like cassiterite and transport these to the recovery plant. Where water is plentiful, as near a sea coast, this practice is efficient but may have severe environmental impact on the local habitat. It is now discouraged in developed countries. All dredging, e.g. a bucket ladder dredge, where buckets revolve in a swaying manner on a boom digging out sediments, or a drag line dredge, which is a mobile washing and recovery plant fed by conveyors, or an offshore suction dredge using sand and gravel pumps, create disturbance to the primary environment. In the offshore domain, the impact of dredging on benthic and mobile life forms is generally adverse, though re-colonisation is rapid.

In shallow mineral deposits extracted by underground mining, the *room and pillar method* is adopted. The mined out spaces constitute the rooms; in between, pillars support the roof. But in the long-term, unless the vacant spaces are filled up by sand, the land subsides here and there, creating a pock-marked appearance on the surface. Where *longwall mining* is applied, e.g. to mine tabular veins or stratiform mineral deposits, the entire material is removed along the advancing mine face, leaving nothing behind to support the roof permanently. Consequently, this practice creates extensive subsidence of ground. Where veins are steep-dipping and comparatively thin, land degradation as a *direct* offshoot of mining (underground) is relatively minor, although recent subsidence of land (November 1994) around the Badia

Copper Mines of East Singhbhum, Bihar (worked by the Indian Copper Corporation) shows that land subsidence also affects underground metal mines. Extreme landscape degradation includes subsidence of/over abandoned stopes. Slow subsidence in such areas is punctuated by episodes of sudden collapse.

Open cast mining causes the maximum damage to land, vegetation and indigenous biota with overburden dumps spreading toxic matrial (in metalliferous mines), and noise and dust (from blasting) adding to the burden of ecological stress. Dredging operations cause destruction of aquatic life and generation of a large sediment plume down-current. Underground mining has a less adverse impact, although subsidence of land, leaching of pollutants to surface and groundwater from ore dumps, waste dumps and tailing ponds, specially around old mines and other associated damage to land and vegetation require specific treatment.

In extra-peninsular tracts, mining activities on unstable slopes can trigger landslides, either due to cut in slopes where the rock layers dip at about the same angle and direction as the average slope of the land surface, or due to the presence of smectite-type clay, which absorbs large quantities of water and becomes soft and weak after heavy rainfall during the monsoon months. Seismicity generated by blasting of a mineral deposit can cause landslides in potentially landslide-prone areas, as also loading of the upper part of a vulnerable slope. The geologist must examine the aerial photographs of the area very carefully, supplement this by ground mapping and evaluate the susceptibility of the mining area to landslides. The air photos will reveal not only fresh scars of recent landslides but also those modified by erosion, vegetation and anthropogenic interferences. For each rock type, there is a critical slope angle. Where slopes are steeper than the critical angle, landslides could be generated by mining activities. Susceptibility to soil slip and debris flow after bouts of intense rainfall must be investigated. The interested reader may consult *U.S. Geol. Surv. Circular*, 880, 1982, 49 pp. and the textbook edited by R.L. Schuster and R.L. Krizek entitled *Landslides—Analysis and Control,* Transportation Research Board, National Research Council, Special Report 176, 1978, National Academy of Sciences, Washington D.C., for detailed guidance on landslide evaluation.

CONTAMINANTS

Mining and smelting cause extensive contamination. In a recent study of ice cores from Greenland, French scientists discovered that snow falling at the time of the ancient Greeks and Romans between 500 BC and AD 300 contained an unexpectedly high concentration of lead (*New Scientist*, 1st Oct., 1994, p.14). Such contaminants have a long life. In course of mining alone, the soil and water systems of the neighbourhood may be contaminated by airborne or waterborne natural or man-made substances. The important types are discussed below.

(1) Radioactive Material

Low levels of ionising radiation which may be in the form of charged alpha and beta particles or in the form of neutral gamma rays damage the DNA (deoxyribonucleic acid) located within the genes of all living cells. The total effect is of three types: (1) radiation sickness and even death by acute non-genetic damage; (2) delayed somatic damage manifested as cancer, birth abnormalities and early death; and (3) genetic damage on reproductive cells. Whereas the standard permissible annual level of radiation for the general public is 1 milliseivert and the recommended annual limit for nuclear workers is 20 milliseiverts, higher doses received by Japanese and Russian (Altai region around the Polygon test site) civilians led to fatal infectious diseases or pneumonia in children, lung, blood, bone and skin cancers and cataract of the eye (Rob Edwards, *New Scientist*, 13 May 1995, 14–15).

Uranium mining and milling is presently a significant source of environmental contamination. By 1990, the Soviet Union itself had accumulated approximately 5 billion tons of uranium mill tailings with an annual production of 6–7 million tons coming from uranium mining operations. The total contaminated area is estimated at 600 sq. km. By AD 2000 Russia is planning to cover its mill waste with a 1.5 m-thick clay top covered with grass. How far this will stop leakage into the food cycle and for how long is not known.

In the U.S.A., the total contaminated area from uranium mill tailings is about 4 sq. km, run in. The new US regulations require that new tailing piles must be smaller than 40 acres with no more than 10 acres uncovered at any one time. Multi-barrier repositories are also being used to remediate tailings in the U.S.A.

In India, the Atomic Energy Regulatory Board is entrusted with enforcing safety regulations. In river courses, lake beds and sea floor sediments, the diagnostic isotopes are ^{137}Cs, ^{60}Co, ^{90}Sr, ^{228}Th, ^{232}Th, ^{234}Th, ^{238}U, ^{55}Fe, ^{226}Ra, ^{210}Pb, ^{212}Pb, ^{214}Pb, ^{40}K, ^{238}Pu ^{241}Am, ^{144}Ce, ^{95}Nb, ^{106}Ru, ^{95}Zn, ^{99}Tc, ^{129}I and ^{7}Be. In water columns, radionuclides include ^{137}C, ^{90}Sr, ^{226}Ra, ^{238}Pu, ^{241}Am, ^{99}Tc and ^{129}I.

Some of the large inventories of radioactive waste have already been released into the environment. Human exposure to radioactive sources at a level of tens of curies can result in significantly harmful effects. A curie is 3.7×10^{10} nuclear disintegrations per second. It has been estimated in the U.S.A. (D.J. Bradley, C.W. Frank and Y. Mikerin, *Physics Today,* April 1996, 40–45) that the total amount of radioactivity released by the Soviet Union is 167.4 million curies and by the U.S.A. only a meagre 2.6 million curies! Figures for other countries like the U.K., France, China etc. are not even available. More than 2 billion curies are certainly in global circulation. Nuclear weapons create a variety of radioactive isotopes. Linus Pauling (*No More War!* New York, 1958) was the first scientist to call attention to the menace of bomb-produced ^{14}C. According to his calculations, the quantities of this longlife isotope discharged between 1952 and 1958 would ultimately produce about two million embryonic and neonatal deaths and 'will cause many millions of people to suffer from minor hereditary defects'. Other fatal isotopes are ^{131}I (half life: 8 days), ^{137}Cs (half life: 30 years) etc. In ten years time since the explosion of the Chernobyl reactor in the Soviet Union on 26 April 1986, there have been 43 deaths during the early days and 800 confirmed cases of thyroid cancer among children in Belaraus, Ukraine and Russia; and according to WHO estimates, the radioactive iodine (half life: 8 days) would cause, by cascade effect, thyroid cancer among 16,000 more children in the next four decades.

Because of its chemical similarity to K (an important nutrient) ^{137}Cs gets accumulated by plants and animals. In some regions of the U.K., recycling of ^{137}Cs in upland areas led to controls on the sale and slaughter of sheep (*NERC News*, Autumn 1996, 28–9).

Another isotope of great potential hazard is ^{90}Sr. It has been observed that ^{137}Cs in liquid wastes get bound to clays at lake bottoms, but ^{90}Sr gets easily into groundwater systems. Radon emissions into the hydrologic cycle are also damaging.

Increased incidence of cancer and birth deformities are reported among workers of the monazite-bearing sand of Kerala and among the villagers around the Jaduguda uranium mine, Singhbhum, Bihar.

Clay minerals in the area around atomic test sites can absorb high doses of radioactive elements like Cesium 137, which get into the cycle: water $\rightarrow$ plant $\rightarrow$ lower order animal $\rightarrow$ human being. Reports of far field groundwater contamination from the Pokhran implosion site in Rajasthan afford an example of prolonged effect reaching remote areas. Diseases and deformities in Rawathbata area near the Rajasthan atomic power station are also suspected to be induced by radioactivity.

(2) Particulate Material

Some of these may be harmful. For example, some forms of asbestos are known to cause lung cancer. Clay minerals in groundwater, specially around the sulphide and radioactive mineral workings, are carriers of contaminant elements due to their cation exchange capacity.

After India attained Independence, there has been a boom in mining activity, as would be apparent from Table 10.1.

Table 10.1: List of mines/producing leaseholds of major minerals

Mineral/Metal	*No. of producing leaseholds*[A] *(1951–52)*	*No. of mines*[B] *(1992–93)*
Apatite and phosphorite	9	12
Barytes	35	28
Bauxite	9	193
Chromite	15	22
Copper ore	10	14
China clay	22	15
Dolomite	11	133
Fireclay	17	154
Gold	8	8
Gypsum	42	48
Kyanite	10	10
Iron ore	13	265
Limestone	85	627
Magnesite	5	21
Manganese ore	211	184
Mica	66	100 (approx.)

[A]P.K. Ghosh, *Directory of Indian Mines and Metals*, MGMI, Calcutta, 1952, 208pp.
[B]S.K. Choudhuri, *Minerals and Ecology*, Oxford & IBH, New Delhi, 1994, 133–44.

This list excludes graphite, diamond, emerald, beryl, bentonite, calcite, chalk, varieties of clay (pottery and other uses) corundum, felspar, fullers earth, garnet and other heavy minerals recovered from placer sands (of Orissa and Kerala), ochre, dimension stone, stone for ballast, chips etc.

Let us consider a few specific examples. Around the Amjhore Pyrites Mine in Sahabad district, Bihar, the hill slope where the mine dumps carrying pyrite, galena etc. accumulate has been the source of contamination of the countryside for nearly three decades. No baseline data were collected before mining started. Its impact is undefined; no monitoring system has been installed, and restitution is too costly to undertake. Travel a few miles, and you will see the extensive damage to the countryside by the limestone mines of the Rohtas stage. There are as many as 627 working limestone mines in India, producing 75 million tonnes of material per annum for steel plants and the cement industry, pockmarking the countryside, spreading aerosol, damaging the crops of the cultivated lands around and displacing local habitats of both wildlife and indigenous people. The essential raw material for cement manufacture is limestone, which is obtained by open cast mines. To produce a tonne of cement, 1.5 to 1.6 tonnes of limestone are normally required. To cater to a one million tonne per year cement plant, one has to remove 1.5–1.6 million tonnes of limestone, with an additional quantity of up to 1 million tonnes of material in the form of overburden, waste rock and rejects. Thus an area of 21,400–128,000 sq.m comes under mining operation every year for such a plant, depending upon the thickness of limestone. Such extensive land degradation leaves its impact on relief, hydrologic regime, air, forest, agriculture, wildlife etc. There are long stretches of abandoned, water-logged quarries which are unusable.

In the Dehradun–Mussorie belt, there are 50–60 mines of limestone, producing about 1.5 million tonnes of material for the steel industry every year. This being an area of tourist interest, land degradation became a prominent issue and a public interest litigation was filed in the Supreme Court. The Court directed that all the mines in the area should be closed down in phases as the leases expire.

This case illustrates four points:

(1) The bizarre pricing policy of our economists, who appear to believe that exponential growth can go on for ever in a finite world. Current pricing of metals and minerals totally ignores the cost of environmental damage and the cost of replacing or substituting for a diminishing resource.

(2) The absence of an effective preventive machinery which would automatically have ensured simultaneous restitution of damage to the land and the hydrosphere as mining proceeds.

(3) The growing awareness of the common man in the country about the urgency of environmental protection.

(4) An enlightened and supportive judiciary who have already created benchmarks for future executive decisions.

Notwithstanding the hopeful trends, the corrective steps taken so far, even where protective measures are officially in place, are inadequate. The polluter still does not pay. This would be clear from Malanjkhand (M.P.), where copper ore is mined in large open cast mines. Tailing ponds have been constructed 13 km away from the mines and check dams have been built to prevent contamination of surface water downstream. But there is no monitoring system to keep track of the diffusion of heavy metals and acid from the mines and tailing ponds into the groundwater, nor of the spread and impact of aerosol by blasting in the mines. The silent spring of degradation could be running unchecked. Nowhere except in the Dariba-Rajpura lead zinc mines in Rajasthan are the tailings put back into the underground openings. In the Khetri copper field and Zawar lead-zinc mines, the levels of Cu, Pb and Zn in the neighbourhood soils and sediments are several times higher than in the undisturbed environment (A. Haque and V. Subramanian, *CRC Critical Reviews in Environmental Control,* 12, 1982, 13–68). In the Rangpo Zn-Pb-Cu sulphide mine of Sikkim, the steep left bank slope of the Teesta river contributes to easy and efficient dispersal of the mine waste into the fast flowing river, although the waste dumps, the tailing dumps and stocks of non-saleable lead concentrates constitute point sources of contamination. The effluents from the concentration plant include cyanides and xanthates. Mining activity here commenced in 1966. Besides the defacement of land around the mine site, the health of the local inhabitants needs to be monitored for adverse impact of contaminants from the mine. Heavy metals introduced into the hydrosphere by tailing discharges exist in relatively unstable forms and are more easily absorbed in short-term biogeochemical cycles than detrital natural silicates. This creates serious risks for the health of human and other life forms. Even in the humid tropical environment of coastal Orissa, where post-monsoon biotic resurgence is very strong, damage has been severe. Compare two sets of air photographs of the Daiteri Range and the Damsal Valley (near the trijunction of Cuttack, Dhenkanal and Keonjhar districts), one taken before 1960 and the other after 1985. You would find the ravages of iron ore and chromite mining. In this once-densely forested, elephant- and tiger-infested area there are many pockmarks of abandoned quarries and dumps. Unlike the limestone mines of Dehradun, tailings from the iron ore mines on the hill tops of Bihar, Orissa, Karnataka and M.P. may not attract attention, because tourism is not a major industry in such malarial jungles where tribals dwell. But these brown and red powders travel downslope into the major river systems like Karo, Baitarani, Indravati, Tungabhadra etc. In areas around iron and manganese ore quarries, well water is locally contaminated with diesel or excessive haematite silt. During the rainy season, the rainwater and the groundwater are normally collected in pits, which are pumped out to the nearby stream. This contaminates the drainage channels downstream and seeps into the river-side wells of downstream villages. The manganese ore mines of the Koira-Jamda valley in Orissa and of the Sausar belt in M.P. and Maharashtra have accumulated century-old dumps around water-logged quarries, the countryside scraped barren like a moonscape at places. A large portion of land in the heart of the Bisgod Forest, Uttar Kannada district, Karnataka has been stripped of vegetation cover, leading to erosion of top soil, excessive silting of the Kali river and landslides (e.g. in Hosmane village) as a result of manganese ore mining by a number of companies.

While it is nearly impossible to correct the damage wrought over a century of rampage, it should now be mandatory to collect baseline data on the environment covering soil, water and vegetation as a necessary component of prospecting and exploration.

(3) Inorganic Compounds

Inorganic compounds including the material mined out and the stock required for mining operation may contaminate both soil and water. These include the following.

(a) Heavy metals: Heavy metals are usually defined as metals with density more than 5 g/cm^3. This group comprises nearly 70 elements, but only some species are so far known to be ecologically significant. These are listed in Table 10.2.

Lead is a powerful toxin to the central nervous sytem. It has the capacity to seriously affect brain development and function. The amount of Pb in the atmosphere has increased a hundred-fold from the period of ancient silver mining (vide Chapter 1). Analysis of lake sediments from various parts of Sweden found a peak in Pb accumulation around 2000 years B.P. (counting from AD 1950 backwards). Steady increases that began around 1000 years B.P. reached 10–30 times the background value by the beginning of the Industrial Revolution and accelerated during the last two centuries, peaking in around AD 1970. Records in ombrogenic bog at Etang de la Gruyere, Switzerland show high Pb values for the last 2000 years. Similar records with peaks in Pb concentration during Roman times have been reported from peat bogs of Central Europe, northern Scotland and parts of England.

The current problem of Hg pollution, induced by the gold rush at Serra Pelada in the Brazilian Amazon, is a mild version of the Hg pollution in South and Central American silver mines in the past by Spaniards. Between AD 1580 and 1900, annual loss of Hg from the silver mines during metallurgical processing averaged 612 tonnes per year and totalled about 200,000 tonnes in all. One can imagine the extent

Table 10.2: Ecological classification of important heavy metals (after W.E.H. Blum, *Ceres* 135, 1992, 42–4).

Element	*Density (g/cm)*	*Essential for plants or animals*	*Known as pollutant*
Ag	10.5	–	x
Cd	8.7	–	x
Cr	7.2	x	x
Co	8.9	x	x
Cu	8.9	x	x
Fe	7.9	x	x
Hg	13.6	–	x
Mn	7.4	x	–
Pb	11.3	–	x
Mo	10.2	x	x
Ni	8.9	x	x
Tl	11.9	–	x
Th	11.5	–	x
Sn	7.3	x	x
U	19.1	x	x
V	6.1	x	–
W	19.3	x	x
Zn	7.1	x	x

of human tragedy which followed in the wake of such ignorant rapacity. Hg pollution around the Kolar gold mines would also be significant.

Besides metalliferous deposits, acidic mine drainage from coal mine discharge is also capable of transporting large quantities of transition metals. A study in the Mahanoy creek, a tributary of the Lower Susquehanna River, Pennsylvania by K.J. Breen and A.J. Gavin of USGS (*EOS*, *Trans. AGU*, Spring Meet. Suppl. 76(17), 1995, S 113) showed that transfer from the creek to the river per day is of the order of 2000 kg of Fe, 1400 kg of Mn, 0.7 kg of Cu etc. Transport of metals was found to be mostly as suspended particulates or colloids in water.

Heavy metals get incorporated in soil in the following three ways: (a) mechanical mixture of heavy metal compounds within a horizon of the soil; (b) uptake of heavy metals by soil microorganisms and plant roots, depending on soil pH, Eh etc; and (c) absorption-desorption by ion exchange at the surface of humic substances, clays and iron and manganese oxides, including chelation (strong complex bonds), occlusion within oxide minerals, freshly precipitated by capillary transport, cation exchange into clay mineral structures, precipitation and dissolution as carbonates, phosphates, etc. In the fifties and early sixties, some Japanese industries were dumping Hg into Minamata Bay. The Hg contaminated the fish which were later eaten by the local people. The resulting Hg poisoning caused appalling deformities in children. This came to be known as Minamata disease. The toxic effect of Hg is enhanced after it is converted to methyl mercury by microorganisms. Downstream activities related to mining normally lead to extensive pollution of great physiological significance. In the Rhine river, Hg, Cd, Cu and some Cr come mainly from metal and chemical plants, whereas Ni, Zn and some Cr come from the sewage effluent as a result of corrosion of pipes and home appliances. Pb is essentially contributed to the hydrologic regime of urban and semi-urban centres by gasoline. These heavy metals are locally so abundant that they settle in the sediments, e.g. at Rotterdam port, where dredging led to resuspension of metal-laden sediments in nearby estuaries. Such baseline data are lacking for the major Indian ports, where dredging is routinely undertaken.

(b) Anionic elements and complexes: Cl, S, P, F, NO_3, NO_2, NH_4, HCO_3. When water bodies are charged with acids from sulphide mines, major changes in the ecosystem are effected. Just as hydrologic pathways determine which minerals come into contact with water and the duration of their reaction (for deep circulation), the mineralogy of the host rocks is an equally important factor in hydrologic sensitivity. Carbonate rocks and reactive silicate rocks (mafic to ultramafic, igneous) rapidly react with H^+. Groundwaters in such environments are not likely to be unusually influenced by chronic acidification as a result of leaching of mine dumps. On the other hand, in areas made up of sandstone, shale, granite, schist, phyllite etc., the groundwater is susceptible to acidification, because the constituent minerals either do not react or react very slowly with H^+. French potash mines in Alsace are estimated to add 130 kg of chloride to the Rhine river every second. Sodium chloride, which is mined as an associated material, gets dissolved from the dumps and spread into the orchids of Dutch flower growers. Since 1992, the damage has been partly brought under control by holding back leakage from the dumps. Metals mobilised by acidic water can pose a threat to health. Such water is usually characterised by pH of 4.0–5.5 and high Al concentration, displaced from exchangeable sites of clays. It is important to bear in mind that high Al damages plant life, since it interferes with root function and inhibits the uptake of essential elements like Mg, Ca and P. As pH level decreases, the species diversity of the biological community is impoverished; insect, amphibian and fish populations die out; mammals

and birds which depend on these food chains get reduced in number and variety; and populations of acid tolerant species increase. High concentration of H^+ ions and toxic metals like Al, Cd, Cu, Pb, Hg, etc. cause osmoregulatory failures or irreversible loss of NaCl from body fluids in aquatic organisms, leading to fatality. Although many fine details of how the damage spreads in organisms are yet to be unravelled, acid infiltration—either episodic during early monsoon or chronic in poorly buffered waters—can have serious health problems for both human and other life forms (O.P. Bricker, *Quart. Jour. Geol. Soc. Lond.* 143, 1986, 621–6).

(4) Organic Chemicals

Organic chemicals include many synthetic materials used in mining establishments for ancillary requirements of the mining camp. These include carbon tetrachloride and other low molecular weight chlorinated hydrocarbons, pesticides like DDT, toxaphene, endrin, methoxychlor, lindane, benzene and other organic contaminants. In S. Korea in the early nineties, some local industries had dumped 300 tons of phenol into the Naktong river. Phenols used in the production of printed circuit boards are known to cause cancer and to damage the nervous system. This river was the main source of water for around 10 million people downstream, and a minister of the government had to resign on this score.

Water quality is very sensitive to organic pollutants. Monitoring it poses complex problems. The reason is that there are thousands of organic constituents as against a few dozen harmful inorganic chemicals. It is not possible to isolate and analyse each of the organic chemicals separately for monitoring purposes. So these are grouped into different categories depending on their effects. These are: (1) adsorbable organic halogens (AOX) which include primarily compounds with chlorine; (2) detergents; (3) hydrocarbons; and (4) humic acids. DDT and other insecticides used in mining camps belong to the first category. These are not produced or used any more in many advanced countries. The present trend in detergent manufacture is to reduce anionic surfactants—the active ingredients of old detergents—and permit only biodegradable detergents. This brings down pollution significantly. Hydrocarbons are more readily biodegradable than halogenated compounds of the first category. Humic acids are essentially harmless.

One common measurement of the effect of organic pollutants is the Biological Oxygen Demand (B.O.D.). *This has to be measured within 5 days from the time of collection of the water sample.* Bacteria and nutrients are added to the water and their consumption of oxygen is measured in milligrams per litre of water. Another index is the Chemical Oxygen Demand (C.O.D.) in which concentrated sulphuric acid and chromium are used to estimate the maximum possible oxygen consumption of the sample.

For understanding the composition of organic molecules, a recent development is the two-step, laser desorption, mass spectrometry (L^2 MS), much like the electron/ion microprobe for inorganic molecules. Lasers of different wavelengths (tunable lasers) can be used to volatilise neutral molecules from grain surfaces. Using the principle of resonance-enhanced multiphoton ionisation (REMPI), specific organic molecules or a cluster of similar structured organic compounds like polycyclic aromatic hydrocarbons (PAH) can be selectively ionised; and from the vaporised desorbed species, these ions can be related to specific mineralogical and textural sites via a mass spectrometer with on-line attachments of optical microscope and video camera (J.H. Hahn, R. Zenobi, J.L. Bada and R.N. Zare, *Science*, 239, 1988, 1523–5).

It is important to remember that for tropical life forms there are no safe lower limits of long-term exposure to organic contaminants. Mine dumps, oil and gasoline from mining camp vehicles, aerosol from blasting in open cast mines and untreated domestic wastes in humid tropical environments provide enough potential for strong point source contamination.

TRACING THE SOURCE

Locating and hydraulically containing a groundwater contamination plume is a complex problem. Uncertainty in: (a) source location; (b) source loading time; and (c) aquifer heterogeneity causes great uncertainty in remediation. Data on mean hydraulic conductivity and its variance in space are sparse. This leads to speculations and unfounded panic, much to the detriment of acceptable levels of mining operation.

As a result, sins of the past may be assigned to the present activity wrongly but unwittingly, unless dependable baseline data are gathered before the new operation begins. It is the responsibility of the prospecting geologist to generate these data on the basis of careful sampling and accurate analytical determinations in standard laboratories.

Given the baseline data and the nature and extent of the planned mining operation, predictive modelling of geochemical processes which could get involved in contaminating the neighbourhood of a point source can be attempted, if we have specification of appropriate sorption and reaction phenomena either by using heterogeneous phase equilibria or by defining the stoichiometry and rate of non-equilibrium reactions. Without detailed data on the mineralogy of the excavated rocks and soil and chemical analysis of natural groundwater composition in the surrounding area, predictive modelling is virtually unconstrained. Mass balance geochemical modelling helps to build up plausible geochemical processes, if the chemistry of the rocks, soils and groundwater are available. Mass balance modelling assumes a steady state flow path by the reactions within the uncertainty of: (1) the analytical data; and (2) redox processes introduced by microorganisms. Since the latter play a dominant role in humid tropics, it is inadvisable to ignore biological transfer mechanisms of contaminants.

Inorganic contaminants from a mine spread through particulate, colloidal and solution phase associations. Discrimination of transport processes needs sophisticated sampling and chemical-mineralogical analysis with the help of scanning electron microscopy-energy dispersive X-ray (SEM-EDX) (for the particulate components), analysis of filter digests in AAS (vide Chapter 4, for specific needs of AAS vis-a-vis elements under determination) for the colloidal fractions (between 0.45 micrometres and 10^4 Daltons) and of the filtrate for soluble components. Adsorption of toxic chemical species (both natural and industrial) on common surficial minerals is of great importance in spreading pollution. Study of mineral surfaces, particularly of sulphides, of weathered feldspars etc. is greatly aided by Auger Electron Spectroscopy (AES) and X-ray Photoelectron Spectroscopy (XPS). Microbiological measurements include direct counts and Most Probable Number (MPN) determinations of methanotrophs, sulphate reducing bacteria and methanogen.

Predictive models indicate not only the possible extent of contamination in a space-time frame but also the best sites for monitoring both conservative and non-conservative contaminants, appropriate waste disposal locations and the likely efficiency of different mitigation strategies. The interested reader should consult L.F. Konikow, *U.S. Geol. Surv. Water Supply Paper* 2044, 1977, 43 pp., for an illustration of a predictive model, developed for tackling groundwater contamination affecting a large area between the Rocky Mountain arsenal and the South Platte river.

Where mining activities are in progress, environmental control measures include the following elements:

(1) Installation of areas of compensatory plantation, barrier zones etc.
(2) Careful storage of topsoil in protected/walled pits.

(3) Physical and chemical cleaning of water discharging from the mine and the stacks. The quality of groundwater is indirectly improved by building large reservoirs of rain water around open cast mines.
(4) Aerosol can be contained by: (a) using a suitable dust collector during drilling; (b) removing topsoil completely before blasting; (c) concreting the roads used by loaded dumpers or sprinkling water over the roads regularly; and (d) large-scale replantation around the mine.

In lateritic tracts, saprolite acts as a reservoir for contaminants due to high porosity of the matrix. During remediation, the matrix changes its habit from a sink to a secondary source.

When the large open cast sulphide mines of Malanjkhand will be abandoned, surface and groundwater flowing into the old pits will create environmental and economic liability. Before such risks assume serious dimension, it is useful to model the problem of contamination from abandoned and flooded open cast sulphide mines. The radial flow equation and numerical methods have to be used to solve such non-linear and analytically intractable problems. A common, erroneous notion is that landforms can be easily rehabilitated at former mine sites by re-laying the soil cover and re-plantation. The magnitude of recharge beneath rehabilitated landforms controls the degree of dispersion of toxic levels of pollutant elements, like U, Hg, Pb, etc. (vide Table 10.2).

A broad idea of this hazard can be formed by using the chloride balance of the aquifer. The mass balance is given by the formula

$$V_R C_R = V_P C_P - V_S C_S \quad \text{(i)}$$

where

V = volume of water per unit area;

C = concentration of chloride;

R, P, S = recharge, precipitation, streamflow.

The fraction of precipitation leaving the catchment as streamflow is estimated from the mean runoff coefficient r, so that

$$V_S = r\, V_P \quad \text{(ii)}$$

and equation (i) can be rearranged as

$$V_R / V_P = (C_P - r\,C_P) / C_R$$

Estimation of r is not however very simple; it is dependent on rainfall intensity, total annual rainfall, antecedent soil moisture at various periods of the year, soil type, topographic slopes etc.

A comparatively simple way to measure rainfall-induced infiltration rate through the rehabilitated landform is by using a lysimeter, buried beneath a top clay-rich cover.

Given the multi-facetted environmental impact of mining (and downstream beneficiation and metallurgy) and centuries of ignorance about the resultant damage to life forms, it is no wonder that awareness has brought in its wake many stringent regulations in advanced countries like the U.S.A. It has been estimated that the direct cost of federal environmental, health and safety regulations in the U.S.A. is around 100 billion $ annually. There is a growing consensus that re-allocation of a part of the expenditure from regulation to productive programs like 'health and food for all' is necessary, and that regulatory decisions should be based on cost-benefit analysis, quantified wherever possible with best estimates and a clear description of the uncertainties in the estimates. In the U.S.A., this procedure was adopted for phasing out lead from gasoline and banning of certain asbestos products. Environmental activism in developing countries like India is generally bereft of hard data. Populism must be replaced by a critical analysis of a core set of economic assumptions and variables like social discount rate, the value of reducing risks of premature deaths and accidents, of improving health, etc.

MONITORING SYSTEM

The lack of quality and comparability of chemical measurements performed for monitoring of the environment has often hampered a correct interpretation of the geochemical pathway, residence time and contamination trend of a variety of elements and compounds. International commissions have recognised the glaring unreliability of analytical data from various laboratories. In some fields, task forces have been set up for a fully-integrated quality assurance program for the chemical determinations.

The impact of a well-designed monitoring program cannot be overemphasized. The best way is to develop a model that tries to predict how the ecosystem will respond to perturbations by mining activities. Information from the first phase of the monitoring program could then allow progressive refinement of the model as well as creating new perception about the extent of reversible interventions. In the absence of a clearly-articulated concept about the potential impact, monitoring programs do not attract continuing public support and funding. A clear choice of what should be monitored and what need not depends on correct identification of the *minimum number of sensitive parameters* which would reflect the overall change in the ecosystem. Another shortcoming of some monitoring activities is the lack of a proper analytical protocol and coordination among agencies about what should be sampled, how, when and why. A clear example is the 1990 report of the United Nations Group of experts on the Scientific Aspects of Marine Pollution, who 'despaired over the lack of international standards that would help ensure comparability of information collected by monitoring programs'. The UN group concluded that 'many of the measurements taken in the previous decade were of little use in assessing trends in marine pollution because of uncertainties over quality control' (M.L. Weber and J.A. Gradwohl, *The Wealth of Oceans,* W.W. Norton, N.Y., 1995, 256 pp.).

Human civilisation cannot do without mines and minerals. But it is important to define for each habitat the limits to which mining of rocks and minerals could proceed before damage becomes irreversible. Environmental Impact Assessment Reports on mines and prospects do not provide such estimates even now, although there is a fuzzy awareness of environmental impact occasionally leading to debates on TV and politically motivated agitations. Mining affects ecosystems no doubt; and its impact reverberates over many facets of the living and non-living world. But hard science with clear modelling studies and quantified statements are still uncommon. In tropical countries particularly, limited and local interventions due to mining over a few decades may not create any irreversible damage. But how much damage could one inflict without purchasing a one-way-ticket to destruction is not known. Such modelled experiments are badly needed.

Installation of efficient monitoring systems is still an optional route for mine management in India, although how long this will be allowed into the next century is difficult to predict. Ideally, each prospecting program should create a benchmark data base before mining starts, so that future perturbations could be measured, if and when necessary. Sometimes it is needed for the defence of the mine owner; the reason being that whenever a large area is contaminated, it becomes quite difficult to pinpoint the source of the contamination, unless specific tracers are used. Not so problematic are radiation-related contaminants. In India, around each nuclear power plant, whether it is a uranium processing plant, a fuel fabrication unit, or a power station, there is an Environmental Survey laboratory, which gathers samples on an hourly/daily basis of vegetables, water, air, fish, cereal, goat's thyroid etc. to compute effective total radiation dose per person. These laboratories are independent of the Nuclear Power Corporation and provide the data to the Health Physics Division of the Bhabha Atomic Research Centre, Bombay. Unfortunately, such monitoring systems were not installed around the mines.

The changes induced in the environment by mining have to be monitored both daily and seasonally every year (separate pre-monsoon, monsoon and post-monsoon measurements) under the following heads.

(1) Air: Ambient air quality in respect of suspended particulate matter (SPM), NO_x, SO_2, CO and dust fall rate. High volume samplers with suitable calibrations are needed. In case of chimneys, tracer isotopes can be used for mapping the spread of the aerosol (vide Chapter 4).

Air samples should be collected for 8 hours duration at each station at a flow rate of 1.0–1.5 m^3/min. SPM is computed by weighing filter paper before and after sampling in a Mettler or any other suitably sensitive electronic balance. SO_2 and NO_x in air are collected by bubbling the air sampled in specific absorbing solution at an average flow rate of 0.2 lit. per min. for NO_x and 0.5 lit./min for SO_2. The impinger samples are put in an ice box immediately after collection and transferred to a refrigerator till these are analysed. CO can be measured by automatic instruments like the 'Environment S.A.' CO/11M, France. This is based on infra-red Absorption Gas analysis.

(2) Surface and ground water: Selection of monitoring stations in any fluid regime requires the identification of dominant flow directions as well as the location of residential and other sensitive areas. For example, if the wind blows towards NW over a major part of the year but monitoring stations are set up NE of the project area, the readings will be of no use. For surface and groundwater regimes, monitoring stations must be sited lower down the hydraulic gradient. Stream baseflow chemistry strongly reflects the nature of the watershed and is better suited for monitoring of pollution than lakes, which register a combined impact from aerosol, groundwater and surface flow.

Water Quality study[1] involves estimation of suspended and dissolved solids, chloride, sulphate, fluoride, nitrate, B.O.D. (Biochemical Oxygen Demand), C.O.D. (Chemical Oxygen Demand) etc., besides heavy metals occurring in the rocks and minerals of the mine area. Samples have to be collected from open drainage channels, wells and impounded water reservoirs. The pH, temperature and conductivity have to be measured in the field. This is not yet a common practice in our country. The observations have to be seasonal (pre-monsoon, monsoon and post-monsoon). The samples must be separately analysed for suspended particles and for dissolved components.

The MPN index for bacteriological parameters has to be measured according to the standard method given in IS-1622 (Indian Standards Institution). In fact in humid tropical areas, bacteriological monitoring is essential for public health. Microorganisms are known to be very efficient in extracting Cu and other metals by oxidising the sulphur that binds the metals. The flip side of this environmental menace is the discovery of a new technique known as biohydrometallurgy which is already in operation in old uranium mines of Canada and gold mines of S. Africa. As much as 30 per cent of the copper produced in the U.S.A. is extracted this way (John Merson, *New Scientist*, 4 January, 1992, 54–6).

Underground water quality is monitored by direct sampling of deep tube wells or boreholes, wherever available. Resistivity profiling at 50–100 m intervals can indicate the spread of acid water from mines and mine dumps. Resistivity of fresh water is 60–200 ohm-m, whereas that of acid water is 6–12 ohm-m. Usually, various modes of electrode spacing in a Wenner array are tested for best response. Measurements should be undertaken at different seasons, wherever possible. Borehole geophysics is also used in environmental applications (C.J. Mwenifumbo, *The Canadian Mining and Metallurgical Bulletin*, 86, 1995, 43–9).

In the new Republic of S. Africa, Section 2.11 of the Minerals Act (August 1991) stipulates that all existing mines must implement an environmental management

---

[1]*Note:* The permissible levels of some of the parameters are as follows:
All heavy metals except
Fe: less than 5 p.p.m.
Fe: less than 10 p.p.m.
B.O.D.: less than 30 mg/l
C.O.D.: less than 250 mg/l
Suspended solids: less than 100 p.p.m.
It would be obvious that the analytical instruments and laboratory conditions must be superior to those in many of our universities.

program. This should include remedial measures to ensure that no pollution will occur when a mine is closed. Pollution around an abandoned mine generally spreads through surficial flow of contaminants into the soil during rainfall, leakage into groundwater, mass movement of material from waste dumps, slime ponds, ore dump, rock dump, stream sediments etc. Where there is a natural flow of groundwater into the abandoned workings, groundwater contamination cannot be ruled out. A common procedure for measuring the groundwater flow pattern in such cases is to monitor the wells around or to dig a series of trenches around the mine and record the direction of flow in various seasons. Concurrently, samples of soil and water are collected for analysis. The soil and dump material are studied and tested for mineralogy, particle size distribution, pH, electrical conductivity and concentration of Ca, Mg, Al, Mn, Fe, Co, Ni, Cu (bivalent and trivalent separately), Zn etc. Since metal ions and toxic salts are brought into solution more readily in acid condition where pH is less than 5.5, great care has to be taken around sulphide-bearing mines. In tropical countries, high surface temperature of the dumps in the summer months, frequent presence of *Thiobacillus ferrooxidans* cultures on the crust of such dumps and high moisture content ensure a high rate of sulphate generation. The water samples have therefore to be analysed for the following anionic radicals: NO_3, SO_4 , Cl, HCO_3, CO_3 besides TDS (Total Dissolved Solids), hardness and alkalinity. The maximum permissible limits are as follows:

pH	:	6.5–9.5
Electrical conductivity	:	300 mS m^{-1}
NO_3	:	10 mg l^{-1}
SO_4	:	600 mg l^{-1}
Cl	:	600 mg l^{-1}
TDS	:	2000 mg l^{-1}
Hardness	:	650

Acidic mine drainage water has the best chance of neutralisation in carbonate- or clay-rich areas, having Ca, Mg, Na and K as predominant cations and a flat surface topography of the surroundings. In mine sites on undulating topography, the groundwater gradient has to be delineated correctly to estimate the possible limit of contamination. In many areas, contamination tails are noticeable for more than ten km downstream.

RECLAMATION

The elements of reclamation of land are as follows:

1. Selective removal, storage and preservation of top soil.
2. Segregation of oversized and unwanted rock fragments which may impair the growth of plants.
3. Stockpiling of waste matter and overburden for refilling or back filling.
4. Proper compaction and grading of reclaimed area to control erosion.
5. Plantation of grass for protection against erosion and growth of soil.
6. Creation of water reservoirs and gardens where possible within the excavated sectors.

Recovery is non-linear with respect to time and intervention can only accelerate some phases of the process. Where land has not been stripped of topsoil, substantial recovery is possible in as few as 3 to 5 years with intensive management (V.M. Kine and E.A. Howell, in W.R. Jordan III, M.E. Gilpin, J.D. Aber (ed.), *Restoration Ecology*, Cambridge Unmersity Press, 1987, 75–83) but more typically may take 20 years. In order to be effective, a long-term reclamation programme is needed.

In the bauxite mining fields of Darling Range, Australia, conservation measures are based on a careful population study of the rarer species, range of mobile species, minimum sustainable size of each ecological habitat, the varieties of habitats existing in the region, supplemented by low-level aerial photography.

Treatment of Contaminated Water Source

Cleaning up contaminated underground water resources is very expensive. Remediation by *natural attenuation* is recommended if: (1) there are large areas around the zone of contamination free from habitation, (2) there are no wells or receptors down-gradient near the contaminant plume and (3) contamination source is under remediation with an installed monitoring system, equipped with a network of multi-level wells and models of flow. An understanding of the microbial community structure is also essential, since microbial degradation of chlorinated hydrocarbons and solvents often produces highly toxic metabolic byproducts.

Once the potential contaminant radicals have been correctly identified and the migration pathways (including extent and concentration of the contaminants and their residence time) outlined, there are various known remedial measures. These are first tested on bench- and pilot-scale so that appropriate design criteria are established and then introduced on a long-term basis. The various processes include: (1) steps for surface flow control, such as contour grading, surface sealing and replantation over the landfill dump; (2) creating an underground barrier between the groundwater and the landfill; (3) chemical immobilisation of waste by coagulation, pH adjustment, oxidation, resin stripping etc; (4) biological treatment, both aerobic and anaerobic; and (5) excavation and reburial at distant places. Essentially, the techniques attempt at either reducing leachate generation or controlling its movement. For further details of the available routes, the reader may consult Larry W. Canter and Robert C. Knox, *Groundwater Pollution Control,* Lewis Publishers Inc. Michigan, 1985, 526 pp.

Treatment of Degraded Land

Treatment of contaminated ground is difficult and costly. One way is to dilute the high level of contamination of the soil by mixing it with non-contaminated matter like clays and oxides, which have high sorption capacity. Mixing with organic matter does not help immediately.

Another technique is to adjust the pH and Eh of the soil by liming or aeration. This does not remove the heavy metals but their mobility is reduced.

A third method is to select from the locality itself plant species which are fast growing, primary colonising in nature and which could improve the soil by leaf litter decomposition. It has been observed that such post mining rehabilitation is aided by including legume species in early surface replantation. This contributes to organic matter accumulation and generation of a nitrogen pool comparable with that of a native forest. A recent experiment by the NEERI scientists with MOIL (A.S. Juwarkar et al., *Minerals and Ecology,* Oxford & IBH, New Delhi, 1994, 95--102) has revealed that manganese mine dumps can be reclaimed successfully (Mn being a growth-promoting metal) by planting saplings of teak, neem, shishum etc. after treating the top layer of the dump with pressmud, biofertilisers at the rate of 50–100 tons per hectare.

Wherever reclamation is planned, the action program should first be tested in small experimental plots before committing large funds. A common shortcoming of reclamation through planting new species including legume and grass on the sites of old spoil dumps is that arrangements for soil turning, water supply during dry seasons and protection against grazing is inadequate, leading to reversal of remediation after a few years.

Where heavy metals are a source of contamination, microorganisms could be tried as biological filters for polluted water, particularly in marshy tracts. Rushes such as cats tails (*Typha latifolia*) collect microorganisms that metabolise heavy metals around their roots. Under such a set-up, plant species which would absorb low-level pollutants and would not go further upwards in the food chain are introduced. Genetic engineering to create or find new bacterial strains that can stand up to the presence of heavy metals that poison the microbes is now under way (A.S. Moffat, *Science*, 1994, 778–9). Biotechnologic cures could evolve in due course.

Today mining is the single most damaging activity for the environment in the countryside. The essence of managing the environment in a world of rising population, expectation and information exchange would involve continuous upgradation and innovation of mining techniques and pollution control technologies. It is not feasible to stop mining and other related activities under the ill-defined garb of 'sustainable development'. The modern world cannot afford to consider environmental protection without regard to costs. In the U.S.A. alone, businesses, states and cities now spend more than US dollars 100,000 million annually to comply with federal environmental laws and regulations (R. Stavins and T. Grumbly, Making the Polluter Pay, *SPAN*, 36(1), 1995, 42–7). Such 'command-and-control' regulations with a sluggish bureaucracy are known to be inefficient and static. A realisation is therefore emerging that the differences among individuals, firms and regions tend to be ignored, unless a market-based approach is adopted for environmental regulations. Too many regulatory burdens might kill mining activities of all kinds, thus affecting economic growth.

At the same time, emerging portents of critical environmental problems on a global scale such as the decline of sea urchins, birds and amphibia, bleaching of coral reefs, the appearance of phytoplankton blooms, cancer epizootics in fish 'add up to a whole flock of miners' canaries singing' (Norman Myers, *Science*, 269, 1995, 358–60). In a recent statistically representative study of international public opinion, which reveals substantial concern about the environment in both developing and industrial countries, David Bloom (*Science*, 269, 1995, 354–8) observed that there is a recognition of the need for strong international agencies in addressing transnational environmental issues.

In South and East Asia, where 'Peace Dividends' are in the form of large multinational investment, the governments face a dilemma. The standards of pollution control in these countries are low and are not comparable to those in the advanced countries. Goods can be manufactured here at lower costs no doubt with lower investment in environment-friendly technologies. But the global market for such goods is bound to shrink; the demand from European and American companies in their own countries for internal tariff protection against what they perceive to be unfair trading practices, such as 'dumping' or selling goods at uncompetitive prices to capture foreign markets, is likely to become more strident, unless the Asian countries adopt equally rigid and testable environmental standards. Exploration and extraction technologies in the mineral industry will face increasing pressure in the next century.

Recent experience in different parts of the temperate belt shows that it is possible to restitute old ecological habitat by careful intervention. One well-documented example is the recovery of eel's habitat in the Rhine river within two years after pesticides from a Sandoz warehouse near Basel got washed into the Rhine during a fire in November 1986. A growing awareness of the human heritage will make us all regulate future mining and development even in the developing countries so that these do not turn into dumping grounds for banned technologies. This presupposes a generic awareness on a global scale and at least high school level science education among the populations.

FURTHER READING

D.R. Gates, *Environmental Geology*, John Wiley & Sons, N.Y., 1991, 701 pp.

A.D. Bradshaw and J. Chadwick, *The Restoration of Land: The Ecology and Reclamation of Derelict and Degraded Land*, Blackwell Scientific Publishers, Oxford, 1986, 317 pp.

E.S. Lyle (Jr.), *Surface Mine Reclamation Manual*, Prentice Hall, N.J., 1986, 299 pp.

L.W. Canter, *Environmental Impact Assessment*, McGraw Hill, N.Y., 1977.

J. Satsmadjis and F. Voutsinou-Taliadouri, An index of metal pollution in marine sediments, *Oceanologica Acta* 8, 1985, 277–84.

B.G. Prusty, K.C. Sahu and G. Godgul, Metal contamination due to mining and milling activities at the Zawar zinc mine, Rajasthan. 1. Contamination of stream sediments, *Chemical Geology*, 112, 1994, 275–91.

A. Paithankar, *The Impact of Mining on the Environment: Problems and Solutions*, Balkema, Rotterdam, 1994, 452 pp.

K. Spitz and J. Moreno, *A Practical Guide to Groundwater and Solute Transport Modeling*, Wiley-Interscience, N.Y., 1996, 461 pp.

11

Pattern and Range of Industrial Specifications: Some Examples

The mining industry has to depend on a reasonable measure of consumption by indigenous mineral-based industries in order to ensure a dependable and stable market for its output. Inspite of global and regional trade agreements, excessive or total dependence on export markets can only lead to wide fluctuations of sale from year to year in terms of both quantity and price, unless there are firm long-term contracts. The new arrangements under WTO are not likely to be universally benign either. A stable mining industry of a country should normally rest on a large industrial base, although the reverse is not true, as we can see from the Japanese example. The present century has witnessed strange and unorthodox manipulations by multinational and G-7 mining companies—mining in one country, smelting in another, the profits going to a third country. With increasing environmental concern, there is also a latent urge among mining companies of the advanced countries to avoid the high cost of pollution in their own backyard and procure semi-finished metals from other countries for their industrial needs. In this international game, detailed specifications are very commonly kept a trade secret—*and no generalisation is valid.*

This is not difficult to understand. Industrial specifications for any mineral at any place and time depend upon:

- size, organisation and geographic distribution of the industry in the country and in the world;
- state of technology;

- demand-supply relationship;
- need for the mineral in various strategic industries;
- state of R & D and the emergence of substitutes;
- requirements of environmental control in the area;
- regional and global security environment; and
- extent and efficiency of recycling of waste products etc.

Given such a large number of variables, specifications change from time to time. To give you an idea of the range of variations in specifications, some gross outline specifications for some mineral commodities are given here. These are not to be taken as absolute values for defining the economics of a deposit.

BAUXITE

About 95% of the total world production of bauxite is now consumed in the production of alumina, the remaining 5% being used in refractory, chemical, abrasive, cement, iron and steel, petroleum and plastics industries.

The Indian Standards Specifications of bauxite for use in the production of alumina by the Bayer process and its subsequent use in the production of primary aluminium metal are given in IS:5953–1985. Some of its important features are given in Table 11.1.

Within this generalised framework, the specifications of different companies fluctuate. For example, the National Aluminium Co. (NALCO), drawing its supply from the Panchpatmali (Orissa) laterite plateau over migmatised khondalite, specifies a minimum of 42.5% Al_2O_3 , a maximum of 25.6% Fe_2O_3 and a maximum of 1.65% reactive SiO_2 (i.e. silica bound in clay minerals) whereas the Bharat Aluminium Co., another Public Sector industry, which draws upon bauxite from laterite plateaus over Deccan basalts specifies a minimum of 44.4% Al_2O_3, a maximum of 5.76% reactive silica and a maximum of 25.25% LOI. The physical and mineralogical characteristics as well as the nature of distribution and operational efficiency of the mines play some roles in these varying specifications. The specifications of a mineral, even under the same management and constant technological and market conditions, depend upon its geological environment, and are so designed in the light of available technology that the product fetches the optimum return.

Table 11.1

Constituent	*Percentage by weight*	
	Grade I (*Essentially gibbsite*)	*Grade II* (*Mixture of gibbsite & boehmite*)
Total Al_2O_3 (min.)	40	47*
Total available alumina (min.)	36	43
Total SiO_2 (max.)	4	4
Al_2O_3/SiO_2 (min.)	12	12
$Fe_2O_3 + TiO_2$ (max.)	30	30
P_2O_5 (max.)	0.20	0.20
V_2O_5 (Max.)	0.20	0.20
Loss on Ignition (LOI) at 1100°C (min.)	20	20

*Normally 1–2% diaspore and 5–7% boehmite

Table 11.2

Constituent	*Gujarat*	*Lohardaga*
Al_2O_3	55–58%	55% (min.)
Fe_2O_3 (max.)	3%	4.5%
TiO_2 (max.)	3%	11%
CaO	1.5%	1.5%
LOI (min.)	34%	26%

This point will be manifest in the specifications of bauxite for the refractory industry within India. In Gujarat, where the bauxite underlies marine Eocene beds, the limits of Fe_2O_3, TiO_2 etc. are lower than in Lohardaga, Bihar where the bauxite is associated with laterite over granitic rocks (Table 11.2).

The typical average Al_2O_3 content of bauxite in the world's leading bauxite and alumina producing region (6.65 million tonnes in 1989–90)—the Darling Range of Australia—is 30–35%. Approximately 3–4 kg of bauxite are required there to produce 1 kg of Al_2O_3

In the chemical industry, one of the most important criteria is that the bauxite should have a high $Al_2O_3 : Fe_2O_3$ ratio. Al_2O_3 should be at least 58%. But such stringent specifications are not followed by many companies, e.g. Hindustan Heavy Chemicals, who specify that bauxite should be in lumps, and should contain 50–

60% Al_2O_3, 0.5–3% non-reactive SiO_2, 0.1–0.6% CaO, 3–5% Fe_2O_3, 0.5–6% TiO_2 and 20–25% LOI. In the abrasives industry, the minimum Al_2O_3 content of calcined bauxite is required to be 80%. The maximum permissible silica content is 7%. Alkalies must be very low to minimise the formation of glass and TiO_2 should not exceed 4%.

For the indigenous cement industry, the specifications of bauxite are not stringent. For high alumina cement, Al_2O_3 should be 38–56% and Fe_2O_3 between 10 and 18%. Low iron cement requires less than 6% SiO_2. But when the same bauxite is exported to the cement industry in the Gulf countries, far more stringent specifications are laid down as follows: Al_2O_3: 50% min.; (Rejection below 48%); Fe_2O_3: 15% min.; SiO_2: 4% max.; TiO_2: 3.5% max.; CaO: 4% max.; Magnesia: 3% max.; LOI: 28% max.; Moisture: 5% max.; Size: 100% below 100 mm.

CHROMITE

Chromite is an important alloying element in ferrous metallurgy. Nearly 65% of global consumption of chromite is in this field. Out of the remaining, approximately 22% are used in refractories and 13% in the chemical industry. The specifications of chromite for the metallurgical industry (IS: 10818–1984) are given in Table 11.3.

Table 11.3

Constituents (on dry basis)	*Grade of feed for*			
	Low carbon ferrochrome	*High carbon ferrochrome*	*Silico chrome*	*Charge chrome*
% Cr_2O_3 (min.)	48	48	48	44
% Total Fe as FeO (max.)	15	16	15	18
% Al_2O_3	13	13	13	10
% SiO_2 (max.)	5	8	10	12
% CaO (max.)	5	5	5	5
% MgO (max.)	14	16	14	12
% S (as SO_3)	0.1	0.1	0.1	0.14
% P (as P_2O_5) (max.)	0.005	0.02	0.02	0.2
Cr:Fe (min.)	3:1	2.8:1	3:1	1.6:1
MgO:Al_2O_3	–	1.2–1.4	–	–

It will be seen from the above that low-grade chromite is utilised in the manufacture of charge chrome. The metallurgical industry prefers hard lumpy chromite, although fines and concentrates which are predominant in the Sukinda ultramafic field, Orissa, can be used for smelting in an electric furnace.

For the refractory industry, chromite should invariably be hard and lumpy, fine-grained and free from serpentine. The specifications according to IS: 10819-1984 are given in Table 11.4.

The foregoing specification appears to be more rigid than the U.S. National Stockpile specification which requires a minimum of 31% Cr_2O_3, 60% or more of $Cr_2O_3 + Al_2O_3$ with a maximum of 12% Fe, 5.5% SiO_2 and 1% CaO. The high alumina chromite of the Sittampundi complex, Tamilnadu would satisfy the U.S. specification. The Indian specification is more rigid.

Similar differences exist in the specifications of chromite for the chemical industry. IS:4737-1982 specifies the characteristics of chromite for the chemical industry as given in Table 11.5.

Table 11.4

Constituents (on dry basis)	*Grade I (% by mass)*	*Grade II (% by mass)*
Loss on ignition (max.)	1.5	1.5
Cr_2O_3 (min.)	50	40
Total Fe as FeO (max.)	18	18
Al_2O_3 (max.)	14	14
SiO_2 (max.)	4	12
CaO (max.)	0.8	0.8
MgO (max.)	15	15

Table 11.5

Constituents (on dry basis)	*Grade %*
Cr_2O_3 (min.)	44
Total Fe as FeO (max.)	20
Al_2O_3 (max.)	14
SiO_2 (max.)	7
CaO (max.)	3
MgO (max.)	14

On the other hand, the U.S. National Stockpile specification requires the mineral to contain not less than 44% Cr_2O_3 and not over 5% SiO_2.

In all such cases, the specifications at the shop floor level are found to be somewhat more flexible depending on the demand-supply position, cost of mining and transport, physical state of the ore etc. Even in the case of the refractory industry, blended feed containing a fraction of low silica, friable ore mixed with lumpy, high silica chromite is used for making ordinary refractory bricks, since the reserve of high grade lumpy ore in India is very modest.

COPPER ORE

Most of the ores currently extracted and processed are made up of disseminations or aggregates of chalcopyrite, bornite and chalcocite in silicate rocks. These are subjected to crushing, fine grinding and concentration by flotation. Oxide deposits containing malachite, azurite and chrysocolla are leached with dilute H_2SO_4 to dissolve the copper. Dump leaching, heap leaching etc. with or without help from microbes (like Au and U, discussed in Chapter 10) are other techniques for metal concentration.

In ore beneficiation, copper recovery falls off as the copper content of the ore declines. Material containing less than 0.4% Cu may not prove to be economically minable unless the associated metals are of high value, e.g. Au, PGE, Ag etc. Costs of producing copper are variable, depending on the location of the deposit, physical characteristics of the ore, methods of mining and extraction, efficiency of the operations etc. In terms of percentage of the cost, the following is a thumb rule: 15% for mining, 25% for beneficiation and 25% for smelting and refining, leaving the remaining 35% for overhead including taxes, mine development, exploration, R & D, etc. It would be clear that open cast operations are cheaper per ton of ore raised. As the mine gets deeper and underground, the need for raising the average grade becomes stronger till a stage is reached when conventional underground mining has to be abandoned for the time being. The Mosabani copper mine in Singhbhum, Bihar went down to more than 1000 m below the surface before closing down. At its terminal phase, economics played a greater role than down depth continuity.

GRAPHITE

The major uses of this mineral are in refractories, carbon raising and foundry mould facing. It is also used as a lubricant, in special packings, pencils, electric motor and generator brushes, paints, polish, rubber and explosives.

Given such a wide array of uses, different types of graphite are mined. The three principal types are lumpy, amorphous and crystalline flake. Lumpy graphite is divided into a number of grades, depending upon the size. The size classification is as follows. *Lump*: from walnut to pea. *Chip*: from pea to wheat grain. *Dust:* finer than 60 mesh. Amorphous graphite is graded essentially on graphitic carbon content, which should be above 50%. Flake graphite must have a minimum of 85% graphitic carbon and must be – 8 mesh to 60 mesh in size. It is a common practice among tradesmen to blend different grades of graphite and obtain a final product which has the best performance for the specific industry. This is generally kept a secret.

GYPSUM

High purity gypsum is used in the manufacture of ammonium sulphate fertiliser. Less pure gypsum is used in Portland cement manufacture. It is also used for moulding and in the manufacture of Plaster of Paris. The industrial uses are specified in Table 11.6.

Another important use of gypsum is in improving alkaline soils. For such use, the material should contain a minimum of 70% $CaSO_4.2H_2O$ and the Na content should not exceed 0.75%. There are other specifications for the use of gypsum as an extender in the paint industry (IS:69-1950), for the ceramic industry (IS:2333-1981), for the manufacture of plaster boards (IS:8272-1976) etc.

GLASS SAND

For most of the glass produced, silica sand is the main raw material. Various types of glass produced in India include glass bottle, sheet glass, wired and figured glass, vacuum flask, laboratory equipment like pipette etc., glass shells, fibre glass, flint glass, opthalmic glass, glass for bangles etc. A minimum of 96% of SiO_2 is essential,

Table 11.6

Constituent %	*Uses*			
	Surgical Plaster Grade 1	*Fertiliser Grade 2*	*Pottery Grade 3*	*Cement Grade 4*
Free water (max.)	1	–	1	
CO_2 (max.)	1	–	3	
SiO_2 and other insolubles (max.)	0.7	6.0	6.0	
Iron and aluminium oxide (max.)	0.1	1.5	1.0	
MgO (max.)	0.5	1.0	1.5	3.0
$CaSO_4 . 2H_2O$ (min.)	96.0	85–90	85	70–75 (80–85 for exportable variety)
NaCl (max.)	0.01	0.003	0.1	0.5

but for high-quality optical glass, the minimum for SiO_2 is 99.8% with not more than 0.02% iron oxides, 0.1% of CaO + MgO and 0.1% of Al_2O_3. TiO_2, Cr, Co and Mn are also required to be very low, not exceeding 1 p.p.m. each. The physical specifications as set by the American Ceramic Society require that 'All sand should pass through 20 mesh screen, 40–60% should be retained on a No. 80 screen and not more than 5% should pass a No. 100 screen'.

IRON ORE

Iron ore usually consists of variable mixtures of magnetite (Fe_3O_4. iron content 72.4%), haematite (Fe_2O_3: iron content 69.9%) and goethite ($Fe_2O_3.H_2O$: iron content 62.9%). In India, the reserves are mostly of haematite and are classified as very high grade (with greater than 65% Fe), high grade (62–65% Fe), medium grade (less than 62% Fe) and unclassified (where sampling is not very detailed). Physically, the ore is classified as lump ore (particles 8 mm or larger) and fines. Sinter feed consists mainly of fines larger than 100 mesh, while fines smaller than 100 mesh are classed as pellet feed. Besides, the present technology prefers low alumina, high silica ores, whereas Indian ores, on account of their genetic association with the lateritisation process, are rather high in alumina. Phosphorus content should be less than 0.045% for Bessemer ore but can be as high as 0.18% in non-Bessemer ore. Mn content is also an important parameter for classifying the end use.

LIMESTONE AND DOLOMITE

The major uses of limestone are in the cement and steel industries, whereas dolomite is used largely in the iron and steel industry as feed for the blast furnace to improve the fluidity of the slag, for maintaining the slag basicity in the steel converter and to produce dolomite bricks and mortar for the refractory industry.

In the blast furnace, limestone is the main flux for smelting of iron ore. Upto 6% acid insolubles in the limestone can be accepted. However, the content of alkali elements has to be very low. In conventional open hearth technology of steel making, limestone with upto 3–4% silica was acceptable; but with the introduction of the basic oxygen furnace (B.O.F.) for reducing energy consumption and improving the yield of metal, the limestone is required to have 53–54% CaO and less than 1% SiO_2. It is an illustration of how the resource position changes with a shift in technology. In the fifties and sixties, the open hearth furnace was the general route for steel making. We had sufficient reserves of SMS grade limestone, e.g. in the Katni-Satna area. The moment B.O.F. technology came in, all these deposits became sub-marginal, and new deposits are tapped from places like Rajasthan, Himachal Pradesh, etc. far from the steel plants.

While the dolomite required for a blast furnace has fairly broad specifications, the refractory or converter grade dolomite requires less than 1% SiO_2, most of which is located in the Himalayas.

LEAD ORE/LEAD-ZINC ORE

Notwithstanding environmental hazards, demand for lead and lead-zinc ores will continue to rise with the increase in global population in view of the manifold uses of these two metals in ammunition, communication equipment, radiation shielding, car batteries, paints, construction industry, galvanised steel and zinc-based coatings, brass and bronze, chemicals, rubber products, etc.

Average minable grade is 5–6% Pb in lead ore without recoverable Ag, Au and Cu. In ores with other high-cost by-products, 3% Pb and 1% Zn are generally considered economic if the shape of the orebody permits systematic underground mining.

Simple lead ores are readily concentrated by flotation; over 90% recovery of the metal is effected in concentrators and smelters. On the other hand, the beneficiation of zinc ore is a complex process, and varies according to size and interlocking of the grains, the mineralogical diversity (including oxidation or coating on the surface of sphalerite) etc. As a result, a zinc-rich ore requires a higher grade or cheaper development cost to break even. The average grade of ore in the Rampura-Agucha deposit in Bhilwara district, Rajasthan is 13.5% Zn and 1.97% Pb. This is, however, a very high-grade deposit; the tenor of minable zinc ore in the world ranges from 3% onwards, averaging around 5%.

MANGANESE ORE

The term manganese ore is restricted by the U.S. Bureau of Mines to those ores which contain 35% or more of Mn. Those containing 10–35% Mn are called ferruginous Mn ore, and those containing 5–10% Mn are called manganiferous iron ore. The major use of Mn is for the production of iron and steel, principally in the form of ferromanganese and silicomanganese. The specifications for these feeds are as follows: Ferromanganese (Mn: 74–78%; Fe: 6–8%); Silicomanganese (Mn: 70–74%; Si: 16–20%); Chrome-manganese (Mn: 20–25%; Cr: 50–55%); Spiegeleisen (Mn: 15–30%; C: 4.5–6.5%). Other uses are in the manufacture of dry batteries, chemicals, paints, pigments, etc. In India the grades of raw ore are classified on the basis of MnO_2 content into Grade I (greater than 46%), Grade II (44–46%), Grade III (35–43%), Grade IV (34–25%) and Grade V (less than 25%). It would be obvious that for manufacture of both ferromanganese and silicomanganese, high-grade ores are essential. For the U.S. National stockpile, manganese ores are divided into three categories: metallurgical, battery and chemical. The metallurgical grade requires a minimum of 44% Mn, battery grade a minimum of 68% MnO_2, and chemical grade a minimum of 80% MnO_2.

ROCK PHOSPHATE

This is used in the manufacture of phosphoric acid, elemental phophorus and fertilisers. Its specifications for manufacture of elemental P in India are as follows: P_2O_5: 24% (min.); SiO_2: 20% (max.); Fe: 3% (max.); Al_2O_3: 7% (max.).

SILLIMANITE AND KYANITE

There are no prescribed Indian standard specifications. Sales are normally based on chemical composition and physical properties as agreed between the two contracting parties. In general, however, an Al_2O_3 content of more than 59%, SiO_2 less than 39%, Fe_2O_3 less than 0.75%, TiO_2 less than 1.25%, and CaO + MgO less than 0.20% are preferred in the international market.

The physical characters of these minerals are as important as their chemical composition. Lumps are preferred, with not more than 1% passing through 60 mesh seive. For fine sillimanite, abundant in placer deposits, marketability is the most serious problem.

Mineral specifications in different industries have changed rapidly during the last 50 years. The following generalisations can be made:

(1) Changes in technology and end use create unexpected changes in mineral specifications.

(2) There is a progressive shift towards specialised needs and specifications for the different user industries as well as a larger recycling of waste.

(3) With lowering of tariff and trade barriers across the world, indigenous resources of low grade may no longer enjoy any preference in the local market. Present industry frequently discards wastes with higher metal concentrations than what is found in commercial ores. Once this attitude changes and environmental costs are added, it may be cheaper to import a metal than to set up an industry for marginal profits.

(4) In the search for high grade mineral deposits, leadership in exploration techniques and international tie-ups will play a more decisive role in the next century than what we have seen so far. The country which falls behind in exploration, mining and metallurgy will be condemned to be a captive consumer of products. Such a country becomes a net importer of goods and services. The threat of 'economic terrorism' to such underdeveloped countries

will loom large in the second half of the next century, unless the prevailing socio-economic paradigms shift substantially in the near future.

(5) A vibrant R & D is the *sine qua non* of survival and prosperity in the next century. Recent attempts at the Fairview mine, S. Africa to pretreat refractory sulphide ores for gold recovery provide one such example where commercial biomining for gold has become operational after extensive pilot-plant-scale validation by Gencor (Pty.) Ltd. (*Science*, 6 May, 1994, 778–9). Sadly, comparable attempts by Indian companies (if there are any) are not known.

FURTHER READING

Indian Bureau of Mines Mineral Facts and Problems.
Indian Bureau of Mines Commodity-wise Monographs.

12

Geotechnical and Geohydrological Measurements

A working mine depends on two separate branches of earth science: economic geology and engineering geology. No wonder one of the best economic geologists of the Geological Survey of India, C.S. Fox, had also authored a standard textbook on Engineering Geology (1935, D. Van Nostrand Co., London). The geologist exploring a deposit has to provide basic data to the mine designer about the strength of the mineral-bearing ground, including the wall rocks, stability of the hill slope, frequency of earthquakes, best alignment for driving an opening into the hill face, rate of seepage along fault zones and other site-specific data. In all large mining camps, the geologist has also to locate non-mineralised rocks within a short distance from the site, which could be used as concrete aggregate. Such rocks should meet certain physical and chemical specifications. The rock should be fresh, strong, durable and on breaking should yield a product which does not contain a large proportion of platy or elongate fragments. Such specifications are usually satisfied by igneous rocks. River gravels, sulphate/sulphide-bearing rocks, carbonaceous rocks etc. are undesirable.

Some minerals like opal, chalcedony, acid volcanic glass or similar material with cryptocrystalline form of silica sometimes react with cement which has an alkali content (Na_2O + soda equivalent K_2O) of more than 0.6%, causing expansion and disruption of concrete. This is known as alkali aggregate reaction.

In the deeply-weathered Peninsular tracts of India, the strength of rocks is severely reduced within the zone of weathering. Any underground mine has to be so designed that the roof support system can bear the lithostatic load of the superincumbent mass. For example, in Sukinda, it has been observed in course of drilling that the zone of weathering is at places more than 100 m thick. If and when underground mining of the chromite deposits of this field is planned, the low strength of the saprolite zone has to be kept in view while designing the roof support system in the upper levels of the underground mine. The geologist has to delineate the nature and depth of the weathered zone within the mine area, either by deep pitting or by dry drilling.

The Rangpo sulphide mine in Sikkim illustrates some facets of the problem. The rock mass through which the adits have been driven are so broken that much effort is required to avoid sudden collapse and stoppage of mining operations. Under extreme geotechnical hazard, even a high-grade mineral deposit becomes uneconomic.

In the case of underground mines, the three most important geotechnical factors are rock weathering, structure and groundwater conditions. In tropical countries, rock weathering pervades the upper levels, penetrating locally as tongues down to 100 to 150 m below the ground. Surfaces of structural weakness and their orientation with respect to the excavations have to be studied carefully for minimising failure of the excavations. Besides their orientation, the spacing and widths of the individual fractures are to be recorded systematically over statistically representative study areas, so that sensitive sectors could be strengthened by an efficient grouting programme. Grouts are of two types: particulate grout (cement and clay) and non-particulate grout (silicate and organic polymer). The objective of such grouting is to fill and seal all pore spaces and fractures within the target zone of the rock body. Very thin fractures with wall separation less than 10 microns do not allow grout to flow in and seal.

In mountainous terrains with high rainfall, the shearing strength of a rock mass may fall below the stress induced by high pore water pressure to result in landslides. Such areas should be avoided for mining, although the risk of landslide can be reduced by implanting horizontal or gently inclined bores, together with a system of surface drainage to reduce infiltration.

Geohydrological measurements are equally important. Except for extreme cases, like mining below the sea bed as at Cornwall, U.K., the general practice is to avoid as far as possible excavations through zones of very strong hydrostatic pressure. The exploration geologist has to forecast the behaviour of groundwater in new mines and to suggest ways of development which would create the least difficulties. In monsoonic tracts of the Indian Peninsula, shallow groundwater table is liable to create problems in open cast quarries during the rainy season, including local collapse of benches and water-logging of the lower levels of the quarries. Through pumping at an appropriate rate, the quarries could be kept operational during the monsoon. Water-filled abandoned mines, specially where new underground developments are planned, are more dangerous. A sudden rush of water into the new openings may be fatal to the workers below. In such areas it is advisable to drill a few holes through the abandoned mines (in case mine plans are not available) and take up long probe drilling ahead of the mine faces to avoid serious consequences. Even in hardrock areas, there could be deep aquifers fed from major river courses. In the course of exploratory drilling of the Rakha Mines sector of the Singhbhum copper belt, it was observed that water was gushing out from some of the deep boreholes intersecting the lodes at depths exceeding 300 m vertical depth. Obviously, when the present mine reaches such depth, pumping of water could become an important additional cost in the workings. Normally, at depths of 1,000 m, groundwater ceases to be a source of serious problem in underground mines unless there are deep aquifers and/or strongly fissured ground. Where a mine opening is close to a river course, it is necessary to keep its minimum elevation at least 4–5 m above the Highest Flood Level (H.F.L.), so that the mine is never inundated by flood water.

HAZARD POTENTIAL OF WALL ROCKS

Broadly, the exploration geologist can use the following thumb rules for anticipating potential geotechnical and geohydrological hazards.

Geotechnical Hazards

1. *Hard, compact, homogeneous rocks:* Ideal for roof of underground workings.
2. *Hard gneissose or schistose rocks:* Properties of individual beds, density of joints, and the nature of joint in-fillings control the strength of the underground mine. Light- to medium-support might be needed.
3. *Densely jointed rocks:* Incapable of carrying overburden load. Backpacking of natural arch space needed.
4. *Rocks with clayey joint infillings:* Likely to have low cohesive strength with clay infillings weakening the mass substantially. If one measures only the compressive strength of a fresh rock sample in the laboratory and ignores the frequency and distribution pattern of clay-filled joint surfaces, the geotechnical assessment will be wrong. What is needed is to estimate the rock body behaviour en masse and in situ. If there are interlacing openings in a hard and compact rock

body, which is to support arched roofs, insist on adequate lining of the openings.

It is common knowledge that failure at shallow depth both in underground and open cast workings by way of roof collapse or sudden subsidence of the ground is essentially caused by the proximity of a free boundary of the rock mass. At great depths, on the other hand, confining pressure enhances the strength of the rock. Exceptions to the rule are examples of violent rock-burst whereby parts of the walls of deep underground workings spall off suddenly into small rock fragments or splinters, e.g. at Kolar Gold Field. This is caused by sudden release of strain under the lithostatic load of the overburden. This could be fatal to the workers in the vicinity. Normally, rock bursts affect more brittle and harder rock types in a mine, particularly where strain is localised. Extensive perforations into the overlying mineral-bearing ground are a contributory factor.

The problem of subsidence by mining initially received serious attention due to surface damage, since caving of the ground under human habitation caused occasional injury and loss of investment. Subsidence must be prevented where there are towns nearby, since it would affect the layout of drainage, underground pipes and cables. Special care has to be taken where there are water courses above mine workings. Presently, subsidence within underground mine workings is equally a subject of enquiry. In metal mines, controlled subsidence reduces mining cost in some methods of stoping. Locally, subsidence is planned for filling voids, e.g. in deep-seated sulphur deposits recovered by hot water.

In open cast mines, where the dip is steep and the rock is hard and homogenous, slides develop on slopes of 45° and more; but where the rocks are layered (like slates or schistose or banded quartzite) slides can develop on slopes of 30°. Waste rock dumps should not be sited near the boundaries of such quarries to avoid excess weight of the dumps triggering failure of the walls. Schistose footwalls are always a source of slides. Flat-lying strata are generally more stable in open cast mines.

Instances of sudden subsidence of underground mines with severe ground shaking, often accompanied by air blasts underground, are known from abandoned and inaccessible workings in Lake Superior Copper district. One must always provide against such contingencies. If the excavation is filled wholly or partly by natural or artificial support or by special types of roof bolting, subsidence may be controlled but not prevented. Timbering used to be popular for supporting small stopes of metal mines at shallow depths. Where the rocks are sheared, schistose, sheeted or jointed, rocks may yield along shear and joint planes at depths of 300 m or so by slow and silent creep. It is therefore important to allow ample margins of safety to support the load along shafts and over drifts and cross cuts.

For shallow mines, particularly where mining goes on fitfully over decades, one must be prepared to anticipate the risk of subsidence of ground. Subsidence of ground has to be tackled imaginatively. To claim that mining underground would invariably lead to subsidence of the surface at a later date, e.g. at Badia (Bihar) and that the mine owner is not responsible after the lease expires is to ignore the needs of other people. Sandstowing, for example, can be adopted in suitable instances. In all underground mines, one has to delimit the potential area which could be affected by subsidence, depending on the size and shape of the workings, their disposition in depth and the nature of formations including their shearing strength. It is advisable to undertake regular seismic monitoring for forecasting sudden breakages. Subsidence normally starts at places where the gravitational force exceeds the shearing strength. The actual failure takes the shape of a near vertical surface in its upper part, curving inward as an arc to the bottom. At shallow levels particularly in underground stopes, subsidence fractures start as steep-dipping tension cracks, following downwards into bedding planes or joints or fractures. The method of mining, the pattern of blasting, and the rate of mining are all critical in controlling subsidence.

It is possible to monitor the rate of ground subsidence by time series observations of a number of benchmarks, both on the surface and underground and measuring the rate of change in R.L. In mining blocks with old workings, accumulated water in the upper levels may lubricate clay-rich zones in fractured ground and trigger off sudden subsidence. It is therefore a common practice to thoroughly drain neighbouring low lying ground before starting new mining operations in a partly exploited area.

In deep open cast quarries, the bench height and the overall slope of the quarry must be so designed that the gravitational load of the free face does not exceed the shearing strength of the material in wet condition. Otherwise during the monsoon months, the weight of material on the unsupported faces of the quarry would lead to sliding en bloc. Many managers of small, private mines leave the footwall side relatively undressed. This is a risky practice. Where saprolite forms a part of the wall rocks, one must not exceed the limiting slope of 30° and bench height of 3 m. Otherwise there might be subsidence after intense rainfall.

Even in comparatively shallow excavations, like quarrying for building stones, it is essential to study the pattern and frequency of joints carefully, in addition to measuring the thickness of individual bands, nature and depth of weathering, colouration pattern, grain size variation, if any, and permeability and porosity characters of the rock. Since joints are regularly spaced subparallel surfaces, their orientations are critical for taking out large blocks intact. In granitic terrains, joints frequently occur in two or three sets—one nearly parallel to the banding and the others at right angles to it. Such joints are usually called master joints, if they are persistent, strongly developed and are spaced sufficiently apart. For any prospector searching for building stones, such joints are a boon, if these are not infiltrated by weathered products and zones of discolouration. In lateritic tracts of Peninsular India, such discoloured zones are common. Downwards, these are usually tongue-shaped and more than a few meters thick. In relatively arid areas, hard massive granites and gneisses are commonly seen as bald, domical lumps or as tors of gigantic blocks on steep-sided barren hills. These form as a result of sheet structured joints on three or more sets. Similar sheeted structures are also noticed in some Vindhyan sandstones, which have provided beautiful architectural raw material by virtue of their uniformly fine grain size, sober colour and the ease with which the material can be mined and dressed. Hard rocks like charnockite, which are now in great demand overseas, are not so easy to dress and polish; it is necessary to use cutting and polishing machines for such hard rocks. This needs larger investment. In such cases the prospector must be sure that the material will be easily quarriable in abundant quantity, free from veins of unwanted shades and composition. A careful evaluation of the geotechnical property of the rock mass, including the ability to retain high polish, forms an essential component of its economic evaluation.

Geohydrological Hazards

1. *Unconsolidated sands and gravels:* Highly permeable.
2. *Limestones and dolomites:* Potentially cavernous and karstified.
3. *Zones of deep Tropical Humid Weathering:* Irregular tongues of highly porous and permeable zone containing intermittent boulders of hard basement down to 100–200 m below the ground.
4. *Granite and quartzite:* Permeability high along zones of jointing, fracturing and faulting, some highly water charged.
5. *Folded terrain of slate, schist and phyllite:* Moderate permeability with subtle contrasts between different bands, particularly in peneplained terrain. In the Himalayas, fractures and faults as well as margins of silicified zones have high permeability. The copper bearing quartz vein at Shumahal in Anantnag district,

Kashmir, having a spring in its vicinity and the Rangpo copper mine in Sikkim with mild seepage, are examples.

The basic concepts of groundwater flow stem from Darcy's law which states that the flow rate through a porous medium is proportional to the head loss and inversely proportional to the length of the flow path. The relevant formulae are as follows:

$$Q = K\,i\,A = K\,A\,\frac{h_1 - h_2}{L} \qquad \text{(i)}$$

$$V = K\,i \text{ or } K = \frac{V}{i} \qquad \text{(ii)}$$

$$K = L/t \qquad \text{(iii)}$$

where,

V = velocity; L = length of the flow path; t = time

i = hydraulic gradient $\frac{h_1 - h_2}{L}$

A = area normal to the direction of flow, L^2

Q = rate of flow $\frac{L^3}{t}$

h_1 and h_2 = water level or potential at two points on a line parallel to the direction of flow

L = length of flow path between h_1 and h_2

K = proportionality constant known as the coefficient of permeability or *hydraulic conductivity*.

In a porous medium, this varies for different fluids depending on density and viscosity. Since the term fails to describe 3-d flow characteristics of an aquifer adequately, the term *transmissivity* is used. This is equal to the average permeability multiplied by the saturated zone thickness. Field measurement of hydraulic conductivity can be made by measuring the time interval for a water tracer such as a dye (sodium fluorescein) or a salt (calcium chloride) or radioisotopes (tritium - ^{3}He, ^{60}Co or ^{131}I) to travel between two observation wells or test holes. The tracer is injected into one hole and thereafter samples of water are taken at intervals from the other hole to determine the passage of the tracer. This method has serious drawbacks. It presupposes an accurate knowledge of the flow direction in advance of the experiment and a uniform transmissivity of the saturated zone, and requires that the two holes be placed close together. This is a self-defeating procedure if the value is to be used for regional application.

An alternative technique is the point dilution method, where the tracer is introduced into the well and mixed thoroughly. Thereafter the concentration of the tracer is measured in the well at regular intervals of time. As water flows into and from the well, the resulting dilution curve is taken to define the local groundwater velocity.

Hydraulic conductivity (*K*) describes the resistivity of a medium to fluid flow. It is scale-dependent. If laboratory measurements on small samples or piezometric tests yield low values, these should not be extrapolated for large volumes of rock.

The best method of estimating hydraulic conductivity is by using the pumping test of wells. Based on observation of water levels around pumping wells, both the rate of fall of water level during pumping and rate of recovery after cessation of pumping, a *K* value for the whole area under study can be computed.

Hard rock areas need not necessarily have very low *K* value. Traditionally, the crystalline rocks were considered to be impermeable. But recent findings show that these have varying degrees of conductivity. The very deep well at Kola Peninsula in the former Soviet Russia was found to contain open, water-filled fissures at more than 12,000 m depth. The conductivities determined in gneiss and granitic rocks from the Black Forest of Germany vary from $K = 3.5 \times 10^{-10}$ m/s to 8.7×10^{-7} m/s and the associated transmissivities range from $T = 1.0 \times 10^{-7}$ m^2/s to 4.7×10^{-3} m^2/s. Thus the fluctuations range over several orders of magnitude.

Another fundamental parameter is longitudinal dispersivity (α), which describes the local variations in the velocity field of a groundwater solute in the direction of fluid flow. This parameter is very important for defining the transport of dissolved contaminants through groundwater. Like hydraulic conductivity, its value is also scale-dependent. In carbonate reservoirs, it has been found that the relationship of longitudinal dispersivity to scale is exponential until an upper bound is reached after which it remains constant with scale. Moreover, in such rocks, it is proportional to the square root of hydraulic conductivity. In a new field, it is essential to undertake a tracer test by injecting a tracer in a central well and measuring the transport in radially-spaced wells up to a lateral distance of 100 m from the central input well. The value of 'α' so obtained will be applicable to distances up to a few km, provided the medium remains identical.

In general, it must be borne in mind that fractured rocks are more conductive. This is why granitic rocks are more conductive than gneisses.

Some other related expressions are given below:

(a) Porosity: It is a non-dimensional value that expresses the ratio of the volume of pores to the total volume of a porous material, and is usually expressed as a percentage.

$$P = \frac{V_p}{V} \times 100$$

where V_p is the volume of pore space.

(b) Hydraulic head: This is the total fluid potential above a datum plane and may be expressed by the Bernoulli equation

$$\frac{p_1}{\gamma} + \frac{V_1^2}{2g} + z_1 = \frac{p_2}{\gamma} + \frac{V_2^2}{2g} + z_2 + h_l$$

where p is pressure, γ is the specific weight of water, V is the velocity of flow, g is the acceleration due to gravity, z represents elevation at different points and h_l is the head loss.

(c) Average flow velocity: This is discharge velocity divided by porosity. Discharge velocity of a porous medium is defined as the volume of water that flows per unit time across a unit cross-sectional area normal to the direction of flow.

An essential part of geohydrological studies for a mining project is modelling of groundwater flow in a general 2-d system. This is required both for pollution monitoring and impact studies as well as for ensuring sustainable yield in mining regions, where surface runoff is meagre. Common hydrological settings include one- and two-dimensional confined and unconfined aquifers, mixed confined and unconfined flow, circular recharge areas in closed valleys, heterogenous aquifers etc. Modelling can be attempted by combining many elementary analytical solutions, each of which explains a specific aspect under investigation (e.g. water courses, percolating water-filled quarries, flow within and below weathered zone, etc.). Each provides an elementary contribution of its own by which mass conservation is ensured in the equation.

PARAMETERS TO BE MEASURED BEFORE MINING

A simple list of hydrological and geotechnical measurements to be made following preliminary exploration of a mineral deposit and before preparation of the Detailed Feasibility Report is given below.

Geotechnical Parameters

(a) Bulk specific gravity, grain size distribution and porosity of the lithotypes.
(b) Resistance and expansion characters of the rock mass when in contact with water.
(c) Permeability in bulk.
(d) Compressive and shearing strength of the rocks.
(e) Resistance to excavation.
(f) Historical analysis of past earthquakes in the area.
(g) Records of past avalanches, subsidence and other geohazards in the area.

Geohydrological Parameters

(a) Depth and slope of groundwater table.
(b) Proximity to a river.
(c) Inflow from aquifers and piezometric surfaces of different horizons to determine the direction of underground flow.
(d) Permeability and porosity of the rock formations *in bulk*.
(e) Indications of karst, if any.
(f) Distribution of faults and fractures and their water content.
(g) Pumping test to establish the conditions of groundwater flow (hydraulic conductivity, interconnection, etc.) and the depth of lowering of water table under different rates of pumping.
(h) Sources of drinking and industrial water and their geochemical and bacteriological analysis.

In the course of the last two decades, geotechnical studies to identify suitable waste disposal sites have become common, both for major townships like Bangkok and for radioactive waste disposal or containment. The ground rules are as follows:

(1) The site should be sufficiently distant from human settlements.
(2) The subsurface lithology should have very low permeability, low porosity and deep water table with a high degree of ability to retain harmful substances.
(3) The topography should be as flat as possible, but well above the highest flood level during the rainy season.
(4) The risk of earthquakes and avalanches should be very low.
(5) Areas with continuous forest cover, agricultural activities, water courses, other natural resources at shallow depths and of special tourist, religious or cultural interests are to be avoided.
(6) Limestone terrains or other localities with karst type drainage are to be avoided.
(7) Groundwater recharge areas are to be avoided.

In the past, radioactive wastes from mines, including tailings from treatment plants, were dumped on the surface and held in tailing dams. This is an extremely hazardous practice. At Rum Jungle, Northern Territory, Australia, such a tailing dam overflowed durng the rainy season about 20 years ago, leading to the death of plants and fish. At Grand Junction, Colorado, U.S.A., 30,000 tonnes of tailings were used as landfill on which buildings, including a school, were constructed! This led to increase in infant death rate and in pulmonary carcinoma.

For low-level risks, it is frequently observed that some compromises are made with adequate protective measures for containment of pollution. For example, in the case of low-level radioactive wastes like the monazite sands of Kerala, the following are some of the options available:

(1) use of ion exchange media as part of the liners or barriers for attenuation of radionuclides;
(2) use of a cover system in the beneficiation plants for radon gas control and attenuation;
(3) containment and isolation of the storage dumps of beneficiated products using a surface cap and a liner system around and below for encapsulation;
(4) building bentonite slurry walls for hydrological isolation; and
(5) use of other passive systems.

But where highly radioactive end products are sought to be stored in containers in deep underground vaults, the hydrologic regime, seismic hazard and other pathways of accidental leakage and contamination have to be carefully examined by both surface and underground measurements. Ideally such localities should be in the heart of a desert, underlain by massive, fine-grained igneous rocks, free from joints and faults with no past record of earthquakes above M_b 3 and negligible records of Holocene geomorphologic changes, like relict terraces, fault line scarps, etc.

Geotechnical and geohydrological studies for identifying safe sites for nuclear waste repositories are currently not standardised. As a result, controversies erupt. For example, the proposed low-level nuclear waste dump at Ward Valley, California, designed to hold waste from utilities, hospitals and laboratories in California and other states was investigated over a decade by the U.S. Geological Survey, the Environmental Protection Agency of the U.S.A., the Metropolitan Water District of Southern California etc. The site was declared suitable. But in 1989, soil tests conducted at the site (porous desert soil) detected tritium, deposited on the surface by fall-out from nuclear tests in the 1950s and 1960s at depths of 30 m. At that rate, it is felt by some, liquid radioactive waste could sink from the dump to the water table, 210 meters below in about 200 years! To resolve the ambiguity of such extrapolations, Lawrence Livermore National Laboratory (LLNL) has been entrusted with a study to find out how fast radionuclides deposited decades ago, including ^{36}Cl and ^{14}C are migrating through the Mojave soil. The answer is critical to save California's water supply.

Investigations for high-level waste repositories are equally tricky. At Yucca Mountain, Nye county, Nevada, it is not yet known whether the waste will leach out of the large metal canisters during the next 10,000 years or whether the heat generated by the waste's own radioactive decay will affect the stability and porosity of the highly fractured host rock. Initial geotechnical appraisal of the Calico Hills tuff considered it to be essentially unfaulted and unfractured. Subsequent excavations have shown that there are vertical fractures which could act as fast paths for water to flow into and through the tuffs. This has occasioned a shift in exploration. Below the level where the repository is planned, it is now proposed to drive a few drifts. Tracers would be injected in gaseous and liquid form from horizontal holes within the tuff at higher levels and their arrival would be observed in other holes and galleries excavated below the injection holes. This will be followed by overcoring of a number of selected holes by larger diameter drilling along the original configurations. Samples so recovered would permit observation of imbibation of tracers into the fractured walls and test the ability of the rock to absorb radionuclides.

In some countries, it is proposed to use highly alkaline (high pH) cements in underground vaults for storing radioactive waste. The high pH cement surrounds the waste and immobilise radioactive elements like U and Pu. Additionally it is predicted that alkaline water seeping from the cement into the repository rocks will interact with them, precipitating new minerals into pre-existing pores and fractures. This will limit the dispersal of radionuclides into the groundwater. Minerals of the zeolite family can incorporate significant quantities of radioactive elements and afford potentially useful lining to repositories.

In the U.S.A. alone, 29,000 tonnes of nuclear waste from civilian reactors—an amount that grows by 1,900 tonnes every year along with 50 tonnes of high grade radionuclides, such as ^{137}Cs from the nuclear arsenal, are waiting for permanent burial. Recent research suggests (R.F. Service, *Science,* 270, 1995, 1762) that high-grade nuclear waste containing upto 10% plutonium by weight could possibly be fused in alkali-tin-silicate glass and safely stored for thousands of years. But low-level wastes are a different proposition altogether. Neither in the G-7 countries nor elsewhere has a standard protocol been evolved for safe storage of such bulky contaminants. This should form an important agenda for international collaborative research.

FURTHER READING

H.E. Mckinstry, *Mining Geology*, Prentice Hall, Inc., N.J., 1948, 680 pp.

M. Kuzvert and M. Bohmer, Prospecting and Exploration of Mineral Deposits, *Developments in Economic Geology*, No. 21, Elsevier, Amsterdam, 1986, 508 pp.

D.K. Todd, *Groundwater Hydrology,* John Wiley & Sons, N.Y., 1980, 535 pp.

H.M. Haitjema, *Analytic Element Modelling of Groundwater Flow*, Academic, California, 1995, 394 pp.

K. Spitz and J. Moreno, *A Practical Guide to Groundwater and Solute Transport Modeling*, Wiley-Interscience, N.Y., 1996, 461 pp.

Appendix I

Checklist Before Investment in a New Mine

A: Average financial structure of a mining project

1. Debt (major) approx. 60%
2. Shareholder's equity (minor) approx. 40%

B: Possible sources of failure of the venture

1. Errors in ore reserves: a minimum proved + probable reserve life of 7–9 years needed to cover the scheduled life of long-term debt
   N.B.: *Reserves to be independently checked by a reputable firm; assay to be re-validated in internationally recognised laboratory by fresh sampling.*
2. Delay in completion of preliminary work: In case of cost or time overruns, if sponsors fail to provide:
   (a) all excess funds; or
   (b) standby line of credit from commercial banks;
   (c) certain percentage of overruns;
   (d) persuade host government to provide for overruns.
3. High cost of operation: Low cost operations less risky; flexibility in operation (e.g. preferential extraction of higher grade ore or reduction in stripping ratio) a positive factor.
4. Price fluctuation:
   (a) taxation on the basis of revenue actually earned preferable to computation on the basis of spot values;
   (b) if cost of participation is not treated as deductible from Income Tax;

(c) absence of a carefully designed hedging program to lock in fixed prices for a proportion of total sales.

5. Foreign Exchange: Where chronic shortage of F.E. affects a mining project. For access to F.E. for operations and debt payment, it is preferable to have sale proceeds to be denominated in hard currency and paid to an account where expropriation is unlikely; e.g. in private banks.
6. Political Uncertainty: Project sponsors can take out policies and assign benefits to lenders. Insurance agencies such as MIGA (World Bank), OPIC (U.S.A.) and UDC (Canada) specialise in such insurance and provide coverage for expropriation, war, civil unrest, inconvertibility, etc.
7. Absence of security:
   (a) Fixed assets to be mortgaged.
   (b) Moveable assets (e.g. bank accounts, inventories) to be covered under a floating charge with or without overall guarrantee from the host government.
8. Conflict of interest with host government:
   (a) Lender's risk assessment model for expropriation etc., should be weighted by analysing historical facts of a specific country, rather than on subjective sentiments.
   (b) Clauses to be incorporated stating that sponsor's title to concession cannot be revoked by government, even where prompt payment of royalties and rent cannot be ensured all the time.
9. Environmental damage: Environmental Impact Study or Assessment (EMS/EMA) essential before mining. Expert to be appointed and monitoring system installed for observance of environmental standards.

For all non-renewable resources, one World Bank expert recommends an investment decision based on the following:

(a) expected duration and earnings from extraction;
(b) discount rate;
(c) net profit minus funds needed for re-investment for replacement of exhausted resources.

For example, if the benefits from coal mining are to be assessed, part of the revenue from the sale of coal has to be invested for an equivalent quantity of solar or wind or OTEC power; it has to be deducted from the total profit and the remaining amount should be reflected in GNP.

Appendix II

Checklist for Rapid Evaluation of Partly Explored/Developed Prospect

This varies from one deposit to another.

1. Dimension of the deposit
   - (i) Plan with scale (desirable scale 1:1000 with both geological and topographic features)
   - (ii) Deposit boundary defined by:
     - (a) boreholes at close intevals;
     - (b) pits and trenches;
     - (c) Mostly exposed surfaces; or
     - (d) imaginary models.
   - (iii) True thickness measured by:
     - (a) boreholes at right angles to the dip of the deposit;
     - (b) pits and trenches down to the bottom of the deposit;
     - (c) exposed scarp sections; or
     - (d) extrapolations from other areas.
   - (iv) Representative samples from the deposit recovered by:
     - (a) boreholes with at least 90% core recovery from the zones of mineralisation;
     - (b) channel samples from pits;
     - (c) channel samples from outcrops; or
     - (d) extrapolations from elsewhere.

(v) Total volume and tonnage of deposit mined out and run of mine (R.O.M.) grade of raisings on monthly basis.

(vi) Total duration of mining operation with records of shut down, if any.

2. Variations of grade.

a. (i) Names of laboratories where analysis was undertaken;

(ii) List of elements analysed;

(iii) Methods and instruments used for analysis;

(iv) Percentage of duplicate samples cross-checked with actual records of deviations between original and duplicate values;

(v) ranges of difference among borehole, pit, stack and bucket samples;

(vi) Range of difference between *in situ* grade of each block and R.O.M. grade (where mining was undertaken);

(vii) Actual reports from user's laboratories and differences between the sender's and recipient's labs.

b. Methods of sampling followed

Initial weight/steps of size reduction/final size/quantity of sample taken for digestion/reagents used for digestion and hours of digestion

3. History of accidents in the mining operation

Dates, months, years, report from authorised agencies with causes.

4. Hydrological data

5. Engineering data on strength of different types of rocks and mining methods followed

6. Monthly report from the company's geologist and mining engineer with special emphasis on delays, difficulties, development work, OMS, recommendations (bad grammar, mis-spellings, incorrect use of technical terms to be carefully listed to judge the capability of the technical personnel employed)

7. In case there are underground workings,

(i) scale used for mapping and survey

(ii) methods of survey adopted

(iii) frequency of structural data plotted

(iv) spacing of channel samples

(v) dimension of sampled ore blocks left inside the mine between different levels for future mining

(vi) groundwater condition in the levels opened as well as within depths considered for future mining

(vii) actual disposition of faults with estimated amount and direction of throw in each case

(viii) condition of roof and walls of the mines
(ix) analysis of gases inside the mine
(x) location of dumps in relation to future mine development
(xi) access mode—incline or shaft
(xii) 10% site check to validate the records—choose spots on the basis of random numbers of gridded zones—consult any book on statistics.

8. Water filled workings: data from long drill-holes ahead of the advancing face Actual rate of pumping followed
9. Records of ground subsidence/slumping of benches/stability of old stopes/geodetic measurements *on time series* of rate of change in elevation of benchmarks over and around the underground developments.
10. Categorisation of reserves:
    (i) by sampling at 5 m interval— Proved Block plus 10% tonnage around the Proved Block
    (ii) by surface sampling through drill-holes and pits at 25 m interval (grid)—Possible

Note: Where there are no records of past mining, there are no proved reserves.

Appendix III

Some Important Economic Indices and Problems in Environmental Accounting

Gross Domestic Product (GDP): Total production of a country measured *as the monetary value* of all final goods and services produced; or the expenditure on goods and services produced; or the income received from goods and services.

Gross National Product (GNP): (Total GDP + share dividend payments + interest + profits + rents flowing into a country) MINUS (share dividends + interest + profits + rents flowing out of a country).

Per Capita GNP or GDP: GNP or GDP divided by the total population. Net National Product (NNP) = GNP MINUS an allowance for depreciation of capital (e.g. cost of replacing machinery).

Standard System of National Account (SNA): GNP MINUS value of natural capital depletion, degradation and defence expenditure.

The present trend is to generate Integrated Environmental and Economic Accounts (IEEA) rather than a cost-benefit analysis on the basis of Hoskold's formula. But the more elaborate it is, the more curious it turns. As D. Duthie, *New Scientist*, 1993, 858 remarked:

Present GNP statistics are like sausages: readily consumed by economists, politicians and the media, but most prefer not to dwell on what does (and does not) get into them.

Problems

(a) Who will prepare the physical account which records the changing state of environmental resources (e.g. depth of topsoil in cm; live timber in cubic meters, etc)?

(b) Who will develop consistent valuation techniques to transform physical accounts in physical units into financial accounts which can be integrated into SNA (Standard System of National Accounts)?

(c) Who will calculate the Sustainable Measure (SM) which is equivalent to the amount of potential investment to generate new Natural and Fabricated capital MINUS Depreciation of Natural and Fabricated capital?

A large and inefficient state control does not provide a convincing set up anywhere to meet such goals.

Appendix IV

Checklist of Environmental Baseline Studies for a New Mine

1. *Agriculture and land use*
   Types and quantity of crops raised annually and their end use and market value; nature and thickness of topsoil; type and quantity of fertilisers used; extent of irrigated vs. non-irrigated land; swamps and ponds; fisheries and annual value of catch; area used for habitations; building material used; forests, grasslands, length and type of drainage courses; annual discharge; major, minor and toxic element geochemistry of soil, water and sediment in the drainage courses.
2. *Socio-economic set up*
   Population, employment pattern, industrial structure, level of education, possible impact of mining and related activities on local structures, available social services, mortality trend, health and hygiene including incidence of cross-cultural infections like AIDS, and others.
3. *Tourism*
   Annual frequency, earnings, facilities, nature of tourists, i.e. country or place of origin, age.
4. *Roads and traffic*
   Sources of road metal; type and width of roads in existence; maintenance authority; budget; type and frequency of vehicles plying and vehicle repair facilities; depots of fuel and lubricants—their distance and rates.

5. *Landscape and amenities*
   (a) Flat/Rolling/Mountainous: per cent and distribution.
   (b) Barren/Shrubland/Forested: per cent and distribution.
   (c) Rainfall pattern and temperature ranges for the last 30 years, if available.
   (d) Nearest markets and railway stations/seaports/airports and mode of access.
6. *Air quality and dust*
   Abundance of toxic gases, suspended particles, dominant directions and intensity of wind, including incidence of hurricanes and past record of damages.
7. *Surface and groundwater*
   Quality and quantity available;
   Depth and water table;
   Toxic elements in groundwater, if any.
8. *Noise and vibration*
   Average and maximum level of noise;
   Seismic risk;
   Risk of landslides in unstable slopes.
9. *Ecology and wildlife*
   Variety and density of wildlife;
   Presence of any endangered species;
   State notified reservations of land.
10. *Archaeology and heritage*
    Old monuments or habitations;
    Places of pilgrimage;
    Unusual geological or anthropological features.
11. *Safety*
    From hostile natural forces like volcanism, tsunamis, cavings by collapse of land due to past mining activities.
    From man-made disasters like uprising, local rowdies, activists, etc.

Appendix V
Some Common Conversion Factors

Multiply		*By*	*To obtain*
		Length	
micrometer	(μm)	0.00003937	inch
millimeter	(mm)	0.0394	inch
centimeter	(cm)	0.3937	inch
meter	(m)	3.281	foot
kilometer	(km)	0.6214	mile
		Area	
Square centimeter	(cm^2)	0.1550	square inch
square meter	(m^2)	1.196	square yard
		Volume	
cubic centimeter	(cm^3)	0.06102	cubic inch
litre	(l)	1.057	quart
		Mass	
kilogram	(kg)	2.205	pound avoirdupois
megagram	(Mg)	1.102	ton

Subject & Locality Index

C

D

E

F

L

M

N

O

P

R

S

T

U

V

W

X

Y

Z

Author Index

D

E

F

G

H

I

J

K

L

M

N

O

P

R

S

T

V

W

X

Y

Z